HOW DEMOCRACIES PERISH

JEAN-FRANÇOIS REVEL

HOW
DEMOCRACIES
PERISH

with the assistance of
BRANKO LAZITCH

translated from the French by
WILLIAM BYRON

PERENNIAL LIBRARY

Harper & Row, Publishers
New York, Cambridge, Philadelphia, San Francisco
London, Mexico City, São Paulo, Singapore, Sydney

HOW DEMOCRACIES PERISH. Translation copyright © 1983 by Doubleday & Company, Inc. Originally published as *Comment les démocraties finissent,* © Editions Grasset & Fasquelle, 1983. All rights reserved. Printed in the United States of America. No part of this book may be used or reproduced in any manner whatsoever without written permission except in the case of brief quotations embodied in critical articles and reviews. For information address Doubleday & Company, Inc., 245 Park Avenue, New York, N.Y. 10167. Published simultaneously in Canada by Fitzhenry & Whiteside Limited, Toronto.

First PERENNIAL LIBRARY edition published 1985.

Library of Congress Cataloging-in-Publication Data

Revel, Jean François.
  How democracies perish.

  Translation of Comment les démocraties finissent.
  Reprint. Originally published: Garden City, N.Y. : Doubleday, 1984, c1983.
  Includes bibliographical references and index.
  1. Communist strategy. 2. Communism—1945– 3. World politics—1945–
4. Democracy. 5. Soviet Union—Foreign relations—1945– . I. Title.
HX518.S8R4713 1985   327.1'1'091717   85-42926
ISBN 0-06-097011-1 (pbk.)

85 86 87 88 89 MPC 10 9 8 7 6 5 4 3 2 1

TABLE OF CONTENTS

PART ONE   HOW DEMOCRACY FACES ITS ENEMY

1	The End of an Accident	3
2	A Willing Victim	7
3	Tocqueville's Mistake	12
4	Survival of the Least Fit	16
5	The Fear of Knowing	21

PART TWO   THE REALITY OF COMMUNIST
EXPANSION

6	After Poland: An Autopsy	33
7	The Territorial Imperative	55
8	The Unilateral Arms Race	66
9	Persuasion by Force	75

PART THREE   THE TOOLS OF COMMUNIST
EXPANSION

10	Global Strategy and Active Vigilance	89
11	Long-range Vision and Hindsight	99
12	Attack, Always Attack	109
13	Playing Hot and Cold	123
14	Dividing the West	136
15	The "Struggle for Peace"	144
16	Ideological Warfare and Disinformation	160
17	Piracy and Perversion	188

PART FOUR THE MENTALITY OF DEMOCRATIC DEFEAT

18	The Fault Lines	215
19	Where Cowardice Began: The Berlin Wall	230
20	The Phony "Cold War"	241
21	On the Inventor of Détente	258
22	Yalta: The Myth of Where It All Began	264
23	Miracle in Moscow: The Comedy of Succession	277
24	The Double Standard	295
25	The Two Kinds of Memory	318
26	The Democracies Versus Democracy	338

CONCLUSION NEITHER WAR NOR SLAVERY

Index   361

PART ONE

HOW DEMOCRACY FACES ITS ENEMY

THE END OF AN ACCIDENT

DEMOCRACY MAY, after all, turn out to have been a historical accident, a brief parenthesis that is closing before our eyes.

In its modern sense of a form of society reconciling governmental efficiency with legitimacy, authority with individual freedoms, it will have lasted a little over two centuries, to judge by the speed of growth of the forces bent on its destruction. And, really, only a tiny minority of the human race will have experienced it. In both time and space, democracy fills a very small corner. The span of roughly two hundred years applies only to the few countries where it first appeared, still very incomplete, at the end of the eighteenth century. Most of the other countries in which democracy exists adopted it under a century ago, under half a century ago, in some cases less than a decade ago.

Democracy probably could have endured had it been the only type of political organization in the world. But it is not basically structured to defend itself against outside enemies seeking its annihilation, especially since the latest and most dangerous of these external enemies, communism—the current and complete model of totalitarianism—parades as democracy perfected when it is in fact the absolute negation of democracy.

Democracy is by its very nature turned inward. Its vocation is the patient and realistic improvement of life in a community. Communism, on the other hand, necessarily looks outward because it is a failed society and is incapable of engendering a viable one. The

Nomenklatura,[1] the body of bureaucrat-dictators who govern the system, has no choice, therefore, but to direct its abilities toward expansion abroad. Communism is more skillful, more persevering than democracy in defending itself. Democracy tends to ignore, even deny, threats to its existence because it loathes doing what is needed to counter them. It awakens only when the danger becomes deadly, imminent, evident. By then, either there is too little time left for it to save itself, or the price of survival has become crushingly high.

In addition to its external enemy (once Nazi, now Communist), whose intellectual energy and economic power are primarily destructive, democracy faces an internal enemy whose right to exist is written into the law itself.

Totalitarianism liquidates its internal enemies or smashes opposition as soon as it arises; it uses methods that are simple and infallible because they are undemocratic. But democracy can defend itself only very feebly; its internal enemy has an easy time of it because he exploits the right to disagree that is inherent in democracy. His aim of destroying democracy itself, of actively seeking an absolute monopoly of power, is shrewdly hidden behind the citizen's legitimate right to oppose and criticize the system. Paradoxically, democracy offers those seeking to abolish it a unique opportunity to work against it legally. They can even receive almost open support from the external enemy without its being seen as a truly serious violation of the social contract. The frontier is vague, the transition easy between the status of a loyal opponent wielding a privilege built into democratic institutions and that of an adversary subverting those institutions. To totalitarianism, an opponent is by definition subversive; democracy treats subversives as mere opponents for fear of betraying its principles.

What we end up with in what is conventionally called Western society is a topsy-turvy situation in which those seeking to destroy democracy appear to be fighting for legitimate aims, while its de-

1. Voslensky, Michael, *La Nomenklatura: Les Privilégiés en URSS*, Paris, 1980. The book was recently issued in English (Garden City, N.Y.: Doubleday, 1984) under the title *Nomenklatura*.

fenders are pictured as repressive reactionaries. Identification of democracy's internal and external adversaries with the forces of progress, legitimacy, even peace, discredits and paralyzes the efforts of people who are only trying to preserve their institutions.

Already besieged by this combination of hostile forces and negative logic, the democracies are also harassed by guilt-producing accusations and intimidation that no other political system has had to tolerate. Like the "industry of vice" that reform groups used to talk about, there is now an "industry of blame"; it promotes the now universally accepted notion that everything bad that happens in the Third World is the fault of forces necessarily and exclusively located in the "more advanced" or "rich" countries, meaning, in almost every case—and for good reason—the democracies.

The major shareholders in this industry of blame are, first, the despots who oppress the peoples of that unfortunate Third World with impunity. Next come the Communist countries, exploiting the underdevelopment abroad that they cannot remedy at home and converting the poor nations into totalitarian military fortresses.

Here too, in what are termed North-South relations, the democracies' foreign and domestic enemies are converging; their maneuvers are of no help at all in improving the lot of the poor countries, but they are marvelously effective in undermining the democracies' confidence in their own legitimacy, their own right to exist. The "progressive" support some Westerners give to the worst of the Third World regimes is merely a geographical relocation of what for sixty years was "progressive" support of the Soviet Union and, later, of Mao Tse-tung's China: complicity by a part of the Western left *against* the peoples of the less developed countries and *with* the tyrants who enslave them, brutalize, starve, and exterminate them. A shameful distortion of a noble cause!

It seems, then, that the combination of forces—at once psychological and material, political and moral, economic and ideological —intent on the extinction of democracy is more powerful than those forces bent on keeping it alive. Democracy is not given credit for its achievements and benefits, but it pays an infinitely higher price for its failures, its inadequacies, and its mistakes than its adversaries do. The aim of this book is to describe in detail the implacable democracy-killing machine this world of ours has become. There may be some satisfaction in understanding how it works, even if we are powerless to stop it.

2

A WILLING VICTIM

DEMOCRATIC CIVILIZATION is the first in history to blame itself because another power is working to destroy it. The distinguishing mark of our century is not so much communism's determination to erase democracy from our planet, or its frequent success in pursuing that end, as it is the humility with which democracy is not only consenting to its own obliteration but is contriving to legitimize its deadliest enemy's victory.

It is natural for communism to try with all its might to eliminate democracy, since the two systems are incompatible and communism's survival depends on its rival's annihilation. That the Communist offensive is more successful, more skillful than democracy's resistance will be seen by history as just another example of one power outmaneuvering another. But it is less natural and more novel that the stricken civilization should not only be deeply convinced of the rightness of its own defeat, but that it should regale its friends and foes with reasons why defending itself would be immoral and, in any event, superfluous, useless, even dangerous.

Civilizations losing confidence in themselves: an old story in history. They stop believing they can survive, because of an internal crisis that is both insoluble and intolerable or under threat from an external enemy so strong that the civilization must choose between servitude and suicide. I do not believe democracy is in either predicament, but it acts as if it were in both. What distinguishes it is its eagerness to believe in its own guilt and its inevitable result. Democracy's predecessors hid such beliefs as shameful even when they thought, or knew, they were doomed. But democracy is zealous in devising arguments to prove the justice of its adversary's case and to lengthen the already overwhelming list of its own inadequacies.

Are these inadequacies real or imaginary? Some are real, of course, just as there is real cause to blame specific democracies or the democracies in general for some of the injustice and misfortune in the world. But many of these alleged inadequacies and much of the democracies' responsibility for the world's ills are exaggerated or conjectural or purely imaginary. And besides, are those real faults serious enough to provide moral justification for totalitarianism to exterminate the democracies? And why are the imaginary flaws so widely credited in the democracies themselves, which thus consent in their own calumniation?

If democracy does succumb, it will not be to the sort of internal crisis, an essential lack of viability, that nearly wrecked it between the two world wars. From 1919 to 1939, the democracies seemed to be eaten from within by an irresistible malady that raised a rash of right-wing dictatorships. One after another, they capitulated to authoritarian or totalitarian governments born of the democracies' inability to govern themselves. In Central Europe, almost none of the parliamentary regimes established after World War I were still functioning ten years later. In Western Europe, first Italy went fascist, then Portugal, Germany, Spain. Of the great European powers, only Britain and France remained faithful to democracy, and in France it was so feeble, so incoherent, and so beleaguered that there were grave fears for its survival.

The situation now, as the century nears its end, is nothing like that. Non-Communist Europe's political health is satisfactory. For the first time since 1922, when Mussolini took power in Rome, all of Western Europe is democratic. The Greek colonels' seven-year dictatorship (1967–74) ended with their fall and a reinforcement of democracy there. In Spain, the putsch dreaded since 1975 was tried and failed. The most dangerous, most unrelenting attacks against democracy have come from the revolutionary left: red terrorism in Italy, Spain, and West Germany and a minority attempt in 1975 to saddle Portugal with a Communist military dictatorship.

Despite these trials, the old democracies have held firm and the new ones have survived and even developed. The laborious effort the left periodically makes to frighten people with the specter of a neo-Nazi peril in Europe always collides with the brute fact that none of the fascist movements in Europe today has reached party status or has managed to elect a member of any parliament. The publicity that raised France's obscure, marginal "New Right" to fame in 1980 attested mainly to the need for the left to invent an enemy to its liking so as to hide its real enemy, communism, from itself. The New Right is an intellectual and moral freak with absolutely no political weight. In fact, unlike the situation common before the war, no influential political figure today openly advocates the overthrow of democracy. And if such a figure were to surface, he could never dream of carrying through his program.[1] Rightist or "black" terrorism's foreign origins and support are far less discernible than those of leftist "red" terrorism, but both emanate from the same inability to recruit more than a tiny following by legal means. The stupidly inflated notion of an "extraparliamentary left" that flourished in Italy and Germany around 1970 expressed nothing more than the revolutionary left's inability to seduce enough voters into making it parliamentary.

Considered in isolation, then, democracy has been expanded and consolidated since World War II. True, few countries possess it, but in these its support as an institutional system is now, more than ever in the past, virtually unanimous.

Yet, while the democratic system as an institution is no longer challenged from within, the societies, civilization, and values it has created are being increasingly questioned. Self-criticism is, of course, one of the vital springs of democratic civilization and one of the reasons for its superiority over all other systems. But constant self-condemnation, often with little or no foundation, is a source of weakness and inferiority in dealing with an imperial power that has dispensed with such scruples. Believing it is always

1. The neofascist Italian Social Movement (MSI), although excluded by Italy's other parties from the "constitutional arc," nevertheless supports the country's institutions and opposes violence.

right, even when the facts say it's wrong, is as blinding and weakening to a society as to an individual. But assuming it is always wrong, whatever the truth may be, is discouraging and paralyzing. Not only do the democracies today blame themselves for sins they have not committed, but they have formed the habit of judging themselves by ideals so inaccessible that the defendants are automatically guilty. It follows that a civilization that feels guilty for everything it is and does and thinks will lack the energy and conviction to defend itself when its existence is threatened. Drilling into a civilization that it deserves defending only if it can incarnate absolute justice is tantamount to urging that it let itself die or be enslaved.

For this is really what's at stake. Exaggerated self-criticism would be a harmless luxury of civilization if there were no enemy at the gate condemning democracy's very existence. But it becomes dangerous when it portrays its mortal enemy as always being in the right. Extravagant criticism is a good propaganda device in internal politics. But if it is repeated often enough, it is finally believed. And where will the citizens of democratic societies find reasons to resist the enemy outside if they are persuaded from childhood that their civilization is merely an accumulation of failures and a monstrous imposture? At both ends of the democratic world's political spectrum there is agreement with the Soviet Union's rationale for its plan to destroy the liberal societies—from radical critics out of conviction, from conservatives out of resignation.

While the principle of political democracy may no longer be contested from within, it is under worldwide attack as it has never before been in its brief history. And that attack, which is being waged with unexampled vigor, scope and intelligence, is catching the democracies in a state of intellectual impotence and political indolence that disposes them to defeat and makes a Communist victory probable, if not inevitable.

It is also possible that democratic civilization will not die forever, that it is merely at the close of a cycle, the end of a first period of individual freedoms as modern democracy understands them.

All mankind would then come under Communist domination. Later it may rise against communism, which would then have no outside accomplices to support it, no future victims to enslave, no capitalist economies to keep it alive. It would not have the slightest excuse for its inability to manage a human society and could no longer resist its subjects' rebellion; it could not, after all, imprison or exterminate everybody. Thus, after a few centuries, when mankind has paid off its mortgage to socialism, a new democratic cycle could begin.

3

TOCQUEVILLE'S MISTAKE

WE MUST RAISE a parricidal hand against our father Parmenides, says the Stranger in Plato's *The Sophist*, and reexamine a central thesis of his philosophy. It is with the same *Filial Feelings of a Parricide*, to borrow a title from Marcel Proust, that I raise a question, if not a hand, against Alexis de Tocqueville.

I do not mean to suggest that his work doesn't deserve the repute it has finally won—on the contrary! It is a lone haven of grace and reliability among all the terrible monuments of political philosophy, all those revered writings by both the right and the left that for two centuries have vied in prescribing the extermination of half the human race and the reeducation of the other half. What consoles me for my audacity in correcting Tocqueville is that, on one point, I think he was simply too pessimistic.

He foresaw that democracy could suffocate itself, in a sense, by following its own logic to its extreme. This has been noted before in his writing, but it's one aspect that has been less emphasized than others. Tocqueville described this ultimate phase as a mild dictatorship of public opinion, an age of homogeneous feelings, ideas, tastes, manners that enslave the citizenry, not to an external force, but to the omnipotence of their will toward consensus. The more perfect egalitarian democracy becomes, the more naturally its citizens resemble each other, the more they will all freely desire the same things. Diversity would gradually be banished from such a society, not by censure, but by general disapproval or mere indifference. The majority's omnipotence would eliminate even the urge to stray from prevailing opinions. Original minds that work against the popular grain would gradually wither—those, that is, that were not stillborn—not because of persecution, but simply for lack of an audience, for lack even of anyone to contradict them.

Equality of status, the basis of democracy as Tocqueville understood it—that is, equality not of riches, but before the law—engenders uniformity of thought. When the two forms of equality are coupled, they breed an offspring that nullifies or, at least, renders unrecognizable the original idea democracy had about its future development. For what they produce is the growing role of government, the modern government of which democracy's children ask everything and from which they consequently accept everything. Each individual is isolated from all the others by the very equality of their status and their identical freedoms.

Tocqueville the visionary depicted with stunning precision the coming ascension of the omnipresent, omnipotent and omniscient state that twentieth-century man knows so well: the state as protector, entrepreneur, educator; the physician-state, impresario-state, bookseller-state, helpful and predatory, tyrant and guardian, economist, journalist, moralist, shipper, trader, advertiser, banker, father and jailer all at once. The state ransoms and the state subsidizes. It settles without violence into a wheedling, meticulous despotism that no monarchy, no tyranny, no political authority of the past had the means to achieve. Its power borders on the absolute partly because it is scarcely felt, having increased by imperceptible stages at the wish of its subjects, who turn to it instead of to each other. In these pages by Tocqueville we find the germ both of George Orwell's *1984* and David Riesman's *The Lonely Crowd.*

In one sense, history has endorsed Tocqueville's reasoning and, in another, has invalidated it. He has been proved right insofar as the power of public opinion has indeed increased in the democracies through the nineteenth and twentieth centuries. But public opinion has not grown more consistent or uniform; it has in fact become increasingly volatile and diversified. And the state, instead of gaining strength in proportion to its gigantism, is increasingly disobeyed and challenged by the very citizens who expect so much from it. Submerged by the demands on it, called on to solve all problems, it is being steadily stripped of the right to regulate things.

So the omnipotence based on consensus that Tocqueville forecast is only one side of the coin of modern government. The other is an equally general impotence to deal with the conflicting daily claims made on it by constituents eager for aid but less and less willing to assume obligations. By invading every area of life, the democratic state has stuffed itself with more responsibilities than powers. The very contradictions among special interests that are as legitimate as they are incompatible, all expecting to be treated with equal goodwill, show that the state's duties are expanding faster than its means of performing them. There is no denying how burdensome a tutelary government is on society—provided we add that its expansion makes it vulnerable, often paralyzing it in its relations with client groups that are quicker to harry it than to obey it.

This sort of behavior splinters democratic societies into separate groups, each battling for advantage and caring little for the interests of others or society as a whole. Public opinion, instead of being united by uniform thinking, is fragmented into a variety of cultures that can be so different in tastes, ways of living, attitudes and language that they understand each other only dimly, if at all. They coexist but do not mingle. Public opinion in today's democracies forms an archipelago, not a continent. Each island in the chain ranks its own distinctiveness above membership in a national group and even higher above its association with a group of democratic nations.

In one sense, we do live in a mass era as residents of a "planetary village" where manners and fashions blend. But, paradoxically, we also live in an age of the triumph of minorities, of a juxtaposition of widely differing attitudes. While it is obvious that the passion for equality, identified by Tocqueville as the drive wheel of democracy, generates uniformity, let's not forget that democracy also rests on a passion for liberty, which fosters diversity, fragmentation, unorthodoxy. Plato, democracy's shrewdest enemy, saw this when he compared it to a motley cloak splashed with many colors. In a democracy, he said, everyone claims the right to live as he chooses,[1] so that ways of living multiply and jostle each other. To Aristotle, too, liberty was the basic principle of democracy. He broke this down into two tenets: "for all to rule and be ruled in turn" and "a man should live as he likes."[2] In American democracy, the right to do one's own thing is as much or more cherished than equality.

The ideological and cultural wars among the islands in the archipelago now take precedence over defense of the archipelago itself. In Holland in 1981, a considerable share of public opinion, questioned about its feelings on Poland and Afghanistan, declared that the Dutch lacked a moral right to criticize Communist repression or Soviet imperialism "as long as housing conditions in Amsterdam fail to meet the highest standards of modern comfort, as long as women remain exploited and the legal rights of heterosexual married couples are denied to homosexual married couples."[3]

Tocqueville's vision of a society becoming democratically totalitarian through absolute agreement among its citizens has not come true. In our time, the system described in the last part of *Democracy in America* is in force in the truly totalitarian societies, the Communist societies. This by no means confirms Tocqueville's hypothesis, since none of these societies became totalitarian by democratic means.

Among democracy's enemies, it's an old obsession to predict— with aims and arguments wholly opposed to Tocqueville's, of course—the stealthy transformation of democratic regimes into authoritarian states. It's a way of denying that democracy is real or even possible. The world today refutes that theory. Democracy is less than ever threatened from within. But it is more than ever menaced from outside.

1. Plato *Republic* 8.
2. Aristotle *Politics* 6, 2.
3. Cited by Michel Heller in *Sous le regard de Moscou* (Paris: Calmann-Lévy, 1982), p. 72.

4

SURVIVAL OF THE LEAST FIT

THERE IS A widespread belief that a society's survival depends on its ability to satisfy its members' needs. Relying on this notion, many Western leaders and commentators point to the chronic anemia of the Soviet economy, which seems not only to be irremediable but to be growing steadily worse, and see in it the imminent collapse of the Soviet empire, or at least a forced slowdown of its expansionary momentum.

Others, however, find cause for alarm for the democracies in communism's extraordinary incompetence: unrelieved internal failure, they fear, drives the empire's masters to seek external success. I hasten to add that whichever of the two theories is favored, Western governments' conclusion is that the Soviet Union must be appeased. If it is true that the Soviet imperialist drive is slowing down for lack of fuel, why whip it up with tough diplomacy? And if its temper is being darkened by internal bankruptcy, wouldn't Western inflexibility provoke a disproportionately violent Soviet reaction? Do we want them to blow up the planet?

A striking illustration, this, of the maxim Montaigne used as a chapter heading: "By various means we reach the same ends."[1] From different premises, our diplomats of both schools reach the same conclusion: that not only must we avoid overresistance to Communist imperialism, but we should try to buy it off with economic aid. If communism's leaders are going soft, we should show them that softness pays; if their subjects' poverty is making them

1. *Essays*, bk. I, chap. 1.

increasingly irritable toward the rest of the world, we must ease that poverty to cool their anger.

Failing any benefit to the democracies from Soviet economic weakness—and, for the moment, they disavow such base desires—the only question remaining is whether this persistent weakness can cause the empire to collapse under its own weight. It seems to me that the answer must be "yes" in the long run, but not soon enough to change the balance of forces in today's world.

It stands to reason that a social system that in three quarters of a century has merely perpetuated its people's shortages of food and medical care is doomed to disappear someday. But not in time to change the near future for us. The Soviet Union survived its economic failures even in the days when it was far less of a power than it is now. Police repression is seamless, the compartmentalization of people and regions is effective in nipping organized protest in the bud; the great mass of the population, deprived of any basis of comparison, is largely unaware of other standards and styles of living. Because of these factors, it is hard to see what could force the Soviet state in the short run to replace its military and imperialistic priorities with an intensive program of internal economic development and social progress. Besides, such a program would be impossible to undertake without immolating the existing political system, which is the strongest brake on development.

Above all, and this is my principal objection, the idea that an authoritarian political system must collapse because it cannot provide a decent life for its citizenry can only occur to a democrat. When we reason this way about the Soviet empire, we are simply ascribing democracy's operational rules and attitudes to a totalitarian regime. But these rules and attitudes are signally abnormal and, as I said earlier, very recent and probably transitory. The notion that whoever holds power must clear out because his subjects are discontented or dying of hunger or distress is a bit of whimsy that history has tolerated wondrously few times in real life. Although they are forced by the current fashion to pay lip service to this cumbersome idea, nine out of ten of today's leaders are careful not to put it into practice; they even indulge themselves

in the luxury of accusing the only true democracies now functioning of constantly violating the precept. But then, how could totalitarian rulers break a social contract they've never signed?

As things stand, relatively minor causes of discontent corrode,
disturb, unsettle, paralyze the democracies faster and more deeply
than horrendous famine and constant poverty do the Communist
regimes, whose subject peoples have no real rights or means of
redressing their wrongs. Societies of which permanent criticism is
an integral feature are the only livable ones, but they are also the
most fragile. They will continue to be the most fragile as long as
theirs is not the only system in the world and must compete with
systems that do not burden themselves with the same obligations.
We must not ascribe this kind of fragility to totalitarianism; it is
exclusive to democracy, along with another kind that needs identifying.

The more problems a society solves, the more perishable it becomes; conversely, the fewer it solves, the longer it will survive.
Tocqueville noticed—and history has borne him out—that a society rebels against authority in proportion as its needs are met. In
other words, the more largely claims are satisfied, the more aggressively they are made, especially when there is ample hope of constantly gaining further advantages. This presupposes an already
substantial level of prosperity and freedom. The third quarter of
the twentieth century, the period when they grew richest and most
free, was also the period in which the industrial democracies became increasingly unstable, explosive, ungovernable. In short, it's
not stagnation that breeds revolution, not repression, but progress,
because it has already created the wealth that makes revolution
viable.

This "law" of Tocqueville's needs some moderating. Of course
there have been uprisings caused by poverty, although, in the
Third World, even these are often triggered by a beginning of
modernization and improvement and by the conviction that the
means to a better life do exist. We must nevertheless concede that
the law gains in validity as societies grow more complex, less fearful of treating with a government that is—or is thought to be—

versatile and efficient and anchored in a democratic tradition. To be effective, the law requires that a society be capable of standing up to the state, which really means becoming stronger than the state. Neither the Soviet Union nor China meets these conditions. There the state is everything, civilian society nothing; economic stagnation and social sclerosis foreclose all hope, and the absence of freedom blocks the spread of discontent.

Monumental internal failure, then, will not make Communist states disintegrate or keep them from being imperialistic and hence dangerous to the democracies. State power and society's happiness are unrelated in a totalitarian context. We often hear it said that the Soviet Union is too weak, its economy too discredited for it to defeat us, that democratic capitalism has won the race between the two systems by a wide margin and has proved its superiority. Besides, the argument goes, aren't the Communists always pestering us to help them with credits, food, and technology?

When alarmed associates asked former French President Valéry Giscard d'Estaing why he was so patient with Moscow, he replied that after World War II his teachers at the Ecole Nationale d'Administration* depicted the Soviet economy as the standard by which all others were judged. Thirty years later, Giscard commented, a teacher who began his course on that note would be a laughing stock to his students. Everyone knows, the ex-President said, that the Soviet Union is too weak for us to fear.

I repeat, it is a mistake to ascribe democratic logic to a totalitarian system. The democracies trim their military spending when the economy goes sour; the Communist countries do not. Revision between 1948 and 1980 of judgment on the Soviet economy reflected the ignorance, the credulity or the dishonesty of Western economists after the war, not any objective deterioration of the Soviet system since then.

In fact, Giscard's argument is self-defeating, for the extreme weakness of the Soviet economy after the war, when the system's fundamental sterility was aggravated by the damage suffered in

---

* The school that trains most of France's top government officials and many of its leaders in trade and industry.—TRANS.

1941–45, did not prevent the U.S.S.R. from expanding dramatically throughout the world in the ensuing thirty years. Nothing has slowed the rapid progress of Communist imperialism—not the bankruptcy of communism and the fierce police repression in the satellite countries, not poverty, not the failures of all attempts at economic redress in the Soviet Union itself, under Khrushchev and later under Brezhnev, either via Lysenko's clownish "dialectical materialist" biology or the very materialist but not at all dialectical aid received from Western taxpayers. Indeed, the Soviet advance has speeded up since 1970.

Communism's final paroxysm will doubtless come someday. But this will not happen soon enough for the democracies to make it the key to their strategy of survival in the immediate future. Communism may be a "spent force," as Milovan Djilas has repeatedly said. Some might even call it a corpse. But it is a corpse that can drag us with it into the grave!

5

THE FEAR OF KNOWING

To SOME PEOPLE, it is a truism hardly worth saying that communism's aim is world conquest, that the Soviet Union—the leading Communist power in seniority and resources—has made great strides toward that end, especially since World War II, and that it is now in a position to advance still farther and faster. To others, this is a twisted obsession, a systematized frenzy nourished by reactionaries, revanchists, "Manichaeans," and warmongers of every stripe.

One of the objectives of this book is to determine which of these two points of view is the less delusive. There must be a way for us to rise above all the shouting and collect the facts or, at least, the clues that can help us find the truth—to determine, at any rate, which is the more reasonable assumption.

From the outset, we must insist that those democracies anxious to preserve their system, if there are any, adopt the more pessimistic approach, out of sheer prudence. Insurance protects you from hail and floods, not from fair weather. Throughout this book I will reiterate that the Western weakness for taking the optimistic view has never been and cannot be a good way to formulate foreign and defense policies. I would even say that conditioning us to think it is shameful to defend ourselves is one of the most successful of the Communist propaganda ploys. "How easy it is to manipulate naive people," Communist leaders must gloat, "to persuade innocents, who negotiate on the assumption that you only mean well by them, that you're just a poor, terrified little thing longing to be appeased forever by, oh, almost nothing—merely the loss of their independence."

Isn't there nevertheless reason to think that Western pacifists may be right on one point: that we must beware of the ideas some people in the democracies hold, in the best of faith, about communism? Doesn't history teach us that in times of conflict or tension each antagonist suspects the other of plotting aggression?

We never see ourselves as aggressors. Almost always, our own aggressiveness, our intransigence, is presented and sincerely felt as a reply to threats from the other camp. By acting as though we were under threat, don't we risk actually inviting threats, pushing the Communists into behaving as we expect them to? This is the basis of all the peace propaganda issuing from the Soviet Union and its many allies in the West. Again, the best way to distinguish real danger from mere phobia, real aggression from hysteria, is to study the facts, actions, situations, comparing them over periods of ten, twenty, thirty years. The best way to find out if a policy of expansionism exists is to see if there has been expansion.

You certainly do not have to be obsessed to find a sort of Soviet conspiracy everywhere in the world. It isn't, strictly speaking, a conspiracy, which is a single operation carried out in a limited period of time. Feeling out the terrain everywhere, hunting for territory to annex or for political advantage, is in the nature of the Soviet machine, its normal way of functioning, just as Japan's genius is shown in expanding trade and a constant search for footholds in new markets.

Conspiracy is too mild a term for what the Communists do. They have an overall plan that they follow methodically, patiently, relentlessly. They announced their intentions early in this century, they began to fulfill them under Lenin, and they've been at it ever since. To them, a defeat is never final; they can wait and try again, changing tactics when necessary.

Communism's victories, however, are more often than not final and irreversible because, in a matter of months after each Soviet advance, the West accepts the fait accompli and acknowledges the U.S.S.R.'s ill-gotten gain, territorial or political, as a rightful acquisition; questioning this by any form of "interference," even verbal, is seen as a danger to peace. The democracies act—abstain from acting, rather—this way because they have no long-range counter-strategy and, especially, no common plan uniting them all.

For example, the restoration of totalitarianism in Poland in December 1981 again caught the West unprepared. Coming after the invasion of Afghanistan, after the row over the 1980 Olympic Games and the quarrels over intermediate-range nuclear weapons, the Polish crisis dramatically highlighted the lack of coordination and foresight in Western policy. Yet the Western powers cannot say they hadn't the time to plan for every contingency. In Poland, the Soviets restored Communist order without intervening openly as they had in Budapest in 1956 and Prague in 1968.

This Soviet success illustrates a fact worth repeating: that the Communists have an overall strategic concept in Europe, Asia, Africa, Latin America, the Caribbean, the Indian Ocean. But the West waits to react until the U.S.S.R. has moved, and then the riposte is generally no more than a vague attempt to save face with words rather than any active reprisal. Since 1981, Afghanistan has become old hat. We've almost forgotten the Afghans. Any obstacles the Communists are meeting there are being put up by the Afghan resistance, not by the West, which has purged its mind of the problems of reprisals against the invader and aid to the victims. Not even evidence revealed in January 1982 that the Soviets are using yellow rain in chemical warfare against the Afghans aroused any special feeling in the West. And, after the few months needed to exhaust our compassion, we have also half forgotten the Cambodians and the Cuban and Vietnamese boat people.

The fact that changes in the balance of power in recent years particularly threaten Western Europe because of its proximity to the U.S.S.R. does not mean that the world situation should be seen exclusively from a European, or even a Western, point of view. Asia, Africa, Latin America, Oceania are all, in varying degrees, theaters of confrontation where the gigantic world match is being played.

For this is now a single rivalry, in which all the continents, all nations and peoples, whatever their systems of government, their levels of development, or their alliances, are involved and interdependent. Since around 1975, one player has seemed to dominate the match: the Soviet Union. The powers it is attacking merely deplore its aggressiveness and quarrel among themselves about how to reply; meanwhile they send out endless signals of moderation in the hope of inspiring a spirit of saintly emulation in the Soviets.

What is really behind their passiveness? Is it inevitable? Does it conceal a calculated policy or a lack of political analysis? Is the West resigned to Soviet domination, or is it simply waiting for a better opening to counterattack? What, ideally, should we do and what, in fact, can we still do? Answering these questions is the purpose of this book.

Before deciding what is good and what is bad, we have to understand what the situation actually is. Identifying good and evil, whether in terms of morality or of our interests, is a matter of subjective choices. That an African country has become a Soviet satellite is good in some eyes, bad in others. But the first thing to determine is whether the country *is* a satellite and, if so, when it became one and how many other African countries are liable to follow it into the Soviet orbit. Such and such a European statesman may honestly believe that the least damaging course for the future of Europe is to negotiate an agreement with the U.S.S.R. giving Europe autonomy in return for recognition of the Soviet empire in Central Europe and for turning a blind eye to Soviet expansion elsewhere in the world. Is this a good or bad policy? Not all Europeans will see it the same way. But, first, we must know if such a policy is really being pursued, to what extent, by how many countries, and with how much public support.

How can we make value judgments—remembering that the values will vary with each individual's ultimate goals—about actions and facts we haven't yet established as real or important? Yet it is around the circulation of facts that the taboos are strongest in the evolution of public information and debate into national policy. The fear, or hope, that an event might serve a given view of the world, a given network of alliances and interests, takes precedence over precise knowledge of that event, the overall situation that made it possible, the power balance it reveals. As a rule, concern that a fact might influence public opinion in a way we dislike overrides our curiosity about it and our honesty in making it known. Hence the barriers to establishing a running chart of the world balance of forces. Yet such a chart, even if it is reduced to nothing more than the elements we're sure of, is indispensable if we are to understand our position, choose the directions in which we can move, and evaluate our means for reaching our objectives.

It's a difficult task, since it is at the fact-finding stage that refusing to know becomes censorship. I must insist on this machinery of self-censorship that persuades so many people that the Red Army and the KGB operate only in the fervid imaginations of anti-Communist fanatics. One of the Kremlin's chief assets is the repugnance on the part of many Westerners to recognize Soviet expansionism for what it is. Anyone calling attention to it is likely to be thought an obsessive, a nut.

This is not true in Europe alone. For example, the author of an article in the July 1981 issue of *The Washington Monthly* derided Professor Richard Pipes of Harvard, then an adviser to the White House, because he believed the Soviets have a master plan. This was taken as a sign of madness. In France, I was authoritatively assured, Giscard d'Estaing was "exasperated" by the "obsessions" of Alexandre de Marenches, then head of the French secret service. Giscard also viewed the invasion of Afghanistan as a careless Soviet mistake. The veteran George Kennan, once the State Department's top Sovietologist, who later taught his specialty at Princeton, told the *U.S. News and World Report* (March 10, 1980) that when the Russians moved into Afghanistan "their immediate objective was purely defensive." Against whom? We're not told. And we are tempted to reply that even if this were true, it would make no difference to us, much less to the Afghans.

Early in 1979, Giscard ordered the cancellation of two large contracts for the sale of warplanes and electronic equipment to China "so as not," he explained to me, "to accentuate the Soviets' complex of encirclement." In the United States, Representative Patricia Schroeder (Democrat, Colorado) replied to the aforementioned Professor Pipes on the same subject, declaring that the United States has no interest in heaping fuel on the flames in its relations with Russia by giving military aid to China.

The position could be sound—it all depends on the outcome. But what incontestable Soviet concession can be cited in return for French cancellation of the China contracts? None. Did France or the United States win Soviet agreement to stop selling weapons to any of its satellites—Cuba, Ethiopia, Angola, Nicaragua? No. Henry Kissinger reports in his memoirs that State Department bureaucrats and members of Congress concerned in the 1970–72 negotiations on mutual reduction of forces *assumed that the Soviet Union wants peace* and reasoned as though only the United States could be considered aggressive. Requests from President Nixon and his Secretary of State for increases in the defense budget were regularly refused by Congress as provocative; in Vienna, meanwhile, the State Department's disarmament negotiator skillfully undermined Kissinger's efforts to win agreement.

There is a common line of behavior in all this: we deliberately adopt the policy most favorable to the Russians (that they are similarly generous toward us seems improbable, to say the least). This peculiar turn of mind was summed up by the Czechoslovak Karel Kosik. "In politics, the loser is the one who lets himself be swayed by the other's arguments and who judges his own actions through his adversary's eyes."[1]

Naturally, in foreign policy one must take the rival country's viewpoint so as to try and understand its policy and anticipate its future moves. But this is exactly what the West does *not* do. Instead, we think what the U.S.S.R. *wants* us to think—for example, that economic sanctions would increase Soviet intransigence and would turn out badly *for us*. What we *do* is accept the principle of nonreciprocity of concessions as a legitimate rule. We see ourselves as aggressors when we react, if only verbally, to Soviet aggression.

1. Cited by François Fetjö in *Histoires des démocraties populaires* (Paris: Seuil, 1969), vol. II, p. 263.

For example, a Reaganite congressman from Iowa said in January 1982 that the administration had alienated the young with its "hard-line foreign policy." That young Americans oppose even a remote possibility of reviving the draft is only human. But it is astonishing to hear talk of a "hard-line policy" when they are only being asked to *register* for a call-up that will probably never come, with nothing said about a peacetime draft. What, then, would a "soft line" be?

It is considered good form always to adopt the most indulgent outlook for the Soviet Union and the most optimistic for the West. Yet I must insist that foreign and defense policies must be based on worst-case hypotheses that anticipate the least favorable developments for ourselves. We are not covered unless we do this. If a man comes at you in the street holding a gun in each hand, it's one chance in a million that he's just a guy from a shooting gallery taking his stock back to the fairgrounds. It would certainly be reckless to take that as your *only* working hypothesis.

There can be a number of causes for this passivity, this deliberate blindness: a conviction that the U.S.S.R. is so strong and its future expansion so certain that we have no choice but resignation; persistent identification of communism as *the* political left, despite a sharp shift of opinion away from it, and associating anti-Sovietism with the political right; the notion that what was once American dominance put the Soviets on the defensive and, consequently, that the more the West relaxes its pressure, the more peaceful they will be. Even conservatives seldom risk naming the threat of totalitarianism as the greatest menace of our time, for fear of seeming fanatical. Democracy, on the defensive against an all-out totalitarian offensive, dares not admit it is fighting.

Yet never has such an admission been more warranted. Of the sixteen North Atlantic Treaty Organization members, only Turkey again strayed from democracy toward the end of the 1970s, and even there a 1982 referendum gave its military dictatorship a kind of legitimacy. But all seven of the "richest" nations, spread over three continents, are democratic. There was no such honorable level of democracy among the forces fighting the Germans in 1914–

18 or among the Allies in World War II. And yet, today, it is increasingly frowned on to state plainly that democracy is struggling against totalitarianism. Good taste demands that the fight be dressed in more neutral colors that show communism in a less pejorative light: a conflict between East and West, between capitalism and socialism, between the two superpowers.

Fear of knowing always leads to fear of calling things by their names.

During a luncheon at the State Department in January 1982, I heard one high official say, "We Americans are not solving problems, we *are* the problem." In Europe, fear both hidden and open of the United States is so violent that, deep down, some Europeans are prepared to accept Soviet domination just to see the Americans destroyed. This covers a broad spectrum, from the Christian-Marxists on the left to those Gaullists on the right inspired by the teachings of Charles Maurras.[2] In his movement's magazine, *Elements*, the French New Right's theoretician, Alain de Benoist, judged "decadence worse than dictatorship," that is, that an "Americanized" West is worse than communism. "Some people," he concluded, "are not resigned to the idea of having to wear a Red Army cap some day. True, it is not a pleasant prospect. But we cannot stand the idea that we will eventually have to spend the rest of our lives eating hamburgers in Brooklyn."[3]

In another issue, De Benoist praised the anti-Americanism of the French Socialist Minister of Culture who, during a UNESCO conference in Mexico City, spoke as an implacable champion of cultural xenophobia. "[Minister] Jack Lang," De Benoist wrote, "delivered what may have been the most important speech in contemporary history since General de Gaulle's address at Phnom Penh."[4]

It is interesting, though not surprising, to see the extreme right, in condemning free enterprise, pick up the same arguments the non-Communist Marxist left has been using for years and is still

2. Maurras (1868–1952) was a right-wing extremist French author and political theorist.
3. March–April 1982.
4. October–November 1982. On De Gaulle's speech, see pages 121–2.

using. That the terminology of some leftists has thus returned to
its true sources is clear from this assertion by De Benoist. "The
truth is that there are two distinct forms of totalitarianism, very
different in their natures and effects, but both dreadful. The first,
in the East, imprisons, persecutes, ravages the body; at least it
leaves hope intact. The other, in the West, ends up creating happy
robots. It air-conditions hell. It kills the soul."[5]

In assessing the relative gains made by democracy and its enemies, we must pay increasing heed to the myriad backfires of will-
ful ignorance being set to divert attention from the spreading con-
flagration.

---

5. Remarks to the XVth conference of the Groupe de Recherches et d'Études sur la
Civilisation Européenne (GRECE), reported in *Le Monde* of 20 May 1981.

PART TWO

THE REALITY OF
COMMUNIST EXPANSION

6

AFTER POLAND:
AN AUTOPSY

AT A SUMMIT MEETING in Versailles early in June 1982, six of the seven industrialized countries immediately formed a united front against the seventh, the United States. The reason was the Americans' insistence that the Europeans raise the interest rates on their loans to the Soviet Union—specifically, to deny it the preferential rates usually accorded the poor countries. Why not, the United States objected, charge the U.S.S.R. the normal rates? Why shouldn't it at least pay the rates the Western countries charge each other? The Europeans refused, arguing that higher interest rates would not improve Soviet behavior in international relations.

So, after a dozen years of pleading that economic aid to the East bloc would pacify the Soviet Union, the Europeans in 1982 declined to reduce that aid because it would not make the Russians less belligerent. Incoherence on a grand scale! Economic cooperation did not bring the hoped-for détente, but neither would noncooperation. That's a fine, blind maze we've shut ourselves into; appeasement and reprisal, we find, are equally incapable of making the Communists behave themselves and of slowing their aggressive drive. By this reasoning, our only choice is whether we're going to pay to be rolled, and we are opting to die paying. For after openly confessing that all the calculations on which they'd based their hopes for détente have come to nothing, the Europeans are capping it all by acting like unmitigated suckers with a prodigality surprising in countries plagued by a persistent economic recession.

At Versailles, President Reagan finally had to settle for vague European promises of "heightened vigilance" in their economic and technological dealings with the East. A fuzzy phrase, the sort of flowery communiqué language that automatically precludes any practical follow-up. Yet it was fiercely criticized the next day by Soviet commentators irritated by the verbal liberties the Europeans had allowed themselves toward Moscow. True, their anger was tempered by their very well-founded satisfaction that the United States, to quote *Pravda*, had not won "a complete victory for their position." It's the least they could say.

Now, this was six months after the declaration of martial law by the Polish Government, yet American appeals for European firmness had already been scaled down to very modest goals. There was no more talk of wholesale cancellation of aid as a stern warning to the U.S.S.R. Economic sanctions had come down merely to a question of withdrawing the Soviet privilege (of low interest rates), which seemed the minimum the West could do. And even this struck the Europeans as so exaggeratedly severe that the United States was again thought of as the real aggressor, the power that was disturbing the world's tranquility.

Half a year had been more than enough for the West's spirit of passiveness to learn to live with Poland's martyrdom. This is the standard period after each new Soviet thrust, all the time needed to overcome our strongest resentment. A resurgence of repression in Poland early in May 1982 failed to arouse even a hundredth of the previous winter's indignation that had sparked so many protest demonstrations in the West.

By this time, everyone had concluded from the Franco-German summit conference in Paris on February 24, 1982, that the party really responsible for the international crisis created by the crackdown in Poland was, after all, the United States. Hadn't the Americans, by trying to forge a common Allied policy, simply been using the crisis to sow discord between France and West Germany? Besides, the Paris communiqué implied, what did Soviet repression in Eastern Europe or in Afghanistan matter compared to the far more unforgivable American crime of maintaining high interest rates? The Soviet aim of transforming the Polish crisis into a Western crisis was a resounding success.

And so it had been almost from the start, with no effort on Moscow's part, beginning on December 13, 1981, when the Polish people were brutally awakened from their dream and led back into the prison of totalitarianism. By complying with the Kremlin's ultimatum, Poland's storm troopers had not only reestablished Communist order in Warsaw, but had established disorder in the West as well. A firecracker in a henhouse could not have touched off any more harmonious, coordinated, appropriately intelligent flapping and cackling than the December 1981 Polish countercoup aroused among Western nations.

That the power play in Poland became a drama for the democracies once more highlighted the incompetence of their diplomacy, of their intelligence services, and, especially, of their governments. The Soviet leaders had done their homework, or their bureaucrats and technical advisers had done it for them. They had found a way to limit the penalties that a replay of their Budapest and Prague invasions would have brought down on them. Western imagination, however, had stretched no farther than a repetition of those Red Army offensives. It never occurred to Western planners to wonder if the U.S.S.R. might hit on a form of repression other than the slightly too obvious and repetitive one of sending in the tanks.

In the eighteen months separating the start of the latest workers' uprising against communism in Poland and the December 13 police clampdown, the West had not strained its brains trying to anticipate all the possible variations on Soviet repression or to work out the necessary countermoves. Again, we did not act, we reacted. And our reaction took the form of agitation within the Western camp rather than a reply to the Soviet initiative. We have granted the Soviets a monopoly on action. In this chess game, the U.S.S.R. is always playing white, with the advantage of the opening move; when it's black's turn to play, all the West does is make a clumsy sweep that wipes the board clean.

Because we allow ourselves to be surprised by Soviet moves, such reactions as we have are improvised, ephemeral, and disorganized. After we failed to devise an effective, coherent response to

the invasion of Afghanistan and, through two years of silent inertia, had finally ratified the Soviet occupation there, a new tune was
struck up in the West. "If the Russians touch Poland," it went,
"they'll have gone that one step too far that we will not tolerate
under any circumstances." We had quarreled among ourselves over
Afghanistan, under the Communists' alert gaze; we had even failed
to agree on a boycott of the 1980 Moscow Olympics. After July
1980, the West justified its inertia with the notion that riling the
Soviets could disrupt the process of democratization in Poland.

Well, Western reactions to the December 1981 repression of the
Polish workers' Solidarity movement may not have been as morally disturbing as our reaction to the Afghanistan invasion, but
neither did they show any more sign of planning. Our behavior
amounted to absolution of the Communists. Indeed, criticism in
the West of Soviet boss Leonid Brezhnev soon shifted to President
Reagan, even though he had waited two weeks—because Secretary
of State Alexander Haig was anxious to handle America's allies
with tact—before condemning the Soviet Union. Haig's anxiety
reflected an odd distortion in the problem's focus, but it did the
United States no good, of course: the Allies were angry with the
Americans anyway for almost making them feel remorseful and
almost proposing that they do something.

In short, the Soviets succeeded in the twin project of stepping on
Poland while setting the Europeans against the Americans. They
operated with total impunity, at least as far as we were concerned;
such problems as did arise for them stemmed not from our firmness but from the Poles' resistance.

The West's display of cowardice after the Soviet grip closed
again on Poland confirmed the crushing victory the Soviet Union
had won in the struggle over application of the 1975 Helsinki
agreement.

In essence, the agreement provided for a swap. The West presented the U.S.S.R. with two lavish gifts: we recognized the legitimacy of the Soviet empire over Central Europe, which it had illegally grabbed at the end of World War II, and we offered massive
and almost interest-free economic and technological aid. In return,

the Soviet Union promised a more moderate foreign policy and respect for human rights within its empire.

Only an unfathomable lack of comprehension of communism's real nature could have made Western statesmen take that second proviso seriously; in any case, it quickly became clear that the promise was merely a joke designed to liven up dull Politburo meetings. But the topper was that Western governments, ever prompt to anticipate the KGB's wishes, were the first to proclaim that insisting on enforcement of the article was a provocation of the Soviet Union. President Carter's obstinacy in promoting a human-rights policy throughout the world was soon assailed as interference in other countries' internal affairs and a threat to peace—except, of course, in Chile and Saudi Arabia.

Humiliation followed for the West at the 1978 Belgrade conference, which had theoretically been called to verify that the Helsinki agreement was being applied. Without any superfluous hesitation or temporizing, the Soviets simply refused to take part in the work of the human-rights commission. Nevertheless, in 1980 we rushed merrily to a follow-up conference in Madrid, to go once again through the same vain farce that, for the democracies, remained as pointless as ever. Doubly pointless, in fact: since the Belgrade conference, the Soviets had invaded Afghanistan and colonized vast segments of Africa, thus shattering the credibility of the other Soviet promise at Helsinki, for moderation in foreign policy. So all that remained of that celebrated pact was the Western contribution: economic aid to the U.S.S.R. and recognition of its empire. By their concrete actions after the reestablishment of real and total socialism in Poland, the West Europeans staunchly affirmed their unshakable determination to live up unilaterally to their Helsinki commitments without so much as pretending to ask anything in return. Even the few concessions made by East Germany to ease restrictions on travel between the two Germanies were revoked at the end of 1980.

To grasp the full effect of the martial-law declaration in Poland on December 13, 1981, and especially the West's reaction to this Soviet gambit, we must not lose sight of the overall stakes. For eighteen months, the Soviet Union had been faced with the resistance of a whole people in its largest and most densely populated European colony. It was contending with a peaceful revolution it could not put down by any of its usual methods. The few whiffs of apparent liberalization granted by an overwhelmed Polish Communist Party did not begin to satisfy the people's passionate longing for freedom. But Soviet military intervention would probably have involved more drawbacks than benefits for the Communists; its duration and repercussions would have meant an overall setback to them at a time when the Soviet presence in Afghanistan was still causing keen irritation, if not effective opposition, in the rest of the world.

Moreover, while the Polish economy was collapsing, economic difficulties were also increasing sharply inside the Soviet Union. The Kremlin could not afford to lose the West's financial support for itself or its satellites. It had to achieve a tour de force: to subjugate the Poles while maintaining the economic privileges granted by the democracies and the political privileges won at Helsinki. With these, and protected by the mythology of détente, the U.S.S.R. could extend its conquests and reinforce its military strength. Moscow's game was to preserve these benefits despite the martial law in Poland.

For the democracies, the challenge was to profit from the weakened position of a Soviet Union awash in trouble in both Afghanistan and Poland by trying to force it into the path of genuine détente as the West had originally envisioned it; this was, especially, a chance to slow Soviet expansion and stall its efforts at destabilization on five continents. There was also an opportunity to win Soviet agreement to truly balanced arms limitation, not merely to a reduction in Western weaponry.

Obviously, the democracies could not dream of making the slightest show of armed force. The problem was what it has always been: how to use the economic and political means we have to moderate Soviet policy. Such tactics have never, to my knowledge, endangered the peace, whatever is said by Westerners toeing the Communist line. In fact, they perfectly fit the definition of peacetime diplomacy. No one can be accused of warmongering because he seeks to suspend or curtail favors that are never repaid. Consequently, the only real question after the December 13 declaration had nothing to do with military posturing. It was whether the democracies were going to consider the Polish declaration as intolerable and end the era of unilateral Western concessions. There would have been nothing wild or dangerous in such a stance; in dealing with a Communist world tormented by its inner contradictions, it might even have been reasonably effective.

But the West never tried to play its hand, not even in a limited way. It just surrendered immediately. From the day martial law was declared, the democratic governments trumpeted that nothing had happened. And you can't react to nothing, can you? French Foreign Minister Claude Cheysson saw this in a flash; on the evening of that December 13, he was the first aboard with an announcement that "of course, we'll do nothing." It was more than a creed, it was a prophecy—the only true one any politician has made in a long time. French President Mitterrand "condemned" and "reproved" the "emergency regime" in Poland, but referred those curious about France's concrete policy to an upcoming statement by Prime Minister Pierre Mauroy in the National Assembly.

In his address, Mauroy said that "for the moment, the events now occurring [in Poland] remain within a national context" of "internal sovereignty"; France, he said, would help the Poles "return to the path of democratic renewal."

Thus the French President and Government endorsed the fiction of a purely Polish operation, again more than satisfying Soviet hopes; Moscow did not need to try hard to put across its propaganda twaddle because this twaddle was exactly what the West wanted and pretended to believe to excuse its own passivity.

Buffeted by unexpectedly large protest demonstrations, the unequivocal firmness of the non-Communist trade unions, and the almost unanimous complaints of France's intellectuals, the French Government had to fall in quickly with public indignation and admit that the Soviets were responsible for the events in Poland. But the West German Government waited nearly a month to follow suit. After a vacation in the Florida sunshine, the then West German Chancellor, Helmut Schmidt, met with President Reagan in Washington on January 6, 1982. In return for relaxation of American opposition to the West Germans' contract with the Soviet Union for supplies of Siberian natural gas, the President extracted a promise that Bonn would explicitly name the U.S.S.R. as the real instigator of repression in Poland.

Schmidt complied during a televised press conference I saw retransmitted. Sighing heavily, coughing up scraps of phrases separated by long and dismal silences, smiling sadly with the angelic bitterness of a martyr about to make the supreme sacrifice, he began by complaining of harassment by American newspapers over the previous month on the issue of Poland. He could not, he regretfully declared, make out what the Americans really wanted because of alleged contradictions in American officials' viewpoints.

Schmidt reiterated that economic sanctions would not bother the Kremlin and so none would be useful. At last, in a kind of rattle made almost inaudible by the weight of his sorrow, he managed to murmur that the Soviet Union *probably had a hand* in the declaration of martial law in Poland. I imagine that history textbooks a century from now, which will all be identical after communism's global victory, will say that before the press conference that day Schmidt was tortured and drugged by the CIA.

Mild as it was, the Chancellor's statement immediately drew down Moscow's thunder. Bonn and Washington were accused of interfering in Poland's internal affairs. It was the West, it seemed, not the Soviet Union, that was really meddling in Poland, just as it was the Soviets who were "defending" Afghanistan from "Western intervention by the American-Zionists."[1] Soviet leaders would be foolish to forego the delicate pleasure of bombarding the world with this arrant nonsense, since the Western governments never ridiculed it as it deserved and since a substantial part of Western public opinion believed it and concluded that the only real aggressors were in the West. Meeting in extraordinary session in January 1982, the NATO member states thought it a triumph that they

1. *Pravda*, 5 August 1981.

were able to agree on a communiqué. At that point, the democracies no longer hoped for a concerted line of action that might influence the Soviet Union; all they hoped for was to agree, barely and painfully, on the wording that would least divide them.

The democracies' moral battle against the reenslavement of Poland, then, took the form of immediate surrender. They would have surrendered, that is, if public opinion hadn't forced their governments, especially the French, into a posture of—purely verbal —heroism. France's Socialist administration, mortified in the week of December 13–20 by the lively reaction of the country's intellectuals, its non-Communist labor unions, and the crowds that poured spontaneously into the streets to protest, understood its mistake. It fired up its tepid early response and improvised some martial speeches that, we must objectively recognize, contrasted completely with its actions. Mitterrand was primarily anxious not to break the Socialist-Communist alliance in the government.

The French Communist Party, flanked by the labor-union federation it controlled,[2] not only rushed to support police terror in Poland but campaigned for it so aggressively that the party's general secretary, Georges Marchais, even bestowed the ignominious label of "phony left" on three Socialist-leaning newspapers—the dailies *Le Monde* and *Le Matin* and the weekly *Nouvel Observateur*— that were outraged by the repression. Yet *Le Monde*'s outlook had been acceptable to the Communists at first; in an editorial headed "Let's Keep Our Heads," editor in chief Jacques Fauvet had counseled the West to avoid risky provocation and urged it not to add fuel to the fire. This was precisely the argument the Communists used until public excitement over Poland subsided.

Many in France had excused the inclusion of Communist ministers in the Mauroy government in the spring of 1981 by saying that their power was limited and that Mitterrand would impose his policies on the Communist Party. But when the Polish crisis erupted, the French Communists again unfurled their banner of pro-Soviet servility while blithely remaining in the cabinet alongside a Socialist Party that had, at least verbally, turned anti-Soviet.

2. The Confédération Générale du Travail (CGT).

That Mitterrand kept the Communist ministers on clearly shows which of the two parties intimidates the other. To contend that the Communist ministers personally made no public statements is evasive hypocrisy. What counts, what has political weight, what influences public opinion and hampers or helps the President is not what individual ministers say or do not say—they are mere pawns supplied by the organization—but what the party says and does. In this case, the Socialists tolerated its saying and doing the opposite of what the government said and did without booting its ministers out of the cabinet.

President Mitterrand's second concern, after that of keeping the Communists on his side even if they did attack his position on Poland, was to win back the support of France's intellectuals. He ordered an improvised evening for intellectuals and artists at the Paris Opera so that they could show their support both for the Mauroy government and the oppressed Polish people, with emphasis on the former. Unfortunately, the evening was dominated (ignorance? or provocation?) by such pro-Castro and pro-Soviet writers as Gabriel García Márquez and Régis Debray, despite the odd injection of a few business "moles." Even if it had been less ambiguous in tone, this "charity" event would not have accomplished much.

A month later, the Americans put on a TV show called "Let Poland Be Poland," in which top people in show business made a fine display of democratic and pro-Polish sentiments that were heartily approved by lovers of Poland everywhere. We had better believe that both events made the Kremlin quake. Perhaps it will counter with an evening of anticapitalist ballets so resoundingly hard-lined as to shame the warmongering Yankees of the military-industrial complex and the "American-Zionist conspiracy."

France's moral resistance, the main effect of which so far had been to flatter the country's cultural establishment, did not entirely sacrifice politics to esthetics, however. The broad policy lines were still being stressed. From the start, the French Socialist Party undertook *to prevent conservatives from demonstrating in favor of Poland.* Some Socialist officials even greeted Gaullist leaders marching in protest in Paris with shouts of "You have no right to be here!" "Socialist Leadership Denounces Opposition Hypocrisy," headlined *Le Monde* on December 19, 1981. This, five days after the unleashing of terror in Poland, was what was mainly worrying the Socialists! You had to be Socialist—and allied with the French Communists—to have the *right* to criticize the Polish dictator, General Wojciech Jaruzelski, and the Soviet Union. That way, it would remain a family quarrel. What an admission! True, the Socialists also attacked the French Communist Party and the CGT for supporting the December 13 coup. But what did this matter, since the Socialists continue to govern with the Communists? We can imagine with what exquisite mockery Soviet rulers contemplated the surrealistic foolishness of French Socialists criticizing martial law in Poland yet excommunicating others who also condemned it while governing alongside still others who supported it.

Moscow had manifestly won the psychological battle. Discord among the democratic allies and among the political parties within each of the democracies overrode their resolve to unite in opposition to totalitarian wrongdoing. Clearly, such an anemic and confused reaction in even analyzing the danger could not produce coherent action. Disagreement in perceiving and interpreting events cannot lead to formulating and executing a suitable common policy.

The irresolution of those socialists, like the French, who cling to orthodox Marxism derives from their insistence on seeing rebellion by people under the Communist yoke as a process of *socialist reform*. To a petition from writers and artists irate at the flabbiness of France's diplomatic response to Polish martial law, the Socialist Party replied with its own petition (an odd procedure by a party that includes the nation's President, its Prime Minister, and an absolute majority of its Parliament) on December 18, 1981. "These tragic events," it said, "coming after those of Czechoslovakia [in 1968] and Hungary [in 1956], demonstrate that socialism cannot be built when [a nation] opposes its people and scoffs at democracy."

Well, maybe it can! The history of the twentieth century has drilled into quite a few skulls that, unfortunately, socialism cannot be built any other way. Nothing could be more absurd than the notion, so widespread before December 13, 1981, of a "process of democratization in Poland." Do the decomposition, the putrefaction, the mortification of a whole system deserve to be dignified with the label of progress simply because the system is socialist? It's as though we'd said that the fall of the Third Reich in 1945 signaled the democratization of naziism. When socialists do admit that workers, intellectuals, whole peoples have risen against communism in East Berlin, Hungary, Poland, Czechoslovakia, they hastily qualify it by saying that the insurgents' real aim was to prove that socialism and freedom can be reconciled. Ritual attempts by the rebels to win partial liberalization by presenting it as the best way to consolidate socialism are designed merely to beguile their oppressors—with precious little success so far!

That Western historians have failed to see the obvious—that most of these misery-ridden people are rebelling against socialism itself, to overthrow it and not to amend it, even if they can't say so openly—shows the favoritism communism has so long enjoyed in the West. It is not thought indecent to say that in some places the masses have rebelled against capitalism, even when it isn't true. But that they might rebel against socialism as such is out of the question! Enticed by exotic forms of socialism whenever the tired slogan of "socialism with a human face" is revived in conveniently faraway places, Marxists cut and run with laughable speed when the experiments turn tragic. Never mind if people suffer; it's the future of socialism that counts! On December 14, 1981, the Young Christian Workers, a French Marxist-Christian movement, exorcised the supreme threat by announcing "We insist on condemning the attitude of those on the right who are trying to seize on the events in Poland to oppose change in France." We know that in the French political lexicon "change" has been synonymous since the spring of 1981 with socialist-Communist government. Even if the Poles perish, their regrettable bad luck must not be allowed to besmirch the image of socialism and so alter the untouchability of "change."

A grand display, this, of political egotism, coming after so many socialist disasters throughout the world. Such sophistry has finally sickened the stomachs of so many intellectuals that Mitterrand ought not to be surprised that so few thinking men have rallied to the "French-style socialism" he represents. The situation now is almost the reverse of what it was in the two decades after World War II. Then the eggheads sang the praises of the Soviet Union, of China and Cuba, while the politicians, especially those in government, repeatedly warned against the Soviet threat in particular and the dangers of communism in general. Since 1970–75, it's the intellectuals who are warning against the Communist menace while their governors do their best to ignore or mask it.

Since 1970, social democrats and conservatives have been more tolerant of Soviet misdeeds and more docile in response to Moscow's ultimatums than, say, the Italian Communist Party. Its leader, Enrico Berlinguer, protested louder after December 13 than did West German Social Democrat Willy Brandt. Don't worry, though: the shouting doesn't always match the policy. The choristers often seem to be singing the wrong parts in a score that ranges from leonine roaring to companionable silences and murmurs of grief. But when the time comes for action—or, rather, inaction—they're all together again, perfectly in tune. Then there isn't the slightest divergence in the West, among parties or among nations.

Not basic differences, anyway. You see, the democracies have invented an explanation for their inertia: each remains passive because the others have. Martial law in Poland sparked a crisis in the Atlantic Alliance. The Soviets shrewdly guessed that no member of the alliance really wanted to adopt sanctions against them and that each would justify itself by blaming its allies for its own cowardice. In fact, the crisis in the alliance that the media talked so much about was a spurious quarrel: each ally played the goat on behalf of the others. False though it was in substance, the row brought real divisions into interallied relations in the forms of mutual recrimination, new moral slights, a storing up of future rancor that presaged more complete paralysis and greater impotence later on.

For it is a mistake—and a suspect one—to rush to assume after each new Soviet encroachment that sanctions would be useless. This is particularly unacceptable when it comes from exponents of détente. They cannot argue that Western economic aid would fertilize love of peace in the U.S.S.R. by hoisting the empire out of its economic pit and at the same time maintain that withdrawing our aid would not in the least disturb the Soviets. Yet this is what Chancellor Schmidt declared during his Washington press conference. The incoherence of ideas here reveals how false the arguments are. Either Western economic cooperation is negligible to the U.S.S.R., which makes the whole theory of détente absurd, or it's important to the U.S.S.R. and suspending it would be an effective sanction.

It's the second alternative that's true. If you want proof, just watch the alarmed, frantic activity of pro-Soviet elements in the West as soon as sanctions are mentioned. Western aid is very important to the Communist world, although we must add that it has also become very important to the West—more important, it must be admitted, because the West is virtually incapable of reducing its living standards even slightly to achieve a political end. Totalitarian states, on the other hand, can always safely impose a little more poverty on their people (barring accidents, of course) because their societies are kept in what Michel Heller has called a situation of "controlled scarcity."[3]

Détente was not a dream, then, it was a trap. The "weapons of peace" worked very well for the U.S.S.R.; the West, especially West Germany, was tied up by its economic aid and outstanding loans to the East.[4] Soviet pawns could be advanced because the West could not counterattack without lowering its living standards, increasing unemployment and losing the money its banks and governments had lent the East. It is wrong to say that economic sanctions would

3. Michel Heller and Aleksandr Nekrich, *L'Utopie au pouvoir* (Paris: Calmann-Lévy, 1982).
4. *Les Armes de la paix* (Paris, Denoël) appeared early in the 1970s. In it, international lawyer Samuel Pisar argued that by trading with the Soviet Union the West encouraged it to become democratic and peaceful. The book deeply influenced Giscard d'Estaing during his term as President.

not affect the Soviet Union. On the contrary, they constitute tre-
mendously telling reprisals. But they also imply serious difficulties
for the West. The question is, which is more worth safeguarding,
our independence or our economic advantages?

It's all the more pressing a question because the economic advantages we grant the Soviet Union enable it, directly or indirectly, to
bolster its military potential. The process is direct when we ourselves finance transfers of strategic technology; it is indirect insofar
as we help relieve the Communist countries of their intolerable
poverty or lend them the hard currencies they need to buy from
the West the manufactured goods they cannot produce enough of
for themselves. This spares the Soviet Union from having to raid
its military budget for funds to satisfy urgent civilian needs. After
December 13, 1981, the Western powers could have imposed sanctions against the Soviet Union that, without constituting aggression, would have plunged the U.S.S.R. into serious difficulties. For
refusing to renew loans or sign contracts cannot in itself be considered aggression.

We could have begun by recognizing the insolvency of the Polish
state, which not only could not pay its debts when they fell due but
could not even pay the interest on them. Declaring it bankrupt and
suspending all loans to the East would have had a political impact
even before its economic consequences were felt: the drying up of
part of the resources available to finance Soviet expansionism.

But what was the Soviet Union to conclude when, after taking a
step we had warned it not to take, it continued to enjoy the same
advantages we had been granting it all along? The reasons given
for not declaring Poland bankrupt neglected this essential political
factor. Moreover, they were not convincing technically. Just to
amuse our readers, we might recall the statement by Prime Minister Mauroy that to deny loans to Eastern Europe would mean "accepting the idea of an economic blockade" and would be a "grave
act, an act of war." Just how is a refusal to make a bad loan an act
of war, and what has it to do with a blockade?

The State Department's objection was more serious: declaring
Poland bankrupt would panic the Third World, where many coun-

tries are as deeply in debt as Poland and equally insolvent. The answer: agreeing to reschedule those countries' debts while denying the same service to Poland would have been an excellent way to underline the move's political nature.

Another objection: in refusing to fatten the Polish public treasury, we would not so much punish the country's leaders as its people, who would only sink deeper into poverty. It's a decent motive. Unfortunately, however, recent history proves that standards of living in the Soviet Union and its European satellites reached their lowest point since World War II during the ten years we were flooding their governments with loans. From 1970 to 1980, the democracies lent the Soviet bloc seventy billion dollars, yet food shortages there were never so acute, except in Hungary, as they were in 1980–82.

It is legitimate to infer that this money was not used for the well-being of the masses. If it was employed to reinforce the states' military and police power, as it appears to have been, then the loans served to increase the oppression of the masses, not to ease their poverty. In Western financial circles, the argument was, in the words of Citibank President Walter Wriston, that "forcing Poland into default on loans to American banks would push the Eastern European nation into the arms of the Soviet Union." As though it weren't already there! Speaking on the CBS program "Face the Nation" on January 24, 1982, the banker declared, "If Poland were to be defaulted, Russia would have achieved the objective which it has been seeking since Catherine the Great, which would be to make Russia Poland's only friend."

Why, of course! Isn't that the real risk? When we weigh the historical knowledge and political flair of some of the West's most influential business leaders, we understand why the elite of the Soviet Nomenklatura loves to deal with them. They're so easy to trick, and they spread the nonsense the Communists give out as disinformation. Besides, these financiers must know that by imposing a "transferable ruble" on the COMECON (Council for Mutual Economic Assistance) countries in 1976 the Soviet Union cornered most of the hard currency the West had lent its satellites; from then on, they have merely fed the Soviet economy.

The practical upshot of this string of arguments is that the United States Treasury paid the banks the installments the Poles could not meet, which amounts to financing repression in Poland with the American taxpayer's money.

What's more, a look at the list of credit openings to the Soviet bloc during the first half of 1982 tells us that at no time did the process slow down; it also shows that the Soviet Union needed and will continue to need them badly. This wrecks the notion that sanctions are ineffective. Throttled by scarcity that had gone out of control, the Soviets persuaded the United States to reopen negotiations in April and May 1982 for the purchase of American grain. By giving in to pressure from American farmers, the Reagan administration naturally supplied a good argument to the Europeans, who were anxious to go ahead with their part of construction of the pipeline that will bring Siberian gas to Western Europe.

Politically and morally, America's capitulation is no more excusable than Europe's. In practice, however, the two transactions are very different. The Americans are selling wheat to the Soviet Union for cash at going world prices; they are not giving anything away except for the money, or most of it, that the U.S.S.R. needs to pay for its purchases. But they are not delivering advanced technology with military applications or giving the Soviets a way to blackmail the West by suddenly cutting off energy supplies. Creating this energy dependence in the West is as blamable as it is pointless; we now know that natural-gas reserves in Northern Europe are so large that the European democracies could have passed up a deal with the Soviets that is both dangerous and economically ruinous.

Each type of economic sanction the democracies could have used against the Soviet Union had drawbacks that inspired caution; not all of these drawbacks were imaginary. It is nonetheless surprising, in the Polish crisis as during the Afghan situation, that, as luck would have it, all the measures discarded by our leaders as ineffective or dangerous were exactly the ones available to us. In an interview with the Washington *Post* in June 1982, President Mitterrand, while reaffirming his determination to contain Soviet ambitions, also declared that economic reprisals "lead to war" and that he would avoid them. He thus endorsed the position of his Prime Minister—or, rather, the Prime Minister had simply been speaking for the President. France has been particularly zealous in its refusal to wield economic weapons; it even agreed to take over the 15-percent share of the cost of building the trans-Siberian gas pipeline that the Soviet Union had contracted to pay.[5] By an intriguing coincidence, our firmness is intractable only when it has no practical consequences; it dissolves whenever there's a chance to give it concrete form. But then, the French are not the only ones to suffer this strange run of bad luck.

In this system, political sanctions are no more welcome than economic penalties. The West had a powerful counteroffensive instrument after December 13: it could have denounced the Helsinki agreement and refused in February 1982 to return to the Madrid Conference on European Security and Cooperation, already the scene of a year's totally sterile discussion about applying and extending the pact signed with the U.S.S.R. in 1975. Let's not forget that it was the Soviets who had long wanted this agreement that was so providential for them. The West had a strong card to play by coolly declaring the pact invalid on the ground that it had clearly been violated in Poland.

Instead, France and West Germany argued in support of the Soviet position by harking back to the 1945 Yalta agreements—or, rather, to an imaginary version of them. Far from legitimizing the Soviet occupation of Poland, the Yalta agreements called for free elections there, which the Soviets, naturally, never allowed. In a remark that sounded oddly like the most visceral kind of anticommunism, Stalin once told an American at the Potsdam conference a few months after Yalta that any freely elected government would

5. This came to an extra $140 million "lent" by nationalized French banks at the government's order.

be anti-Soviet, and the Soviet Union couldn't allow that.[6] Stalin's clear-sightedness, combined with American passivity, enabled the Russians to grab Poland and the other satellites that today comprise the Soviet bloc in Europe.

His tactics are understandable. It is less clear why Western leaders have always—as both Mitterrand and Schmidt again did in 1981—propagated the Yalta myth. Why is it that even those who are most conscious of the Soviet menace let themselves become unwitting champions of precisely the position Moscow wants to see prevail? They did this again, not surprisingly, in explaining why they were returning to the Madrid conference instead of scrapping the Helsinki pact, as they should have done, since it provided for human rights and freedom in the East bloc.

The Soviets thrive on conferences, summit meetings, visits, friendship treaties. The sheer fact of meeting with us gives them a chance to drown their acts of aggression in speeches. It took them several months after they invaded Afghanistan to persuade Western leaders to meet with them again. After their power play in Poland, however, they needed less than two months. Again, it was the democracies that circulated among their own citizens the empty slogans by which they justified their knowingly falling back into the trap. The Americans and Europeans agreed to believe that attending the conference would give them an opportunity to demand "explanations" about Poland and to keep both sides talking to each other. "We are not the ones," said France's Cheysson, "who will break off the talks here. We must avoid showdowns. A few weeks or months of reflection would probably be useful, but we must pursue the discussion within the context of the Madrid conference and that would be easier if General Jaruzelski kept his promises [sic]."

So it would. But for that, we first needed people stupid enough to believe Jaruzelski's promises. "As long as the Madrid conference remains a forum," it was declared in West Germany, "the Kremlin

6. P. E. Mosely, *The Kremlin and World Politics* (New York: Vintage, 1960), cited by Jean Laloy in his article "L'Europe depuis 1945" in the magazine *Commentaire*, no. 14.

cannot duck the controversy over Poland." As we shall see, there would be no difficulty in keeping the conference going. As long as controversy was all Moscow had to fear . . .

According to French Prime Minister Mauroy, the Helsinki pact should be used "to relentlessly point up the inner contradictions of the U.S.S.R. and its friends."

No doubt the idea that their inner contradictions might be shown up by the dreaded French dialectician made the Soviets quake with terror. But they didn't show it. When the Madrid conference resumed on February 9, 1982, the Soviets and the Poles adopted a policy of obstructionism and somehow managed to make the West look ridiculous; Western leaders who had naively gone there and wasted their time, their saliva and their taxpayers' money were made fools of by the masterly hand of Moscow.

Once more, "détente" had been fruitful for communism. Again the West had invented a series of quibbles to avoid taking the simple, obvious step that would have put the Soviets in real trouble. Our diplomats once more found a way to act against our honor and our interests. The Soviets even scored a new feat, a great "first" to their credit: they prevented Foreign Minister Cheysson from talking. After the meeting in which he had failed to win the floor, he declared sheepishly, "I don't really understand the attitude of the Eastern countries." A bit of realism, at last!

This rapid overview of some typical Western reactions in the six months following the re-Bolshevization of Poland has by no means exhausted a subject that Polish resistance has kept at the boil since the December 13 crackdown. Brief as it is, however, this summary amply illustrates the basic issues we are dealing with here.

A pragmatic thinker might, of course, argue that neither the democracies' honor nor their interests were really at stake in the Polish affair. In 1938, the democracies had a treaty with Czechoslovakia, which they nevertheless allowed Hitler to invade, thus breaking their word while preparing their own ruin. But no treaty linked us to Poland in 1981; the country's subordination to the Soviet Union was a long-standing situation that had simply been renewed and consolidated in the guise, what's more, of an internal political arrangement. However morally legitimate people's feelings may have been over Poland's anguish, reasons of state perhaps counseled respect for the compromise reached in the Helsinki pact and, before that, at Yalta—even if the Yalta agreements have been fictionalized. Is anything more constraining, after all, than the fables everyone believes?

Because we followed this line of reasoning, we refused to interrupt our economic relations and strategic talks with Moscow, as we could have done on the grounds that it violated a status quo in Eastern Europe . . . in which we had really concurred all along. Indeed, which informed Westerner ever believed that after Helsinki freedom would be restored to the Communist countries? Knowing socialism to be incompatible with human rights and the satisfaction of people's most elementary wants, we could have foreseen—we *did* foresee—further revolts in the Soviet empire. There have been uprisings since then, and there will be others, so let's not feign surprise every time they happen. This is part of the situation forced on us, against our will, in the final phases of World War II. It is against this background that we must build our security and find an acceptable modus vivendi with the Communist superpower.

This is the case made by spokesmen, both professionals and volunteers, for the Soviet Union in the West. Far more important, it is also advanced by a majority in the Socialist International, followed —preceded, rather—by conservative nationalists, with France's heirs to Gaullism at the head of the column.[7] Some Western Marx-

7. An article by Maurice Couve de Murville, a former Foreign Minister and Prime Minister under General de Gaulle, appeared on page one of *Le Monde* on February 13, 1982. It was headlined "Economic Policy and National Dignity." With the West then debating the construction of a Soviet gas pipeline and the West European dependency on the U.S.S.R. this threatened to create, one might at first have thought the article was about the benefits and penalties of the Franco-Soviet agreement. Not at all! What had aroused the old statesman's alarm, stirred his anger, and inspired his warning was a meeting organized by the *International Herald Tribune* between American businessmen and members of the French Government for vague talks about possible American-French economic cooperation, especially the chances of American investment in French industry. When French capitalists, encouraged by the state, lend money to the Soviet Union at preferential rates, sell it equipment on ultra–long-term credit, and get no thanks but insults, France's "national dignity" is never compromised. But when American capitalists consider risking their money

ists even bolstered their practical arguments with a moral prop of debatable elegance: that because few of the Central European countries in the Soviet bloc were democratic before 1939, they have no business demanding their freedom now. By this token, neither ex-Hitler Germany nor formerly fascist Italy, ex-Salazar Portugal, ex-Franco Spain, nor once-Pétainist France, not to mention a host of other peoples now enjoying democracy, should have had the right to aspire to it. They ought to be only too happy that, at best, they have mended their ways enough to qualify for communism. It's a grand theory, and it did flourish among French leftists in 1975 as justification for an attempt by Stalinist Portuguese Army officers to take over in Lisbon.

A central strand connects all the elements in this dialectical panoply, political, ideological, economic, strategic and historical: they all present things as the Soviet Union would like them to be believed. In practice, it's a code that comes down to two precepts. First, we should not deprive the U.S.S.R. of the Western supplies that help it to increase its power. Second, we should not exert any pressure on it, however slight, when it is rendered vulnerable by an internal crisis of the system or when an expansionist venture backfires, like the war in Afghanistan. Add a third precept: our neutrality need not be rewarded; the West must not insist on Soviet reciprocity for its discretion.

I am not saying this policy is good or bad. Indeed, good or bad for whom? I am not trying to convince anyone to change it. I am describing it. This book is not a sermon. I want to record, not to convert anyone. Recording, however, implies evaluating the fruit of this line of diplomacy, assuming that it is fruitful, and trying to find out who is stockpiling the biggest share of the harvest.

---

by investing it in France under normal market conditions, they are striking at the nation's honor.

7

THE TERRITORIAL IMPERATIVE

Observing the Western muddle after the invasion of Afghanistan and the restoration of totalitarian order in Poland does at least refocus one's attention on a principle of Soviet power that is too often neglected, probably because it is too simple, too archaic, and too obvious: the principle of territorial occupation. It applies to all the varieties of communism—in Vietnam, in Cuba, in China—and especially, in the most expansionist of them all, to the Soviet Union's brand of communism. The secret of Communist imperialism is that it is still territorial imperialism.

These days, the great Western theoreticians in the art of politics expatiate, they cavil, but they do not agree on the most perfidious forms of neocolonialism and indirect expansion, the subtleties of economic imperialism and cultural domination, the march of the multinationals to the pounding of legions of Toyota panel trucks and cans of Nestlé's concentrated milk. The Soviets, meanwhile, have built and are continuing to build their empire on old-fashioned foundations. They are keeping to the much safer and time-proven system of territorial annexation and direct appropriation. For they know that terrain is not really yours unless you have political and military control over it and, preferably, have won the international community's recognition that you have a right to rule there, either in your own name or in that of a theoretically independent, sovereign state that is actually subject to you alone.

Few historians discoursing on the "two imperialisms"* point out

* That is, Soviet imperialism and alleged Western imperialism.—Trans.

that since 1945 the two imperialisms have moved in exactly opposite directions. Since the Second World War, the major excolonial
powers that make up today's capitalist world have abandoned, willingly or not, the territory they had annexed over the centuries.
Spain long ago lost its vast American possessions. Since then, the
former overseas holdings of Britain, Holland, France, Belgium,
and Portugal have become a crowd of independent nations. In
some cases, decolonization went ahead with speed and intelligence,
in others slowly and stupidly, with terrible carnage, but in the end
it was done everywhere. It is interesting to note that the colonial
powers that tried to resist the trend were disapproved of by the
other capitalist countries; they were isolated even among their allies and forced to give in. Just how much real independence many
of these new Third World states have is a matter of considerable
debate. The fact remains, however, that aspiration and accession to
independence on the part of any group with even the slightest
claim to statehood is one of the great postwar historical phenomena.

At a time, then, when territorial annexation, once considered a
legitimate reward for military superiority, has given way to peoples' right to self-determination and national status, only the Soviet Union continues to grow by means of armed conquest. In the
1940–80 period of decolonization, when the old empires were restoring independence to or conferring it on the territories they had
subjugated over the centuries, the Soviet Union was moving the
other way, appropriating a number of foreign countries by trick or
by force.

I would hesitate to weary the reader with a list he should be able
to find in the encyclopedias and history books if it were not that
most of these reference books, reflecting Europe's cultural Finlandization, shamelessly gloss over the brilliant achievements of
Soviet expansionism.

By what right, for example, did the U.S.S.R. cling after the war
to the countries Germany ceded to it as payment for its neutrality
under the 1939 Hitler-Stalin treaty sharing out a dismembered Europe? This is how the Soviets acquired the Baltic states, eastern

Poland, southern Finland, and part of Romania (Bessarabia and southern Bucovina). I grant that it was Germany that later broke the treaty and invaded the Soviet Union, which, it is worth recalling, would have liked nothing better than to go on enjoying its fruitful cooperation with the Nazis. Involuntarily and oh how regretfully, Moscow had no choice but to switch camps. Indeed, it *was switched* by Hitler.

Was this any reason for the democracies not to reconsider what Hitler had bestowed on Stalin? Fighting alongside the Allies in the second phase of the war of course gave the U.S.S.R. the right, as it did to all the victors, to recover its own territory intact. But this did not authorize it to expand, as it alone did, at the expense of other martyred countries and certainly not to keep the proceeds of its collusion with the Nazis. Yet not only did the Allies fail to challenge these ill-gotten acquisitions, but they even threw in a few gifts, such as East Prussia, Ruthenia (a part of Czechoslovakia), the Kurile Islands, and the southern part of Sakhalin Island (in the Sea of Okhotsk, north of Japan). No popular vote, no referendum or plebiscite was organized or even contemplated through which to ask all these Poles, Lithuanians, Estonians, Letts, Romanians, Slovaks, Germans, and others if they wanted to become Soviet subjects. The Allies shut their eyes firmly to these annexations, a disconcerting application of the principles guiding their destruction of naziism. Absorption of these countries into Soviet territory, so prodigiously contrary to the principles of that period of decolonization, revived the practices of a monarchist Europe that died two centuries ago. It constituted what may be called the first wave of imperialism and the first zone of national annexation.

The second wave led to the creation of a second imperial zone, that of the satellite countries.

Just how Eastern and Central Europe were subjugated is too well known to need repeating here. The technique used in this form of colonialism is to set up the facade of an ostensibly independent state. Administration of this state is entrusted to loyal nationals who function as provincial governors and who are allowed only a few minor departures from the Soviet system, as long as they don't tamper with its essentials. In practice, the democracies very quickly recognized the Soviet Union's right to quell by force any disturbances arising out of demands for genuine independence in the European satellites. In other words, they soon agreed to view the European satellites as appendices to Soviet territory, a de facto situation that the Helsinki pact would legitimize in 1975.

The third wave and third zone of Soviet territorial conquest covered more distant countries that have been annexed or subjected to Soviet control since 1960. Some of these countries, including Cuba and Vietnam, are satellites in the strict sense; another, South Yemen, has been working since 1982 to destabilize the neighboring state of North Yemen. For, driven by unflagging effort, the Soviet advance never stops.

Then came the African satellites: Angola, Mozambique, Ethiopia, Madagascar, Benin, Guinea, and other, lesser, prey, often colonized by mercenaries from other satellites—Cubans or East Germans. These are more fragile protectorates, subject to the sort of accidents that caused the fall in Equatorial Guinea (the former Spanish Guinea) of dictator Francisco Macías Nguema, who, with the help of Soviet advisers, had exterminated or exiled a good third of his country's population in only a few years.

Fragile though they are, these distant protectorates must nevertheless be considered satellites insofar as their policies, armies, police, transport, and diplomacy are in the hands of Soviets or Soviet agents. To stay within the strict limits of my subject, however, I will deal in this chapter only with territories directly occupied, directed and controlled by the Soviet Union or its delegates. Elsewhere I will examine the countries that are manifestly under Soviet influence—such as Algeria and Libya—and the so-called nonaligned countries, for most of which, and really for their movement as a whole, nonalignment has long since been merely a name that is misleading, false, and fraudulent.

In the long-range Soviet view, any country is a permanent candidate for promotion to a higher category, from nonaligned to protectorate and up to the rank of inalienable satellite. Soviet leaders thus show, clearly and consistently, that in their eyes the only serious form of imperialism is territorial occupation, physical presence on the ground. If they cannot annex a territory, they resort to the next best thing: installing a government loyal to them, which applies their proven methods of assuming monopoly power by gradually eliminating the non-Communist parties. This is what the Sandinistas have done since 1980 in Nicaragua, where iron-fisted, Cuban-trained leaders have repeated the process developed in Central Europe after World War II. To prepare it for satellite status, the U.S.S.R. has enmeshed Nicaragua in friendship treaties, sent it military advisers, appropriated its ports as naval bases and taken fishing rights, cynically adopting the most outmoded and profitable standards of colonial exploitation. Off Angola, for example, Soviet trawlers have swept the sea clean of fish and spoiled the ocean floor by abusive use of the outlawed suction method of fishing, which destroys the fauna and flora on the seabed; there have been no objections from the Angolans, who have no means of surveillance and whose government cares little anyway about Angolan interests.

The fine points of "invisible," "indirect," or "hidden" imperialism, of the "domination effect" and "dependence," are so many jokes, suitable for capitalism; the Soviets prefer the security of real presence and direct or proconsular rule. All the Communist countries think and act this way. Communist China no sooner consolidated its authority than it invaded, occupied, annexed and destroyed Tibet. Communist Vietnam lost little time after securing its (at least nominal) independence before invading Cambodia and subjugating Laos. Communism's bosses know there is always a difference in kind between vague "dominant relationships," which are intrinsically fluid, and territorial zones, which figure on a map and whose ownership no one can challenge without being accused of disturbing international order.

The primarily territorial nature of Soviet imperialism is one of the secrets of its irreversibility. Alliances with independent states can be altered or abrogated at any time; General de Gaulle took France out of the NATO military command; since 1975, West Germany has shown neutralist tendencies and opened the possibility that Soviet diplomacy might one day separate it from the Western camp. The expulsion of Soviet advisers from Egypt by Gamal Abdel Nasser's successors was a lesson to Moscow that no country can be held permanently unless it is given a Communist regime wholly shaped in the standard satellite mold. Arguing that Cairo's action proved the Soviets can be made to retreat from an acquired position fails to take into account that Egypt had never been a true satellite. In the Soviet view, the case simply proved that half measures can never guarantee anything, that security in a colony lies in bringing Communists to power who, if trouble arises, can be relied on to call for "fraternal assistance" from the Soviet Union or one of its offshoots.

Soviet leaders are the first to believe—there is no evidence to the contrary—that shared power is threatened power, from within as well as without. This is why they succeed so well wherever they do make a breakthrough in grabbing a monopoly of power and masking this with the legal fiction of a seemingly sovereign state.

Economic imperialism alone no longer gives an empire the irreversible status guaranteed by territorial occupation that is confirmed by international treaties. It is Communist propaganda, as the Kremlin well knows, that pastes the label of imperialism on what is often no more than normal economic life obeying the laws of the market. And these laws, subject to the vicissitudes of efficiency, productivity and innovation, dictate that a dominant position is subject to perpetual and rapid change; we have seen such positions pass from Britain to the United States to West Germany to Japan to South Korea, from the industrialized countries to the oil-exporting countries, and so on.

The Soviet leadership does not like this; it wants stability and permanency. For the same reason, economic imperialism, which is merely one aspect of imperialism, is never so easy as when it is waged in the protected preserves of the Soviet satellites. Let's not forget that among the great powers it is the Soviet Union that grants the least aid to the less developed countries but which unrestrainedly exploits any Third World nation that falls within its orbit. Soviet money given to Cuba is not economic aid, it is the wage paid to a mercenary soldier—costly, no doubt, but it certainly does not exempt Cuba from being exploited. This is an old-style colonial arrangement under which the colony supplies cannon fodder and slaves for the Soviet Union, along with some raw materials, in exchange for cash that provides higher living standards for the narrow class of Cuban proconsuls, governors, functionaries and police.

The primacy of the territorial imperative explains the monotony of the maneuvers by which the Soviets patiently enlarge their empire. There is no reason to vary a highly refined procedure that always catches the West unprepared and leaves it petrified with surprise. It is instructive to note that the excuses, so gross as to be insulting, that served as the pretext for invading Afghanistan at the end of 1979 were the same ones used for the annexation of Georgia in 1921.

Georgia had originally been one of three Transcaucasian republics that were independent of Moscow. In free elections on May 26, 1918, the Bolsheviks received a negligible share of the vote, as usual.[1] As in Afghanistan fifty-eight years later, the Kremlin's puppets in Georgia appealed for the Red Army's help. The republic was invaded, occupied, annexed. And, as in Afghanistan, the occupying power was held in check by fierce local resistance. In 1924, insurrectionists even succeeded in liberating half of Georgia; the rising was drowned in blood by the aptly named Red Army, but only with the aid of heavy armored and air reinforcements. As it did after the Afghanistan invasion, an "indignant" West was content to "follow the events in this part of the world attentively so as to seize the opportunities that might arise to assist this country's return to a normal situation by peaceful means in accordance with the rules of international law."[2] You'd think you were reading the communiqué cooked up in January 1980 by the French President and the West German Chancellor.

While Georgia was the first country forcibly annexed by the

1. Menshevik Social Democrats, 640,231 votes; Armenian Nationalists, 73,654; Georgian Nationalists, 51,427; Moslem Party, 47,808; Revolutionary Socialists, 40,196; Bolsheviks, 24,513; Cadets, 14,475.
2. Resolution adopted by the League of Nations on September 24, 1924.

Soviet Union, Outer Mongolia had the honor, also in 1921, of becoming the first Soviet *satellite*, again thanks to a method so well
designed from the start that it has been used unchanged many
times since, most recently in Nicaragua. In 1921, according to the
1931 Soviet Encyclopedia, there were 164 Communists in Outer
Mongolia and 99 members of the Young Communist League. Not
very many, in truth. Enough, however, to allow the Communist
Party to propose to the other parties, representing the peasantry,
the formation of a national-front government (here we go!) to oppose "Chinese domination." As soon as the front was formed and
became a provisional government, the Communists grasped the
levers of power, as they would later in Hungary and, more recently, in Nicaragua. Their allies, unmasked as counterrevolution-
aries and bedecked with the exquisitely Mongolian epithet of "feu-
dal-theocratic elements"—an ingenious phrase, and one to bear in
mind[3]—were eliminated. All that remained after that was for an
improvised "national liberation" army to appeal for "fraternal assistance" from the Red Army, which never needs coaxing to do its
fraternal duty. On June 13, 1924, a Mongolian People's Republic
was proclaimed and rapidly attached to the Soviet Union by a web
of "friendship" treaties, mutual assistance treaties, cultural, economic and military treaties and heaven knows how many others.

In 1968, the Red Army moved into Prague; Czechoslovakia was
"normalized" in what Western leftists saw as Soviet rejection of
"socialism with a human face"; that is, Czechoslovakia became a
battleground for conceptions of socialism. Comintern veterans recognized the essential element in this: recuperation of a key territory. One of them, a French communist named Laurent Casanova,
unshakable even though he had fallen into disgrace with the party,
replied to a condemnation of the Russian operation by fellow Communist Philippe Robrieux, who has since left the party. "You don't
understand," Casanova said. "The Bohemian quadrilateral must be
held in order to hold Europe." Robrieux reported these comments

3. At every party congress since World War II, the Mongolian People's Revolutionary Party has used this wooden, vaudeville-style political jargon so peculiar to the
Communists; its resolutions frequently include the phrase "liquidating the vestiges
of feudalism."

by highly placed French Communists: "Our Soviet comrades are acquiring a fleet and the means of intervention, including marines, which can go into action anywhere . . . They will cruise on every ocean, go to every point on the globe."[4]

The only conception of socialism that still stands up after the system's general collapse as a model is that of territory, the criterion of acknowledged land ownership. Ideological struggle is aimed solely at sapping the resistance of those opposing the extension of territorial boundaries. For example, only a project of gradual annexation of the area around the Persian Gulf, where rich and poor countries alike buy most of the fuel they need, gives meaning to the invasion of Afghanistan, the erection of a pro-Soviet regime in Yemen, the work of the Communist Tudeh Party in Iran in the interim before the mullahs' mad, chaotic power disintegrates. Western leaders in the late 1970s who refused, out of intellectual sloth or fear of action, to see in these separate elements the matching parts of a long-range, overall plan will have to bear heavy responsibility for what befalls our descendants.

Territorial imperialism has two main advantages.

The first is that it cannot be fought without the governments combating it becoming, in theory, aggressors and violators of international law. We all know that the Communist potentates the Soviets have set up in Kabul since 1978, most of whom have zealously killed each other off or been assassinated by the Soviets themselves, have merely been Moscow's tools. In practice, however, even if the democracies have provisionally refused to recognize them, their governments have nevertheless been Afghanistan's legal administrators; we cannot attack them or send troops to aid the Afghan rebels without officially going to war against Afghanistan. And this is a step that cannot be taken in today's circumstances, least of all by the democracies, unless their help is requested by Afghan authorities—a privilege usually reserved for the Soviets.

Everyone knows that the Warsaw Government merely represents the Soviet occupier, that it exists by force alone, and that free

4. Philippe Robrieux, *Histoire intérieure du Parti communiste* (Paris: Fayard, 1982), vol. III, p. 73.

elections would sweep Poland clean of communism, as they would any other country that has experienced Communist rule even for a few years. But the fact remains that, on paper, the governments in Warsaw and the other satellite capitals represent legitimate sovereign states freely allied with the Soviet Union; to attack Poland in order to free the Poles from tyranny would be an act of war against an independent nation and its great ally. In short, to be outraged by the misery and repression in the East is to disturb international order, whereas objecting to misery and repression in a country under Western influence, in Latin America, say, is to work in the cause of progress. Again, the rules are rigged so that communism cannot lose, since it does not require democratically expressed approval. The democracies cannot win because they are not authorized to defend their interests unless all the conditions of the highest democratic morality are met.

In other words, by the consent of the international community, East Germany and Hungary and Cuba are recognized as being the *property* of the Soviet Union in the territorial, cadastral sense of the term, but there is no question of recognizing Morocco or Guatemala as the property of the United States. This leaves the Communists free to foment guerrilla action against the governments of Morocco and Guatemala—regimes that are certainly questionable in any democrat's view—without being accused of breaking international law. But the democracies may not foment guerrilla warfare against governments that, from a democratic standpoint, are even more illegitimate, like those in Poland and Czechoslovakia, without starting an East-West war.

In practice, of course, the notion of stirring armed rebellion in a Communist satellite is pure fantasy. While the Soviet Union can easily create or support dissidence in any Western country by manipulating a handful of fanatics, it is totally impossible for a Western power to do the same in an East-bloc country even with the backing of three fourths of that country's population. Totalitarian systems know how to defend themselves. On this point, too, the essential factor is that the Soviet empire's territorial legitimacy is its guarantor of indestructibility. Soviet imperialism is irreversible not because it is invincible, but because it achieves recognition as legitimate under international law; sooner or later, de facto power is accepted as rightful power. This ties the democracies' hands. And it is why the Soviets insist that "recognition of the territorial changes that supervened in Europe as a result of the Second World War be taken for granted," as Brezhnev put it in his report to the twenty-fourth Soviet Party Congress in 1971. The West did exactly that in 1975 when it signed the Helsinki agreement—an imperial gift to Moscow for which nothing but words was demanded in return. To the honorable, a word is a bond, but to the Communists, a bond is nothing but words.

Territorial imperialism's second advantage is that it is renewed, fortified and justified by its very success. The wider an empire is, the more it is threatened and, accordingly, the more it must expand to neutralize further threats. When you have invaded Afghanistan, you are automatically threatened by Pakistan, with which you did not previously have a common frontier. We have heard ad infinitum about the Soviet Union's "fear of encirclement," the greatest strategic farce of modern times. Obviously, the wider your ring of borders spreads, the more countries you come to touch on, and these all become potential centers of aggression against you. The simplest way to neutralize a potential center of aggression is to install a friendly government there. But this friendly power, while no longer a threat to you, is in turn exposed to the hostility of the countries beyond it, the countries against which it buffers you. In fact, your real frontier becomes that of your new friend. And since this friend also has the right to suffer deep feelings of insecurity, it will surely appeal for your fraternal assistance. We know it will not appeal in vain.

Let's be logical: the only way for the Soviet Union to make certain its borders are not threatened, that they are fully secure, *is to have no more borders at all* or, if you prefer, borders that coincide with the entire world. Only then will "peace and security" be guaranteed to all mankind. And it is because they absolutely must have this guarantee that, as Brezhnev also told the Soviet Party Congress, "the total triumph of socialism throughout the world is ineluctible."

8

THE UNILATERAL ARMS RACE

AROUND 1978, the democracies realized that the Soviet Union had surpassed them in military power. Roughly a decade of détente had produced, first, a worldwide extension of Communist territorial domination and, second, a decisive weakening of the Western powers' security. For the first time since the Atlantic Alliance was formed, the West's power to discourage or to repel a direct Soviet attack on their territory, and so to resist pressure against their political independence, became doubtful.

In September 1979, Henry Kissinger admitted that seldom had a group of nations let itself slide so quickly and willingly into a position of military inferiority, and he deplored his own share in this paradoxical decline. I am tempted to complete his thought by saying that the West knowingly let its military power slip. We find many examples in the past of nations and empires defeated with surprising ease because, out of ignorance or arrogance, they slept while their future adversaries improved their techniques and tactics. At the outbreak of World War II, the democracies were surprised by the growth and improvement of the Nazi Army. But this had been accomplished rapidly, behind the Allies' backs. In 1939, France was convinced its Army was the best in the world. A mistake, no doubt, that led logically to its defeat in 1940.

Far less logical is the consent of today's democracies—open-eyed, without illusions—to the deterioration of their defensive capacity vis-à-vis an enemy coyly described as "potential" when in fact it is increasingly arrogant and enterprising. The democracies of the second half of the twentieth century have had all the time and information needed for correct evaluation of the growth of Soviet military strength. Indeed, throughout this period the media, with a gravity and precision unknown in less trying times, have kept the public constantly informed of the West's decline; leading publications in all the democratic countries have been careful since the era of détente opened to assign defense news either directly to experts whose job it is to think about defense strategy or to competent journalists who have kept a large audience regularly and clearly up-to-date on this difficult issue. With two exceptions—the Communist press, which takes the Moscow line, and some of the big West German weeklies, which underestimate the Soviet military threat in the hope of encouraging bilateral Russo-German détente —newspapers in the democracies, especially since 1975, have reported the balance or imbalance of East-West forces with greater impartiality than ever before. And they have done so despite the reluctance of some newspapers, styled "neutralist" in Europe and "liberal" in the United States, to recognize the startling increase in Communist military power.

Naturally, since there is always an audience for political nonsense, we see a whole menagerie of propagandists and opinion molders rushing noisily through a classic act in the repertory: demonstrating that the notion of a Soviet arms buildup is either false or is a mark of the Kremlin's desire for peace. Conversely, the West's efforts to make up what is now conceded to be its military inferiority are denounced as warmongering.

How true it is, as Demosthenes told his fellow citizens twenty-four centuries ago, that "it is those who advise you to defend yourselves who are said to press for war." In his vain effort to incite Athenian resistance to Philip of Macedon's drive for hegemony, he described with troubling precision some of the eternal springs of what can be called the psychology of advance surrender. "As soon as Philip is mentioned, one of his agents among you immediately rises to tell you how sweet it is to live in peace, how costly to maintain an army. They are out to ruin you, he cries. Thus he persuades you to put everything off and give your enemy the time and means to achieve his ends undisturbed. You win a brief respite, but someday you will have to admit how much this respite has cost you. [The agents] beguile you—and earn the pay they were promised."[1]

Let's leave aside for a moment the question of whether the reversal of military superiority was directly caused by détente, that is, whether it could have happened without Western economic and technological aid to the Soviet Union. According to some experts, the growth in Soviet armed might since 1970 would have occurred even without Western aid, at the cost, if necessary, of further reducing living standards in the Soviet Union and its satellites. All the experts agree, in any case, that détente at least lulled Western vigilance, stopping or slowing the development of Western defenses while the Soviets continued their buildup. The basic American idea of détente beginning in 1970 was to freeze by treaty the military parity the two superpowers had just reached. This did not, of course, mean completely halting weapons production; it would merely guarantee that if one side added to or modernized its arsenal, the other side would follow suit.

These agreements led to a spectacular drop in American defense spending. The Soviet Union, on the other hand, violated or circumvented them, either through technical subterfuges that enabled it to give its nuclear weapons more punch without increasing the number of missiles, by reinforcing the military sectors not covered by the treaties, or by refusing or dodging the inspections provided for in the agreements. Besides, so many obstacles are raised to inspection in a totalitarian empire that the idea is simply illusory. So, for ten years, the Soviets profited from all this to pursue what has justly been called a "unilateral arms race."[2]

We can gauge the results of this uncontested race from a single, simple fact: in 1970, the Soviet Union was superior in conventional forces while the West was ahead in nuclear armaments; since around 1980, the Soviets have led in both categories. They have increased the power and the quality of the U.S.S.R.'s conventional

1. Demosthenes, *Oration on the State of the Chersonesus*, paras. 52–53, 59, 64.
2. Albert Wohlstetter, "Is There a Strategic Arms Race?" in *Foreign Policy*, 1974, nos. 15 and 16.

forces, especially its tanks and naval equipment for nonnuclear use, thus assuring the inferiority of NATO's conventional defense. The experts are still debating whether the Soviet Union has also achieved overall nuclear superiority—and it is a sign of the times that it is being debated at all—but its atomic arsenal is certainly large enough now to *neutralize the American deterrent.*

It is superior in Western Europe, at any rate. Until 1970, the European allies were protected from possible attack by Warsaw Pact forces by an American retaliatory nuclear capacity that the U.S.S.R. could not match. Ten years later, Soviet attack strength is equal to the reprisals it risks: its intermediate-range SS-20s directly threaten Western Europe's vital centers and could preventively annihilate the few atomic weapons stocked there, including the French nuclear strike force but (temporarily) excluding submarine-launched missiles. Hence the all-out Soviet campaign since 1979 against the modernization of NATO nuclear forces, especially the stationing in Europe of American intermediate-range Pershing II missiles designed to counterbalance the SS-20s. Even the Pershings will only partially correct the East-West nuclear imbalance in Europe unless supplemented by other materiel. But the program immediately became a symbol of Western Europe's political will in dealing with the Soviet Union.

Since the late 1940s, the keystone of Western security was American nuclear credibility. The term means, first of all, a conviction on the part of both the Soviets and America's allies that the United States would reply with atomic weapons to Communist aggression and, second, that there would consequently be no Communist aggression. In this second proviso lies the essence of what is called deterrence. When awareness dawned, around 1978, that American nuclear credibility had not survived détente, nothing was done except to recognize that America's nuclear strength had weakened. Kissinger was only drawing the irrefutable conclusion from the new balance of power when, in a widely criticized speech in Brussels in September 1979, he warned America's allies that they should no longer rely on strategic guarantees "that we Americans can no longer give, or could not carry out if we gave them because we would risk the destruction of civilization."[3] At the time, Kissinger was simply a private citizen, yet the storm his speech raised was as great as though he had spoken in the name of the United States Government.

Whatever the merits of his statement, it is interesting in that it shows that the Soviet nuclear potential need not surpass the West's by very much to nullify deterrence. This is why it is pointless to argue over which of the two superpowers holds overall strategic superiority. That there is any argument at all shows that, at the very least, the two sides are closely matched overall, which is enough to cancel America's deterrent power.

It can be objected that deterrence thus becomes reciprocal and that this balance, this parity, has created what is, after all, a healthy situation in which neither superpower can attack the other's camp without opening itself to mortal danger. The objection, typically, is based on the postulate—as false as it is widespread—that there is a perfect strategic and political balance between East and West. *In fact, overall nuclear parity between the United States and the Soviet Union means overall weakness of the democratic camp* versus the forces of totalitarianism.

For America's nuclear superiority only compensated for general Western inferiority in all other military areas. Yet between 1975 and 1980, the West's overall inferiority increased and America's nuclear superiority vanished or, at any rate, lost the margin of security on which deterrence was based. American nuclear deterrence was already unsuited to thwarting the imperialistic drives launched or extended by the Soviets everywhere in the world. You can repel an organized outlaw band with a battery of artillery if you have no rifles, but artillery is useless against a pickpocket or against small, scattered aggressor units. There was no justification in any treaty—or in the magnitude of the threats—for a nuclear alert when Afghanistan was invaded, when Cuban and East German troops colonized Angola and Mozambique, when Soviet bases

3. Henry Kissinger, "NATO, the Next Thirty Years." The speech was given worldwide press coverage.

were established in Madagascar; atomic weapons are even less appropriate in terrorist or guerrilla destabilization operations.

Since an atomic reply is ruled out in such cases, and because the democracies lack both the conventional military means and the political will to block these varied and widespread thrusts, the Soviets expanded almost without risk even in the days of American nuclear supremacy. The only time a nuclear alert was called was in the fall of 1973, during the Israeli-Egyptian Yom Kippur War, when the Russians threatened to intervene to save an encircled Egyptian army.

This was a full-scale war between protégés of the two superpowers. But Communist imperialism usually maneuvers skillfully in areas where fighting is unofficial. It advances masked behind revolutions, wars of "national liberation," appeals for help from "friendly governments," guerrilla actions, and "desperate" terrorists battling the despotism of a Giovanni Spadolini or a Felipe González. Swamped, swindled, tormented, the democracies could not benefit from nuclear superiority even if they had it, since it is useless in such situations. They have always lacked adequate conventional means of retaliation. And the shortage is becoming more and more acute, despite such occasional rearguard actions as the 1979 French landing in Zaire to repel a Katangan attack organized by Cubans based on Angola. Generally speaking, Western public opinion, media, and opposition political parties are becoming increasingly hostile to this kind of operation. So Soviet military dynamism enjoys nearly total latitude in most areas, the democracies being almost inoperative at virtually every possible phase of intervention and counterthrust. Moreover, the West lacks coordination in blocking this worldwide encirclement, usually confining itself, after each new setback, to internecine quarreling over what to think about it all.

Nor was any thought generated by the radical change in the threat hanging over the democracies' own territory, especially among the European members of the Atlantic Alliance.[4] Develop-

4. This is highlighted by Pierre Lellouche in his study "European Security in the 1980s: An Attempt at Synthesis and Prediction" in the volume published by the

ment of European defense since the critical period of vulnerability began has been tributary to internal political quarrels, to European resentment of the United States and vice versa, and to self-seeking calculation by the European governments, each of them anxious to retain as many exclusive economic advantages as possible by perpetuating a defunct détente with the Soviet Union. If we add to this picture a growing cowardice and docility in the face of Soviet pressure, we understand why it is so easy for Moscow to terrify Western public opinion and to break Western leaders' really not very stubborn resolve to accept the two lynchpins of future European security: the neutron bomb and the new generation of American missiles in Europe.

The neutron bomb is the only weapon that would have made up for our inferiority in conventional forces. A tactical nuclear weapon, it is the only one that can stop an armored invasion with pinpoint accuracy, killing tank crews without destroying cities and buildings, without harming the civilian population (which, in the circumstances, is by definition friendly) or contaminating the air over an area larger than the target. Propaganda by the Kremlin's friends in the West, campaigning against adoption of the neutron bomb, represents it as a "capitalist" weapon because it kills men without obliterating equipment and property, which can be salvaged when the holocaust is over. Salvaged by whom? By the multinationals, I suppose. Clearly a plan, say the partisans of Western unilateral disarmament, framed by the military-industrial complex to wipe out the populations of Italy, West Germany and Holland so that it can lay hands on those countries' factories, homes, nightclubs, stadiums, sentry boxes, airports, churches, beehives, triumphal arches, tunnels, restaurants, and prisons. In other words, offering neutron bombs to NATO was part of a diabolical American plot to slaughter the Europeans and take over their property.

Everyone knows that the most intelligent creatures on earth live in the Western part of Eurasia. Surely they will not fall into so

Institut Français des Relations Internationales on *Dimensions nouvelles de la sécurité de l'Europe*, Paris, 1980. Lellouche explains how the Soviets succeeded in neutralizing Western deterrence.

crude a capitalist trap. With laudable consistency, President Carter canceled plans to arm NATO with neutron bombs, thus showing that the Americans, fat-witted as they may be, can rise to the level of European sensitivity when it is well advised. Once more the Soviets had rescued us from the imperialist Yankee stranglehold; now they gaze at us with the happily sanctimonious smiles of killers whose victim voluntarily shed his parachute before jumping out of the plane.

The job of raising Europe's moral standard regarding the new American missiles was more difficult. In December 1979, NATO's members decided to deploy Pershing II and cruise missiles no later than 1984; this martial spasm shook them so deeply that they still haven't gotten over their fright. Nevertheless, Moscow's propagandists had to reach an elusive target: cancellation of a measure already adopted in principle.

A two-pronged offensive of harassment and corruption, along with resurrection of the old "peace movement," did wonders. With their usual warm, cordial good humor, the Soviets offered to "freeze" the situation and negotiate: in other words, to keep their SS-20s trained on Western Europe and, meanwhile, to open discussions—doubtless protracted—on the nondeployment of the new NATO missiles. Brezhnev even announced that, if the offer were taken up, the Soviet Union would deploy no further SS-20s in Europe, a brilliant use of the old Soviet rule that "once I've gotten everything I want, I ask for nothing more."

Brezhnev did, however, ask one more little thing: denuclearization of Northern Europe, meaning that NATO would drop its guard in Scandinavia. Added to Soviet destabilization of Turkey and attempts to blackmail Spain, first into refusing to join the Atlantic Alliance and, when that failed, into reversing its decision to join, the new proposal laid a solid foundation for creation of a Europe united from the Urals to the Atlantic.

Moscow's official charmer in charge of grand reunions was Vadim Zagladin, first deputy chief of the Soviet Communist Party Central Committee's international department. He rushed into print in Le Monde on March 17, 1982, to lay out "six Soviet ideas for security." These really came down to a single idea: "We are the strongest and we intend to remain so."

Despite the ritual illusions Westerners predictably cultivated concerning Yuri Andropov's peaceful intentions, Brezhnev's successor did not alter anything basic in Brezhnev's tactics. Like his predecessor, he alternated threats of world war with proposals for general disarmament. The proposal of a general nonaggression pact that he outlined during a Warsaw Pact summit meeting in January 1983 contained nothing new. Andropov's aim was to persuade the West to call some kind of a conference early enough for Moscow to finagle at least a postponement in NATO's missile-deployment timetable without committing the Soviets to anything firm thereafter.

This was the same old game: offer the West conversation in exchange for a concession, a promise of discussion in return for real renunciation of its missile program. As matters stood when Andropov succeeded Brezhnev, the only way to restore a power balance and reduce tensions was unilateral Soviet arms reduction. Andropov's objective, however, was to persuade the West that world peace depended on its accepting Soviet military superiority once and for all. The long campaign to dismember the West's security apparatus had already ended in success for Moscow. All that remained was to preserve and, if possible, augment the advantage it had won.

9

PERSUASION BY FORCE

"WHAT COUNTS," Lenin wrote, "is to be the strongest."[1] The Soviet Union's real gains in terms of territorial occupation and military power have produced a very precise, very concrete result: a steady increase in its ability to impose its political will.

Having solidly established its domination or influence over a growing number of countries; active on every continent and on or under every ocean; equal or, more often, superior to the democracies in most forms of land, sea, conventional, and nuclear armaments, the Soviet Union bends the democracies to its will in most of their confrontations—this not merely because of the democracies' mysterious propensity to bow, but simply because they are frightened. And they are frightened because the U.S.S.R. has become the strongest, because they have become the weakest, and so, in the daily practice of diplomacy, they are compelled to docility by the sinister shadow of Soviet superiority looming in the background. The nations of Western Europe are reduced to disguising their increasingly habitual surrenders as "resistance"—to the United States.

It is this contortionism, for example, that has added spice to the choreography of the incredible ballet they danced in 1982 around the trans-Siberian gas pipeline. Always the great innovator in the technology of bowing and scraping, West Germany received Leonid Brezhnev with considerable pomp one fall day in 1981 while the Communists were massacring the Afghans with renewed vigor

---

1. And he added, "And to win at the decisive moment at the decisive place."

and were preparing to bludgeon the Poles with a stout blow against "foreign interference." What was most atrociously delicious, most foolishly abject in all of this was that during the visit of that cadaverous Muscovite potentate hundreds of thousands of West Germans demonstrated, not against the senile puppet who represented on their soil the most actively bloody imperialism of the day, but against the United States. Not against the Soviet missiles aimed squarely at Western Europe, but against the *still nonexistent* American missiles that were to counterbalance them.

Had President Reagan been the visitor, we would have understood neutralist demonstrations in his presence against the *plan* to deploy the new NATO missiles. But since the good Brezhnev's hostility toward the plan was already firm, it would not seem to have needed further encouragement. What was the point, then, to this absurd demonstration before Brezhnev against the absent Reagan? For partisans of unilateral Western disarmament, any time would have been proper and useful to promote their cause *except* during Brezhnev's visit. The marshal-president really needed no convincing—indeed, he was the last man in the world the pacifists would have had to pressure into supporting the weakening of NATO. Then why the surrealist and not very heroic burlesque of booing the cuckolded husband under the happy lover's windows?

I wondered about this for a long time. And, as Rémy de Gourmont said, "what is terrible about the search for the truth is that you find it." Especially when it's simple: since everybody couldn't have gone crazy at once, the only plausible reason the Germans had for their massive anti-Reagan demonstration before Brezhnev was to woo Brezhnev.

To woo the strongest, that is—one of man's two or three oldest passions and, contrary to what might be thought at first, not one of the most self-seeking. To many people, bowing before the strongest of them all is a pleasure in itself. For what interest could a national of West Germany, of Western Europe, have at this point in the twentieth century in sharing the seedy, mindless existence of the average Soviet citizen? Only a spirit of sacrifice, of self-immolation would drive him to it, an edifying negation of his lust for life, a saintly renunciation of freedom and dignity—with, I concede, a grain of utilitarianism. For self-interest, after all, obliges us to observe the commonsense maxim that when there is no choice it is better to flatter the master than to anger him.

The most important feature of the debate on modernizing NATO forces has been that, all along, the Europeans have seemed less concerned with adopting the best possible course for their defense than with what the Soviet Union might think of their policy, with whether it will sit not too badly with the Kremlin. Even back in 1975, Giscard d'Estaing, when he was the President of France, pointed out a drawback to a current plan to strengthen European defenses: that it might displease the Soviets. Since examples in history are rare of an alliance deliberately seeking to please the power whose aggressiveness it is supposed to be combating, Giscard's objective seemed comic at the time. But it in fact foreshadowed a line of thinking that was to spread widely during the years that followed. While the Soviet Union obviously would not dream of consulting the democracies before deciding on a new military program, it has come to think it has the right to a voice in NATO planning. And the worst of it is that the Europeans themselves have gradually slipped into the habit of thinking it normal to have to account to Moscow, to owe it explanations. One day the Soviet Union warned France its foreign policy was becoming too Atlantic again, the next it hinted at punishment for Spain's impertinence in joining NATO; in March 1982, Brezhnev made an "arms control" proposal that amounted chiefly to a warning that the West risked reprisals if it deployed the new American missiles in Europe.

Was a nuclear-armed Soviet spy submarine careless enough to let itself be trapped in a Swedish bay? In the time it took—never very long—for Stockholm to bow and escort the sub out of the bay, Moscow got the point: that excuses are decidedly superfluous. Nor was it to offer excuses that the Soviet ambassador to Rome phoned the Italian foreign ministry seven times in one day in January 1982 after another Russian submarine wandered into Italian territorial waters off Taranto. No, the purpose of those seven phone calls to the Farnesina was to put Italy on notice not to go back on its agreement to help build the Siberian pipeline despite "intolerable pressure" from the Americans.

Persuasion is the reverse of deterrence. The less confidence the American deterrent inspires, the more easily Moscow imposes its will on the Europeans without having to use force. The peculiarity and the advantage of military superiority consist precisely in obtaining without going to war the same results that a war would bring. This is, indeed, the only constant law of diplomacy. If we keep it in mind, we are less surprised that European "pacifists" feel threatened not by the Soviet missiles pointed at them, but by the American missiles destined to protect them from the SS-20s. The pacifists know that in life it's the weaker who is called an "aggressor" by the stronger for attempting to remedy his weakness.

And yet, writes François de Rose, "nothing is further from the truth than the belief that the American missiles based in Europe would give the United States a first-strike capacity against the Soviet intercontinental missiles and so upset the balance between the great powers."[2] Without the neutron bomb and the Euromissiles,* Europe's defense would be a shambles; this would confirm Soviet military superiority and, consequently, the political subordination of the Western European democracies. "If the decision to deploy [the Euromissiles] is revoked," de Rose wrote in the same article, "it would end the linkage between the European theater and the American strategic system, that is, the kingpin of deterrence." This is why the Soviet Union and its allies in our countries have worked so tenaciously to bring about the annulment of the decision to deploy the Euromissiles. For the Soviets, separating Europe from its American ally would open the way to political domination of the countries west of the iron curtain.

Such a break would be fatal to France's defenses. For it is a mistake to think that French military independence from the

2. This great expert in strategic problems points out that "the four silo fields west of Moscow are the only ones the 108 Pershing missiles could reach out of 21 deployed throughout Soviet territory. An attack by the Europe-based missiles alone, therefore, would leave intact the great majority of the 1,398 Soviet missiles for a counterstrike against American territory." From "The Primary Obligations," in *Le Monde*, 21 May 1981.

* The term used for American nuclear missiles stationed in Europe.—Trans.

NATO command and its autonomy of decision regarding the use of its nuclear strike force would guarantee the nation's security if the Atlantic defensive system should degenerate. The force would not make the country invulnerable, in a sort of ex post facto vindication of Gaullist diplomacy, if the American nuclear guarantee were nullified. Only its inclusion in the overall Atlantic system gives it whatever weight it may have. This certainly is how the Soviets see it; they invariably count the French missiles as part of the total Atlantic nuclear arsenal. This is also the view of President Mitterrand, who, alone in the Socialist International with Italian Socialist Party leader Bettino Craxi, came down firmly in favor of deploying the Euromissiles in Western Europe as a *preliminary* to any discussion with the U.S.S.R. on nuclear-arms limitation. Most of the other socialists, including the French, of course recommended the good old tactic of prophylactic capitulation: "Let's surrender first and negotiate later." French defenses dissociated from a European environment of strength could not alone ensure the country's invulnerability—far from it!—or its indefinite political independence.

It is in the light of European political subordination to Soviet military power that we must reexamine the development of the Siberian pipeline issue after the reestablishment of totalitarian order in Poland. True, Europeans' "resistance to American imperialism" had long been merely the visible face of their submission to Soviet imperialism. But this is particularly striking in the case of the gas pipeline. When none of the economic arguments advanced is entirely convincing, only politics can explain how, by a sort of miraculous predestination, European decisions always end up conforming with Moscow's wishes. This is why the project went ahead despite the profound change in the international situation that had occurred since its inception.

The deep-lying, still unavowed explanation of the European attitude towards the pipeline is that the Soviet Union's economic exploitation of Western Europe is in fact already well under way. Given the balance of military-political power, West Europe no longer dares say no, and it vents its irritation at its own cowardice on the United States. The remarks this elicits from some European politicians are splendidly farcical, or would be if these officials' decisions were not based on such "analyses." For example, a French Socialist cabinet minister named Roger Quilliot declared in the National Assembly that "I consider the financial policy of the United States more of a threat to the West than a hundred Soviet divisions."[3] Less amusing, but more redoubtable because of the speaker's greater influence, was British Prime Minister Margaret Thatcher's declaration of support in the House of Commons on July 1, 1982, for the German-French stand on the pipeline. She harshly criticized Washington's decision to ban the use of equipment made under American license in building the line. The ban, said the Iron Lady suddenly transformed into a Cotton Lady, *violated contracts* signed by European companies with the Soviet Union. It's a specious argument because it expresses the reason for the row in purely commercial terms, ignoring the question of strategic priorities and the danger of again using Western technology for the Soviet Union's benefit, and at no cost to Moscow.

A few days later, on July 5, 1982, the London *Times* picked up the argument. The majestic daily's first aphorism: *economic sanctions have never served any purpose.*

I admit this amazed me. I seemed to remember how insistently the British had urged their allies to impose economic sanctions against Argentina when it invaded the Falkland Islands a few months earlier. I recalled how openly London had rejoiced when the European Economic Community unanimously agreed to do so. I could still see the two Prime Ministers, France's Mauroy and Britain's Thatcher, vying in eloquence at a banquet given by the Franco-British Council in Edinburgh on May 15, both praising a European decision taken with a speed matched only by its severity. Some European countries that traded heavily with Argentina, especially Italy, paid a stiff price to prove their faithful friendship to Britain. The argument about saving jobs in Italy and in Europe

3. *Le Monde,* 27–28 June 1982. Note that the French Socialists were blaming the poor results of their management of the country on high American interest rates long after the rates had fallen.

that had served so well in the quarrel over the Siberian pipeline had suddenly lost all its pertinence when it came to punishing Argentina, a weak country, and not the powerful Soviet Union. I merely note that the big mouths that had remained shut and the purses that remained open to the Soviet Union after its invasion of Afghanistan now, in the Falklands affair, regained all their natural dimensions and mobility.

Plunging into his argument with thoughtful gravity, the *Times*'s editorial writer then delivered himself of his second aphorism: *the West cannot restrain Soviet expansionism with economic weapons.* It was lucky for Britain that its allies had not adopted the same doctrine four months earlier in connection with Argentine expansionism. There is an odd paradox in the notion that by barring the use of certain American patents in building the Siberian pipeline the United States had *struck a blow at Western friendship*, whereas this friendship was reinforced by the embargo against Argentina. The *Times* therefore deplored what it called *the injustice of the American decision regarding Europe*, which, the newspaper spelled out, *is in a position of weakness because its industry depends on Moscow for jobs.* It could not more ingenuously have cast a crueller light on the real motive for the lack of anti-Soviet sanctions. It was the West, according to the *Times*, that was economically dependent on the Soviet Union, not the other way around. The editorial ended on the same note of disillusioned quietism on which it began, affirming that *trade is not a reliable weapon either for improving relations or for sanctioning misdeeds.*

This profound adage is all the more convincing for the fact that the Soviets and the Europeans work marvelously together in giving it concrete substance. The Soviets take care of validating the first condition: they do not temper their relations with the rest of the world at all despite the trade credits granted them. The Europeans devote themselves with touching scrupulousness to applying the second condition: they never use trade to sanction Soviet misdeeds.

In the quarrel between the United States and the Europeans over the gas pipeline, we must remember that the Reagan administration did not ask its allies to break off all economic relations with Eastern Europe, any more than it would have broken off its own. All it asked was that the Soviets be made to pay a fair market price for the services, goods, and technology furnished to them. The dispute did not hinge on the principle of providing these supplies but on the credit facilities accorded by the Western Europeans. It was the aim of the United States to force the Soviet Union to pay the allies in hard currencies rather than see the West continue to furnish both the supplies and the money to pay for them. If this were done, it was hoped the Soviets would henceforth have less money for military expenditures than they had during the ten years of détente, when the Soviet military budget was four times that of Western Europe in terms of its percentage of the gross national product and triple that of the United States. In the American national budgets during the euphoric years of détente, defense spending was cut 35 percent in constant dollars.[4]

This, Reagan told a summit meeting at Versailles, near Paris, in June 1982, was the vital issue. Three weeks after the meeting ended without agreement, the White House indicated that it might rescind its embargo on the use of American-licensed equipment for the gas pipeline if the allied governments raised the cost of their loans to the Soviet Union. It is all very well to lend billions of dollars to such Communist governments as those in Poland and Romania, but must we continue to lend them fresh money when they fail to repay the old loans or even meet the interest on them despite the low rate?[5] I am among those who think that the United

4. According to a report to the Joint Congressional Economic Committee by the Defense Intelligence Agency on June 29, 1982, annual military expenditures in the Soviet Union, which had been running to 12 to 14 percent of the national wealth, were said to have risen in 1982 to between 14 and 16 percent of the GNP. The United States spent 4.9 percent of its GNP on defense in 1980 and 5.7 percent in 1982. Although the Soviet GNP is below that of the United States, military expenditures in the U.S.S.R. are higher than the Americans' in constant dollars: for 1980, the last year for which figures are available, the Soviet outlay was $252 billion versus $168 billion for the United States (*International Herald Tribune*, 22 July 1982).
5. Despite Hungary's "new economic mechanism," whose miracles have been so loudly sung in the West, the country was unable to service its debts in 1982 and had to solicit fresh loans to bring in hard currency and partially repay its creditors. A group of Western banks saved it from bankruptcy in July 1982.

States should have maintained its embargo on grain sales to the Soviets, whatever the cost in domestic politics and in subsidies to American farmers, because this sacrifice would have endowed the country with incomparably greater moral authority. But it must be admitted that the kind of trading the Americans do—delivering wheat to the Soviet Union payable immediately in hard currency —conforms to the rule they are asking the Europeans to follow. Our aim should not, of course, be a total blockade of the Soviet empire, which would be utopian and unrealizable, but to bring our dealings with it back within the jurisdiction of the laws of the marketplace, to force the Soviet Union to face economic facts by offering it trade, not aid, and certainly no privileges. It is this return of East-West transactions to normal trading conditions that the European governments have refused.

In the case of the pipeline, the extremely low-interest loans customarily granted to the U.S.S.R. will bear extraordinarily heavy consequences. The exploitation of Siberian natural gas that we are making possible will bring the Soviet Union a considerable strategic profit: the gas transported via European Russia will spare the country an energy crisis by partly replacing oil, which will thus be available in greater quantities to the armed forces and for export. For the Soviet Union's two vital problems in the 1980s are the preservation of its military superiority and its hard-currency earnings. The gas pipeline will unquestionably help it solve both. Why must Western technology, some of the secrets of which have been embargoed by contract precisely for strategic reasons, be used to weaken the West itself?

All the disputes among Westerners about possible economic sanctions following the invasion of Afghanistan, the repression in Poland, the destabilization of Central America, ended in victory for the Soviet Union without its having to try very hard. The Europeans defended its cause against the United States.

This success is richly promissory for the leaders in the Kremlin. Perhaps the supreme defensive instrument democracy still has for insuring its survival is its capacity to provoke—or, at least, to avoid preventing—a global crisis in the empire. This is, at any rate, the only weapon it has left. Since 1945, the democracies have been unable to contain the Soviet Union's territorial gains and have deprived themselves of the right to challenge them by recognizing the sovereignty of states that were, for the most part, under Red Army occupation. The democracies signed all the treaties, especially in Helsinki, that confirmed the Soviets' conquests. Then they dropped all insistence that Moscow respect the Helsinki clauses signed in exchange for the Western gift. Finally, the democracies let themselves slip to a level of military vulnerability that makes it impossible for them to impose their political will on the Soviet Union—that, on the contrary, forces them to submit to Moscow's. That the problem of restoring military parity is also merely a source of dispute among the Western powers reinforces their inferiority.

But they still have their economic weapon, since, even in a recession, capitalism continues to fulfill its role as volunteer nursemaid to socialism. The democracies have neither the energy nor the skill needed to roll back Soviet imperialism whenever and wherever in the world it advances. They do not react rapidly enough, they lack military flexibility, their domestic politics are much too complex, and their diplomats much too timorous for them to intervene, even verbally, every time communism takes another step forward, in Madagascar, in Suriname, or in Honduras. So the sole resource left to them would be to exploit the empire's intrinsic and incurable cancer; in other words, to slow its expansionism by trying to wither the trunk instead of rushing around trying to lop off the tips of the imperial branches, for these are too luxuriant a growth to keep up with. This pressure on the center is what might be called, in the jargon of the Helsinki pact, the "third basket" of resistance to totalitarianism, since the first two were, for the democracies, dangerously empty. This is a course of action that some of the most perceptive of the Sovietologists, such as Richard Pipes and Martin Malia, think is possible and even unavoidable.

But why expect democracy to become more agile and decisive than before in profiting from communism's debility—especially when it seems more reluctant than ever to do so? Democracy has always held excellent cards to play against communism; it is the way it plays them that's disastrous. I am therefore intellectually delighted but skeptical in practice when, for example, I read these lines by Malia: "The only way to help Poland is to do everything we can to extend the crisis to the whole Soviet bloc and to the Soviet Union itself. I know that when such a suggestion is made, one is accused of warmongering. But this crisis will occur anyway; we are involved in it anyway. We have, in any case, to make a decision. So it might as well reflect our political will."[6]

Reflect what? Political will? That's a commodity we lack in the West.

The Soviet Union is gaining ground against us economically the same way it is gaining territorially and in the arms race: by force. It is undoubtedly sick, very sick. It will die, that's certain, not as "we other civilizations" shall, for we are all mortal, as any reader of Paul Valéry knows, but because it is in and of itself a society of and for death. But the prime question of our time is which of the two events will take place first: the destruction of democracy by communism or communism's death of its own sickness? It seems to me that the second process is advancing less rapidly than the first.

6. Martin Malia, "La Pologne: une révolte contre l'Empire soviétique," in *Commentaire*, no. 18 (summer 1982).

PART THREE

THE TOOLS OF COMMUNIST EXPANSION

10

GLOBAL STRATEGY
AND ACTIVE VIGILANCE

THE AMBITION TO conquer the world has two different sources in the mental equipment and political training of Soviet leaders. One is the classic, traditional, permanent image of "world revolution," the certainty that all humanity is destined to become Communist. The other is a sense of the Communist system's inherent fragility, shown by the tendency of all peoples under its yoke to try to evade it or shake it off whenever a crack in the wall of police repression gives them a chance.

This second cause for the Soviets' expansionist gluttony has given rise to the thesis, highly esteemed in the West, of Soviet psychological "insecurity." It is this obsession that is said to explain, even to excuse, the aggressiveness of Communist foreign policy. If insecurity is understood in a territorial sense—of frontiers too insecure to safeguard a nation's existence, like those of Israel since its foundation—then it seems frivolous to think there are valid reasons for such a feeling in the U.S.S.R. Its neighbors have better reason to feel insecure, as do the neighbors of Vietnam and Cuba. The only border the U.S.S.R. may have had to guard against a potential aggressor rather than from the flight of its own people has been, for many years, its frontier with China, since China is the only country to have laid an official claim to territory annexed by the Soviet Union—something no capitalist power would have the effrontery to dare. The democracies are totally outside this quarrel between two Communist empires, and they have scrupulously avoided trying to inflame it. But Peking's threat to the Soviet Union is extremely slight in view of the Soviets' enormous military superiority over China, which could not even whip the Vietnamese Army.

If there is a threat to the empire, it does not come from the capitalist world, which is inclined to the defensive and which has doubtless been temporarily saved by dissension among the Communists rather than by any Machiavellianism of its own, a skill the democracies have lost. In fact, the much-bruited "encirclement" of the Soviet Union by a capitalist world allegedly determined to destroy it—the supposed justification for the country's persistent mistrust of the democracies—comes down to a few scattered operations in 1918–19, during the civil war in Russia; these were disconnected and were never followed up. No large-scale military operation has ever been mounted to bring down the young, or old, Soviet state. On the contrary, capitalist economic assistance in 1921 cushioned the bankruptcy of the Soviets as it has so often since.

No state, no empire since the world began, no human group, from the humblest tribe to the most far-flung federation, has ever enjoyed absolute invulnerability or total exemption from threats to its security and resources. But, until the rise of the Soviet empire, none had concluded that it had a right to appropriate the entire planet before it could set its mind at rest. Few empires have been as sheltered as the Soviet regime is behind its thick geographical buffer, thanks to its now almost unrivaled military strength and the virtual self-sufficiency in energy and foodstuffs it could have if —but this is a different problem—it only knew how to exploit its resources.

Any feeling of insecurity that might haunt the Nomenklaturas in power in the Soviet Union and all other Communist empires is not even due to fear of domestic insurrection. This does happen, but perfectly organized police terror guarantees that uprisings are short-lived. What the feeling of insecurity stems from is the humiliating, stabbing certainty that as long as a non-Communist society exists anywhere in the world, the empire's subjects will try to escape to it, or at least will dream of escaping. The Communist world really is a fortress under siege—but from within. It is the first society condemned to live behind walls to protect itself not from incursion from outside, but from exodus from within, or the desire for one. So long as in all the waters of the earth there is a single rock where socialism does not reign, there will be boat people. The twentieth-century socialist societies are the first to be totally closed and enclosed, where even thinking of leaving is a crime. The first of their size, at any rate; their predecessors, the Inca empire, for example—the Nomenklatura of old Peru—were, in size and population, tiny in world terms.

Think of the cost of spying on people, of hemming them in, of jamming airwaves, of censoring printed matter, speech and telecommunications—in short, the cost of maintaining the vast, parasitic bureaucracy trained in surveillance and repression. It is disagreeable for the Nomenklatura to live with the constant, disquieting feeling that its subjects are only there because they can't get away. It's the kind of doubt that will finally wear down even the least suspicious of men. No human being, no matter how tough, can find moral comfort in spiritual schism, in appearing as a benefactor of humanity when the only takers of his benefactions are those who cannot avoid them. The only way to fix things so that no one wants to escape from prison is to turn the whole world into a prison. Or, to forget about metaphors, the only way to convince oneself and the rest of humanity that the socialist system is best is to see to it that there are no other systems.

Hence the worldwide insatiability of Communist imperialism. The great empires of the past grew to a point of equilibrium, at which they stopped growing in exchange for implicit recognition of their dominion by the other powers. With time, they even tolerated decentralization of power, progressive autonomy of local authorities in distant provinces. The Roman, Arabian, Ottoman, Spanish and British empires all moved, by various ways and guided by their particular political customs, along these parallel routes toward final consolidation of their frontiers and dispersion of internal authority; with these came a growing right of each part of the empire to develop its distinctive personality.

The Soviet empire is the first in history that can neither be substantially decentralized without risking immediate disintegration nor halt its expansion. For communism, incapable of engendering a viable society, cannot tolerate the continued existence of other societies to bear witness against it; each such society would by its very existence be an indictment of socialism, a point of comparison by which to judge its unrelieved failure in terms of human happiness.

Once they were replete, the old empires tried mainly to insure that they were left in peace; they found a modus vivendi with their rivals, gave free rein to their proconsuls, sultans, or viceroys and entered an era of a "concert of nations," of balance of power, and, at home, of a diversified civilization that produced cultures as creative and sumptuous as those of the Hellenistic Greeks and the Moslems in Spain. Diversity of "cultures" is unknown in Communist countries, first because there is no Communist culture and second because all Communist societies, even those that have broken with Moscow, reproduce essentially the same model, obey the same genetic code, with only infinitesimal variations deriving from the personal idiosyncracies of their leaders.

As for a balance of power, beginning with a "concert of Europe" democratic diplomacy's error has been precisely its trust in patterns inherited from the nineteenth century, its belief that the Soviet Union too could be persuaded to halt its expansion in exchange for concessions that are a little costly, perhaps, but seem to be final. The most recent of these errors—and the most ingenious, since it codified this belief in an elaborate theory—was committed by Henry Kissinger. His theory was wrong[1] because it failed to take account of the specificity of communism, as that of naziism had been ignored before World War II: that they are systems whose survival depends at every second on a plan for world domination, both as fantasm and as realpolitik. Concessions do not appease the gluttony of such systems, they stimulate it.

Keeping this final objective constantly in mind, Soviet leaders know that to draw a little closer to it every day requires unfailing active vigilance, and they never cease to demonstrate in what eminent degree they possess this sense of active vigilance. Their great

1. See Chapter 13.

talent is their ability to act against the slightest point of resistance at any moment anywhere on earth. Nothing is negligible to them, any position is worth occupying, from the tiny island of Grenada, in the Caribbean, which became a "popular democracy" in March 1979, to vast Ethiopia.

Their active vigilance, however, does not primarily take the too blatant form of enlarging zones of influence and increasing the number of their friends. It usually begins with quiet feeling-out of the terrain that either goes unnoticed or shines with innocence, as, for example, in that cloud of agreements on fishing and fisheries that the Soviets extort from the most unexpected countries everywhere in the world; these provide a point of entry—for use of a port, installation of a base, the operation of spy ships, not to mention the fruitful pillage of fishing grounds. Soviet imperialism excels not only quantitatively, by the weight it brings relentlessly to bear on areas that might crack, but also qualitatively, by its variety of means, ranging from a multiplicity of "friendship treaties" with other countries to terrorism, implanted or encouraged in those very countries, as well as a full line of "customized" procedures.

Diverse though they are, these procedures obey a common principle: to exploit crises, to profit whenever an adversary has to drop his guard, to infiltrate every crack. Barring errors, the Soviet Union advances when it can't lose. Or, if its move does fail, the blame must be made to attach to one of the empire's valets, not to its rulers. From this point of view, the war in Afghanistan certainly resulted from an underestimation of the Afghan people's ability to resist.

We have already noted that Soviet expansion took its two longest forward leaps since the war at two moments when the West's guard was down or when the democracies were paralyzed. In 1945–50, taking advantage of the vacuum left by the rapid and thoroughly irresponsible departure of American forces from Europe, the Soviet Union imposed communism on all of Eastern and Central Europe except Austria. In 1975, the Vietnam debacle and the removal from office of President Richard M. Nixon left the United States cataleptic. Western Europe, sprawled on the sofa of détente, ecstatic over America's humiliation and over the Helsinki agreement, was determined to see nothing reprehensible in anything the Soviet Union might undertake. In less than five years, the U.S.S.R., the strongest but one of the Asiatic European powers, became a world superpower, spreading stout branches and promising shoots into Southeast Asia, Africa, the Middle East and Central America. These gigantic advances exemplified the Soviet precept that military superiority should not be used to make war if it can be avoided but to impose the U.S.S.R.'s will without a fight. It's a Communist rule the Western Europeans would do well to keep in mind. They are wrong to think the only alternative facing them is invasion by the Red Army or total freedom. Conditional liberty is also a possibility.

While the balance of military power determines in a very general way whether confrontation is possible, it is usually less of a factor than timeliness in deciding in detail how that confrontation will end. Another example can be found in the Soviet Union's exploitation of all kinds of crises and revolutions. During a January 1982 conference devoted to pacifism and the European-American crisis, Alain Besançon noted that the international Communist movement, led by the Soviet Union, seldom if ever triggers revolutions; it grabs power *inside* a revolution.[2] It infiltrates revolutions and infiltrates governments, and this is impossible to combat by military means. From this, lovers of totalitarianism draw the satisfied conclusion that force can never triumph over people's hope for independence and freedom. Mistake! Confiscation of revolutions and freedom movements by communism is the surest way to stifle those hopes. The Nicaraguans are among the most recent to have learned this when, between 1979 and 1981, they exchanged one form of despotism for another. When the international Communist movement tried and failed to capture the Portuguese revolution in midcourse in 1974–75, the Portuguese Communist Party represented slightly over a tenth of the country's voters, as all later elections proved despite the Communists' attempts to prevent vot-

2. A record of the conference, entitled *The Transatlantic Crisis,* was published by the Orwell Press, New York, in 1982.

ing or to discredit its results in advance. If the plot had succeeded, with the connivance of an "armed forces movement" that had long been controlled by agents of the Communist International, it would have established a regime opposed by at least 85 percent of the Portuguese. It is nonetheless likely that at first, anyway, this dictatorship would have been greeted as a victory for democracy and progress by large segments of Western opinion, all aside from the Communists. The democracies could not have delivered a strictly military counterthrust against the perversion of this revolution that had been so long in the making and so skillfully executed. Had they tried, they would have raised howls of indignation from *Western* public opinion.

The Communist plot failed, at least in Portugal itself if not in its former colonies, because of a political battle, a war of ideas, objectively reported by foreign newspapers that are widely read and influential in Lisbon and which, day after day, laid bare the inner workings of the forces involved in the struggle. Most of all, it failed because of the courage of genuine democrats in Portugal who resisted intimidation and exposed Communist provocation.

Fighting a battle of accurate information was not easy. Moscow had mobilized the French Communist Party to beat the big drum of totalitarian propaganda. And the French Communists maintained ideological empire over the Socialist Party and its newspapers. Thus the French Socialist Party split the Socialist International with its campaign to abandon the Portuguese socialists to their fate. Democracy squeaked through to victory, fighting with purely political weapons and—why not say it?—with the truth. Which proves that we are wrong not to use it more often.

Those who still believe in political astuteness, the advantages of an overall strategy, and the efficacy of high-flying Machiavellianism should see an object lesson in the Portuguese conspiracy: if communism had won, the defeat for the democracies would have been grave and costly, but its failure went unnoticed by all but those who were intimately familiar with the event. For the West, which had clearly and openly shown its commitment, the transformation of Portugal, a NATO member, into a "popular democracy" would have meant loss of prestige, a political retreat, and a weakened strategic position. Moscow, on the other hand, went masked, as usual, maneuvering its agents—officially accredited or not—by remote control, intervening only under a pseudonym in the attempted coup d'état. Responsibility for its failure, therefore, fell entirely on the local Communist party and a few harebrained saber rattlers. In any struggle between communism and the democracies waged through intermediaries the Soviet Union will show its hand openly only when it has won, the democracies only when they've lost.

The active vigilance in pursuit of a global vision that gives Soviet foreign policy its stamp of continual effectiveness was nowhere better shown than in Moscow's prompt conversion of its unsuccessful operation in Lisbon into a successful one in Portugal's former African colonies.

Here again, its control over national independence movements bespoke lengthy preparation—the patient placement of the International's agents in positions from which to seize power at the right time—engineering the "liberated" country's skid from one form of colonialism to another in the twinkling of an eye under the pretense of bringing it independence. Communism uses everyone's natural desire for peace as it uses nationalism, to eliminate democratic influence. They function as propellents until they have served their purpose, when they are mercilessly crushed under the weight of a totalitarian system. Even the religious revolution in Iran, so opposed to the Marxist-Leninist spirit and hostile to the language of communism, can nevertheless serve as a vehicle that Moscow has long been ready to commandeer when authority and social cohesion disintegrate in Iran. In the resultant chaos, if it is kept simmering long enough, the Iranian Communist Tudeh Party may find its chance to pose as the only force capable of restoring order. This can still happen despite the arrest of Tudeh leaders by the Ayatollah Khomeini's police.

Pure force functions at two levels in Moscow's imperial advance, the highest and the lowest, the two ends of the strategic arc. First, it functions as a means of overall strategic pressure to enable communism's homeland *to win without war* by imposing its will on big and middle-sized powers, whose will to resist is paralyzed or suspended by their awareness of Soviet military superiority or parity. Second, pure force is used to crush the weak in no-risk operations.

In an article that appeared in 1948, Boris Souvarine explained, with his proverbial but too long ignored perspicacity, that "Stalin's policy is made up of caution, patience, intrigue, infiltration, corruption, terrorism, exploitation of human weaknesses. It only moves on to frontal attack when it cannot lose, against an adversary of its choice who is defeated in advance."[3] The writer recalled a great truth that usually remains oddly buried in history's unconscious mind—that Stalin "only resigned himself to fighting Germany when he was . . . forced to do so by Hitler," but that, on his own, "he would never have gone up against an adversary of his own size." As proofs, Souvarine cited the stab in the back of conquered Poland, the attack on Finland, the invasion of the Baltic states and Bessarabia. It's a list that Stalin's successors, despite "thaws" and "peaceful coexistence" and "revisionism" and "détente," would later lengthen in intrepid expeditions that hung them with heroes' laurels: Berlin, Budapest, Prague, Kabul, Warsaw. Obviously, these were police actions to restore order in the empire's colonies.

Faced with tough and possibly even stubborn foes outside the Soviet sphere, when the odds are less than three to one or, better still, three to nothing in its favor the Kremlin still operates as Stalin did, by "infiltration, corruption, terrorism." In other words, by trickery. When armed force appears necessary or opportune, Moscow prefers to delegate it to a satellite army, like Ethiopia's, or to colonial troops, like the Cuban legionnaires. Communist expansion is based essentially on foresight, preparation, patience, and know-how; it is rooted in the art of using surrogate forces other than communism in dissimulation and perseverance. These are all qualities before which Western diplomacy, hampered as it is by

3. The article can be found in a collection of Souvarine's work, *L'Observateur des deux mondes* (Paris: Editions de la Différence, 1982), p. 86.

self-importance, verbalism, ephemeral vainglory, and domestic squabbling, is virtually fated for discomfiture.

No country or group of countries, no civilization can enforce its will through military power alone. As proof, witness the West's global retreat between 1950 and 1970, when the democracies held military superiority. If they could not profit by it then to impose durable restraint on the Soviet Union, how can they do it now? History has conferred an advantage on the side that has realistic intelligence, that is decisive and unscrupulous. How can that advantage fail to increase now that communism is not only wily, but strong as well?

11

LONG-RANGE VISION
AND HINDSIGHT

THE CONDUCT OF any policy, domestic or international, cannot and should not be wholly a prisoner of precedent. Divorcing oneself from the past can be the best or the worst of things—the best when it eliminates analysis of obsolete elements so as to center action on current ones, but worst when it amounts to a complacent forgetfulness of the lessons of history that can lead to the repetition of old mistakes. Failing to realize that he is facing a new situation is a serious error for a diplomat. But not recognizing an old situation in which he'd been bested before is still more unpardonable.

This is a mistake the Soviets rarely commit. They remember all the West's reactions and lack of reactions—let's say the adversary's, rather, for they never stop regarding us as the adversary, even in periods of so-called peaceful coexistence. Moscow knows the ruts the democracies invariably fall into when faced with a challenge. Their reaction is more often disarray and renunciation than counterthrust and injunction. Moscow knows this; it registered the fact in connection with the oil crisis that began in 1973, with Soviet-Cuban expansion in Africa, after its sabotage of the Helsinki agreement, after the Iranian revolution, with the civil wars in Central America, and in the disputes that followed the repression in Poland. They also know that since 1921 the Soviet economy has periodically been rescued by Western aid; these are concrete actions that far outweigh all the anti-Communist rhetoric the Kremlin hears. They know their deceits and aggressions have never met with lasting reprisals from the West, not even with cancellation of its financial and technological assistance. They know these things and, what's more, they know the West does not know them, that Western public opinion and even the West's governors have forgotten them and will continue to forget them. This allows the Soviets to count on the West's trust, indefinitely forthcoming, renewed and renewable whenever Moscow chooses to repeat its old tricks.

The main lines of the Soviet diplomatic offensives were fixed in the early years of the Communist regime. The intellectual framework of proposals the West sees as new every time it reappears was assembled long ago by the Soviets, along with the techniques by which they milk all their agreements with the West for unilateral advantages. To us, there was the eternal freshness of novelty in our disputes beginning in 1970 about whether to seek economic détente and, in the 1980s, about whether to go on seeking it. But seen from the Soviet side, economic cooperation was simply an example of a proven old formula: "We greatly need technical assistance from the United States and Canada . . . If the Americans keep their promises, the benefit for us will be enormous . . . Agreement with and concessions to the Americans are exceptionally important to us . . . I consider it enormously important to attract American capital to build . . . the pipeline in Georgia. Hammer's son (and partner) is in Russia. He has been in the Urals and has decided to restore industry there . . . Shouldn't Hammer also be interested in the electrification plan so that he may supply not only our bread, but electrical equipment as well (on credit, of course)? . . . With the Germans, the tightening of trade relations is going well. With Italy, it is beginning; she has offered us a loan . . ."

These lines date from 1921! They were taken from notes Lenin sent to members of the Politburo and to Molotov and Mikhailov, the two secretaries of the Central Committee.[1] They show that, very early on, Soviet leaders were extremely clear on their goals, namely, to get the capitalist countries to come to the aid of the Soviet economy whenever it is ailing, if possible at their own expense, and in any case on credit terms so favorable as to border on subsidy. In exchange, the capitalist countries were to be satisfied

1. Nikolai Lenin, *Collected Works*, vols. 44 and 53 of the Russian edition.

either with their own naive faith in the miraculous democratization of communism through the gentle virtues of trade or with promises of restraint in foreign policy that the U.S.S.R. has never kept or intended to keep, as it has almost always admitted, with admirable cynicism, in the most thinly veiled terms. Doesn't it know in advance that the Western countries would forget their previous mortifications, that they would jubilantly rush to resume their old roles as hoodwinked benefactors if only Moscow took the trouble to spruce up a few of its old promises?

This is what happened in 1921, in 1928, in 1947, and especially beginning in 1970. Its record of past experience and its perspicacious vision of the future, based of course on the West's combined amnesia and myopia, enabled Moscow to nip in the bud any Western attempt at linkage, that is, subordination of economic aid to Soviet foreign-policy restraint, stabilization of the Soviet empire, and an end to destabilization in other countries. The Kremlin puts its political objectives before its economic objectives. Lenin himself became aware soon after the coup d'état in October 1917 of socialism's economic sterility and, at the same time, of its prodigious potentialities for world conquest. He thought it periodically permissible to make up for the Soviet Union's chronic economic shortfalls by siphoning off loans, food and manufactured goods from countries with more efficient economies. But he loathed sacrificing a major political objective to temporary material relief. However, there's no need for that: the Soviets know that any spasm of Western insistence on concessions in exchange for aid will soon pass. So they cling tightly to their political advantage and reckon that economic aid will flow to them again sooner or later, in the time it takes for the threatened sanctions to be transformed into the ritual row among the democracies.

If such a quarrel does not arise, or is slow in developing, and the democracies do not bow to Soviet wishes, Moscow is willing to give up an immediate economic gain to maintain intact its capacity for political expansion. This happened when the Marshall Plan was introduced in 1947.

Through Secretary of State George C. Marshall, the United

States offered Europe the means to rebuild its economy—*all* of Europe, including the East bloc and the Soviet Union itself. At first, instead of lambasting American generosity, as it later did, pretending to see the plan as a satanic maneuver by Western imperialism and its "trusts," the U.S.S.R. showed great interest in the offer. Stalin even sent Vyacheslav M. Molotov to Paris to discuss it with the British and French Foreign Ministers. But he quickly realized that acceptance of Marshall Plan aid would hamper the process of absorption and consolidation then nearing fulfillment in satellite Europe and might even shake the totalitarian Soviet system. For an American condition to granting credits was that the beneficiary countries coordinate their reconstruction and harmonize their economies. This was the embryo of the future Common Market. To the Communist leadership, this meant creation of a pan-European network of consultation and exchanges, an imbrication of economies and interpenetration of societies that would in any case have shattered totalitarian power in the satellites and put even Moscow's on shaky ground. How could Czechoslovakia, Poland, Hungary, Romania, East Germany have resisted the attraction of a Western Europe that, in 1950, was about to embark on the most vigorous economic expansion in its history? To force them to remain in the Soviet orbit, to put up with the pervasive beggary of daily life that marks socialist economies, Moscow had to separate them forcibly and totally from the West. So the Soviet Union refused Marshall Plan aid for itself and obliged its satellites to do the same. An ultimatum from Stalin barred Czechoslovakia, which had maintained its hopes until the last minute, from accepting American assistance.

It is a nation's duty, it might be objected, to reject the tying of political strings to economic cooperation. This is the price of independence. In this case, however, the opposite was true: the U.S.S.R. was maintaining its control over countries whose independence it had stolen by force, in violation of all the commitments it signed after World War II ended. It wanted Marshall Plan money while keeping absolute control over its recently won European empire; this was not threatened by any shadow of a political precondition—the Americans never posed any—but by the minimal opening of the empire's frontiers required for economic coordination with the West. It was not every people's right to independence that the Soviets put ahead of economic aid in 1947, but their own right to imperialism and oppression.

They were right, and their long-range view again showed great wisdom since, twenty-five years later, the West returned to the charge and again offered the Soviet Union and its satellites loans, grain, and technology. Moreover, this massive economic aid was later joined to official Western recognition, by virtue of the Helsinki pact, of the illegitimate Soviet empire acquired first by leaving the Red Army in Central Europe after the war and second by a series of Communist coups d'état that completed the integration of this part of the continent into the Soviet sphere. No link between the two periods was seen in the West, nor was it understood that for Brezhnev, intelligently following the Stalin line, *détente was the Marshall Plan minus its drawbacks,* with the added benefit of international legitimization of Soviet conquests.

The Soviet leadership, however, understood this very well. For them, détente was the second phase of an unfinished operation and the fruit of perseverance. For we must not forget that the Helsinki pact was also a Soviet idea, pressed insistently and patiently for some fifteen years in a tireless campaign of persuasion aimed at each of the Western democracies and finally realized in 1975.

An excellent example of long-range vision is Moscow's two-stage (1945–50 and 1970–75) plan to wrest from the democracies the territorial gains it had expected from the Hitler-Stalin pact signed August 23, 1939. As a reward for leaving Hitler free to conquer most of Europe, Stalin figured to obtain, or to be allowed to keep, a number of chunks of territory in the East and North. Hitler made the mistake of attacking the Soviet Union before crushing Britain, which it might have tried again to do in the summer of 1941, before the United States came into the war. He thus turned Stalin into a reluctant ally of the democracies. Yet, paradoxically, Stalin and his successors reaped the same territorial gains, and more, from their unwilling war against the Nazis that they had hoped to harvest from the 1939 treaty.

If Soviet diplomacy is successful, it is not because the men in the Kremlin are endowed with any particular genius. It is because they stick to a method that includes the principles of long-term continuity of action, constant review of the reasons for that action, and acceptance of the fact that solid, irreversible results can be slow in coming. On the other hand, Western diplomacy, however intelligent its practitioners (intelligence that, more often than not, shines outside of politics), is discontinuous. Leadership changes frequently, and the new teams tend to forget or mistrust the reasoning behind their predecessors' decisions. And the democracies' diplomacy is guided by a need to feed public opinion with quick, spectacular results. The upshot of all this is that Western diplomacy is more easily led by the nose than Soviet diplomacy is. Moscow wins the advantage over the long haul, a fact Westerners refuse to believe; to them, the idea that everything the Soviets do is the fruit of long-term calculations is a sign of paranoia. For example, in 1974, during the first oil crisis, and in 1980, after the invasion of Afghanistan, it was considered bad taste in the West to suggest that the Soviets might be trying to weaken Western Europe indirectly through its dependence on Mideastern oil.

Yet in Andrei Sakharov's book *My Country and the World* we find the following passage referring to a period well before the oil crisis, before the Soviets took control in South Yemen and Afghanistan and began the process of destabilizing the Persian Gulf emirates and Saudi Arabia. "I often recall a talk given *in 1955* by a high official of the U.S.S.R. Council of Ministers to a group of scientists assembled *at the Kremlin*. He said that at that time (in connection with a trip to Egypt by D. T. Shepilov, a member of the Central Committee Presidium) the principles of the new Soviet policy in the Middle East were being discussed in the Presidium. And he observed that *the long-range goal of that policy, as it had been formulated, was to exploit Arab nationalism in order to create difficulties for the European countries in obtaining crude oil,* and thereby to gain influence over them. Today, when the world economy has been disorganized by the oil crisis, one can plainly see how crafty and effective is the subtext of the oil policy ('defending the just cause of the Arab nations')—although the West pretends that the U.S.S.R. has played no role in the situation."[2]

I have italicized the words in the excerpt that bring out three facts: how long the plan was in the works before it bore its first fruit in 1973, the clarity of its conception, and the high level of the meeting at which the analysis was made—in the Kremlin itself. The testimony is firsthand, the witness credible, to say the least. True, it was not until 1973 that the threat of an oil shortage and the fact of a severe economic crisis, largely triggered by a quintupling of oil prices, were openly revealed as part of Moscow's plan for domesticating Europe. But let's not forget that in 1956 the Europeans had a foretaste of what the future had in store for them when Nasser, already close to the Soviets, nationalized the Suez Canal. At the time, almost all of Europe's oil was shipped through the canal. The repercussions of that nationalization and the unfortunate Franco-British military expedition into the Canal Zone that angered the Americans, who insisted that their allies break off the expedition at once, trace the outlines of an intrigue that would later become familiar.

I am not suggesting that the West is never wrong. It is not at all in that light that I sought to present the problems in this book. All societies throughout history are both right and wrong, mixtures of justice and injustice. But whatever their respective allotments of vice and virtue, of good and evil, some are eliminated and some do the eliminating. Why and how? This is what I am studying here, using contemporary examples.

When the Soviet Union transformed South Yemen into a satellite, invaded Afghanistan, worked to erode power from within on the Arabian Peninsula, much of world opinion thought it was doing wrong. But almost no one in the democracies is ready to think, or even to envisage the possibility, that these actions are part of a program, a logical one conceived long ago. Sakharov's report reminds us of this. Soviet wisdom in implementing the plan is espe-

2. New York: Knopf, 1976, p. 81.

cially effective because the democracies refuse to see it, refuse to see any kind of plan behind totalitarianism's slow but sure progress throughout the world.

Its progress is not mere illusion. It is rooted in a realistic appraisal of things, and it exploits the West's weaknesses, errors, points of vulnerability—for example, the fact that we are heavily dependent on oil from the Middle East and North Africa, where, by a bizarre coincidence, the two oil-exporting countries, Algeria and Libya, formed early links to the Soviet Union. There is nothing original about exploiting an adversary's weaknesses and seeking out his vulnerable spots. Communism scores its points because it thinks of nothing else, whereas the democracies' concentration is negligent, intermittent, changeable. Communism also advances because there is not an instant when it does not think of the non-Communist world as an enemy to be destroyed, while the democracies imagine they can buy peace by conceding communism a share of the globe. They forget that communism cannot allow itself to stop. It expands or it dies, since it cannot solve any of the internal problems of the societies it creates. What, indeed, would the state do in a Communist society if it did not expand? The Nomenklatura would die of boredom, because its need for action could not be assuaged by the drab management of an economy indissolubly wedded to failure. This is why settling the quarrel over rights and wrongs will not produce a victor. Communism is a better machine for world conquest than democracy, and this is what will decide the final outcome of their struggle.

The democracies tend to seek sweeping, definitive treaties that organize the world for generations to come. They hope that once a balance of power is finally established, once they have achieved this "international community," this "structure of peace," as Kissinger called it, each country could finally turn to civilized tasks: developing its economy, enriching its culture, advancing social justice. All this should proceed smoothly as long as a world parliament, functioning within a stable order, arbitrates the minor conflicts that might crop up. After both world wars, this vision inspired international conferences, peace treaties, the foundation first of the League of Nations and then of the United Nations organization, the charter of which expresses this philosophy of progress through cooperation in a stable world society. This is also the philosophy that motivated the West in reaching the Helsinki agreement in 1975.

For the past forty years, the democracies, seeking what they thought should be a durable global balance, have always been ready to make concessions to the Soviet Union to prove their goodwill and oblige it to show its own. The trouble is that all these treaties, which the West sees as domes of stability, are viewed by the Communists as springboards for destabilization. Communism is not at all interested in replacing the race toward domination with a race toward civilization that it knows it would be doomed to lose. It is greedy for treaties too, but only to receive guarantees, not to give them. A pact is hardly signed before the Communists' active vigilance sends them back on the attack, exploiting the clauses favorable to them and crossing out the others. Everyone is aware of their violations of the Helsinki agreement. But we tend to forget that after World War II Stalin lost no time at all before violating the treaties designed to "rebuild" the postwar world, the agreements signed in Teheran (December 1943), Yalta (February 1945), and Potsdam (August 1945). All the armistice conventions, the interallied agreements, the peace treaties with Germany, Poland, Hungary, Bulgaria, Romania, Korea were broken by the Soviets. Only Austria escaped, a miraculous survivor of the great Soviet sweep, and so did Finland, a semisatellite with a special status. In the same way, the 1973 cease-fire in Indochina was immediately violated by the Communists; North Vietnam's armored divisions completed the conquest of South Vietnam in 1975.

We are dealing here with two kinds of long-range vision. The democracies' is based in law and relies chiefly for respect of that law on the parties' sincerity and pragmatic restraint. The Communists consider nothing but the balance of power and see treaties merely as one of the many ways to lull their adversaries' already somnolent vigilance for a while. When the Soviet Union and the Communist International are in a superior position, they hasten to press their advantage, ignoring treaties; if they are in an inferior position, they fall back temporarily before attacking again as soon as they can. What is more, each phase of a Communist operation is held in reserve, no matter how long the forced interruption, until it can again be connected to the one that follows. Eventually, the past is welded into the general framework of a program that, unlike the democracies', is never left uncompleted.

12

ATTACK, ALWAYS ATTACK

KNOWING THEY CAN trick us without ever undeceiving us, the Communists never accept a retreat or a refusal as final. They return tirelessly to the charge, make the same proposals, infiltrate the same structures, seek the same conquests until they achieve their objectives or replace them with more easily pursued equivalents. They demonstrate this perseverance in both international and domestic politics.

The French Communist Party labored for as many years, between ten and fifteen, to erect their "Common Program" with the Socialists as the Soviet Union did to persuade the West to conclude the agreement on "European security and cooperation" signed in Helsinki. While Western public opinion and Western voters sometimes refuse to be fooled, the same cannot be said for Western politicians, eternally forthcoming, always ready to applaud the most trivial and outworn ideas as dazzling intellectual breakthroughs. What works wonders, again, is Western leaders' ability to forget, their desire, as we have noted, to sign agreements with the Communists that they think are final, their fear of seeming to impede international understanding if they too often reject the same old proposals, even if these are against their own interests. A standard Communist tactic is to mount a propaganda operation to accompany a practical operation. If the latter hits a snag, the former will leave traces in people's minds that will help condition them to give future actions a kinder reception.

In 1958, for example, the U.S.S.R. suggested a nonaggression pact among all the states facing on the Baltic Sea, whether they belonged to NATO or the Warsaw Pact or were neutral. Because of the inequalities of power among the various countries involved, this amounted to proposing total Soviet domination and conversion of the Baltic into a Russian lake. Although the Baltic states resisted the seduction of this magnanimous offer—those that had a choice, that is—the vague ring of the word "nonaggression" was all that sounded in the ears of more distant peoples. How could the notion fail to sink in eventually that a state that spends its time proposing nonaggression pacts could not really be aggressive? Especially when the Soviet premier, Marshal Nikolay Bulganin, shortly afterward proposed that Norway join it in turning the Nordic region into a nuclear-free zone. This implied that Norway and Denmark, NATO's two Scandinavian members, would leave the alliance's military command. It was an astonishingly crude stunt, since even if the U.S.S.R. were to "denuclearize" the part of its territory bordering on Norway, it would nevertheless maintain its atomic strike force intact. But it was a shrewd propaganda move, spreading the impression that Moscow was "against the atomic bomb."

In 1961, Urho Kekkonen was reelected President of Finland after Moscow forced his opponent, a man named Honka, who was considered a sure winner, to withdraw from the election. Two years later, in 1963, Kekkonen revived the idea of a nuclear-free Scandinavia. How amazing that this philanthropic inspiration flooded into his mind in the same year that Moscow tried to station missiles in Cuba!

A climax to this running fireworks display came eighteen years later, in 1981, when the Soviets, decidedly short of imagination if not of tenacity, sang the same old refrain, again calling for a nuclear-free zone in Northern Europe. The West did not seem to recognize the shopworn goods that, in better days, the Kremlin had repeatedly tried to palm off on it. In 1981, as it happened, the days were better for the Soviet Union. Norway's resistance was far lower than it had been, thanks to the reversal of the East-West power balance. So Moscow had no reason to junk its old idea.

No rebuff discourages the U.S.S.R. from persisting in its proposals for disarmament plans that would disarm only the West. In 1957, Polish Foreign Minister Adam Rapacki presented the UN General Assembly with a plan to make Central Europe a nuclear-free zone; it was phrased in such a way as to force the United States to dismantle its whole defensive system in Western Europe while leaving the Soviet offensive system intact. In 1972, Brezhnev offered Kissinger a plan for simultaneous renunciation by the Soviet Union and the United States of the use of nuclear weapons against each other. This "peaceful bomb," as Brezhnev, in a stroke of linguistic genius, decoratively labeled his attempted fraud, came when the Soviets had reached nuclear parity with the United States while maintaining their superiority in conventional forces. Freezing the nuclear deterrent would automatically have meant giving superiority to the U.S.S.R., especially in relation to NATO forces, which could not contain those of the Warsaw Pact without the American nuclear umbrella. Moreover, the proposal was aimed at nothing less than freeing Brezhnev for a nuclear attack against China.

For more than a year, despite the almost comic enormity of his pretentions, Brezhnev insisted with imperturbable aplomb on pressing this gem on the Americans. Kissinger laboriously emptied it of its poison and transformed it into a global promise of mutual restraint. As Kissinger commented on the experience, "Soviet diplomacy knows no resting places. A scheme is presented as a major contribution to relaxing tensions; if we will only accept it, there will be an 'improvement in the atmosphere.' But as often as not, no sooner has one agreement been completed than the Kremlin advances another, which is pursued with characteristic single-mindedness and with the identical argument that failure to proceed will sour the atmosphere."[1]

It is with this spirit, as we know, that the Soviets submerged the West in 1980, 1981, 1982 with "disarmament" plans aimed at halting deployment of the NATO Euromissiles, which still existed only on paper, while keeping their own aimed at Western Europe. In January 1983, Andropov dived into his trunkful of antique

1. Kissinger, *Years of Upheaval*, Chap. 7.

finery and came up with another musty proposal of a "nonaggression pact" with the West. All these offers, the oldest and the most recent, have been part of an extremely judicious Soviet tactic: to impress world opinion with the notion that Moscow is seeking détente and to blackmail it with the specter of a nuclear apocalypse while the U.S.S.R. continues to build up its strategic arsenal. To judge from the results obtained in the past quarter-century, it's not a bad system.

It is in this light that we must learn to evaluate the failures of communism. They occur, of course, but the U.S.S.R. never considers writing a period, marking the end of an effort. It has a decisive asset that is inherent in a totalitarian system: it can afford to wait. This is what it did, for example, in Afghanistan, where its invading army has encountered unexpectedly stiff and tenacious popular resistance. Two and a half years after the Soviets marched in, according to an eyewitness who went there as a reporter in 1982, the Afghan Communist government and the Soviet troops had yet to gain control of the countryside, where 85 percent of the population lives.[2] Western media were retailing the cliché about a "Soviet Vietnam," the "mire" in which the U.S.S.R. would "bog down."

It's a superficial comparison: the Afghan freedom fighters have not been supported and supplied by a superpower with modern weapons, as North Vietnam had been by the Soviet Union and by China as well. The Kremlin does not have to contend with public hostility at home to this distant war, or with a press corps constantly challenging government statements, or with young men dodging the draft and leaving the country (which is impossible for a Communist national anyway). A democracy cannot win a war without its own people's support, even if it has the technical ability to win on the ground. The United States learned this in Vietnam, as the French did in Algeria. Time is not on democracy's side unless public opinion is profoundly convinced that the war is necessary. This is at once its nobility and its weakness, sometimes its strength. Even Israel discovered this law during the war in Leba-

2. Gérard Chaliand, *L'Express*, 16 July 1982.

non, the first of the Israeli-Arab wars in which Israeli public opinion was not almost unanimously behind its government.

The Union of Soviet Socialist Republics, having organically eliminated its public opinion, or, at least, its expression and influence, can wait a very long time, can occupy a country until resistance is worn down. The United States cannot do this because it is harnassed to a need for quick and politically acceptable results. "In evaluating the current situation," concludes the Chaliand report cited above, "we should not overlook an essential factor: time. The Soviets have not yet shown what they can do militarily. They are gradually plugging the Afghan economy into their system. They are in Afghanistan to stay." The indifference of world opinion is no less propitious for this long-term operation than the absence of opinion at home. No Soviet flags are burned in Prague, Budapest and East Berlin, as American flags were burned in Rome, Paris and Bonn during the war in Vietnam. Communist satellites are muzzled, not critical, allies. The totalitarian straitjacket makes demonstrations against Soviet imperialism impossible inside the empire. No Communist general serving a country allied to the Soviet Union could permit himself, while stationed only a few miles from the Afghan frontier—at Peshawar, say—to deliver a sizzling diatribe against the Soviet presence in Kabul, as General de Gaulle did in Phnom Penh in 1966 against the American presence in Vietnam. Even in the democracies, public condemnation of the occupation of Afghanistan comes from isolated groups and individuals; it is a thousand times less virulent and massive than the street demonstrations against the United States during the Vietnam War. The Soviets are discreetly reproached; the Americans were hated ferociously.

And they still are, at every turn. True, the U.S.S.R. is hated far more intensely by the people in the satellite countries than the United States is by the people in the countries with which it is allied. But the Communist-ruled peoples' hatred of communism filters through only in exceptional circumstances, and then its effects are limited and easily contained. Demonstrations in the West against Soviet imperialism are symbolic; some do attract sizeable crowds, like those in support of the Polish people, but, in a few weeks, people lose interest and nothing is achieved. Only skeleton crowds have turned out over Afghanistan and these soon dispersed, which once more wrecks the comparison with the Vietnam War. By 1981, news from Afghanistan had shrunk to brief bulletins and obscure conferences. Yet according to the High Commission for Refugees there were over three million Afghan refugees at the end of 1982, most of them in Pakistan, half a million in Iran; all had fled since the Sovietization of their country began. Since Afghanistan had a population of thirteen million in 1978, an equivalent exodus from the United States would mean sixty million people on the run. The Afghan drainage is comparable in size to that of the Palestinians, but it does not excite the same protests among international progressives. Even solid evidence indicating that the Soviets were using chemical and biological weapons against the Afghan guerrillas was received with indifference by the public and, as was to be expected, by Western chancelleries. We can see how faint the analogy is between Vietnam and Afghanistan, all aside from the very different causes and motives of the two wars. The Soviets have all the time they need. They can compensate for their initial failure on the ground by their endurance, that irreplaceable resource available only to those who are never threatened by domestic strife.

In the Latin American theater, too, the Soviet Union has shown its persistence and its inexhaustible ability to start again from scratch as often as it must. When a Western operation fails, that is usually the end of it because opposition parties and public opinion make it almost impossible to revive an unsuccessful venture. In 1975, the United States Government could do nothing to stop the colonization of Angola by the Soviets' Cuban mercenaries because Congress, traumatized by the Vietnam disaster, simply refused to consider the use of American military forces abroad, no matter where, or even to take a public stand on the situation. A member of President Gerald Ford's cabinet told me at the time, "If I were Kim Il Sung, I would invade South Korea tomorrow morning. We Americans couldn't do a thing about it. We would not live up to our commitments. Under the present circumstances, neither the public nor the media nor the Congress would allow American troops to fight on foreign soil."

A totalitarian system, on the other hand, responsible to no one but itself, can return to the job in hand over and over again, especially since it can hide its failures behind a screen of censorship or distort them with propaganda. Both techniques have been used in Latin America. Soviet-inspired guerrilla risings failed in the 1960s in Bolivia, Peru, Venezuela; massive terrorist campaigns in Argentina and Uruguay succeeded only in bouncing power to atrociously repressive extreme-rightist dictators and unleashing semi-official, uncontrolled counterterrorism. Another failure: the attempt by Salvador Allende, who had been legally elected, but on a minority vote, to turn Chile into a "popular democracy" through confiscation and an internal power grab. It was this setback, as we know, that inspired the famous 1973 series of articles by Italian Communist Party Secretary-General Enrico Berlinguer on the need for a "historic compromise" between the Communists and the parties of the center and moderate right.

After such a crop of failures, any institution other than the world Communist high command would have crossed Latin America off its list. Instead, it redirected its surrogates in Havana toward Africa; Cuban colonial infantry was sent to Ethiopia, Angola and even more remote battlefields. But, while this strike into Africa meant that Latin American operations were suspended for reexamination, it in no way ruled out further attempts at penetration there. The next time, beginning in 1978, the chosen targets were mainly Central America and the Caribbean, and we have seen the results in Nicaragua, El Salvador, Guatemala, Guyana, Jamaica, Grenada, and Suriname.

To avoid any misunderstanding with my readers—those of good faith, that is, for there is no reasoning with those of bad faith—I repeat that in my view the political and social conditions in these countries often explain and justify the popular insurrections that arise there. What I contest is that there is some inherent reason why the ills these countries suffer can only be remedied if they become dominions of the Soviet Union. To encourage them to do this is a betrayal of their peoples' trust that necessarily aggravates their problems and makes them insoluble. The political and social crises in this part of the world are genuine, but rigging them as transit stages to communism is artificial.

It is at the decisive moment in such transfers that imported revolutionary techniques are brought into play: terrorist infiltration, guerrilla operations supported from outside the country, plotting toward monopolization of political power. Why, otherwise, should subversion have appeared in Costa Rica, a small Central American republic that is a model in terms of its standard of living and its fidelity to democratic procedure, a country that *doesn't even have an army?* Another example: Peru. In 1980, after deposing the military-socialist regime that, between 1968 and 1979, had depressed the country's gross national product by 60 percent, the Peruvians chose centrist Fernando Belaúnde Terry as their first legally elected president in a dozen years. Almost at once, as though by happenstance, the country was convulsed by a terrorist campaign that, given its scale, organization, equipment, and leadership, makes any theory that it was a "spontaneous" uprising by angry peasant masses implausible, to put it mildly. Here we have a fine example of the Soviets' tenacity and of their axiom that nothing is ever over; everything must be and is begun again as often as necessary to bring an operation to completion, no matter how long it takes.

As soon as it failed to take over the "Revolution of the Carnations" in Portugal, Moscow pivoted toward the former Portuguese colonies in Africa, and there it was more successful. Although only the part of Angola controlled from the capital, Luanda, was in the hands of the Communist puppet regime, which was entirely sustained by Moscow's Cuban occupation troops, the Soviet Union gradually managed to persuade the West to accept the Luanda Government as legitimate; France, for example, signed a cooperation agreement with it in 1982. Since 1975, Moscow has also been laboring with antlike patience to set up another pro-Communist regime south of Angola, in Namibia, where it is supporting, arming, and financing its spearhead organization, the South West Africa People's Organization (Swapo), an offshoot of the Polisario movement Moscow supports in the North, at the other end of the continent. It abandoned Somalia in favor of that country's larger, more strategic, more powerful neighbor, Ethiopia, since it could not form alliances at the same time with both these hereditary rivals. Then, in 1982, with socialist power stabilized in Ethiopia, the Soviet Union renewed its assault on Somalia. Under the direction of Moscow and of Cuban "advisers," Ethiopian soldiers disguised as Somali rebels were sent in against Syad Barre's anti-Soviet government in Mogadishu. To Moscow, no loss is ever final.

What sturdier confirmation of this rule can there be than the relations between the Soviet Union and Finland? In the wash of neologisms sent up by political hypocrisy, the term "Finlandization" stands out by its longevity. It induces in people's minds the mixture of repulsion, seduction and ambiguity that may explain why some words last. Meaning "barely disguised servitude" to some, to others "the courageous resistance of a small but tenacious country," Finlandization has, for most Europeans, the vague suggestion of a comforting compromise, a chance to become accustomed to their inevitable servitude. After all, don't habit and forgetfulness of the good old days soften the bite of misfortune? A painless transition, snug antechamber to subjugation, Finlandization could prepare us to endure "happiness in slavery" or, at least, condition us for the apathy that makes us indifferent to slavery.

All these stimulating forms of speculation suffer from a common vice: they assume that it was Finland that chose Finlandization, whereas it was the Soviet Union that not so much chose it as imposed it by force and threat; that is as far as the Kremlin has been able to go so far, while waiting for better days. In Soviet eyes, Finlandization is merely incomplete Sovietization, an interim solution to be improved on later. In this, the democracies are making their usual mistakes: ignoring even recent history, interpreting the facts in the way most favorable to Moscow, the way the Kremlin wants them to choose. They are basing their diagnosis on what Moscow *says* and not on what it *does*, falling for the eternal mirage, as we have already noted, of a stable compromise that, at the cost of a few concessions, would supposedly guarantee a "generation of peace."

The Soviet Union brought to bear on Finland all the determination that always stamps its foreign policy. But Finland was no less obstinate and, given the immense disparity of power between the two countries, made maximum use of the meager assets it drew from nature and circumstances. It is fair to proclaim that the Finnish people's courage has always deserved free men's admiration. But it is abject to cite this courage, as Sweden's Olof Palme and West Germany's Willy Brandt, those two beacons of the Socialist International, constantly do, as evidence that Finlandization involves *no* servitude, no amputation of national sovereignty and so can provide the purge needed to treat the languor infecting Western Europe. The Finns were "Finlandized" because they resisted Sovietization with no thought of compromise. Had they said, "Let us accept Finlandization," they would have been Sovietized, not Finlandized. For them, Finlandization was not something they chose but a partial failure of their ability to maintain their national independence. Today, all the gurus preaching the "self-Finlandization" of Europe are, in fact, only the propagandists and propagators of Soviet imperialism.

Finland narrowly escaped becoming Soviet territory on three occasions: in 1918, in 1939, and after the Second World War. Annexed by czarist Russia, it profited from the 1917 Russian military collapse to declare its independence. In January 1918, this was recognized by the Bolsheviks in the way they would later recognize the independence of Georgia, Mongolia and Afghanistan, that is, by fomenting "revolution" through their local agents with the aim of installing a Soviet-style regime. Trotsky sent large shipments of arms to the Finnish Red Guard "revolutionaries." After five months of fighting, nationalist General Carl Gustaf Mannerheim won the war, writing failure to the first attempt to Sovietize the country. In 1932, in a sudden fit of tenderness, the Soviet Union signed with Finland one of those nonaggression and friendship treaties with which it is so prodigal the world over. It distributes them as generously as Don Juan did his promises of marriage; any KGB Leporello could sing the long catalogue of blood weddings that result.

The 1939 Hitler-Stalin pact included a then secret protocol in which Nazi Germany recognized that Finland "belongs in the Soviet sphere of influence," which was Hitler's way of saying that Stalin was free to swallow it up. Endowed, to use gastronome Athelme Brillat-Savarin's words, with "great powers of intussusception," Stalin decided to begin the process of absorption at the end of October, having first, with delicate scrupulousness, denounced the 1932 "friendship" treaty. We know what happened then: to the whole world's astonishment, tiny Finland's troops, still led by Mannerheim, stopped the vast Soviet Army in its tracks. A compromise peace was reached in March 1940, but Finland had to cede the Karelian Isthmus to the U.S.S.R. This had nevertheless been a tie match and so a loss for the Soviet Union, since the initial Soviet objective was total political and territorial annexation of Finland on the pattern used in the Baltic states.

When Hitler turned against his ally in June 1941 and attacked the U.S.S.R., Finland's hatred of the Soviets drove it into the German camp. By 1944 it was on the list of beaten countries, along with Italy, Bulgaria, Romania and Hungary, and this time it had suffered military defeat on the ground, although it had been neither crushed nor occupied. It nevertheless had to accept a treaty under which the Soviet Union sliced off another chunk of its territory. What is noteworthy, here again, is that the Soviet Union won from its involuntary alliance with the democracies the same spoils it had expected from its complicity with the Nazis. In short, as far as Moscow was concerned, after 1945 the democracies kept Hitler's promises.

Semisuccess or semifailure? In any case, the U.S.S.R. was determined not to stop there. It was soon trying to convert Finland into a "popular democracy" by applying the methods it was using elsewhere. In the spring of 1948, a few days after the Communist coup d'état in Prague, a similar plot by Finnish Communists to overthrow the Helsinki Government, in which they participated, was exposed. Better, or worse, yet: it was the Communist Interior Minister, Leino, who, in a fit of remorse, betrayed the plot to his non-Communist colleagues and to the armed forces commander. The military neutralized the "political police," the secular arm of the planned pro-Soviet putsch. Truly, it is difficult to find traitors in Finland. Leino later confessed, "I can now affirm that it is impossible to serve two masters at once, to be both an orthodox Communist Internationalist and a patriotic Finnish farmer."[3] He was a hero, but a hero reproached for the very fact of having saved his country from the U.S.S.R.: Leino was summarily dismissed from the government on the angry insistence of Andrei A. Zhdanov, then a ranking member of the Soviet Politburo.

Technically, this was the beginning of Finlandization. The country escaped becoming a "popular democracy" but had to comply with Moscow's orders. This political abdication, disguised as voluntary cooperation, was the price Finland had to pay to preserve the inviolability of its territory, what was left of it, and the right to live privately in a nontotalitarian society.

With the principle established, the consequences were inevitable: Finland was forbidden to accept Marshall Plan aid; in 1971 it was barred not only from seeking membership in the European Economic Community, but even from signing trade agreements with it. Moscow made the Finns draw back by launching two simultaneous press campaigns, one in the Soviet press, the other in the organs of the French Communist Party, arguing enigmatically but energetically that "any commercial agreement or association with the EEC was a threat to Finland's peaceful foreign policy."[4] Because of this interdiction to exchange Finnish herrings for French melons, "peace" was saved in extremis.

As it had been saved in July 1958. In that year, the Socialist leader, Fagerholm, had won the parliamentary election with a large enough majority to be able to form a government without including the Communists. The Soviet Union recalled its ambassa-

3. Cited by Claude Delmas in *La Finlandisation*, a report by a study group of the Association Française pour la Communauté Atlantique, 1977.
4. *Pravda*, cited in ibid., p. 29.

dor from Helsinki. Kekkonen, President of Finland since 1956, was summoned to Moscow to hear a harangue from Khrushchev, who, "without wishing to intrude in Finland's internal affairs," nevertheless longed to see it "have a well-disposed government." Although Fagerholm had clearly won the popular vote, he was obliged to withdraw his candidacy as Prime Minister. This and the event cited earlier, of the forced withdrawal of Honka in his 1961 race for the presidency against Kekkonen, dispose of the relatively reassuring definition of Finlandization as limited sovereignty in foreign policy and full sovereignty in domestic affairs. This is an entirely false understanding of the term. Soviet diktats concerning Finnish domestic affairs are as frequent and important as those in foreign policy. What is true is that they did not become chronic until 1958. From 1948 to 1958, Moscow had trouble bringing its weight to bear on internal Finnish affairs. It was Kekkonen who made the escalation possible, and this is why he remained President until ill health forced his recent retirement. Such are the rules for fruitful and ever-alert continuity of attention and objectives in Soviet diplomacy.

These case studies show the spirit of constancy in Communist foreign policy. Moments in its history that Westerners seldom think of connecting, or which they consider new departures, shifts in direction, are seen in hindsight to be successive stages of a long-standing and meticulous plan. The intention to absorb Finland, or at least to vassalize it, dates from the very beginnings of the Soviet regime. The invasion of Afghanistan was not at all a mistake; it had been preceded by years of a political and economic stranglehold on the country. Guerrilla activity in Latin America and the Caribbean, relegated to the back burner while the infinitely more profitable process of East-West détente was completed, was brought to a boil again as soon as détente had borne all its fruit. The constant fireworks of propositions for "balanced" disarmament, Scandinavian neutralization, nonaggression pacts, and supposedly equal reductions of the world's atomic arsenals have always been aimed at returning Western Europe to its pre-NATO situation: without its own defenses and without American protection, it could escape servitude only through servility. Such clarity of plan, such obstinacy in its realization, make Western foreign policy seem nothing more than a collection of improvisations. Some Western achievements, such as the Atlantic Alliance and the European Economic Community, have withstood the test of time, even though the original reasoning behind them has been forgotten, which tells on their effectiveness; the early achievements, in any case, have not been brought up-to-date. Overall, however, the democratic powers' foreign and defense policies more often than not confront Soviet concentration and perseverance with their own incoherence and discontinuity.

13

PLAYING HOT AND COLD

IN HIS MEMOIRS, Kissinger compares détente to a high-wire act that the United States cannot carry off unless it hangs negotiation from one end of its balancing pole and confrontation from the other. Never, in his mind or in Nixon's, was détente what it became at the end of the 1970s: a smug, simplistic belief that all differences with the Soviet Union can be settled by negotiation alone, with nothing more than concessions, goodwill and a frantic haste always to take the first step. Détente, wrote the former Secretary of State, could not succeed without both of its components: resistance to every Soviet attempt at expansion and ceaseless negotiation with Moscow.

This marriage of two conflicting diplomatic tactics was dictated by a situation new to humanity, i.e., the coexistence of two nuclear superpowers whose political antagonism is unshakable. Even before the nuclear era, the democracies had learned to their cost how much harm can be done by too accommodating a policy. During the geopolitical face-off that preceded World War II, they thought they could bribe Hitler to be moderate by granting him concessions that, in fact, gave him the time to rearm and then, suddenly, to overrun the Continent.

That's the truth. And it is also true that many characteristics of East-West détente recall that period of disastrous blindness. But, Kissinger warns, this should not make us forget the accident of the First World War, when the nations of Europe, grouped in blocs, encased in pacts, alliances, military security and vigilant resolution, ravaged each other because they had too completely rejected the idea of negotiation. Hence the notion of double-edged détente as both a permanent channel of consultation to prevent the supreme catastrophe and a system of precautions to block Soviet encroachment.

This was a subtle, ambiguous and unusual foreign policy that could have been explained to the American people and applied to East-West relations. Unfortunately, laments Kissinger, we'll never know if it could have worked. It had hardly begun to remodel the practice of international relations when it was undermined by Watergate, which struck its indispensable protagonist, the President of the United States, with political leukemia and stripped him of the authority he needed to be conciliatory or firm as circumstances required. The machine's key part was tossed on the scrap heap, and the motor of détente went haywire, to the sole benefit of the Soviets.

Even without this stroke of fate, détente was prone to untimely compromise by the politicians. In the early 1970s, Congress, backed by the media, saw Nixon as the hawk he always had been. It withheld or haggled over the appropriations needed to modernize America's defenses, which enabled the Soviet Union first to equal the United States militarily, then to surpass it. This deprived Washington of the tools for firmness and knocked one of the components of genuine détente—a détente that was not mere sham— off the balancing pole. During Nixon's first term, Congress slashed the defense budget by forty billion dollars. The dismantling of the country's intelligence and counterespionage services, for highly respectable reasons of political morality, increased America's weakness. In addition, the government's departments, agencies, bureaucrats and the separate armed services all disagreed on a proper doctrine for negotiating the first Strategic Arms Limitation Treaty (SALT), so that the United States, in the person of Secretary Kissinger, arrived at the negotiating table without a clearly defined position.

Then, during the latter part of the decade, the national mood flip-flopped. Congress, the media, public opinion, all the former doves accused Kissinger of letting himself be cheated, of failing to head off a one-way system of détente that benefited only the U.S.S.R.; absorbed to a point of hypnosis by the niggling over SALT, it was said, he woke up one morning to find communism spread out over the world or, at any rate, encamped in a lot of places it had not been before. The same coalition of liberal Democrats and isolationist Republicans who in 1975 had flatly vetoed any effort to reverse the Soviet sweep in Angola now criticized the Administration for its inertia, accusing the State Department of being soft on international communism. In short, during the first half of the period the people of the United States would not hear of anything but conciliation at any price, while in the second half they demanded vigorous action and the laying down of conditions without concessions. But during the first period they had permitted the deterioration of the means needed to enforce the firm policy called for later. Neither American nor world public opinion has ever seized more than one of the two counterweights of détente at a time. But these are inseparable. On several occasions after his expulsion from office, I heard Nixon explain this complex philosophy of true détente as he and Kissinger had conceived it—which, he said, had never been put into practice.

However we may admire the intelligence of this definition of détente as it might have been but never was, the only question that counts now is what the final result was and is. One of the barriers to "genuine" détente was unforeseeable: America's political agony and Nixon's fall. But the others were thrown up by the democratic system itself. That legislatures, media, voters are neither infallible nor entirely logical, nor perfectly informed, nor consistent, that they do not always act in good faith is normal in democratic life. This is why the art of governing is partly a matter of skillful persuasion. Even Nixon's removal—no U.S. President had ever before been forced to resign in mid-term—was part of the workings of democracy. That a diplomatic policy designed to defend democracy was ruined by democracy itself is a natural consequence of the system's structure. If this structure cannot be revised, then democracy is lost. If it can be corrected, then this should have been considered. There are weaknesses hidden in the Communist system too. It is up to us to exploit them. Have we done this? Or have the Soviets exploited ours better than we have theirs? This is all that matters. What's the answer?

In an address on October 8, 1973, to the *Pacem in Terris* conference in Washington, Kissinger subordinated détente to the following three American conditions:

"We will oppose the attempt by any country to achieve a position of dominance either globally or regionally;

"we will resist any attempt to exploit a policy of détente to weaken our alliances;

"we will react if relaxation of tensions is used as a cover to exacerbate conflicts in international trouble spots."[1]

Just rereading these three fine resolutions gives a clear picture of the extent of the debacle. For the three dangerous situations that Kissinger said were incompatible with a healthy understanding of détente have materialized.

Before analyzing why, we might wonder how the Soviets saw détente, what they expected of it, and what they did not under any circumstances want it to be. Totalitarians are obliging: they declare and put in writing in advance everything they plan to do. The democracies normally make the same mistake they made with Hitler in refusing to take these detailed programs seriously because they seem so horrendous. It is a foreordained paradox that they eagerly believe the Communists' pure propaganda, reserving their skepticism for the genuinely revealing doctrinal statements. These they dismiss as mere talk, as efforts at intimidation. Or, committing the constant error of ascribing to totalitarianism the obligations and customs peculiar to democracy, they shrewdly decide that such statements are "for domestic consumption," aimed at "reassuring" one or another faction within the Communist apparatus. But the only way to escape the uncertainties of conjecture is to compare the lists of statements and actions. In the Communists' case, they agree perfectly over the long term.

From the early years of their regime, the Soviets have never ceased declaring that capitalism and communism would have to

1. Cited by Kissinger in *Years of Upheaval*, chap. 7.

fight to the finish for possession of the world. In this fight, Moscow is the seat of the high command of an international organization[2] of which the Communist parties in the capitalist countries are merely one element. World conquest by the Communists may be temporarily blocked; they may be forced into tactical withdrawals, as they were when they adopted the slogan "build socialism in a single country," which seemed to suggest that the U.S.S.R. would stop exporting its revolution. But this was only a pause. Conquest also includes phases of accommodation with capitalism, called "peaceful coexistence" or "détente." It is understood that these remain subject to two conditions: that they be more advantageous to communism than to capitalism and that they impose no delay on Communist expansion.

In 1971, at the dawn of détente, Brezhnev solemnly recalled in his report to the twenty-fourth Soviet Party Congress that the Communists are and will remain combatants. Ten years earlier, Nikita S. Khrushchev, in his report to the twenty-second Soviet Party Congress, outlined his notion of peaceful coexistence. Article One: the Soviet Union will no longer export its revolution. Article Two: the imperialist forces are exporting counterrevolution, which requires a Communist response. "The Communists call on the peoples of all countries to unite," he declared, "to mobilize their forces and, *relying on the power of the world socialist system* [my italics], to deliver a vigorous riposte to the enemies of freedom, the enemies of peace." In other words, revolution won't be exported, but yes it will anyway in competition with the exportation of counterrevolution.

Commenting on this speech in his *Internal History of the Communist Party*, Philippe Robrieux wrote with judicious irony that "there was no better way to say that they would grasp every opportunity to attack, explaining on each occasion that they were only defending themselves. It's an old tactic in human history." He stressed a passage in Khrushchev's speech in which the Soviet

2. The Communist International may exist officially or not, as circumstances warrant, under a variety of names (the Comintern, the Cominform); it can also be eliminated from organizational charts without really ceasing to exist.

leader alluded broadly to the assistance in money and, when necessary, in armaments that the Soviet Union would supply to Communist parties and revolutionary movements throughout the world. "In the same report, the First Secretary specified that the proletariat would have the benefit of powerful international forces possessing everything necessary, moral and *material*, for its effective support."[3]

This cunningly immaculate subterfuge of "defending the peace" was used, among countless other occasions, during the invasion of Afghanistan. Soviet troops, Moscow alleged in 1979, went into the country not to prop up the reviled and wobbly Communist regime set up by a KGB putsch there but to parry imperialist aggression. If those troops are still there, it's because imperialism has not ceased its aggression. Since there was and is absolutely no imperialist aggression in sight, its "cessation" poses an insoluble metaphysical problem. Which means the occupation might go on indefinitely.

What is amazing is that Khrushchev managed to carve out a reputation as an apostle of peaceful coexistence and of a thaw in East-West relations by using nothing but pure ballyhoo, which was his strong point. For he was the man behind the bloody suppression of the revolt in Budapest, the man who built the Berlin wall and tried to station nuclear missiles in Cuba. Indeed, the Sovietization of Cuba, Russian penetration into a strategically vital area for the United States, had begun well before the missiles affair. Contrary to the legend, Fidel Castro was not "pushed into Moscow's arms" by American hostility. The United States had not been at all displeased by the fall of the Cuban dictator, General Fulgencio Batista; it had even indirectly helped it to come about. Castro's rapprochement with the Soviet Union dates from February 1960, at a time when his relations with the United States were still good, well before Washington's first attempts to destabilize his government and even before there was any talk of an anti-Cuban embargo or blockade. As early as the summer of 1960, Khrushchev defied the United States in its own hemisphere by declaring that the

3. Robrieux, *Histoire intérieure* . . . , vol. III, pp. 116–17.

Monroe Doctrine was void and loudly offering his active protection to the new master in Havana. It was not until January 1961 that Washington broke off diplomatic relations with Cuba, two years after Castro seized power—a Castro thenceforth irrevocably and of his own will committed to the Soviet side. Clearly, Khrushchev had a style all his own when it came to peaceful coexistence: pairing pacifism with belligerency, the first in words, the second in actions. Napoleon Bonaparte liked the same double policy; "Always talk peace and think war" was one of his favorite maxims.

If we hesitate to follow Kissinger in what détente might have been but was not, for the West, let us try to understand what it meant to Soviet leaders by putting ourselves in their place, taking the viewpoint of their interests. What did they seek from it, and what did they receive? In any negotiations, any redefinition of foreign policy, one calculates advantages and concessions. Then, after a few years, the results are weighed to see if either side got the better deal.

What advantages did the Soviets expect when they began campaigning for détente, first with the West Germans and then with the Americans? What were their "targets of détente"?

First, international recognition of Soviet territorial gains resulting from the Second World War and from the 1945–50 period in which the Sovietization of Central Europe was completed.

Second, through negotiations on arms limitation, to profit from American goodwill to increase the U.S.S.R.'s military potential.

Third, to obtain financial, industrial, and trade contributions from the capitalist countries that would relieve or at least attenuate the shortcomings of socialist economics.

What concessions or promises did the Soviets have to make to the West in exchange for these benefits?

First, they promised to allow the Americans to conduct on-site inspections to verify that their military strength did not exceed the levels set by the agreements on strategic-arms limitation.

Next, they vowed they would adopt a general policy of restraint throughout the world, or so they led the West, especially Nixon and Kissinger, to believe in 1972–73. This was the notion of "linkage" or "attachment"—the "indissoluble nature of all aspects of détente," as Sakharov put it. Washington and Moscow specifically agreed to use their influence to prevent their respective allies and the countries with which they enjoyed special relationships from undertaking offensive actions, especially military.

Finally, in the most sensational part of the Helsinki agreement, the Soviet Union had to sign a guarantee that it would respect human rights and basic freedoms in the U.S.S.R. itself and throughout the Soviet sphere of influence. Concretely, the agreement was supposed to remove obstacles to the "free circulation of persons and ideas" in both directions between East and West. Including these incredible promises in a treaty that was otherwise so advantageous for the Communists could reasonably be seen by the Soviets as a necessary concession. Their object was to reassure people who, in the West, needed a moral justification that would consecrate the philosophy of détente.

A quick glance at these two lists shows that, for the Soviets, the credit column in this balance sheet is incomparably more substantial than the debit column.

It was soon obvious that the "third basket," as it was called in Helsinki, the one dealing with human rights, was riddled with holes. French President Giscard d'Estaing, who had functioned, at Brezhnev's urging, as the catalyst for the Helsinki conference, persuaded the reluctant Americans to attend. He was poorly rewarded for his zeal. At his first dinner during an official visit to Moscow shortly after the conference ended, he naively proposed a toast to human rights and freedom and to the improvements his hosts had promised concerning them. Furious, the Soviet leadership froze Giscard out the next morning. By a deplorable coincidence, all the members of the Politburo were suddenly as indisposed as they were unavailable: one felt a chill, another had a headache, Brezhnev sneezed nonstop, and all of them vanished. The world watched the humiliating spectacle of a French head of state wandering alone through a deserted Moscow for two long days. Instead of returning at once to Paris, he waited until, at dawn on the third day, he was received by a resuscitated Brezhnev, jovial and patronizing and delighted to have taught a lesson to the insolent greenhorn whose lack of resistance he had correctly gauged.

We know what happened next: the leaders of the "social groups for application of the Helsinki agreement" in the Soviet Union and its satellites were arrested, imprisoned, sent to strict detention camps; permission to emigrate, to travel abroad, to marry someone outside the East bloc became harder than ever to obtain; the movement of ideas and information was as sharply curtailed as that of people, and, after a brief interlude, Western radio programs were jammed more intensively than ever, in defiance of all the promises Moscow had made. And as an edifying crown to this triumph of liberalization and open dialogue, the U.S.S.R. huffily withdrew from the human rights commission at the 1978 Belgrade conference, the first of the periodic meetings scheduled for "verification of application of the Helsinki pact." The subsequent assembly, in Madrid in 1980, was just as much of a success for the Soviets, who stuck to their tactic of flatly refusing to discuss the subject of the conference.

Even after martial law was declared in Poland, Westerners broken to the saddle returned to Madrid in 1982 to go through their paces, chewing over the rotten hay of human rights under the mocking gaze of the Soviet delegation. Not only were the years following the signing of the Helsinki pact marked by tighter repression in the Communist countries, but the Soviet government was ingenious enough even to plead détente to demand—and win —agreement from Western governments and some Western newspapers to stop encouraging East-bloc dissidents. President Ford refused to see Andrei Amalrik. Dissidents were simply people calling for respect of the Helsinki agreement, which the West had signed. In a paradox that will not surprise connoisseurs, the Soviet Union made fewer concessions in the field of human rights during the years of détente than it had during the previous period, when, for example, Nixon and Kissinger had negotiated a considerable increase in the number of exit visas and emigration permits granted by Moscow. In the most ironic switch in this struggle for human rights, President Carter, anxious to be as stern toward the right as toward the "left," made it his duty to impose democracy or, failing this, sanctions on such non-Communist dictatorships as those in Iran, Argentina and Chile; since the Soviet Union remained inflexible, they became the only targets of this campaign for international morality.

Once before, the West had believed in an internal Soviet "thaw." That was between 1956 and 1960, after the Khrushchev report denouncing Stalin's crimes. It failed to see that the report, like the later publication in the magazine *Novy Mir* of Solzhenitsyn's *One Day in the Life of Ivan Denisovich,* challenged Stalinism without questioning the Communist and Leninist system.[4]

It is the purest self-deception to note that Khrushchev, while "wiping a tear from his eye,"[5] authorized the publication of *Ivan Denisovich* in 1962 unless we add the corrective note that the book was later officially declared harmful in the U.S.S.R. and its publication repudiated as an error, one of the consequences of "voluntarism in literature" (everything Khrushchev did would later be condemned in a bloc as "voluntarism" and "subjectivism"); the offending edition of *Novy Mir* was removed from Communist libraries, and Soviet "newspapers" were forbidden to mention its title.

What's more, in 1976 these publications suddenly took to praising the memory of Stalin's overseer of cultural slaves, the lugubrious Zhdanov; on March 10 of that year, *Pravda* exhumed him from the dungeons of history by hailing "his efforts in the fields of science and art." The efforts in question were those of destroying Russian biology by giving the quack Lysenko absolute power in the field and of ambushing Soviet art by eliminating any artist who did not mimic the spiritless daubs of the impossible Alexander Gherasimov and other perpetrators of socialist realism—that "means of moral extermination," as André Breton called it. Most important politically, the rehabilitation of Stalin's henchman

---

4. See Branko Lazitch, *Le Rapport Khrouchtchev et son histoire* (Paris, 1976), pp. 39–40.
5. Solzhenitsyn, *The Gulag Archipelago* (Glasgow: Collins/Fontana), vol. III, p. 476.

Zhdanov was clearly that of the man who gave him his orders: Stalin himself.

"Rulers Change, the Archipelago Remains," proclaims the title of the penultimate chapter in the final volume of Solzhenitsyn's monumental *Gulag*. It is an absurd but logical paradox that, in the same year in which Khrushchev wiped away his tear, he signed a decree reorganizing the labor camps (rechristened "colonies") and introducing a novelty: the death sentence for "terrorist acts against reformed prisoners (in other words, stoolies)."[6]

We have already discussed the second point, Soviet renunciation of expansionism, at length (see "Part Two"). As for any moderating influence Moscow may have brought to bear on its protégés, we have only to recall the military ventures, the terrorist and destabilizing efforts by Castro and Libyan strongman Muammar Qaddafi to measure how seriously Moscow has taken this facet of détente. A highly instructive imbalance: while the French word "détente" has become a household expression redolent of meaning throughout the world, its semantic and diplomatic complement in English, "linkage," has remained so much a dead letter both linguistically and effectively that it must be explained each time it is used. In the phraseology of Soviet leadership, as we have seen, the intensive war Moscow has relentlessly waged everywhere in the world throughout the period of détente, openly or in various disguises, is not imperialistic but a defensive struggle to protect socialism from counterrevolution.

As regards Soviet promises concerning military preparedness, Brezhnev could rightly boast in his report to the twenty-fifth Soviet Party Congress in 1976 that his country was achieving superiority. We have already noted (Part Two) that détente coincided with a boost in Soviet strategic capacity. As soon as the SALT I agreement was ratified and while talks were getting under way on SALT II, the Kremlin found ways to get around the bans and ceilings agreed on. "Two weeks after the June 1973 summit," Kissinger wrote, "the Soviets conducted their first MIRV tests on

6. *Gulag*, vol. III, p. 493.

their SS-17 ICBM, the new missile that was to replace the obsolescent SS-11. *A strategic revolution was now only a question of time.*"[7]

This was even sooner than expected. In 1979, when the still-unratified SALT II accord was signed, many Western experts estimated that before 1985 Soviet superiority over the Americans would vary from three to one to three to two, two to one or even seven to one, depending on the types of weapons involved, the targets and the launching methods. And this SALT II accounting concerned only those missiles aimed at the United States, ignoring the shorter-range missiles and planes targeted on Western Europe, which were not regulated.

How did the United States get into this fix? SALT I, signed in 1972, froze the *number* of missiles authorized for both sides but did not specify their *size*. The Soviets had merely to undertake a program of giant missiles (the SS-18s) within the original framework to attain superiority in magatonnage without violating the letter of the agreement. Behind a facade of equality, the Soviets achieved strategic superiority. This is why, when negotiations were resumed in Moscow in March 1977, just after Jimmy Carter's accession to the White House, the Americans insisted that the number of SS-18s be reduced by half so as to restore genuine parity. We recall the sensational turn events then took: the Russians "lost their tempers." Khrushchev's slogan "We will bury the United States" was not realized in the economic sphere he had in mind but in armaments.

But any purely military analysis must be matched by a political analysis. Westerners opposed to reinforcing our defenses maintained that the Soviets had no intention of waging a nuclear war against the United States, which would leave three fourths of their own territory in ruins even if they won, or of invading Western Europe. Perhaps. Why indeed would the Russians go to war if they could win without it most of what a war might bring them? They translated their military superiority into political domination.

In short, they garnered the advantages of détente without having

7. My italics. MIRV: Multiple Independently Targetable Recovery Vehicle. ICBM: Intercontinental Ballistic Missile.

to concede anything in return. And the West quickly formed the habit of not insisting on such concessions; even hinting at doing so soon became synonymous with provocation. Trying to link continued economic collaboration with respect for human rights or the withdrawal of Soviet troops from Afghanistan or freedom in Poland was viewed as warmongering, as imperialism. How could the Kremlin help but see détente as a great victory? What was more natural than Andropov's call, as soon as he came to power, for a "return to a policy of détente"?

The democracies, on the other hand, could hardly claim they had achieved their goals for détente, which were to ensure Western security in exchange for economic, technological, and financial aid to the East, to resist nuclear blackmail while avoiding nuclear war, to restrain communism's global aggressiveness and—the supreme dream—to oblige it to respect human rights. It is very difficult for a statesman to disentangle the snarl that immediately occurs in his mind between the merits of a policy as they were originally calculated when he envisioned the future success of his plan and its final results. The harder you try to focus his attention on the policy's real consequences, which are all that count for his fellow countrymen, the more energetically he refers to his earlier projections, the ones on which he wishes to be judged. Like Kissinger, Nixon maintained that "the failure was not of détente, but rather of the management of détente by U.S. policymakers."[8] He contrasted "hardheaded" détente as he would have managed it had he remained in office to "softheaded" détente as it was conducted contrary to his ideas before and after his resignation. But when has a policy been judged on what it might have achieved?

Kissinger has no more right than Nixon or any other statesman to claim that privilege. The rule in the art of governing is to accept the verdict of results. Theory exists in action only in the action itself. It never occurs to anyone to criticize a successful policy on the grounds that the ideas behind it were wrong. Then why praise a losing policy just because the ideas that inspired it were right?

8. *International Herald Tribune*, 23 August 1982.

14

DIVIDING THE WEST

DIVIDING ONE's adversaries, one's rivals, even one's associates and allies has always been among the most respected forms of diplomacy. In Marxist-Leninist terminology this is called "exploiting the contradictions" of capitalism and imperialism. Certain decisive improvements have been brought to the procedure in communism's diplomatic relations with the democracies.

The first is the recognition that the art of dividing the enemy camp is a one-way operation: the Communists can sow discord among the democracies without being divided in turn. When a break occurs inside the Communist world, it is never the fault of the West, which is usually caught entirely by surprise and which thinks of profiting from it only later, or partially, or not at all. The second improvement is almost miraculous: it flows from the democracies' propensity to quarrel almost unprompted among themselves when they have to deal with totalitarianism. Third, these spontaneous dissensions among the democrats occur in periods of rising totalitarian aggressiveness as well as when the Communists propose and obtain détente. When the totalitarian threat grows, there is disagreement on how to reply to it. When it seems to diminish, each of the democracies falls into the trap the Soviets have set for it by making it think it will be its "most favored partner."

These procedures are used to divide the Europeans from the Americans and among themselves. In particular, Moscow has always profited adroitly in Europe from the splitting up of Germany. By its thoroughly outrageous annexation of the part of Germany it liberated from the Nazis, rejecting any peace treaty that

would reunify Germany and setting its acquisition up as a supposedly independent East German state, the Soviet Union established
a permanently vulnerable area in Central Europe, dividing the
German people in two and giving itself a weapon for unending
blackmail.

In fact, the theme of "dividing the West" that provides the heading for this chapter really runs all through this book, for it is indissolubly associated with all the other methods used to weaken the
democracies. The few examples given in this section, supplemented by the many more offered in other chapters, are designed
mainly to point up the creative enrichment Soviet methodology
brings to the rudimentary Machiavellianism of old-style diplomacy.

In military policy, for example: during the SALT talks, which
centered on intercontinental missiles and disregarded the East-
West arms balance in Europe, the European governments' refrain
was that this was an unacceptable Soviet-American "condominium" erected "over the heads" of the Europeans. When the United
States then offered to station intermediate-range missiles in Europe to counterweigh the SS-20s the Soviets had deployed during
the SALT talks, the Europeans *also* protested against this and
against the neutron bomb, even though these new defenses constituted the answer to their previous complaints about a "condominium." Wouldn't they have reinforced European defensive autonomy?

It was apparently child's play for the Kremlin to exacerbate
these contradictions. Having abandoned any attempt to make the
Soviets respect the Helsinki pact and the principles of reciprocity
in détente, Europe tried to institute a division of labor in which, as
Kissinger cleverly remarked, it took charge of reconciliation and
left firmness to the United States. This attempt at job specializa-
tion flattered an old European illusion that it could function as
mediator between East and West without committing itself to a
"policy of blocs." This laudable objective accentuated the inequality between the two worlds, since the East really remains a bloc,
with all the efficiency derived from unified policy conception and
command, while the democracies remain separated. Although

Europe's desire to play a special diplomatic role is praiseworthy, the way it has set about doing this is less creditable. There is nothing very remarkable in the discovery that it is easier to thwart your allies than your enemies, to ruin your own family than your rivals, to be more "independent" of your doctor than of your disease. Whenever a major issue of confrontation arises between East and West in which Western firmness is vital, the Europeans rush to beg —indeed, to summon—the United States to show restraint and goodwill toward the Soviets, and they hasten to assure the Soviets that, thanks to Europe's mediation, American aggressiveness will be defused. Moscow skillfully cultivates European vanity, persuading one or another country of moderate importance that it enjoys a "special relationship" with the Soviet Union and can rise "above blocs." Wholly imbued with this very ambition, the country courted by Moscow thenceforth tends to view the United States as a treacherous saboteur of its global influence.

This is a well-known and certainly not new tactic in Moscow. Almost routine, in fact. For example, in 1967, well before the official period of détente began, Brezhnev told Wladyslaw Gomulka, then the dictator of Poland, "Take De Gaulle, for example. Didn't we succeed without the slightest risk in opening a breach in imperialistic capitalism? De Gaulle is our enemy and we know it. The French Communist Party, which is narrow in its concepts and sees only its own interests, tried to set us against De Gaulle. Yet what did we achieve? A weakened American position in Europe. And it's not over yet . . ."[1]

Moscow is cunning in placing the Europeans in a situation in which the defense of their dignity coincides miraculously with the safeguard of Soviet interests. The 1982 dispute between the Americans and the Europeans over the trans-Siberian gas pipeline is a prime example of this happy coincidence. I have already discussed this exemplary episode (chapters six and nine), but I would like to return to it from the point of view of that honor so often invoked by the Europeans.

Each of the European countries pleaded its national honor and

1. Erwin Weit, *Dans l'ombre de Gomulka*, Paris: R. Laffont, 1971. Weit was Gomulka's Russian translator.

"respect for contracts" to justify its fidelity to the pipeline project. Similar business ethics were not required of the Soviet Union, however, which never felt it had gone back on its own commitments because it had forgiven a number of colossal violations of the principles of détente. Moreover, the European position implied that the rule of respecting a contract was sacred only in relations with the Soviet Union, not in those with the United States. In all the wrangling, the Europeans completely neglected to mention the contracts between the American firms holding the patents on the equipment at issue and the European companies planning to transmit pipeline-construction technology to the Soviet Union. Yet these agreements were extremely explicit. The Europeans had not been forced to sign them. So there was no reason for them to shout about violation of their national independence when the United States insisted that the contracts be respected; whether Washington was psychologically wrong in doing so is another question, but its legal rights were clear. All the contracts at issue stipulated obedience to the 1949 Export Administration Act, and the European firms knew this when they signed them.

The clauses these companies accepted were abundantly clear. Under Alsthom's contract with General Electric, for example, Alsthom had to promise GE it would not export to countries in "group Y" any equipment marked "A" without "the prior authorization of the U.S. Office of Export Administration." "Y" is a code letter for a group of countries which includes the Soviet Union; "A" designates the disputed rotors and turbines over which the United States sought to retain embargo rights. With other French, British and West German firms and the European subsidiaries of American companies, Alsthom had to accept GE's conditions even though it risked later refusal of authorization to sell the equipment to the U.S.S.R. It also agreed to keep up-to-date on American export regulations and to conform to any changes in them.[2]

2. Here is an extract from the English-language version of the clause in question: ". . . to facilitate the furnishing of data under this agreement, Alsthom hereby gives its assurance, in regard to any General Electric origin data, that unless prior authorization is obtained from the U.S. Office of Export Administration, Alsthom will not knowingly . . . export to any country [in] group Y any direct product of

The governments of Europe, both socialist and conservative, lied to their people in concealing that, by entirely explicit agreement, equipment manufactured under license by European firms was contractually liable to embargo because it was catalogued as strategic. These governments led their citizens to believe that the United States was trying to curtail their sovereignty, as though the American President had suddenly taken it into his head to bar France and Britain from selling tomatoes and bicycles to the Soviet Union. The Europeans may have had a right to question the Americans' *political* analysis of the situation, to plead that international tensions were not so high as to warrant application of the embargo clause on equipment defined as strategic. They nevertheless had no right to howl outrage, pretending not to know about the restrictive clause, or to claim "respect for contracts" as a reason for violating it.

Meanwhile, it occurred to the Sakharov Committee, the Frankfurt Association for the Defense of Human Rights, a few labor leaders and a handful of journalists to point out that much of the labor used in building the pipeline was probably slave labor from the gulags, in keeping with a long-standing Communist tradition in big works projects. The French Government, suddenly nervous as well as amnesiac (had Europe's politicians forgotten *The Gulag Archipelago?*), instructed its ambassador in Moscow to go to Siberia to "investigate" the matter. "At last an occasion for outright hilarity in the Politburo," wrote one commentator familiar with the situation.[3] When we remember that diplomats assigned to Moscow can travel only to strictly defined areas, we can guess how much leeway the French ambassador was given to conduct his "investigation," which, needless to say, died at birth.

On the other hand, *L'Humanité*, a French Government newspaper (since it is the leading organ of the French Communist Party, which is allied with the government and has ministers in the cabinet), took care to supplement any ambassadorial inadequacy by

such technical data if such direct product is identified by the code letter A. Alsthom further undertakes to keep itself fully informed of the regulations (including amendments and changes thereto) and agrees to comply therewith."
3. Jérôme Dumoulin, in *L'Express,* 13 August 1982: "Le Goulag et le gazoduc."

sending one of its own notoriously independent and impartial reporters to Siberia. The report the paper published[4] was such as to quiet the most ticklish consciences: not only, it told us, are the pipeline workers there of their own free will, but they receive Himalayan-high wages and go about their work with a socialist-realist jubilation worthy of the great days of Stalin's "radiant future." What's more, the article informed us, work on the project is not at all behind schedule, contrary to false Western allegations. The Soviets, *L'Humanité* asserted, could have done nicely without American technology, could have manufactured their Soviet rotors and turbines that would have been better than the American equipment. In short, it was out of pure charity that they did their shopping in the West.

A few skeptics nevertheless quibbled about the distinction to be made between political and common-law prisoners. In which category did the slave laborers on the pipeline belong? Holy and incurable ignorance! Again, democratic distinctions were being applied to a totalitarian system. For whom were Solzhenitsyn and Vladimir Bukovsky writing? Don't we know that no Communist ever carried out a major public works program without resorting to slave labor? When a Communist state is short of free labor, it launches, say, a "drive against hooliganism" that brings in the few hundred thousand fresh slaves it needs. These waves of arrests maintain the Soviet forced-labor contingent at a permanent level of around three million. In *The First Guidebook to the U.S.S.R. Prisons and Concentration Camps*,[5] Avraham Shifrin superimposed the pipeline route with wonderful precision on a map of the camps. According to Bukovsky's calculations in *To Build a Castle*, "estimating the average detention time at five years and the maximum percentage of repeaters at 20 to 25 percent, a total of nearly a third of the country has gone through the camps. This high criminal percentage is artificially maintained by the state for primarily economic reasons." By "artificially maintained by the state" Bukovsky did

4. On August 27, 1982.
5. Published in Switzerland (Stephanus edition) in 1980 and cited in the Dumoulin article mentioned above.

not, of course, mean that the government promotes crime but that it suddenly takes notice of an exceptional number of supposed criminals—"parasites," "hooligans," "vagabonds"—in Soviet society whenever it needs to resort to mass arrests to augment the labor supply. For camp labor is inherently necessary to the sagging edifice of Soviet production. This is why Cuba and Vietnam pay part of their debts to the U.S.S.R. by sending it forced-labor contingents, just as, in ancient times, a conquered people's tribute to the victor had to include a certain number of slaves. No sham "investigation" by the ambassador of an irresponsible French Government is going to extirpate a custom rooted in the very foundations of a collectivist economy and without which communism could not survive. "If a general amnesty were suddenly decreed," Bukovsky believes, "it would trigger an economic catastrophe."

However divisive the pipeline quarrel may have been, however complex and difficult to resolve, there is at least one thing certain about it: it continued and ended exactly as the Soviets wished. Their success even exceeded their hopes: not only did the project proceed uninterrupted, but it raised a row in the West that dealt a devastating blow—another one—to the Atlantic community.

Thus the Soviet Union pocketed a greater profit than any it could have earned by granting the Polish people the right to self-determination. It must be admitted that such divine surprises do not encourage good behavior. Two years of bleeding the Afghan people and bludgeoning the Poles and reaping not reprisals but, as the French Foreign Minister said, "a gradual divorce" between Washington and Europe is surely enough to put the men in the Kremlin in a cheerful and confident mood. The best part of it is that Moscow did not even have to take a hand in all this or make the slightest effort. The usual machinery of intestine transatlantic warfare switched itself on automatically; tension between Europe and the United States rose spontaneously, as usual. By July 1982, when the French Minister handed down his "divorce" decree,[6] the Atlantic Alliance was nearly at the breaking point.

6. The statement was made during a French television program (channel 2) on July 21 and reported in the following day's issue of *Le Monde*.

Whether Moscow is faced with a difficult situation in Poland or in Afghanistan or in its own economy counts for very little in its ledger, then, since every crisis in the East ends with the weakening of the West. As for the aggression and subversion the Communists use to enlarge their sphere, the West can neither cancel them through reconquest, which is banned on principle and, often, by treaty, nor avert them with its now inoperative military deterrent. Nor can it punish them with economic retaliation, for even mentioning this frightens, divides and weakens the democracies. Our democracies' inability to unite gives the Soviet system of expansion an automatic bonus for which there is no precedent so complete in the diplomacy of any other empire, past or present.

15

THE "STRUGGLE FOR PEACE"

THE COMMUNISTS excel in converting ingrained feelings, such as nationalism, and such humanitarian causes as combating racism into instruments for furthering totalitarian expansion, although when they are in power they respect neither the national independence of the countries they control, nor human rights.

To wage their struggle, to tap for totalitarianism's profit the energy men devote to so many just causes in the world against so many evils and inequities, the Communists have always set up front organizations that are not officially Communist but which are Communist controlled and jump to Communist orders with obvious alacrity. These join in propaganda campaigns mounted by the Soviet Union or local Communist parties. The characteristic of these organizations—of women, youth, students, war veterans, parents, artists, mutual aid, travel, etc.—is that top-level figurehead positions are filled with non-Communist celebrities who are motivated by feelings of generosity and, not infrequently, by their own ingenuousness. Positions of real power, especially that of secretary-general, are reserved for members of the Communist party. As many as possible of the organization's lower-level workers, as well as the bulk of the membership, should be non-Communist. This standard distribution of responsibilities is typified in France, for example, by the Movement Against Racism and for Friendship Among Peoples (MRAP), which, behind the noble facade of antiracism, guides its members' energies toward the International's current political objectives. Transnational surveys of the ups and downs and involutions of these groups' propaganda show that, from one to another of a dozen countries, they coincide with amazing simultaneity. Only the Communists can shift scenes that quickly and efficiently.

The "struggle for peace" is a central element in the apparatus of movements, committees, mass organizations, and demonstrations that contribute to the unilateral reinforcement of Soviet power. It exploits such wholly justified and respectable, even indispensable, feelings as fear of nuclear war, opposition to war of any kind, the desire for genuine reduction of armaments and of the risk of conflict. It mobilizes Communist parties and labor unions, of course, but it also enlists a large segment of the Socialist International, the British Labour Party, various religious sects in all countries, and the ecologists, as well as great numbers of the unorganized. A high proportion of the leaders and the troops in these political and spiritual legions are acting on sincere conviction, even if this is not always based on solid facts.

A smaller proportion, but one that many people think represents "the salt of the earth," is made up of Communist agents, professional agitators, and experts in mass manipulation. For example, during the "peace" demonstrations that washed over and into Bonn in the autumn of 1981, any prospective participant anywhere in West Germany could collect his travel expenses and a per diem allowance. Who paid the bills? Or, rather, who could afford to pay them? Not the West German Communist Party, which attracts one half of 1 percent of the vote in every election and therefore has no finances to rely on but its members' dues—a near-zero budget.

There is really no mystery about the financing. What is mysterious is the Communists' artfulness in persuading so many people in the West that "Soviet expansion" is synonymous with "peace." The reasoning behind this is based on the axiom that the enemies of peace are those who oppose the worldwide advance of socialism. For socialism is in essence peaceful. It asks nothing better than to advance peacefully and unresisted. Not until it does meet resistance, for which it is not responsible, is that peace imperiled. For example, it was not the Red Army that chipped an edge off of world peace by crossing the Afghan frontier; the Afghans did this by resisting the Red Army.

All campaigns "in favor of peace" aim at disarming the West and the West alone. When the secretary-general of the French Communist Party visited Réunion, a French island department in the Indian Ocean, he naturally proposed "making the Indian Ocean a peaceful zone," which, coming from him, could mean only one thing: removal of all American and French air and naval forces from the area to make way for the Soviet fleet, the sole conceivable guarantor of "peace."

These good and loyal services are not performed by accredited officials alone. In August 1982, the neutral European countries, including Sweden and Austria and led by Finland, formed a Committee for European Disarmament (CED); this is not to be confused with the European Defense Committee (EDC), which was born dead in 1954. The goal the neutral countries' CED set itself was to restore life to the Madrid Conference on Security and Cooperation in Europe, which was to resume work in November on the application of the Helsinki pact and which, as we know, was bogged down in Soviet obstructionism. According to the CED announcement, however, it was self-evident that the conference's difficulties were the fault of the West alone, especially of the United States, which "does not wish to avoid a war, but to win it." Clearly, in the neutrals' view, the U.S.S.R. is the only power whose behavior in recent years has been peaceful; the notion of disarmament, therefore, could be understood only as Western disarmament.

How did crass Soviet expansionism come to be identified with a desire for peace? By a long and persevering campaign of propaganda and infiltration.

No human being today is against peace. So what we are examining here is not whether peace should be maintained, but how the Communists use the peace slogan as a substitute for war. Reduced to its essence, the advice the Communists lavish on humanity is to avoid resisting their offensives. In practice, naturally, this basic principle cannot be inculcated as is, in its raw state, in the countries the Communists plan to subjugate, however blinded these countries are by their political immaturity. A little tactical refinement is needed. Its function is to impregnate the thinking of bourgeois governments, of capitalist media and public opinion, with the prior notion that communism does not seem dangerous, that it becomes so only when it believes it is being attacked. Driven into people's minds by constant repetition, this useful bit of sophistry is finally accepted as evidence that tension is always caused by the West. Which means that any friend of peace is morally obliged to exert pressure on the democratic governments to disarm themselves and so induce the Communists to do the same, as they will surely do if shown the right path to follow.

This is a particularly sound program because only democratic governments are easily influenced; they are the only ones exposed to whipsawing by their media and public opinion and responsible to their citizenry. In this area as in so many others, the congenital inequality of opportunity between democracy and totalitarianism shines forth. Communist propagandists have an almost clear field in the democracies to exercise their talents and further their cause. They take advantage of all democracy's acknowledged resources, to which, with no risk to themselves, they add a few they prefer not to acknowledge.

Democrats cannot do this to their adversaries. They cannot plead their cause in totalitarian countries, organize groups of supporters, patiently knead the media and the public as if they were so much leavened dough ready to rise, or finance political parties. But Communists in the democracies can work openly to "train" their country's leaders, with the help, if need be, of very special tutors placed adroitly at the rulers' sides; they can also act indirectly on those leaders through public opinion and the press. No mass movement originating in the West can be launched in the Soviet Union to persuade its government to experiment with unilateral disarmament to determine if the West will follow suit. No parliament there will refuse or shave the appropriations requested by the Soviet Minister of Defense. The mere mention of such fantasies immediately dispels them.

So peace lovers, powerless to shake totalitarian governments, however slightly, find it easier to turn their zeal against the more porous fabric of democracy. It is easier to crack a clay jug than a bronze, even if it's the bronze that holds the deadliest poisons. To the antediluvian trick of portraying its attacks as pure defense, communism adds the advantage of being the only system that can orchestrate its music abroad without having to listen to others' refrains at home. As with all circular reasoning, the conclusion here is simply the opening postulate repeated, a postulate that is never proved but that nevertheless is used to prove everything that follows: communism is peace; isn't it therefore pointless, even absurd, contradictory, to campaign for peace in the very citadel of peace?

Soviet leaders deserve credit for their endurance in defending, year after year, a cause they do not believe in. For neither Stalin nor Lenin nor their successors, neither Mao nor Castro nor any other Communist chieftain has ever believed in pacifism. They have never seen it as anything but one of the many variants of idiocy inherent in democratic civilization and as a device for weakening that civilization. When you roam the vast open spaces of Communist leaders' writings, especially those of Lenin and Mao, whose prolixity on paper doubtless came naturally to them, you see in every line that war is central to their ideological system. No matter how poor a Marxist you may be, you cannot help knowing that socialism can't be achieved without violent revolution. This is rudimentary doctrine. Capitalism, we are told, breeds war, which, more or less insidiously, more or less openly, is the international projection of the class struggle. Socialism can eliminate capitalists, either as a class within each country or as a worldwide group, only by using or threatening to use force while holding enough assets to impose its will.

No period of "détente" has ever altered this fundamental historical law, as Brezhnev reminded the 1976 Soviet Party Congress when he said "détente, like peaceful coexistence, does not affect the relations between states. It does not and cannot in any way abrogate the laws of the class struggle." Translated from Communist jargon, this means that détente is a limited tool of official diplomacy that in no way interrupts the historical process of the extension of communism through struggle. Brezhnev's statement was probably formulated by (the late) Mikhail Suslov, which gives it the true stamp of orthodoxy, since Suslov was the Politburo's "intellectual," one of those ideological freezers in which the sacred precepts of socialism are preserved through the ages.

Hence, repression in Poland was seen by the Kremlin as an episode in this ongoing war and not, as from varying viewpoints in the West, as an attack on basic freedoms or a vicissitude in the advent of "democratic socialism." To flirt with such a notion takes all the gullibility of a social-democratic "philistine," as Lenin liked to put it. It was in fact with Lenin and the foundation of the Soviet state that the untouchable principle was born that war expresses a historical law. "Social-democratic pacifism," Lenin wrote, "merely imitates bourgeois pacifism. All the oratorical flourishes of the bourgeois-pacifists and social-pacifists against militarism and war are nothing but illusions and lies." And in October 1914, he added in a letter to Aleksandr Shliapnikov that "the watchword of peace would be a mistake now. It is a watchword for Philistines and popes. Civil war, that's the proletarian watchword." In an article written in Switzerland in 1916, he went on. "Socialists cannot be against all war without ceasing to be socialists. They can never be adversaries of revolutionary war."

Never have the Communists deviated from this dogma—in practice, anyway.

In propaganda and agitation aimed at destabilizing the democracies, however, their tactics are very different. Their adversaries' desire for peace is used as a lever to promote the belief that renouncing self-defense is the best way to avoid war. A pacifist is someone who ultimately sees himself as the only potential aggressor and concludes from this that by ostentatiously laying down his own arms he will avoid all danger of war in the world.

The Soviets realized early on what resources this excellent state of mind offered them. Preparing for the International Conference in Genoa in 1922, the first such meeting in which the Soviet Union took part, Lenin decided to use pacifist slogans for the benefit of the bourgeois and social-democratic states. Until then, the Communist International had condemned all the proposals for arms limitation that had come to light after the First World War. Surprise! The Soviet delegation's first general proposal was for resumption of the disarmament movement. Georghi V. Chicherin, head of the delegation and a veteran Bolshevik, was ordered by Lenin to present the conference with "a vast pacifist program." The disconcerted diplomat protested. "All my life," he wrote to Lenin, "I have fought against these petit-bourgeois illusions and now the Political Bureau is making me support them in my old age. Can you give me precise directives on the subject?"

Very precise directives arrived the next day to calm the naive fellow's fit of intellectual honesty. With it came explanations that, more than sixty years later, still preserve all their Leninist freshness. "Comrade Chicherin, you are too nervous . . . In the name of our revolutionary proletarian party's program, you and I have fought against pacifism. That's clear. But tell me, then, where and when the Party has refused *to use pacifism to break up the enemy, the bourgeoisie.*"[1] The enemy to be "broken up," we notice, is the Socialist International as well as the bourgeoisie, as Lenin makes clear in the rest of his directive.

This established the method, one the Soviets would use in all subsequent "peace offensives." Lenin expressed the principle clearly and concisely. "The Central Committee gives this general directive to the delegation: try to widen as much as possible the gulf between the bourgeoisie's pacifist camp and its aggressive and reactionary camp." He then directed the Genoa delegation to "do everything possible and even the impossible to reinforce the pacifist wing of the bourgeoisie and increase, however feebly, its chances of success at the polls—that is the first task; the second is to split up the countries united against us—this is our double task in Genoa. In no way must Communist opinions be elaborated."

We may admire in passing the Communist art of intervening in

1. My italics. This exchange of letters (February 15–16, 1922) was published in the Moscow *Literary Gazette* on November 5, 1972, to mark the hundredth anniversary of Chicherin's birth.

the democracies' electoral process, and this has been refined since those long-ago days. With the same mastery of the scam techniques that were to become classic after World War II, the Soviet Government in 1922 proposed a "regional conference on disarmament" that would bring Estonia, Lithuania, Latvia, Poland, and Finland to Moscow—five countries, as history attests, on which the Soviet Union would later lavish so many proofs of its love of peace.

Lenin showed how to make peace an instrument of war. His successors realized that giving the watchword was not enough, that they had to take the trouble to organize pacifist movements in each target country and cluster them under an international pacifist movement. To do this, they had only to use the resources democracy offered, the rights it grants everyone to associate, to express opinions, to distribute leaflets, to publish newspapers, to hold congresses, to march through the streets, to cross borders, to open bank accounts, to rent offices and halls, to collect and distribute money, to receive funds discreetly from abroad without notifying the authorities. These are but a few among a myriad possibilities which, of course, are not to be offered to the "enemies of peace" for use against totalitarian regimes.

The target of all the pacifist waves that have rocked the West since this tactic was developed has always been democracy as such. In 1932, the "peace movement" of the moment, called the Amsterdam-Pleyel Movement (after its places of birth), was careful not to attack Hitler, who was about to take power in Berlin. It took only the capitalist democracies to task. After the Hitler-Stalin Pact in August 1939, Soviet propaganda, faithfully retailed by Communists in the West, hammered at the theme that the proletariat must reject and even sabotage the "imperialistic war," that is, the one being waged by the democracies, the "plutocrats of the City."

After World War II, the peace movement expanded all through Europe. Its leaders spread the slogan in the press, among the public and in political circles that "the Americans want war," unlike the Soviet Union, that well-known home of peace. Called the Stockholm Appeal, the movement flourished during the Korean War, a war that began with a deliberate Communist attack ordered by Moscow. Nevertheless, a sizeable and highly influential body of Europeans decided that neutralism was the best safeguard for their security. It was this conviction that scuttled the project for a combined European army, the European Defense Community (EDC); in France, this was strangled by a typical coalition of Communists and Gaullists, with the former skillfully working through the conservatives to align French nationalism with Soviet interests. (I was going to say that the Communists used the Gaullists' disinterestedness, but this virtue did not always shine undimmed among the conservatives who, shoulder to shoulder with the Communists, immolated the EDC on the altar of Gaullism.)

The Soviets lacked neither realism nor results in their peace offensives. Not content simply to maintain a routine climate of defeatism in the West, they pressed for something concrete and succeeded in squelching political and strategic plans that, if realized, would have strengthened democratic Europe. In 1954, the victim was the EDC; in 1979, the drive opened to prevent deployment of the Euromissiles that would modernize NATO defenses. This coincided with the launching of a third incarnation of the pacifist movement in the West. And each surge of this movement in turn has always coincided with a hardening of Soviet diplomatic tactics.

The 1932 Amsterdam-Pleyel Movement got under way before the Soviet Union "turned" against fascism and for nationalistic, jingoist Popular Fronts; local Communist parties' antibourgeoisie, antimilitarist campaigns reached quasi–civil-war intensity that was even more hostile toward social democrats than toward fascism. A quietus was put on this when Stalin ordered a switch that would bring him closer to the bourgeois governments; local Communists were told to ally themselves with the socialists and center parties to form so-called Popular Front majorities.

Then, in 1949, the peace movement picked up steam when South Korea was attacked. This was shortly after the Soviet Union launched the cold war; in 1947, Moscow had organized the Cominform to try to break the Berlin blockade, and Western Communist parties were ordered to take the offensive against their governments. Finally, at the beginning of the 1980s, the U.S.S.R. again needed a switch to divert public attention from the warlike image it had acquired by its exploits in Poland and Afghanistan, its clear and repeated violations of détente, and the increasingly pregnant arsenal that was becoming more and more difficult to hide from the neighbors. Endless processions of pilgrims for peace suddenly and miraculously rose up out of the democratic earth in Western Europe, hordes of penitents moaning in chorus and beating their breasts to implore Andropov's clemency. Would these signs of true repentance inspire his indulgence, even his absolution of the bloodthirsty leaders of the West?

In all the rigamarole with which the Soviets trick people anxious for peace, it is not the longing for peace that is reprehensible but the trickery. The profound hatred of war and the desire for peace at any price that followed the First World War were eminently justified. And who could object to the wish after World War II to make atomic war impossible? How can we fault the motives of the "peace marchers" who, in the early 1980s, asked that their continent not be overloaded with nuclear weapons? But all these movements are drained of their original nobility when they convert themselves into instruments of war, among the many the Soviet Union is using to weaken the democratic camp before attacking it or to force it to succumb even without an attack.

It took Stalin's inimitable aplomb to depict the U.S.S.R. in the West in 1948 as the champion of a "lasting peace" and the United States as a warmonger when Moscow had just annexed, directly or indirectly, the countries it had "liberated," whereas the Americans had swiftly pulled their troops back across the Atlantic once nazism was beaten. Having bundled Central Europe from one form of totalitarianism to another, Stalin must have roared with laughter when his imagination engendered the airy name he conferred on the official organ of the newly organized Cominform: *For Lasting Peace, For Popular Democracy*. A masterpiece of antiphrasis![2] There

2. The name came from Stalin himself. The Italian delegate at the organizational meeting of the Cominform, Eugenio Reale, informed by Zhdanov of the new organ's creation, says he objected. "From a journalistic point of view, I can't see an Italian worker going up to a news vendor and saying, 'Give me *For a Lasting Peace,*

must be a sense of humor in the Politburo too that, since 1980, in these years when Stalin's successors have more than ever extended the use and accumulation of military and police force, has allowed it to chaperone the peace marchers filing through Western Europe.

Words alone, however, could not produce such triumphs. Two other conditions had to be filled: a tight Communist grip on the key posts in the parallel organizations and control of the financing of these organizations by Moscow and its Western representatives.

In the Amsterdam-Pleyel Movement, the two key jobs of president and secretary-general fell, by a happy combination of circumstances, to two men controlled by the Communist apparatus: Henri Barbusse, to whom a Chekist* muse dictated the nauseating pages of his book, *Stalin,* and one Louis Giberti. Fritz Adler, the secretary-general of the Socialist International, entertained suspicions of Giberti that he naively confided to Barbusse in a letter dated July 12, 1932. As though he were telling Barbusse something he did not already know, he affirmed that "Giberti's name is enough to show the maneuvering of the Bolshevik united front." Adler later said he did not know who had named Giberti world secretary of the Anti-War Congress—regrettable ignorance in the man who was supposed to negotiate alongside the person in question. But he was familiar, he said, with this directive from Willy Münzenberg, a high Comintern official and Giberti's boss: "The task of Communist representatives in the mass organizations is to see to it that the secretary is one of them."

This rule has remained in force throughout the century. Fifty years after the Amsterdam-Pleyel Movement, the president of the World Peace Council is India's Romech Chandra, who happens to have belonged since 1951 to the central committee of the Indian Communist Party, has served as editor of its newspaper, *New Age,* and was later named to represent his party on the National Peace Council. Since then, promotion has come fast: from the national council, Chandra moved to the world council, first as a mere mem-

---

For Popular Democracy.'" Zhdanov silenced him with the reply "The name was conceived by Comrade Stalin himself" (told by Reale to Branko Lazitch). ·
* Cheka: the first of the Soviet secret police organizations, formed in 1918 and ancestor of the present KGB.—TRANS.

ber, then, in 1966, as secretary-general, and finally to the presidency.

While the positions of power in peace movements must be held by officials who are openly or secretly Communist, it is equally essential that they be surrounded by a large and, if possible, brilliant group of non-Communists. This was the alibi Barbusse gave in his reply to Adler's letter, stressing that "the great majority of the executive bureau is non-Communist." Later on, the Communist leadership would continue to strive for a mass non-Communist membership, but brilliance became increasingly harder to attract because the discreditation of Marxist ideology has routed the great intellectuals out of the mass organizations. The Amsterdam-Pleyel group recruited such august figures as physicists Albert Einstein and Paul Langevin, philosopher Bertrand Russell, and the novelists André Gide, Romain Rolland, Theodore Dreiser, John Dos Passos, Upton Sinclair and Heinrich Mann. Around 1950, during the period of the Stockholm Appeal, petitions on every street corner bore such famous names as Pablo Picasso, physicist Frédéric Joliot-Curie, and poet Paul Eluard. Fifty years, forty years, thirty years later, compassion for the mentally handicapped, gallantry and respect for intellectually deprived elders restrains us from listing all the non-Communist figureheads assigned to represent the worlds of science, letters, and art in the peace movement.

The movement compensated for its loss of qualitative prestige, however, by substantial quantitative acquisitions: Christian sects of all kinds, ecologists, and heirs to the causes espoused by the rebellious youth of the 1960s—young people who had never lived under a totalitarian system and saw only the democracies' real and, sometimes, imaginary defects. It is quite possible that this larger and more varied clientele has amply compensated the international Communist movement for the loss of most of its bona fide intellectuals. And it has chalked up another gain: the Socialist International, which, since the start, and despite the failure, of détente, has taken positions increasingly in line with the causes and interests defended by the Soviet Union.

The high esteem in which the KGB has always held intellectuals sometimes leads it to inflict more militant responsibilities on them than that of mere figurehead. Among those on whom this honor has fallen is a Danish writer named Arne Herlov Petersen. Here we are getting into the financial side of the peace movement. In 1981, the said Petersen bought a number of full-page advertisements in Danish newspapers to unfurl a vibrant manifesto in support of a plan (already well known to this essay's readers) for "Nordic denuclearization." This is a hobbyhorse Moscow periodically trots out of its stables and tries to sell to the Scandinavian countries in its campaign to turn the Baltic into a Soviet lake.

Petersen's manifesto was presented as a kind of petition sponsored by a bizarre Cooperative Committee for Peace and Security. This had been formed in 1974 after a "peace conference" in Moscow. It was a typical para-Communist organization, but, of course, normal readers of Danish newspapers had no way of identifying it as such. In fact, the bills for Petersen's ads were paid by the Soviet embassy; discovery of this by Danish counterespionage investigators led to the expulsion of Vladimir Merkulov, a KGB officer working behind the cover of his post as second secretary at the embassy. Petersen had also published a pamphlet attacking British Prime Minister Thatcher that he had received from Merkulov. Moreover, the writer advised his Soviet contact on who the "progressive" journalists were in Denmark and how to manipulate them.[3] He was not a member of the Danish Communist Party and was careful not to become one. In this he was just following orders. There are many propaganda agents or "agents of influence," in the West in Petersen's category, innocent-seeming guerrillas. "Progressives" would reply to this that there are surely counterinfluences at work in the Western press. Even if this is so, it doesn't make the match equal. For this, the pro-NATO propagandists would have to be able to foment campaigns not in the Western press but *in the Soviet press*. This is a step into the land of false analogies, one we shall be traveling in yet a while.

The fact, the extent, and the machinery of Soviet financing of

3. This information is taken from a Danish Justice Ministry release on April 17, 1982.

Western Communist parties and mass organizations is well enough known. Only hypocrites and, naturally, the Communists deny it. Hypocrites? That makes quite a crowd, you may say. Some of them will add that non-Communist parties in the West also have secret sources of funds. A fine example of a false analogy. In the first place, laws now regulate the relationships of money and politics in several of the democracies, including some of the biggest. Second and more important, political contributions from business, the labor unions or the government or earned from unorthodox commercial operations are made to *domestic* political organizations and cannot be compared to *foreign* funds paid by a hostile power to corrode another country's independence. Under-the-table domestic contributions may indicate a slackening of political morality, but foreign funds are an attack on the security of the state. The Communist parties and other organizations it supports spend a lot more money than can be justified by their avowed incomes. When an individual's standard of living is radically higher than his declared income would allow, the tax man assumes he is cheating. But, although Communist organizations show the same troubling disparity, the media and the politicians pretend to take them at their word. Of course they know what is really going on, know the circuits through which the Soviet Union helps its own, either directly or by throwing good deals their way. The opulence of peace-movement funds would be inexplicable without this support, which, indeed, is hardly secret at all. "The Congress is not subsidized," declared Barbusse on the eve of the Amsterdam Congress. "It must, so to speak, pay its own way as regards all its expenses . . . Contributions by Congress delegates are not obligatory." A luminous lesson in bookkeeping! To our great relief, historians have since revealed the French Communist Party channels through which the necessary funds flowed to the Movement.

The truth can sometimes be heard from Soviet propagandists themselves: in its bulletin for February 1982, the Soviet "news" agency Novosti remarked that "the Soviet Peace Fund was created in 1961 . . . it provides financial support to organizations, movements and persons struggling to reinforce peace." In *Pravda* on

April 30, 1982, a moving article signed by Yuri Zhukov, chairman of the Soviet Peace Committee, revealed that eighty million Soviet citizens voluntarily deprived themselves to contribute money to the Soviet Peace Fund, that is, to us, dear readers, we the oppressed subjects of capitalist warmongers. It was hard to hold back tears of gratitude a month later, on May 31, when *Pravda* informed the world that Soviet farmers wanted to help us too and that whole kolkhozes had "decided to devote a day's work to the Peace Fund."

This technique of "voluntary" deductions is classic; it allows Moscow to pretend that the KGB's funds are really the proceeds of humanitarian fund-raising. But however prodigal Soviet workers may be with the fruits of their labor, their generosity needs reinforcement that is sometimes provided in colorful ways.

I do not want to give the impression that I have something against Denmark, but, as it happens, in 1975 that country, with Holland, became a switch point for the peace movement. Early in March 1982, Ingmar Wagner, president of the Denmark-U.S.S.R. Association, secretary of the Peace and Security Movement, and member of the Danish Communist Party's politburo, led a Communist delegation to the Soviet Union that was received by Konstantin Chernenko, then an heir presumptive to Brezhnev and later successor to Andropov. While Wagner was away, his house was burglarized. On March 18, members of the Danish Police Narcotics Squad arrested a young man they suspected of being a pusher. In his pocket was the key to a luggage locker in Copenhagen's central railroad station. Instead of the drugs they expected to find in it, the police were surprised to discover a satchel containing thirty thousand West German marks and receipts in Wagner's name for a total of one hundred and fifty thousand DM. The serial numbers on the bank notes were those of bills the Bonn Government had recently paid to the government of East Germany to ransom political prisoners and deliver them to the West. This regular traffic in human flesh has long been one of Communist Germany's main sources of hard currency.

In other words, the Communists begin by extorting money from the West, then reinvest the ransom money in their political war against the democracies. A splendid example of how totalitarianism profits even from its own weaknesses to build its strength. Unable to offer its subjects decent human lives, communism is reduced to preventing them by force from emigrating. Since too many would go if they were allowed to leave at will, communism finds a better use for them: it sells them. And with the money it collects for them, it "struggles for peace."

Others before the Communists knew the art of disguising a certain kind of warfare as "peace." In 341 B.C., Demosthenes tried to open the Athenians' eyes to the "peace offensives" of Philip of Macedon. "Our adversary, with arms in hand and supported by a strong force, covers himself with the word 'peace' while committing acts of war." Philip had his own Afghans and Czechs, for, we learn from Demosthenes, "didn't he tell the unhappy inhabitants of Oreus that he sent them his troops out of friendship, to watch over them?" Only a madman, warned the orator, could "consider as a state of peace a situation that will allow Philip, once he has taken all the rest, to come and attack us here . . . This is naming thus what is doubtless peace for him, but not at all for us." Philip also supported his "peace partisans" among the Athenians, some of them mere innocents, others simply ignorant or indifferent; others, the most active, were paid agents, like the Communists! Their job was to insist everywhere and always that it was Philip who wanted peace and the Athenians who sought war. "This is what he buys with all that money," the orator declared.[4] This is also why Demosthenes spoke in vain, as history records.

---

4. Third Philippic, 6–8 *passim*.

16

IDEOLOGICAL WARFARE
AND DISINFORMATION

IDEOLOGICAL WARFARE is based on the art of liberating people to enslave them—more precisely, to claim to liberate them the better to enslave them, to preach independence so as to force them into servitude. Some religions do believe in redemptive slavery, but their practice does not contradict their doctrine, since slavery is for this life and redemption for the next. But when political ideologies promise happiness in this world, the inherent contradictions of their claims are easy to verify.

It is true that political ideologies also try to establish a contrast between life now and life in the future, trying to redeem present harshness with future felicity. But an irreducible difference will always separate the religious future from the political future: the former arrives after death and so escapes observation, while the second occurs in historical time. Even if humanity is patient enough to let several generations go by before passing judgment, it will sooner or later judge on the evidence. This is why the popular comparison between religious faith and political "faith," especially the Communist "faith," reeks of facility. The dualism of time and eternity, of the natural and supernatural worlds that underlies religious faith cannot form a foundation for political ideology, which seeks to eliminate that antagonism and wrest mankind from the resignation to which its hope in the hereafter condemns it. By plunging men into slavery and poverty, the political ideologues are more adroit than the most deplorable theocrats have ever been, for it is in this life that they promise happiness; they manage to impose their absolutism despite the almost perfect simultaneity between their exaltation of an ideal and its contradiction by experience.

Their success becomes less enigmatic if we remember that totalitarian propaganda is primarily addressed to foreign public opinion. Propaganda is certainly a basic weapon in domestic politics for taking and consolidating totalitarian power. No one has ever said this better than the man who said it first, Adolf Hitler. But once domination is firmly established, the repressive apparatus is adequate to squash freedom and criticism. From then on, state propaganda no longer tries to convince the country's inhabitants; it simply overbears them with its pathetic and burlesque incantation, an insulting antithesis of reality.

But propaganda will always be an effective weapon in foreign policy, helping to open the way to imperialistic expansion, for it is beamed at an audience abroad that is suspended in a kind of vacuum of belief, a never-never land of guileless candor where ideology is considered in isolation from reality. Ideological struggle, psychological warfare, lies, disinformation and intimidation constantly unbalance, impregnate, disorient public opinion and governments in the democratic countries; these are generally easy prey to the trickery the totalitarian mind cultivates better than any other and at which it excels.

Ideological warfare is necessary to totalitarianism but impossible for the democracies. It is consubstantial with the totalitarian mind, inaccessible to a democratic mind. To wage ideological warfare requires, first, an ideology. The democracies do not have one ideology, they have a thousand, a hundred thousand. Democracy is revealed by the mutual criticism of the groups that compose its political and cultural pluralism. Our system is vilified from outside by Communist propaganda and from inside because of the normal workings of those democratic prerogatives that institutionalize diversity. Its variety of groups and interests, critical of themselves and their institutions, is what makes democracy function. But this also exposes it to manipulation from outside; they absorb it in domestic debate that diverts attention from external danger. An interior source of strength in terms of civilization becomes a weakness in competition with totalitarian Communist power, which exists for, and can survive only through, the worldwide annihilation of democracy.

The recurrent idea of an "ideological counterattack" stems from a confusion, an abstract and, thank heaven, mistaken parallel between democracy and totalitarianism. Propaganda is essentially a totalitarian instrument. It requires a monolithic, homogeneous apparatus weighing on a society reduced to silence. It presupposes a country that speaks with a single voice. The modern masters of propaganda have created "unidimensional" communication systems, something the democracies cannot duplicate simply because they are democracies, where every idea immediately engenders a contradictory idea. Propaganda is never the "official" point of view of a democratic state because any such pretention is quickly shredded by political parties, labor unions, churches, interest groups, the media and the intellectuals. How can propaganda contested at its very source alarm distant totalitarian powers? Marxist theoretician Herbert Marcuse's coinage of the epithet "unidimensional" to describe democratic societies is one of the sillier ironies in the history of philosophy, since democracy by its very nature almost infinitely fragments a society's life and thought; Marcuse's neologism does, however, nicely describe totalitarian culture and it alone.

The search, then, for a democratic counterideology to roll back the totalitarian ideology is hopeless. A democratic counterideology is a myth. Democracy must not let itself be circumscribed by the terms of totalitarian thought or try to build an antithetical framework to that thought. Ideology is a lie, Communist ideology is a total lie extended to all aspects of reality. Suggesting that free thought defend itself by inventing a systematized counterfantasy amounts merely to proposing that it commit suicide to avoid being killed. While it is true that nothing more effectively obliterates a mirage than another mirage, it is equally true that democratic civilization should not and cannot survive except by opposing its power of thought to ideology, its sense of reality to the totalitarian lie; its job is to fight propaganda not with counterpropaganda but with truth. Unfortunately, this is not something the democracies are good at.

They are disadvantaged from the start by the long odds against halting the spread of utopian notions with plain facts. And they are unskilled in defending themselves against communism's falsification of those very facts. As weapons in the ideological war, propaganda and disinformation have a double objective: to concoct false images of Communist reality and of its leaders' intentions and to circulate through the non-Communist world the plausible lies and deformed versions of events best calculated to disorganize that world.

More than its predecessors, totalitarian imperialism tries to justify itself with arbitrary assertions of its moral and practical superiority over all other systems. The idea that a nation has the right to destroy or annex its neighbor because it thinks it can govern better became a standing principle of foreign policy only with the advent of the mighty totalitarian regimes of the twentieth century. Old-time utopians built their intellectual models of perfect—hence totalitarian—societies more as monasteries to be protected from outside contamination than as centers of active propagation, conversion and conquest. That a system's function is to redeem the world is a recent notion. The "revolutionary messianism" of the French at the end of the eighteenth century petered out early, turning theatrical and clumsy until a caesarian dictator easily converted it into the driving force for standard wars of conquest. Religious expansionism, Moslem and Christian, though informed with territorial appetites and political ambitions, soon crumbled into a jumble of eccentric regimes and disparate civilizations. The alloy of religious Faith and Interest never reached the devastating and unifying purity of totalitarian Ideology. Free trade became missionary only to unseat protectionism. Modern totalitarianism introduced the idea that what it saw as the worst of systems must disappear to make way for the best, its own.

As long as philosophy has existed, students of political power have examined the characteristics and respective merits of the various forms of government and social organization. Individual nations have sometimes even taken pride in comparing their institutions to others', although it more often works the other way: others' structures are seen as superior, especially if the supposed model is remote enough. But no one before the modern totalitarians ever claimed that the presumed superiority of their own social system conferred the right, even the historical duty, to destroy all others and make the world politically uniform. "You are authorized to survive only if your system is the best": an absurd precept that leads to interminable wrangling and public-relations feuding among regimes parading their advantages and others' disadvantages, real or imagined. Such huckstering has turned the art of governing today into braggadocio; it forces political systems to vie among themselves in word and deed, touches off propaganda wars that are by nature sterile. No, they can be fecund—for the regime best equipped to lie, to dissimulate, to intimidate. Such an offensive can only be fought with the same weapons, but democracy does not possess them.

With communism proclaiming itself the only perfect system in the world and so arrogating to itself the right to force others to imitate it, those systems that have so far escaped this cloning process feel they must talk themselves silly listing their virtues if they are to maintain their right to exist. In doing this, they are playing the totalitarians' game, letting themselves be ground up in the machinery of totalitarian propaganda. They are agreeing to compete under a diabolical rule: that they be able to prove their absolute perfection at all times. The odds against doing this are impossibly long, but if the democracies fail, they consider that they deserve to perish. What civilization could ever feel legitimate under such conditions?

Worse still, communism refuses to abide by its own rule. And because totalitarian societies are hermetically closed, they can escape observation from outside, protect themselves from their adversaries' onslaughts. A Communist frontier is a two-way mirror behind which the system can see without being seen. The empire can operate in adversary countries, but they cannot operate *in* it, although they can bear *on* it, that is, on its government. The Com-

munists can and normally do work simultaneously on governments and on societies as well as *in* societies not yet absorbed into
the empire, trying to mold each separate group to their will. The
more democratic the society, the more freely and openly the Communists can maneuver. But democrats cannot establish direct relationships with a Communist society, with its groupings, its individuals, its nameless masses. They have only the right and the
possibility to deal with official agencies, with the state, for Communist societies are shrouded in secrecy. When societies that are or
purport to be capitalist scrutinize the Communist world from the
reflecting side of the mirror, they see only their own image, reflections of their own disputes. So that when a crisis does arise within
the empire, such as the crushing of the Hungarian revolt, the
Khrushchev report on Stalinism, unusually severe shortages in the
Soviet Union, exposure of the gulag system or of Soviet military
power, the idea the West forms of what is happening is based on
extremely slight real knowledge. And even this serves chiefly to
fuel the internecine struggles within and among the democracies.

Mistrust among rivals working the same side of the political
street is greater than their fear of an enemy capable of running
them off their turf. Aboard the ship of democracy, the threat of a
wreck in which all would perish is forgotten in intrigues for command and struggles for precedence. Faced with the dismantling of
Poland's Solidarity movement or the publication of *The Gulag Archipelago*, Western "leftists" were less upset by the suffering of communism's victims than they were at seeing "rightists" exploit the
"negative aspects" of socialism. When the British Labour Party
voted by a two-thirds majority at its September 1982 conference in
Blackpool to include British unilateral disarmament in its party
program, it was really defying the United States; the vote meant
that Labor's hatred for the Americans was stronger than its desire
for Britain's survival. Few among us have not toyed with the idea
of paying with our lives to destroy a hated enemy.

Communism is lucky in that the forces of democracy tear each
other to pieces over it; its power and influence steadily increase
without its having to lift a finger, except maybe to help things on a

little. Why, for example, should the Soviets have conceded any-thing at all at the renewed disarmament talks in Geneva in 1982 when the Laborites in Britain, the peace movements, the churches and the West German ecologists were striving tirelessly to give them what they wanted: suspension of Euromissile deployment in Western Europe? The Soviets had long since positioned their own missiles; now they could sit back and watch thousands of Western zealots do their work for them by fighting fiercely against the rein-forcement of NATO. For Moscow, it was the better part of wis-dom simply to wait until all these providential currents converged for them. How fragile democratic societies are! Consider that West Germany's whole foreign policy could have been upset by the Greens, the country's ecological party, which got only 5 percent of the popular vote and is openly manipulated from Moscow. How astounding it is that such countries as Belgium and Holland re-main for months on end with mere caretaker governments that could not make the important decisions if a serious threat arose!

The first aim of Communist propaganda, then, is to project to the democratic world an embellished image of the socialist coun-tries and a blackened picture of the others. The second is to deceive the non-Communist nations about the real objective of Communist foreign policy, that is, its pursuit of world domination disguised, as we have seen, as a "struggle for peace." Its third purpose is to intervene invisibly in the non-Communist countries' domestic af-fairs by using false news to trouble public opinion. In the KGB's technical lexicon, this is called "disinformation" or "active mea-sures." While the measures in question are pure trickery, they lead logically to very active results indeed: destabilization, subversion, and terrorism, of which I will have more to say later.

I do not intend to demonstrate again how masterfully and con-sistently Moscow achieves the first of these three aims. It is such common knowledge, so many books and articles have been devoted to proving it that the main problem is no longer one of discovering the truth but of understanding how the Communists manage to conceal it for so long, how the same devices have fooled generations of Westerners and, often, the same generation twice in two similar situations.

Concealment of the famine and mass executions in the Soviet Union during the 1930s was a masterpiece of Communist propaganda and censorship. Although this colossal imposture was finally uncovered—with some difficulty—twenty years later, international public opinion fell for it again when the same thing happened in Asia, i.e., the equally impudent concealment of what really happened in China between the "Great Leap Forward" in 1959 and Mao's death in 1976.

Even if humanity was halfway willing to be fooled, managing to hide from it the real fate of eight hundred million people was no mean trick. Herds of journalists, "experts," illustrious visitors, political tourists, ideological pilgrims and diplomatic ninnies were made fools of by the subsequent disclosures, some by Mao's close companions, of the horror of that sinister period. Since the Communist small-fry have pulled similar stunts on a lesser scale, it is only fair that we lump them in with the giants; such countries as Cuba and Nicaragua, those tiny depositories of world credulity, crouch beside the towering edifices of China and the U.S.S.R.

This persistent Western suspension of disbelief always reminds me of a passage from David W. Maurer's 1940 book *The Big Con.* Some of the victims of Maurer's crooks were so ready to be swindled that they never learned from sad experience. "One dentist from New York State," Maurer wrote, "fortunately having married very well, has been played against the big store more than half a dozen times. He has become somewhat of an institution among grifters. One meets another on the road and asks, 'Do you have anything good in tow?' 'No,' says his colleague. 'Well,' suggests the other, 'why not go up and rope that dentist? He'll always go for twenty grand.' "

It is not my plan here to lead my readers item by item through the annals of Western gullibility. I merely voice my amazement at Communist propaganda's repeated success in duping the democracies. The belief that socialist paradises and radiant futures already exist on earth has fostered the divisions in democratic societies. In the long run, these notions are shown up as lies, but by then they have done their work; for several reasons and in several ways, they continue to govern even minds that have stopped believing them.

First, atrocities and failures that are revealed long after they happen do not have the same impact as they would if they are discovered at once. In 1956, people in the democracies were forced by the Khrushchev report to face the truth about the Stalinist terror; they had no choice but to recognize that instead of improving the lot of the working class the Soviet system had so much worsened it that tens of millions of workers and peasants died of starvation and persecution. By that time, however, all this held no more than historical interest for the West. The disclosures had come too late to purge Western thinking and politics of the golden legend of communism swallowed between the two world wars. The imposture maintained by Soviet propaganda during those years has had a lasting influence on Western countries' internal politics by diverting the left into a feckless fight for, or at least goodwill toward, totalitarian socialism.

Not until 1976 did the West learn that Mao's Great Leap Forward caused massive famine and the death of at least sixty million Chinese and that the Cultural Revolution was precisely the explosion of bloody barbarity Mao had sought. But in 1976, the revelation came too late to expunge from Western minds the image formed in 1960–75 of a "progressive" China, a model of an allegedly non-Stalinist breed of communism, a champion of development to be imitated by the whole Third World. Maoist ideology largely helped create the political climate in those years, the attitudes and sensibilities of the time, the fanatical criticism of capitalism prevailing then—even though working-class living standards in the capitalist countries had never before climbed so high. The showdown among the ruling bureaucracy in Peking after Mao's death left Western Maoists peering into a vast, black hole full of wretchedness and stupidity where they had thought to see a brillian El Dorado, but this did not efface the past ravages wrought by the Chinese illusion. For fifteen years, a lie on a global scale had again distorted public debate, falsified thinking on the fate of humanity by faking the basis of discussion with nonexistent "facts": the supposed success of China's socialist economy and the false legend of a highly civilized Chinese communism.

Similarly, the massive exodus of Cubans in 1980 may have toppled the heroic image of Castro, already badly cracked by information amassed over the years of his rule, but the dictator has nevertheless changed the course of history in Latin America and Africa. That the prestige that enabled him to do so was entirely undeserved only confirms how serviceable good propaganda is and how effectively the Communists use it. And it reminds us once more that retrospective knowledge of the truth by the democracies cannot repair the damage caused by years of ignorance. It is not pure knowledge that is needed in politics, but pragmatic, action-oriented knowledge; knowing the truth is not very helpful once a false idea has taken root.

Disclosures long after the fact are often more irritating than enlightening. The men responsible for détente in 1970–80 resented having to admit its failure afterward. So they did not alter their thinking, they clung to it even harder. The diplomats, politicians and political scientists who had made a heavy intellectual investment in détente over a period of ten or fifteen years and who remained in positions of power or influence after it failed were incapable of fostering a stern public reappraisal of their policy.

Still more unconscious, and so more insidious, is our tendency to maintain habits of thought after we have abandoned the premises on which they were based. Many people now disenchanted with communism continue to reason in terms of the respective strengths of the political right and left, terms that date from the days when communism and its totalitarian sponsors still seemed to them to be springs of social progress. The intellectual framework forged by three quarters of a century of ideological propaganda has thus survived revelation of the true facts about communism and the wreckage of belief in it. This is handed down through the generations in an oral and written tradition that is merely the floating debris of a discredited philosophy—but that can still, somehow, power the old intellectual machinery: another demonstration of the fact that revelations of things well past have only slight practical value. The emotional shock, indignation and horror caused by an atrocity are far more powerful if we learn of it "live" when it happens than if we hear of it in "retransmission" later on.

It can be objected that the Nazis' crimes, which most people learned about after the fact, nevertheless aroused violent feelings of horror. But these were discovered almost immediately after they were committed, for they were perpetrated late in the Hitler period, in 1942–44. To Westerners, especially Europeans, in 1944–45, those years were still the present. The military collapse of the Reich exposed its crimes immediately and completely. Had Germany won the war or negotiated a compromise peace that left the Nazis in power and in a position to cover up what they had done, the truth about the death camps would probably have dribbled out over a period of twenty or thirty years. This would have weakened its effect, leaving the international prestige of Hitler's successors as little tarnished in 1970 or 1980 as that of Stalin's and Mao's heirs was by the long-delayed exhumation of the incredible events in the U.S.S.R. and China.

When we speak of the power of the media, we forget that this is an abstraction, that the media's influence on public opinion and even their very existence depend in practice on a series of preconditions. Some regimes forbid these preconditions, others do not. It is at the ones that do not, those that play fair with information, that the media hit hardest; in the repressive countries, it is strictly no contest. So world opinion, which sees things only from a distance, concludes that the only regimes that do wrong are those which are more or less honest with the media.

During the war in Vietnam, some one thousand correspondents of all nationalities, but mostly American, were permanently assigned to Saigon and the operations zones, all of them conscientiously trying to scoop their competitors on stories and pictures. As has often been noted, this was the first war in history to be televised live, followed hour by hour by a world audience that reacted immediately and violently to it, especially in the United States.

By contrast, Afghanistan was almost completely cut off from the rest of the world after the Soviet invasion in December 1979. No question there, obviously, of a thousand reporters and photographers, of TV crews roaming the country night and day in search of facts the authorities did not want known. Reliable news leaks out of Afghanistan only through clandestine sources who infiltrate the country at high personal risk, and through refugees. Doubtful rumors are as plentiful as hard facts. So that, for weeks and even months, the TV screens that had placed viewers, so to speak, under daily fire in Vietnam were blank and silent about Afghanistan for lack of news.

The newspapers pass on mere scraps of information. For example, during the summer of 1982 they reported, in dribs and drabs, that there was serious terrorism in Kabul, that the occupation army had probably grown from one hundred thousand to two hundred thousand men, that the Soviets were almost certainly using biochemical weapons against Afghan freedom fighters, that the number of refugees in Pakistan alone exceeded two and a half million, which seemed to show that the levels of suffering and atrocities inside the country had become intolerable.

Yet while even patrol-strength skirmishes in Vietnam became instant world events, the facts I have just cited concerning Afghanistan, of much farther-reaching intrinsic importance, appeared in obscure squibs that none but anti-Soviet fanatics could have spotted. Let us assume, for the sake of argument, that both wars are equally condemnable or equally justifiable. We can, again as a hypothesis, place them on exactly the same moral footing. The fact remains that from the crucial point of view of gathering and transmitting the news, the wars in Vietnam and Afghanistan are millenia apart. American and South Vietnamese officials appeared daily before the court of world opinion; the evidence before the court was massive, increasing daily in volume; American public opinion was no more indulgent than the tribunal's foreign judges were.

The Soviet Union, on the other hand, has withheld the relevant evidence on Afghanistan. Lacking solid fuel for its indignation, world opinion has grown torpid and indifferent, as Moscow reckoned it would. Such repercussion as there is on Soviet domestic "opinion" from TV coverage of the war is managed by organizing and rationing information to serve Soviet interests.

In September 1982, perhaps as many as one thousand Palestinian civilians, including women, children and old people, were massacred by Lebanese Phalangists. Television crews stationed in Beirut immediately transmitted pictures of the tragedy to screens the world over. We all know what sorrow and anger they aroused, especially against the Israeli Government, which was later accused by an Israeli investigating committee of an unpardonable failure to intervene in the massacre, even of passive complicity in it. A few months earlier, in February 1982, in the Syrian city of Hama, a bloodbath accompanied army suppression of a religious uprising; the number of victims is estimated at a minimum of several thousand and, if data pieced together from various sources is to be believed, may have run as high as forty thousand. Needless to say, in President Hafez Assad's Syria, a Soviet client state, there were no foreign TV crews around, nor could any foreign journalist dream of trying to visit the scene. Trickling indirectly to the outside world, news of the Hama slaughter was wrapped into a few dry articles that could not possibly have provoked the world outrage inspired by the pictures from West Beirut some seven months later.

No attempt is being made here to excuse either abomination by juxtaposing them; this in itself would be an abomination to which only biased minds could resort. My purpose here is purely technical. I wish only to point out that the mistakes and crimes committed by the nontotalitarian countries boomerang against them in the propaganda war, while those of totalitarian regimes, sheltered behind their screens of secrecy, are only mildly reproved by world opinion; this makes the political cost of error far lower to them than to the democracies. Even leaving aside the bonus in moral indulgence regularly granted to any totalitarian regime calling itself socialist, the *real* inequality of information available gives totalitarianism an edge in the ideological struggle.

It is this privilege that made possible a little-known horror that is nonetheless worthy of comparison with that of the gulags and the Holocaust: the extermination of the Tibetan people and the destruction of their culture accomplished over a twenty-year period almost without the world's knowledge. From 1959, when a Chinese army invaded Tibet, until 1980, when a political change in Peking gave Tibetan refugees in India and Nepal an opportunity to return home to see such remnants of their families as survived, scarcely any news had seeped out to disturb Western sinolatry—nothing substantial and exhaustive enough, at any rate, to shake Western apathy. A few books, a few articles here and there, scattered reports from refugees all went unnoticed. Not many people, probably, were keen on noticing them. Here's cause for meditation on the developing conscience of history: at a time when the entire world was anathematizing the war in Vietnam, an almost flawless program of genocide was being carried out in total secrecy a few thousand kilometers away on the same continent.

The term genocide, too often lightly used, is irreplaceable here. It does not refer to just any massacre, no matter how frightful or murderous. It is a massacre that is coldly decreed, planned and executed by a state, an authority, and that cannot be imputed to even the most inexcusable excesses of an army in wartime. For it was *after* the conquest of Tibet that the Chinese army of occupation set about the physical and cultural liquidation of a defenseless people that had abandoned all but moral resistance.

When the honors were awarded for this enterprise of revolutionary emancipation, after the 1980 liberalization in Peking, the news was, again, received coolly. At least I did not hear of any demonstrations in front of the Chinese embassies in the big democracies. There were none of the processions of which Parisians are so fond. No ecologist, no pacifist, no anti-imperialist rose to perturb, even slightly, the visit of any Chinese dignitary among us. In 1980, after an official trip to China, French President Giscard d'Estaing even insisted, without a trace of embarrassment, on a sightseeing foray into Tibet. Once more, a Communist power had managed to reduce almost to zero the fallout from a crime that would have blackened the image of any Western power for a hundred years.

Testimony by travelers returning from Tibet to Nepal, Bhutan and northern India indicates that, incredible as it may seem, up to 80 percent of the population remaining after the invasion died; in many cases, families of six children were left with only one survivor. Victims who were not murdered outright were felled by those other great pillars of communism: famine and forced labor. Of perhaps one thousand refugees who reached India and Nepal in 1981, more than half had served prison terms; some three hundred had been in prison uninterruptedly since 1959. Working conditions were so hard, both day and night, and food so scarce (a handful every twenty-four hours of *tsampa*, the flour of grilled barley that is Tibet's staple food) that there were always a few people who failed to reply at evening roll call in the camps; they had died, the fugitives said, of exhaustion.

The massacres were particularly ferocious among Tibetan monks. Two hundred of them who remained in the Sechen monastery in eastern Tibet were slaughtered in one day, and this is merely one of many such examples. The Chinese tortured clerics and lay believers who refused to abjure their religion. If the victims moved their lips in prayer under torture, they were beaten to death. One witness told a relative of mine, who is an expert on Tibet and speaks the language fluently, that he had been assigned for a full month to the job of tossing bodies into a gigantic pit. Accused one day of having failed to stack the corpses correctly, which obviously required a certain level of Maoist training, he was forced to go down into the pit, where he sank into the heap of decomposing flesh. He was hauled out just in time to avoid asphyxiation.

The obliteration of Tibet's culture was carried on with almost insane violence, especially after the Cultural Revolution's Red Guards arrived to lend a "spontaneous" hand to the occupation army. Suppose the Nazis had razed every old church in Italy except Saint Peter's in Rome, all the churches and cathedrals in France except Notre Dame in Paris, leaving these two buildings standing only to prove to visitors how calumnious all the rumors of vandalism were. Suppose also that the National Library of France had been burned, and you begin to have a picture of what has happened in Tibet. More than thirty thousand of the country's monasteries and temples were destroyed; hundreds of thousands of woodblocks for printing ancient Tibetan scripture were used as firewood or to build army barracks. The great monasteries at Sechen, Zongsar, Kathog, Dzochen, to cite only the main ones, were razed; only plains are there now that give no hint that the greatest treasures of Tibetan architecture once stood on those sites. Of Ganden, Turphu, Mindroeing, Palpung, nothing but ruins remain. Gone, too, are the five-story Riwotse monastery in the Kham and the thousands of old manuscripts it contained. Over one hundred thousand woodblocks at the great Dershe print shop were saved from burning by a popular uprising that Peking elected not to crush. The sole surviving monastery is the one the world knows, the Potala in Lhasa; damaging it would have been too noticeable.

I have dwelt on the case of Tibet because it seems to me to relegate to its rightful place all the blather about the "power of the media" and the deluge of information supposedly overwhelming modern man. The media have only the freedom they are allowed. Because they are concentrated in the countries to which they have access, they inevitably foster the impression that only in those countries do important events—and, sometimes, crimes against humanity—occur. But they are blind, inevitably, to the countries whose borders are shut to them or where they are prevented from reporting the news freely; in these areas they can be unaware, and can keep whole periods of history unaware for decades, that entire civilizations have vanished.

Perhaps the subtlest form of Communist propaganda is the indirect kind that turns investigators' eyes exclusively toward the capitalist countries simply because the others are opaque. Abundance of information and the severe criticism of events this might entail depend less on the events' importance than on the facilities investigators are given to report on them. Since half the planet is forbidden to them, the other half necessarily becomes the only sector the media can observe vigilantly at all times. Not all the governments in this non-Communist half of the world are democratic, of course. Many dictatorships and pseudodemocracies are to be found in it, but they do not have anything like the means available to the Communist systems for blacking out information entirely and for long periods of time, hiding a physical perception of reality from the rest of mankind. So, stroke by stroke, day after day, a wholly unbalanced portrait of the world is painted.

This, however, is merely the passive phase of the totalitarian regimes' propaganda, the part that results from their unique talent for creating noninformation. It is all to their credit that Communist leaders have not been satisfied with the more or less institutionalized advantage they reap from their mastery of silence. As perfectionists, they go farther, take the initiative, even take the offensive. This is the active sector of the ideological war.

In fact, the Soviets do use the term "active measures" to refer to some of the techniques designed to mislead public opinion in the non-Communist countries. Active measures can often be crude, especially when they take the form of forged documents. Example: the fake letter from President Reagan to King Juan Carlos of Spain in November 1981 containing an offensively worded summons to the King to hustle his country into NATO and clamp down on the parties opposing the policy. Providentially "leaked" to the press and to diplomats attending the Conference on European Security and Cooperation—the one that never accomplishes anything—in Madrid, the forgery was an attempt to rile the Spanish over American "interference" in their affairs and to keep Spain out of NATO. I do not know who the dimwit was who cooked up this foolishness, but it dishonors the KGB, where I imagine somebody knows that the King of Spain has no constitutional authority at all to meddle in such questions. Luckily, the A Service of the KGB's First Principal Bureau, which is responsible for disinformation, usually does a better job than that.

Forgery is only one of the weapons in the huge artillery battery of disinformation aimed at making foreign public opinion, media, governments, and economic decision makers believe what the Soviet Union wants them to believe. The effectiveness of direct propaganda always wanes eventually, since anything from official sources is received skeptically. Disinformation is more subtle; it comes from what seem to be non-Soviet and, if possible, non-Communist sources. Disinformation reached a high point, for example, at the start of the period of détente, when it moved Westerners representing "big capital" and "reactionary" politics to argue for positions favoring the U.S.S.R. Another stroke of finesse: the KGB's slow penetration of Christian churches, panicked by their declining spiritual influence over modern societies, nudging them into adopting a fresh theme, one more "public-spirited" than religion: the struggle for peace or, in the Third World, the "theology of liberation." A bishop is always a bigger draw on such subjects than the Soviet embassy's press attaché.

The best disinformation exploits the secret desires, fears and internal discords of the West and the Third World. It casts its bait and the fish usually bite, taking on themselves the task of elaborating and circulating the false data. For, as Michel Heller wrote, the West incorrigibly "autodisinforms."[1] But since it would be imprudent to rely uniquely on the gullibility of public opinion, it is also desirable to place penetration and propaganda agents and some good old double agents—acting out of conviction, greed, or naiveté—to function as disinformation transmitters at the centers of decision and communications. By no means are all these willing tools Soviet agents: naiveté, especially in tandem with vanity, explains a good many cases of "orientation." Not that I would want to disoblige the professionals by suggesting that their infiltration of the West is nonexistent or even negligible. All I am saying is that the best of the Communist agents (those working among us are excellent and plentiful) can only promote disinformation by touching the real keys to the society in which they operate, just as the art of governing consists in playing on real human passions. Disinformation is rooted in real feelings—anxiety about a nuclear holocaust, for example—to which it skillfully feeds inflammatory arguments.

1. Michel Heller, "La désinformation, moyen d'information," *Politique internationale*, no. 10 (winter 1980–81).

One of its greatest successes was the campaign against the neutron bomb. Since this was the weapon best calculated to counterbalance the superiority of Soviet armored forces, it is understandable that the Kremlin set all its propaganda tom-toms beating to avoid the bomb's deployment in Europe and that Western Communist parties and the organisms they control launched an all-out drive to block the move. But Moscow had to find an image that would strike the imagination, flatter the intelligence and outrage the conscience of a whole segment of public opinion not usually favorable to the Soviet Union. So it invented the slogan that the neutron bomb is a "capitalist" weapon because it kills men without destroying property. It would have been more precise to say the bomb kills soldiers while sparing cities and their civilian population, since it is accurate enough to pierce solids without wrecking them, to wipe out enemy tank crews without ravaging the whole area around a battlefield or contaminating the area's inhabitants.

The "capitalist weapon" catchphrase did its work splendidly. I have already mentioned this campaign, and I would only add here the essential fact that some Western propagators of the idea were voluntary tools in the Communist campaign. There were those among the media who simply closed their eyes and, sometimes knowingly but most often passively, retailed the argument without bothering to examine it seriously. They made no effort to explain to themselves or to the public why NATO wanted the neutron bomb or why the Soviet Union was so set against it. We know what happened: because many Western governments were embarrassed by the public's anger at the weapon, President Carter opted against its manufacture and its deployment in Europe. The Kremlin's operation was a model of its kind, a brilliant success that deserves to remain in the annals of disinformation. By hurling the purely ideological anathema of "capitalist," so irrelevant as to be positively luxurious in its stupidity, Communist propagandists channeled strong currents of opinion to their own use, intimidated part of the media and mystified others until, at last, we ourselves denigrated, and the democracies themselves rejected, a measure that could have reduced Soviet military superiority over the West.

Here again, the inequity of the conditions under which the two camps may fight the ideological battle is flagrant. For the sort of disinformation campaign that eliminated the neutron bomb can only succeed, or be waged at all, in a pluralist society with many different currents of opinion that a disinformer can set at odds. The doors to these societies are wide open to him, and he has helpers within. But the democracies have no such refined propaganda methods, no entry, and no friendly assistants in the totalitarian societies. In this area, at least, the fight is unfair not because of a difference in the experts' know-how, but in the basic differences between the two types of societies.

What social dough could Western propaganda "agents of influence" knead in the Soviet Union? What key posts could they occupy? Can anyone imagine pro-American political parties in Moscow, churches casting come-hither glances at the multinational corporations, television commentators tricked into endorsing the reinforcement of NATO, ecologists preaching unilateral Soviet disarmament, front organizations spreading the good word to a willing press, or a growing tide of protest demonstrations? Or, still less likely, that an accumulation of such pressures could force a helpless Soviet Government to dismantle its Euromissiles? Even as a fable, it's boring: to be interesting, political fiction must have at least a minimum of verisimilitude.

But, you may point out, Western radio broadcasts are beamed at the Communist countries. True enough. But this is a long way from reestablishing a balance between East and West. For one thing, everyone knows where the broadcasts are coming from. They cannot disinform the East as the Communists do the West because they cannot manipulate the Soviet media, cannot induce Communist journalists to publish anti-Communist articles. To disinform, you have to operate on the terrain. In this respect, there is no such thing as equal opportunity.

The Soviet and other Communist governments broadcast as they like to the West, without being jammed. Moscow Radio's shortwave World Service transmits in eighty languages. Quantitatively, the two sides are fairly evenly matched. But this does not apply to broadcast content. Soviet programs are pure propaganda combining verbal aggression and incitation to violence, promoting armed rebellion, especially in the most explosive areas of the Third World. In this as in everything else, the Soviets accuse other countries of doing what they regularly do themselves, while alleging that Western radio stations encourage popular insubordination in the East—an excellent excuse for jamming their broadcasts.

It is true that the Voice of America and Radio Free Europe were criticized for stimulating anti-Communist fervor in the 1956 Hungarian insurgents whom the West then abandoned to Soviet repression. But aside from this dishonorable incident, indeed, perhaps because of the shame it inspired, the Voice of America, Radio Free Europe, Radio Liberty and, most of all, the BBC's World Service have never been so much as suspected since then of broadcasting propaganda; they stress news over psychological warfare. This is precisely what makes them so dangerous to communism, since communism and information cannot coexist. Living in the kingdom of the official lie, listeners in the Communist countries absorb parallel information from the West the more eagerly for knowing that the information they hear is neutral and purged of ideological exhortation. What they want is straight news because that is what they are most cut off from. They are a captive audience—the pun is intentional—for it, and a wholly receptive one.

The British and Swiss broadcasts beamed at the occupied countries during World War II and those to the Communist countries from Western stations since the war are probably the most successful examples of productive message-penetration in the history of modern mass communications. This explains Moscow's attacks against them during periods of East-West tension and its urgent efforts to silence them during periods of détente.

Democracy's only superiority in the ideological war is the truth, even if it is often too unsure of itself to use that superiority. The Communists are addicted to disinformation because Communist propaganda in its raw state is not trusted. This is why, in spreading tales and exciting prejudices that will enlist people in support of Communist policy, they prefer to exploit the bourgeois trust-worthiness of Western information sources.

There seem to be few flaws in the method, since it is used repeatedly, is never changed and still works. Two examples among many illustrate this consistency, one dating from 1952 and the other from 1978. (The Soviet special services have no imagination, and the Western media no memory, so why change the technique?)

In 1952, a prominent Gaullist—the political label was calculated to allay mistrust—leaked what was purported to be a secret document to the French daily newspaper Le Monde. This was the "Fechteler Report," named for the American admiral Soviet officials had chosen as its alleged author. Supposedly outlining American strategic plans in the Mediterranean, the "report" was couched in such outrageously belligerent language that readers could not help seeing it as proof that the United States wanted war—exactly the impression the forgers sought to give. Le Monde closed its eyes and published this improbable document in its issue of May 10, 1952, without checking on its authenticity.

The fraud was quickly exposed. But Soviet publications and news agencies ignored this and went on referring to the report, charging that it "revealed a real war plan against the U.S.S.R."; Western Communist newspapers picked up the refrain, arguing that the "revelation" had appeared in a "big, independent newspaper," an infallible gauge of the report's veracity.

The 1978 fake was even more widely distributed and longer-lived. It took the form of a "practical manual" signed by no less a personage than General William Westmoreland, former American Army Chief of Staff. In it he recommended that American secret services use extreme-leftist subversive organizations operating in the West to safeguard American interests in friendly countries where the Communists seemed about to take power. In other words, the United States was to infiltrate terrorist groups and incite them to make trouble for allied democratic governments guilty of indulgence toward communism. At a time when a number of European democracies were at grips with increasingly troublesome terrorism—in which people were daring to hint at Soviet complicity—the forgers hoped to indict America's secret services before world opinion as the true patrons of subversion.

It was an ingenious idea, but hard to believe. Fortunately, Providence was alert. It took the form of a Spanish journalist, Fernando González, to whom the fake, pompously stamped "Top Secret," was mysteriously vouchsafed. González planned to publish it in the Spanish weekly magazine *El Triunfo* on September 23, 1978. But, in a spirit of self-abnegation rare in journalistic history, the magazine offered to share prepublication rights to the story with the Madrid daily *El Pais*, a newspaper classified as "independent leftist," which ran it as an exclusive on September 20. Since González was a Communist with close links to the Cuban embassy, it was safer to "launder" the forgery by soaking it in the pristine waters of a "great center-left independent daily."

Immaculately scrubbed, the document leaped across the Pyrenees to appear three days later in Paris's *Le Monde* on its way across Europe, stopping en route in the Dutch weekly *Vrij Nederland* on October 7, in the Italian *L'Europeo* on October 16 and, on October 20, in the Greek *To Vima*, which trumpeted its "unquestionable authenticity" and ran it under the headline "A Secret American Manual on Destabilization Operations in Western Europe." At this point, and here is where disinformation becomes high art, the Soviet agency Novosti could pick up the story, citing as its sources these respectable, non-Communist Western periodicals. From then on, pure logic led Novosti and some of its spokesmen in the West to embroider on the story; they later even blamed the CIA for the murder of Italian Christian-Democratic leader Aldo Moro by the Red Brigades, for terrorist killings by the Basque ETA in Spain, and—why not?—occupation of the Great Mosque in Mecca by armed fanatics in 1979.

An exhaustive inventory of disinformation would overflow several fat volumes, so truly worldwide is it and so pervasive. In 1982, for example, Pakistan's antimalaria institute, which had been financed by world health organizations for twenty years and worked in collaboration with scientists from the University of Maryland, was suddenly accused of breeding a special strain of mosquitos with a fatal sting for use in biological warfare planned by the CIA in Afghanistan. Splashed in the Moscow *Literary Gazette* on February 2, 1982, this lamentably crude fabrication was eagerly picked up by the usual pleiad of "independent" newspapers, including such venerable institutions of Asia's non-Communist press as the *Times of India* and the *Pakistani Daily Jang*. As soon as it appeared, the "news" touched off an anti-American riot in Lahore. The antimalaria institute's luckless research scientists had to pack their bags and their mosquitos to avoid being stoned. As it happened, this lively episode came at just the right time to muffle the stories then beginning to circulate about the Communists' very real use of biochemical weapons in Afghanistan, Laos and Cambodia.

This was not a unique case of defensive disinformation. Again in 1982, the Communists managed to commandeer a United Nations report on the economic debacle in Vietnam in which the Hanoi Nomenklatura's ineptitude was made all too clear; the report was censored and then rewritten in a more positive tone. A constructive piece of work, made easier by the fact that, over the years, officials from the Soviet Union and its client states have captured a great many key posts in the UN.[2] This explains how information from Western newspapers and press services cited in another UN report came to be labeled "grossly inaccurate" in comparison with data supplied by Soviet-bloc publications, which were praised for their objectivity and "continuous support" of the world organization![3]

Around this hard nucleus of "active measures" and its outer covering of defensive disinformation float successive layers of gaseous "vague" or "atmospheric" disinformation. This is the twilight zone of information where lies hover in search of an editor who will idly ask some reporter to "check that out for me." It is from this outer air that word arrives of a meeting supposedly organized by the CIA in Geneva to set up the KOR, the Polish intellectuals' defense committee, and that the Israelis had Bashir Gemayel

2. Thierry Wolton, "ONU: l'infiltration sovietique," in *Le Point*, Paris, 4 October 1982.
3. See the story headlined "UN Officials Criticize News Coverage by West," by Bernard D. Nossiter in the *International Herald Tribune*, 16–17 October 1982.

elected President of Lebanon only for the pleasure of assassinating him a week later, since, of course, the Israelis had to be blamed for a murder that was in fact plotted by Syria. This is the area in which the West "autodisinforms" without, needless to say, ever being aware of it. Victims of "vague disinformation" are those who take the Communist view of the world as self-evident. Here is one example chosen at random from among the hundreds in my files, highly illustrative precisely because it was relatively harmless.

On Saturday, March 1, 1980, the 1 P.M. news show on the French Government radio station France-Inter, which covers the whole country, was anchored by Yves Mourousi, a veteran newsman. With President Giscard d'Estaing visiting the Persian Gulf states, a journalist from Kuwait was invited to explain to the program's listeners that: 1) his region was not endangered by the Soviet presence in Afghanistan; 2) the Americans want people to believe there is such a danger to alarm the West over possible loss of its oil sources, using this as an excuse to step up their "intervention"; 3) Giscard's trip was welcome because it would help Arab countries in the Mideast to resist American pressure.

Who was this Kuwaiti journalist and whom did he represent? Not a clue. But a Moscow propaganda line was presented to French listeners as the "Kuwaiti point of view" that implicitly authenticated the "news" with no other comment and no rebuttal.

Pro-Soviet clichés are given privileged, not to say free, entry into the media in the countries communism seeks to destroy. When the media are nationalized, no government control is exercised over this distortion of international news; vague disinformation has equally free rein under conservative and leftist governments. All unawares, the "bourgeois" press, more out of indolence than malice, has largely taken over the after-sales and reconditioning services for the most ramshackle products of Soviet disinformation. And it does not cost Moscow a penny.

True, the Soviet apostolate cannot count on volunteer workers alone to do all its work. Still, the "organs," as the KGB is sometimes called, are endowed with liberal budgets with which to inflame their missionaries' zeal. The KGB's redemptive manna for

Communist parties, front organizations, sympathetic newspapers, discreet friends and devoted agents flows to the West and the Third World through complicated channels that have long since been traced. Even as I write these lines, the morning papers on this October 8, 1982, report that Western intelligence operatives have just found a dummy company in Luxembourg set up by East Germany to provide funds for Greek Communist Party publications. The firm, Press and Printing Development Corporation, had "encouraged" so-called exterior party publications in Greece (that is, those turned out by the pro-Soviet one of Greece's two Communist parties) to the tune of $2.3 million. Heading the company since its foundation in 1977 was one Karl Raab, who described himself as a banker and member of the Central Committee of East Germany's Unitary Socialist (Communist) Party. Mr. Raab's enterprise, the Western intelligence sources said, had for years been financing not only his Greek friends' work, but many other newspapers, magazines, and book publishers throughout Europe that promoted the Soviet line.

The Greek Parliament considered the case. Investigations were launched on an international scale. I have never heard that they came to anything. The Luxembourg company was merely a tiny link in a vast multinational network that has been described in detail by a number of responsible authors. Indeed, the contrast between the lives of luxury led by Communist galaxies in the West and the low incomes they officially declare proves the network's existence. But, out of courtesy, the press and politicians in the democracies pretend to think that "Moscow's gold" is a myth, just as they pretend to believe that Soviet leaders really live on their official salaries, which, as everyone knows, are equivalent to a worker's pay, right? This whopper is another bit of disinformation, circulated, naturally, with the aid of the honorable disinformed, as usual. Could disinformation keep all these improbabilities afloat unless its victims yearned for self-sacrifice?

Every secret service in every country in the world, we are told, has its "action service," its dirty-tricks department, and they all practice disinformation as best they can. Here it is useful to recall the simple truth that democratic societies, and even societies that are neither democratic nor Communist, are penetrable in degrees varying from total ease to relative difficulty but that totalitarian societies are completely impenetrable. A West German Raab could not open a "Press and Printing Development Corporation" in Kiev and begin subsidizing local publications. Which publications, anyway? For the Communist press and the free press have nothing in common but the name. Add to all this the fact that Western special services are periodically attacked and unmasked at home, which is healthy for the democratic process but is nevertheless an advantage to democracy's adversaries. Public censure for the kidnapping of Morocco's Mehdi Ben Barka in 1965 almost wrecked France's counterespionage service, the Service de Documentation et de Contré-espionnage; the CIA's effectiveness was destroyed for several years by the 1975 Senate Intelligence Committee report on it. In the early 1970s, the Italian Government, under pressure from the left, dismantled the SID (Italian Documentation Service), suspected of encouraging rightist coups d'état; during the subsequent six or seven years, this enabled Red Brigades terrorists to murder their fellow countrymen at will in an almost total police vacuum. I would not dream of pleading that these agencies never abuse their power, are never guilty of stupidity or murder. I concede that they deserve to be kept on a leash. The fact remains that such things do not happen to the KGB.

In short, the ideological war is being fought in one direction only. It should really be called a war of lies, since all ideology is a lie. The fundamental lie is surely the association of communism with progress, defense of the poor, the struggle for peace, while all of communism's enemies are identified as "reactionaries," "conservatives," "rightists." This is disinformation's greatest success.

For all practical purposes, there is no way for democrats to combat this. The Communists sap the world in the name of a social model with which those at whom their propaganda is aimed have no experience but which forbids those who are experiencing it even to criticize it, much less alter it. Flaws in the non-Communist systems topple men and parties from power, bring about changes in regimes, eliminate social classes. But the destabilizing effect of popular discontent is almost imperceptible in the totalitarian world because its police system is so highly developed. So the non-Communist societies function permanently in the spotlight of criticism from both the Communists and their own inhabitants. Their defects, real, supposed or exaggerated, are condemned as absolutes, as the only ones on the planet, since the Communists' defects are not subject to daily scrutiny, are seen only as abstractions by anyone not living in the Communist world. The people who do live in it acquire concrete knowledge of those faults, but too late to do anything about them.

In the ideological war, the goal of Communist propaganda is to destroy democracy wherever it exists and to make it an impossibility wherever it could grow. Communism has the means to do this. But the democracies' propaganda cannot destroy communism. At best, democracy can simply try to protect itself. And even this it does badly, if at all.

17

PIRACY AND PERVERSION

Appropriating transport it did not have to build, a qualified crew it did not have to train, passengers who really want to go somewhere, and fuel it did not have to pay for to reach a destination other than the one originally scheduled—these are new political techniques introduced by communism. Trickery here prevails over force—or, rather, precedes it. After seduction and persuasion come intimidation, threats, then terror, and, at the end of a road that is rarely retraced, lies a Communist monopoly of power.

Political piracy, like aerial piracy, rests on misappropriation and parasitism. Situations it never created are invaded from the inside, with minimum brutality and visibility at first. Human hopes, institutions, structures that existed before it did and that owe it nothing are rechanneled to its profit; it annexes them, usurps their watchwords for its own purposes, captures their energy and goodwill, and herds them surreptitiously toward the enclosure where the front organizations are grouped.

Parasitism takes the form of pure absorption through technological pillage, industrial espionage, the economic and financial fleecing of the West. It is active and offensive parasitism when it infiltrates and manipulates terrorist movements that destabilize and weaken the chosen prey of international communism. And it is ideological and political when it perverts the Nonaligned Countries Movement, the Socialist International, the ecologists, the pacifists, the UN (where the capitalist powers pay almost all the costs) and, above all, UNESCO (United Nations Educational, Scientific and Cultural Organization). Add to this the perversion of revolutions and nationalist movements in the Third World; of the Interparliamentary Union (where so-called deputies from the East sit on an equal basis with others elected by genuine popular vote); of the World Council of Churches, which, in opening its doors to Eastern Orthodox churches, was invaded by a heavy brigade of Orthodox popes from the KGB. For communism can also borrow the voice of God to preach unilateral Western disarmament.

It goes without saying that Communist parties in the non-Communist countries also do their utmost to infiltrate and sidetrack target groups, first by utilizing the legal bases they normally acquire under the rules of bourgeois democracy, then, and more important, by expanding from these bases in less democratic ways to seize the centers of political, administrative and financial power. These centers are often hidden and go well beyond what the electorate thinks it has authorized.

In 1973–74, the Portuguese Communist Party tried to confiscate the Revolution of the Carnations and turn Portugal into a popular democracy although it has never drawn more than 15 percent of the vote. In 1981, after its most stinging defeat at the polls since World War II, the French Communist Party was taken into the government (the country's President was constitutionally free to do this even if it did not reflect the voters' wishes) and immediately set about using its position to begin appropriating positions of power in the bureaucracy, sometimes insidiously, at other times imperiously. Special care was taken to gain control over the state-owned radio and television networks or, where direct control escaped the party, to intimidate network news services.

Whenever the French Communist Party gains a foothold in the government, it leaves ineradicable traces in the state apparatus as well as in regional and municipal administrations. With their customary angelism, the Socialists, when they collaborate with the Communists, boast of having "taken them prisoner," arguing that it is "better to have them in than out" so that the numerically superior Socialists can neutralize them. This is forgetting that in any proper flock there are always more sheep than shepherds and sheepdogs. History teaches us that in every country where the

Communists have succeeded in grabbing monopoly power they made their play from a minority position. The organization of a labor union like the French CGT, based on a Leninist model that eliminates internal democracy, is an excellent example of political piracy that converts the union into a lever against the government. France's Socialists learned this in the spring of 1982, during the massive strikes that paralyzed the automotive industry and greatly helped precipitate the Socialist government's economic and monetary rout. A childishly simple double game enables the Communists to combine verbal loyalty to the government with its active destabilization.

Not all the Western Communist parties have been lucky enough to receive a kind invitation to join the government after losing an election. A Communist party out of power is too visible, often too discredited to be used by Moscow as anything but heavy artillery, which is useless in delicate operations. Moreover, the Soviet Communist Party frequently runs into resistance within the Communist International; its naive social-democratic cousins are sometimes easier to manipulate than its brother parties.

This is why genuine political piracy, the most profitable kind, is aimed at organizations that start out being not only non-Communist but often anti-Communist.

Anti-Communist in principle by its very birth certificate is the Socialist International, the social democracy so hated by Lenin. Stalin detested it to the point of supporting Hitler against it: in 1932 he ordered the German Communist Party to give the Nazis a quiet hand in their campaign against the Socialists. And in the early years of the Spanish Second Republic, that is, in 1931–33, the Communists labeled the Socialist Party "social-fascist" and treated it accordingly. The term "social-fascist" was also used by the French Communists to describe Léon Blum's Socialist Party in the 1930s. Communist jargon is international, like Communist policy. But historians of communism, who normally study it only in a single country, do not always notice how closely coordinated changes of policy and vocabulary are throughout the world. This was visible in the Communist parties' experiments with Popular

Front and Leftist Union movements; they joined the coalitions when shifting tactical and strategic requirements dictated and, when it served Communist interests, deserted them with a rapidity that regularly left the Socialists incredulous, stunned, and aghast.

Then, during the profitable period known as détente that began in 1970, while local Communist parties continued to apply this hot-and-cold treatment, a parallel maneuver was superimposed from Moscow: an artful domestication of the Socialist International that we must applaud as an ingenious innovation. Buried in Brezhnev's ritual, hours-long homily to the twenty-fourth Soviet Party Congress in 1971 was an appeal to the social democrats, with whom, announced the secretary-general, the Soviet Communist Party was ready to "develop its cooperation" in the "struggle for peace, democracy and socialism."

What could be more laudable? One after another, delegations from Western socialist parties bustled to Moscow with that prompt obedience that makes Moscow's work so easy in its relations with the democracies. Every time the Kremlin makes an overture, even if it does not offer the slightest guarantees, the slightest proof of good faith, or any shadow of real concessions—indeed, even if the move is an obvious trap—Western leaders generally feel they must respond to it instantly; if they do not, they risk accusation by their own people of rejecting a chance for peace and understanding. So a delegation from the Belgian Socialist Party led off the procession in 1972, signing a prodisarmament agreement with the Soviet Communist Party that amounted in practice to a pact to weaken NATO, of which Belgium is a member. By custom, Western negotiators, those valiant defenders of their peoples' security, never ask the Soviet Union to take the lead in disarmament.

The Belgians were followed to Moscow by representatives of the Norwegian, Danish, Dutch, and Spanish socialist parties; between 1973 and 1977, all of them signed similar agreements with the Soviet Communists that were ratified and reinforced by delegates from the British Labour Party and the West German Social Democratic Party. In 1975, François Mitterrand "led" a delegation from the French Socialist Party that was received by top Soviet leaders;

Suslov, party Secretariat member Boris Ponomarev and Brezhnev himself put on a tremendous act over what they declared was Mitterrand's love of, his obsession for, peace. Said the joint communiqué later issued by the Soviet Communist Party and the French Socialists: "The French Socialist Party delegation expressed its appreciation of the Soviet Union's constructive contribution to the process of international détente . . . the two delegations declared that the imperialists and reactionaries are continuing their attempts to revive the spirit of the cold war." It is noteworthy that the Soviets thus managed to sell their point of view and even their vocabulary to the head of a major Western political party who agreed unreservedly to castigate his own camp. The "imperialists" and "reactionaries" who were "reviving the cold war" could only be the Americans and, more generally, the West, or those in it, at any rate, who were unwilling to accede to all of Moscow's demands.

In 1976, Willy Brandt was elected president of the Socialist International. From then on, Moscow was no longer to deal separately with the socialist parties at the national level but directly with the International. One highly expressive consequence of Brandt's new line was the decision to exclude from the International all the Central European and Far Eastern socialist parties in exile, which until then had been allowed to attend its congresses as observers with the right to be heard.

Following this courageous purge, the renewed Socialist International set up a series of work groups to study the outlook for disarmament. In 1979, an official delegation from the International, called the Work Group on Disarmament Questions, of which the present French Socialist Party chairman, Lionel Jospin, was a member, visited the Kremlin; it was the first Socialist International delegation to set foot there since 1917. Another unit active in 1979 was the Sorsa group, named for the chairman of the Finnish Social Democratic Party, the right man for the job, a zealous workman buoyed by the tireless efforts of the Kremlin's experts on relations with the West, Vadim Zagladin, Ponomarev, and Americanologist Georghi Arbatov.

The invasion of Afghanistan in December of that year only briefly shook the International's faith in the Soviet desire for peace. Soon afterward, a second group was organized, the Palme Committee, which denounced American imperialism, condemned the neutron bomb and campaigned against Euromissile deployment in Western Europe. Only months after the Red Army marched into Afghanistan, Palme, who had demonstrated in the streets of Stockholm ten years earlier against America's presence in Vietnam, visited Moscow to examine with Arbatov ways to counter the warmongering by the United States and other members of the Atlantic Alliance.

In 1981, a group called Scandilux was organized in Copenhagen. It was made up of the social-democratic parties of five NATO countries (Norway, Denmark, Holland, Belgium and Luxembourg) to oppose the modernization of NATO forces and the construction of a French neutron bomb.[1] Dutch Socialist leader Joop den Uyl even called for unilateral disarmament. In July of the same year, Brandt went to Moscow, a trip that earned him the plaudits of the Novosti agency, which lavished special praise on his support for the "peaceful proposal" to create a nuclear-free zone in Northern Europe, that old Soviet hobbyhorse. Novosti could have added that Brandt also exerted pressure on the Spanish Socialist Party, which received considerable political and financial help from the German Social Democrats, to campaign against Spanish membership in NATO despite the deep conviction of the party's secretary-general, Felipe González, that Spain belonged in the alliance.

Whatever we may think of the positions taken by these work groups, even if we approved them, one point is unarguable: the views expressed by the Socialist International concerning the United States, arms reduction, the responsibilities for world tension, NATO European defense and East-West relations very quickly became almost indistinguishable from those of the Soviet Union.

1. A point noted with satisfaction by the French Communist Party newspaper *L'Humanité* on 9 November 1982.

This is equally true of the Socialist International's policies in the Third World. At congresses in Geneva in 1976 and Vancouver in 1978, it voted for more active support of national liberation and revolutionary movements against Third World dictators. Democrats can only approve of these resolutions. One might have thought, however, that the International would find its own policy and, wherever possible, try to improve the chances for political solutions that are equally independent of both types of dictatorship, the fascist military variety and the Stalinist-Castroite-Soviet-Communist brand. Not at all. The International hastened to hammer at democratic regimes in embryo and at the movements aiming to establish them. At the same time, it unreservedly endorsed the Communist definition of "progressive" movements in the Third World. For example, its leaders modestly averted their eyes from the takeovers by totalitarian governments in Nicaragua, Grenada and El Salvador, but they outspokenly denigrated partisans of pluralistic democracy. Castro's official newspaper, *Granma*, in its French-language edition of November 21, 1982, warmly approved the resolution on Latin America adopted by the Socialist International's bureau in Basel on November 8. And it is a fact that there was nothing in the resolution to which Andropov and Castro could not subscribe. I shall return to the questions of Nicaragua and El Salvador; for the moment I would simply like to point out that, again, the new-style Socialist International policy toward these countries was identical with those of Havana and Moscow.

During a Venezuelan television program shortly before the Salvadoran elections on March 29, author Carlos Rangel pertinently remarked, "I consider incomprehensible the attitude of those who, without being Communists, agree perfectly not only with the communist arguments against even organizing elections in El Salvador, but also with the shifts in those arguments. For they have changed constantly. First we were told that the elections would constitute an obstacle to the restoration of civil peace, then that they would be meaningless, and finally that they were risky because they might be won by the extreme right. Each of these arguments contradicted the other two. How could the Socialist International have echoed them so docilely and adopted them as its own as soon as communist propagandists produced them?"

Another objection can be added to Rangel's list: that the arguments were false and could not stand up to examination. First, no election was ever watched by as many foreign observers per square mile as tiny El Salvador's. Second, the party in power, Napoleón Duarte's Christian Social Party, won the largest share (40 percent) of the popular vote but failed to gain the absolute majority it needed to govern, which seldom happens when an election is rigged. It is a known fact that the Salvadoran guerrillas and the Communists, who had urged a boycott of the election, suffered a serious defeat that day because the citizens of El Salvador went to the polls en masse, often risking their lives to do so. This did not prevent the top bosses of the International from declaring a week later, against all the evidence, that the election was worthless because it had indeed been rigged. It is true that Roberto Aubuisson's extreme-right party received a huge 25 percent of the vote, which I deplore, but, one is tempted to ask, whose fault was that? Doesn't it prove that the guerrillas are not as popular as the international left would like to think they are? Be that as it may, the only argument the Socialist International had no right at all to make was that the voting was fraudulent.

My purpose here is not to issue a moral judgment on this flagrant lie. I merely invite the reader to note that in this case, as in many others, the powerful Socialist International's viewpoint is a twin to Moscow's. You will never hear its spokesmen explicitly denounce Soviet imperialism in Africa and the regimes of poverty and terror it has established there. During a decade of virulent Soviet expansionism, the term "imperialism" has come to mean exclusively "American imperialism" to the Socialist International. We may then conclude that in those ten years the international Communist movement has largely succeeded in aligning the Socialist International with its positions on disarmament and the balance of power in Europe and with its policy on which political systems to support and which to oppose in the Third World.

Social-democratic subservience to Communist Third World propaganda is especially surprising because the helplessness of the Communists and their progressive cousins to remedy the poor countries' underdevelopment is one of the most crushing lessons of the postcolonial period. "Popular democratic" regimes in the Third World have aggravated and, in a sense, systematized poverty, disorder, incompetence, corruption and minority privilege in their countries. Very mixed results have been obtained in the countries remaining in the capitalist sphere of influence, appalling or merely bad in some and ranging up through average and good to excellent in others. Results in the Communist-progressive sphere, however, are uniformly disastrous. What's more, these countries' chronic economic anemia is overlaid by the inevitable totalitarian repression, often spiced with an obligatory personality cult, the tribute of an enslaved people to the megalomania of an irremovable despot. "Progressive" countries which, while not dependent on Moscow, have collectivist and bureaucratic administrations are also sunk in famine and shortages that often contrast with the relative prosperity in neighboring nations which have clung to a market economy, even on a small scale. The state of that part of the Third World managed by capitalism merits severe criticism, but not criticism alone; the socialist part deserves nothing but criticism.

The Socialist International's policy since 1976, therefore, is hard to explain by a desire to raise the standard of living of the poor and even harder, I imagine, by concern for the development of social democracy. It is made even less understandable by the fact that of all the industrial powers, the Soviet Union is distinguished by its stinginess in aiding the less developed countries. Western aid in 1980 alone exceeded all the economic assistance granted by the Soviets in the *quarter-century* from 1955 to 1979. And such aid as Moscow did give, parsimonious as it was, went only to countries of which the Kremlin thought to make political use. There is only one sector in which the results have been impressive, however: Soviet arms sales to the Third World. Between 1972 and 1981, the U.S.S.R. hawked twice as much conventional weaponry to the

LDCs as the United States did.[2] True, the cataleptic economies of Cuba, Vietnam, Ethiopia are burdensome to Moscow, but these costs are written off to the welfare of the empire. Given the Communists' squalid showing in the Third World, we should be properly respectful of the political skill with which the Soviet Union has nevertheless fooled people into letting it usurp the role of champion of the poor.

A second brilliant diplomatic success in the way of political piracy and surreptitious annexation following the deviation of the Socialist International into a pro-Soviet channel was the capture of the Nonaligned Countries Movement.

Between the first conference of nonaligneds in Belgrade in 1961, when the genuinely nonaligned position of Indian Prime Minister Jawaharlal Nehru prevailed, and their sixth conference in Havana in 1979, the adjective "nonaligned" had plenty of time to degenerate into a lie. Just the choice of Havana as the 1979 conference site and the election of Fidel Castro, Moscow's number-one field executive, as the movement's chairman showed how distorted the ideal of nonalignment had become. At that sixth conference, Marshal Tito, a few months before his death, fought his last battle to block the Sovietization of the movement of which he and Nehru had been the founding fathers. It was a lost fight; with the collapse of the last independent holdouts, the nonaligned lined up behind the Soviet Union. Begun at the 1970 Lusaka conference, where the members refused to condemn the Soviet invasion of Czechoslovakia, the new alignment became clearer in 1973 at the conference in Algiers. There Castro succeeded, without being voted out of the group, in servilely echoing the Soviet line of the moment, condemning China as well as the United States.

As time went on, the nonaligneds increasingly accepted openly Communist countries as members, avowed and established Soviet satellites, while blackballing other candidates and even forcing out some members that refused to become communism's fellow travelers. Founded to unite those countries, especially the young Third

2. *Le Monde*, 20 August 1982, and the *World Strategic Situation, 1981*, published by the Institute of Strategic Studies in London.

World nations, that preferred to remain aloof from East-West rivalry, the Nonaligned Movement has turned into an auxiliary of the East bloc. Hostility to the United States in particular and to the West in general has become its driving political force, a socialist Third World its central ideology. What makes this degeneration even more absurd is that, like the Socialist International, the nonaligneds preach a doctrine of "North-South relations" that opposes the East-West dichotomy; this is made meaningless by the movement's consistent, sycophantic options in support of Eastern political and strategic interests. India's efforts during the seventh conference, in Delhi in March 1983, to curb the movement's exaggeratedly pro-Soviet stance were really designed to restore the facade of neutrality without which a front organization loses its effectiveness.

To the capture of the Nonaligned Movement was grafted a second offensive, this time with the complicity of UNESCO, which is riddled with Communist infiltrators. It was an attempt to curtail freedom of information and to pirate channels of information for the benefit of totalitarian or, at least, dictatorial governments. Behind this act of larceny was, as usual, a legitimate desire on the part of the young states in the Third World for organs of national information. Nationalism is one of the genuine sources of human energy that Soviet imperialism has learned to capture in extending its dominion, to the long-term detriment, we can be sure, of the independence of nations enlisted in the campaign.

The first open attack came during the nonaligned conference in Colombo in 1976. It was aimed at foreign press agencies and newspapers. With a few minor exceptions, newspapers and radio and television networks in the so-called nonaligned countries are government-controlled. This presents few problems at home. But these governments are irritated by the reporting of a handful of internationally read newspapers and magazines on their actions and on the facts of daily life in their countries, and they are particularly resentful of the big press services, Agence France-Presse, the Associated Press, United Press, Reuter's, etc. These regimes would restrict coverage of their areas to purely national agencies that—

and this is the key motivation—would enable them virtually to hand fashion the public image they want to create of their countries.

As early as 1975, India pointed the way by expelling foreign reporters who refused to submit their stories for official approval before filing them. In late July 1976, a recently arrived correspondent for Britain's daily *Guardian* was forced to leave, after two months of persecution, without having sent his paper a single story. He deserved this, according to Prime Minister Indira Gandhi, because the "British press remains colonialist." This was a particularly lame excuse in the case of the *Guardian*, which in the past had been a determined advocate of decolonization and is now a friend of the Third World.

The principle laid down in Colombo is eminently clear: each Third World nation is the owner of its image, with an exclusive right to portray itself at home and abroad as its leaders wish it to be pictured. Foreign information, reporting, anecdotes, statistics that contradict the official model are imperialist and neocolonialist.

Assigned to enforce this principle, under the patronage of India, its instigator, was a group of Third World agencies responsible for distributing the authorized information emanating from their countries. Operational rules were worked out at a preliminary meeting in New Delhi and ratified in Colombo: at home, government news agencies were to have a monopoly over information, including foreign news. Stories about these countries by foreign correspondents could only be published abroad. New laws were to be enacted that would permit the arrest of any writer judged lying or hostile to the host country. All media were to be nationalized.

These directives were given UNESCO's advance moral approval at a meeting of its Latin American members in San José, Costa Rica, on July 12–21, 1976, where similar resolutions were adopted in clear violation of the UN Charter. When I objected to this Third World censorship a few weeks before the Colombo meeting, a brilliant Moroccan intellectual retorted, "The big newspapers never publish a dispatch from a Tanzanian or Ghanaian agency, never! It is always the news multinationals that are cited, AFP, UP and so on. Why? And why shouldn't we do something about this?"

Unfortunately, the magic word "multinational," supreme stigma though it may be, is just not enough of a prop for the argument. To begin with, the news agencies are not, technically, economically or financially, the multinational corporations that such firms as Philips or General Motors are. They invest no capital, transfer no technology, recruit few employees in the countries where they maintain bureaus. Some professions are by nature international, and agency news reporting is among them. An agency without an international network would be like an airline that served only its home airport. By my Moroccan friend's standards, the most monstrous of all the multinational corporations is the international postal service. Should it be broken up?

Secondly, newspapers subscribe to press services—for a fee, remember—precisely because they provide broad coverage, the more complete and worldwide, the better. Papers can subscribe to one, two, three or four services; more than that would be too expensive, since all the agencies are covering essentially the same stories. It isn't just the African and Latin-American services that have trouble competing with the big four; such European agencies as Ansa (Italian) and Efe (Spanish) can seldom win against them in international coverage. And Japan's position as a "valet of imperialism" does not help its Kyodo agency to break into European and American newspapers with any frequency.

Besides, let's call a spade a spade. There is no point in pretending not to understand that the real aim of this supposed struggle against the "colonization" of information is the creation of state monopolies like Tass and the New China News Agency—neither of which, incidentally, was cited at Colombo or by UNESCO as being among the offending agencies, doubtless because of their well-known objectivity and because they will probably serve as models for the new services.

Fascist censorship is at least honest enough not to go disguised as progressive. The nonaligneds' supreme hypocrisy is to present the domestication of information as democratization. It's very easy:

you win worldwide progressive support by saying that you are nationalizing the press to wrest it from the control of money, then you subject it to the control of your police. But what if the motive of all this "decolonization" of information is merely defensiveness by the power elite in the less developed countries, their anxiety to hang on to their privileges, and not their concern for their peoples' well-being? How many leaders of nonaligned countries truly represent the people they govern? What a contrast: nonaligned governments are being heard—and rightly—louder and stronger all the time, but the people in these countries are more and more silent. Their real lives are increasingly hidden from foreign eyes, from professional reporters and casual visitors alike. The people's voice grows constantly fainter both within and beyond their nations' frontiers. The image they receive of the world, like that the world receives of them, is more and more closely filtered through official censorship. For many people in the world, the irreplaceable and inestimable BBC World Service, the London heart of a twenty-four-hour-a-day broadcasting operation in many languages besides English, is often the sole source of reliable news about what is happening in their own countries. You can't ban the airwaves from a nation's territory, and jamming them, as the Soviet Union does, requires highly expensive technology.

What the less developed countries call freeing themselves from Western imperialism and neocolonialism, if this involves nationalizing the news, means borrowing the worst from their former colonial masters and rejecting the best. It is as though Renaissance Europe, anxious to "liberate" itself from the crushing cultural influence of antiquity, had opted to reject Greek democracy and Roman law but to retain Greek slavery and Roman infanticide. And if we remember that the Soviet Union has failed to honor the provisions of the Helsinki accords on the free movement of ideas and people, we realize that governments' respect for the right to information called for in the UN Charter and the Declaration of Human Rights is shrinking rapidly. The tendency is toward greater restriction. Examples of countries that are liberalizing the flow of information are rare, too rare to offset freedom's losses. Since the vast majority of the regimes in power today is totalitarian or authoritarian, the more or less automatic result is that their organs of information concentrate their criticism on the flaws and failures of the liberal societies and the capitalist system—just as the Communists do.

The Third World has a legitimate need to build its own information network. More than any other world sector, perhaps, given the enormity of its problems, it needs accurate information about itself, not propaganda. But with UNESCO's active help, the Soviet Union plays on Third World defensiveness, exploiting it to create a world system of controlled information. Xenophobia, that degenerate form of nationalism, turns the Nomenklatura of the Third World toward the Soviet model of information management, the most effective for shielding a bureaucracy from independent information. For untrammeled information is the nightmare of all governments; this is true even in the democracies, and it is certainly more acutely felt in the dictatorships.

This convergence of interests provided the impetus for a new drive in Paris in 1981. The setting was UNESCO, whose shocking role as a cultural Trojan horse is becoming more obvious all the time. It is a mournful irony that, to put it mildly, the UN is not opposed to this obscurantist policy on the part of UNESCO, its "cultural" branch in Paris. And the clever touch is that the democracies themselves, through the UN, are financing their own liquidation. Capitalism is the silent backer of pro-Soviet propaganda. In 1979, the UN had 154 member countries, but the United States paid a fourth of the organization's expenses. In 1975 it had paid a third. The share might be justified by America's wealth, but the United States cannot be expected to put up indefinitely without reacting to the perversion by the Soviet Union and its satellites of the UN's specialized branches. Among these is the International Labor Organization, which is so tightly controlled by the East that, at one point, non-Communist Western labor unions temporarily withdrew in protest.

It is probably at UNESCO that the Communist stranglehold is best disguised. International civil servants from East-bloc countries are required, in formal contradiction to the terms of their employment, to go on obeying the orders of their national governments. Those who refuse are sent home, arrested and imprisoned. UNESCO knows this very well, since it has happened more than once to UNESCO personnel. Hence our bafflement when preparation of the organization's preliminary report on "freedom" of information was assigned to a French university professor who is a member of the French Communist Party. Now, he has a perfect right to be a party member; this is among the democratic choices we must all respect. But we may nevertheless wonder if UNESCO acted judiciously, if it took all precautions to guarantee the report's objectivity, when it allotted the task to a representative of an ideology that has never been compatible anywhere with freedom or pluralism of information.

I was among the few, in France at least, who objected at the time to this policy of obscurantism decked out in progressive plumage.[3] A telling sign: the Communist *L'Humanité* immediately assailed me in an article that was unusually virulent even for that frequently vituperative paper.[4] Ferocity and speed of Communist press reaction are always signs that the object of their attack has touched a sore point, has put his finger on a major element of Communist strategy and that the party, the Soviet Union or both are intensely annoyed at having light cast on a key operation. For Soviet imperialism, the confiscation of information in the Third World is a long-range project, a decisive one in which it prefers that its manipulation of UNESCO and the nonaligned countries be neither prematurely nor baldly revealed.

While what may be called these political "embezzlements" are blatant to all save those who will not see, Soviet exploitation and, when necessary, instigation of terrorism is, in the nature of things, harder to spot. Its support of terrorist groups can only be useful to Moscow as long as this link remains impossible to prove conclusively. Filtering cash and arms to terrorists through a string of intermediaries who block positive identification of their original

3. "L'Internationale du mensonge," *L'Express*, 7 March 1981.
4. "Revel au pays des sorcières," *L'Humanité*, 10 March 1981.

sources is a rudimentary part of the KGB's job. This is especially true in connection with terrorists operating in the democracies, which are porous and vulnerable and in which "progressive" public opinion often confuses human rights with the right to be violent.

Because it is an old trick for governments to blame their internal difficulties on foreign plots, prudent commentators and political figures long made a habit of skepticism about the exact extent of Soviet responsibility for the spread of terrorism in Europe since 1970 and in Latin America since 1960 or earlier. As time went on, however, enough circumstantial evidence was amassed to narrow the gap between the opinions these observers expressed in private and those they voiced in public. In private, they had long believed Moscow was supporting terrorism, but they did not abandon their reserve in public until 1980. Then Italian President Alessandro Pertini openly linked the Soviet Union to the Red Brigades and, in Portugal, Socialist leader Mario Soares implicated the Soviets in the terrorist marauding of the Basque ETA in Spain. In 1977, *Le Monde* had opened its pages to defenders of the Baader-Meinhof group with a generosity that indicated some sympathy with terrorism in West Germany; in 1982, however, in reporting on the investigation into the attempted assassination of Pope John Paul II on May 13, 1981, the paper almost unreservedly approved the charge that the shooting had been ordered by the Soviet Union through its Bulgarian vassals.[5] And in a column in the French magazine *Le Point*, the very sober Olivier Chevrillon, discussing a series of terrorist killings in Paris, declared, "The flood of comment . . . neglects one aspect of terrorism today that nevertheless seems as glaringly obvious as Poe's purloined letter. Terrorism, of course, is still what it has always been—a form of madness—but hasn't it also become a reckless auxiliary to [one country's] diplomacy? By showering every kind of *pistolero* with arms and rubles, the Soviets are surely giving themselves an added means of pressure and blackmail against the European democracies."[6]

5. 23 September 1982.
6. 30 August 1982.

French Socialists, once the champions of foreign terrorists, whom they saw as avengers, resisters against oppression, freedom fighters, abruptly changed their tune when they took over the government and the Terrorist International grew a little too active in France. In July 1981, French Interior Minister Gaston Defferre compared the ETA's killers to French resistance fighters against the Nazi occupiers in World War II (the comparison must have struck the young Spanish democracy as beautifully tactful). In a television interview in May 1982, undismayed, as always, by his blunders, Defferre asserted that the Red Army Fraction was fighting "the injustices in its own society," that is, against West Germany, which, when the terrorist acts under discussion were committed, had been governed by Socialists, first Brandt, then Schmidt. He thus espoused the very arguments with which terrorists always justify their crimes against democratic states.

But after a particularly murderous incident in Paris confirmed that big-time terrorism had reached France, Defferre found a new philosophy. "The arms," he told the magazine *Paris-Match*, "are supplied by the East-bloc countries. These countries, which disagree with our policies, and which practice espionage, want to attack our regimes, but with their methods, which are those of terrorism."

Responsibility for public security had revealed to the eminent statesman what everyone else had long since noticed: that socialist democracies are among Terrorist International's favorite targets. After an attack in August 1982 on a Jewish restaurant in Paris that left six people dead and twenty-two wounded, President Mitterrand was questioned about possible collusion between the killers and Eastern European secret services. "It's worth thinking about," he allowed in a suggestively enigmatic manner. What *is* worth thinking about is the timorous languor with which Western European politicians brought themselves to face the fact of a Soviet sanctuary for world terrorism. It is significant that, early in the 1980s, this suddenly seemed self-evident to everybody.

There are so many varieties of terrorism that pinning them all to a single source would border on absurdity. And it would disregard the practical and psychological impossibility that any single force, even Moscow's master destabilizers, could maintain bloody but totally artificial terrorist campaigns in so many countries for very long. Terrorist movements spring from their native soil, which does not always make them morally acceptable; terrorism against a democracy, against the least unjust of societies, can be indigenous but unjustified. Competing with terrorists fighting for democracy or for their homelands against dictators or invaders we find totalitarian terrorists who want nothing less than to impose their obsessions by force on a vast majority that does not want them and has said so plainly at the ballot box.

Terrorism must, however, have local roots to be exploitable. And there is no denying that the Soviet Union and Cuba, its agent in Latin America, have infiltrated *homegrown* terrorist movements, amplified their natural strength, supplied equipment and advisers; when necessary, terrorist leaders have been trained in Eastern European camps that the West has known about for years. The range of possibilities offered has been vast, from Mideastern terrorism through Irish and Spanish separatism and the bloody paranoiacs in West Germany and Italy to the Latin American guerrilla movements. On their own manpower and resources, none of these movements except the Arab terrorists could have gone very far or lasted long. But with so many screens to hide behind, the Soviet Union and its vassals, without ever showing themselves, can maintain a permanent state of insecurity in the Western countries that admirably suits Communist purposes.

The Soviet Union and Communists everywhere protest frequently and vehemently against any insinuation that they are sponsoring terrorism. Compounding the confusion is the fact that Moscow promotes as much terrorist hostility against Western Communist parties guilty of indocility toward it, notably the Italian and Spanish parties, as against the capitalist states. But the ideology motivating the Red Brigades, the Baader-Meinhof gang, and the Basque ETA is nonetheless pure Marxism-Leninism.

Because it publicly and unequivocally condemns assassination— and this is incontestable—the Italian Communist Party (PCI) is highly embarrassed when it is reminded that terrorist theory derives directly from the Communist press of the 1950s and 1960s. The basic themes of all Communist propaganda are the struggle against a bourgeois state, considered dictatorial even when its government is elected, against capitalism's "monopoly of the state," against the multinationals and "imperialism." This was demonstrated, and documented, by a leftist dissident ex-Communist named Rossana Rossanda. In her newspaper, *Il Manifesto*, Mrs. Rossanda analyzed the messages from the Red Brigades and got the impression, she said, that she was leafing through the Italian Party's "family album." As proof, she juxtaposed the terrorists' phraseology with passages from the party's theoretical magazine, *Rinascita*, published, of course, before the "historic compromise."

Alberto Ronchey, one of Italy's best political analysts, was roundly insulted by the party's leading organ, *L'Unità*.[7] Why? In a column written for the Milan *Corriere della Sera* on the causes of terrorism, Ronchey pointed out that while the Christian-Democratic Party's undeniable responsibility in the matter had been widely discussed, a balanced view would require that everyone else's be similarly exposed, including that of the Italian Communist Party. The PCI, Ronchey said, shares the blame by creating a climate that engendered terrorism. First, because from 1969 to 1976 it systematically destabilized an economy that had made a brilliant takeoff in the 1960s, leaving Italy in a badly weakened condition to face the 1973 oil crisis. Second, it orchestrated the pseudorevolutionary vandalism that rocked Italian schools and universities, producing explosive hordes of unemployed college graduates who could not find work partly because there was nothing they knew how to do. It is true that orthodox Italian teaching taught nothing except that society is rotten and must be destroyed by any available means. Communism molded a whole generation that thought anyone who was not on the side of socialism was a "lackey of the multinationals' imperialistic capitalism." The Red Brigades simply took Leninism seriously and acted on its logical conclusions, especially in destabilizing the Italian Communist

7. 10 April 1978.

Party which, they charged, had sunk under its compromise with the bourgeoisie.

On April 7, 1978, an article in *Rinascita* by the secretary of the Communist Federation of Reggio Emilia traced the historical and ideological origins of the Red Brigades. The article was entitled "Reggio, Cradle of the Red Brigades." Its author noted that more than ten of the Brigades members tried in Turin for or suspected of involvement in the kidnapping and murder of Aldo Moro came from Reggio Emilia. "Some young people from our province," he said, "played an important part in organizing the Red Brigades' historic nucleus . . . We must admit that the Red Brigadists also come from our party. They went through a process of crisis and rupture from our party's general line, history and organization."

Simply because the Red Brigades were solemnly repudiated by the PCI, it would be false to claim that communism in general has never resorted to terrorism. Here, as everywhere else in Marxist-Leninist doctrine, we must distinguish between theory and practice. The theory approves of revolutionary terror but condemns individual terrorism. In practice, however, communism has made flagrant use of individual terrorism. We have only to recall the attempt in 1925 to assassinate Bulgaria's King Boris III and his government in the cathedral in Sofia, the urban guerrilla attacks in China, Tonkin (North Vietnam), and Saigon, the kidnapping of generals Kutiepov and Miller in Paris between the wars, the murder of Trotsky, of course; there was also the assassination of Eugen Fried, the Comintern's "adviser" to the French Communist Party's secretary-general from 1932 to 1939, who was murdered by that same Comintern in Brussels in 1943; the killings of Andrés Nin and other Spanish socialists and anarchists during the Spanish Civil War; the murders of a number of former French Communist National Assembly deputies (under cover of the wartime resistance) who broke with the party over the Hitler-Stalin pact.

We also forget that the fascist-style dictatorships in Argentina and Uruguay gained power largely in reaction to years of Red terrorist destabilization in Latin America that was controlled through Cuba. Investigation of a bloody attack in Paris in 1975 showed that the Venezuelan terrorist known as Carlos had been in contact with three Cuban "diplomats" who were expelled from France. Clemens Kapuuo, President of the South-West African Democratic Alliance (Namibia), was assassinated in 1978 by an agent of SWAPO, an organization which does not hide its financial and military links with the Soviet Union and with José dos Santos, the Communist dictator of neighboring Angola. During the 1960s, Ulrike Meinhof was a member of the West German Communist Party and, with her husband, Klaus Roehl, headed the magazine *Konkret*, which was financed by clandestine funds from Prague. It is a mistake to assume that nothing in Communist ideology and practice authorizes the use of terrorism.

Italian terrorism cannot be explained by the country's economic and social problems, which were worse before 1960 than afterward, or by the series of Christian-Democratic "nongovernments," or by that dominant party's corruption. Terrorism has nothing to do with the indignation and spontaneous insurrection of the masses. Its roots are elsewhere. It is based on psychological conditioning, indoctrination, and military organization into small, secret and fanaticized groups that have no need whatsoever of support from a general population whose hostility toward them, in Italy as in Germany, is ferocious and virtually unanimous.

Terrorists in such countries are not fighting for freedom. The Communists are not fighting for the national independence of the people in the Third World or against neocolonialism. The proof of this is that they have grabbed power in countries that had long been independent and nonaligned: Ethiopia, for example, and Afghanistan. It is a lie that the Communists are fighting for democracy: the proof of this is that they have tried to overturn democratic regimes in such countries as Venezuela and Portugal, that they methodically try to topple democracy wherever it exists. It is true that in Cuba in 1959 and in Nicaragua in 1979 the *guerrilleros* overturned dictatorships, but only to replace fascist dictatorships with Communist dictatorships. I have already referred to Peru, where the country's return to democracy in 1980 immediately sparked a terrorist movement of astonishing efficiency that, curiously, had spared the military dictators in 1968–79, probably because, while ruining the country and plunging its people into poverty, the generals had taken their places in the sacred ranks of Third World Communist sympathizers.

Just as an example, what motivated the ETA's murder of the general commanding the Brunete armored division in Madrid in November 1982, *less than a week after legislative elections that gave the Socialist Party an absolute majority in the Parliament?* It could have had only one objective: to prompt the Spanish Army to try again to eliminate democracy in Spain. What other aim could the ETA have had during that period when an interim government handled only day-to-day business and the future Socialist government had not yet taken over? Had the Basque extremists merely sought greater autonomy for their region, they could have waited until the new government took power and could receive their demands; there was time enough to resume their killings if the demands were rejected. Assassinating the general at that time could only reduce the chances of favorable consideration of ETA's demands by the new Socialist Prime Minister, who would have had to show exemplary firmness in the circumstances. No, there is no plausible explanation for the crime but a desire to destroy democracy.

We note that it was a social-democratic government that was placed in difficulty by this operation even before it had time to assume the country's direction. Similarly, Socialist Bulent Ecevit was the first to be submerged by a rising tide of terrorism just after the Turkish Government abolished its state security courts in 1973 in a move toward greater democracy. Ecevit was forced to declare martial law; defeated in the next election, he gave way to a rightist government that was equally powerless to halt the terrorism and was in turn ousted in the 1980 military coup d'état, when the Turkish constitution was suspended. In short, the Turkish terrorists' first victim was democracy.

The Soviet Union gained ground in two directions there: in a key NATO country, terrorism first swept democracy away, without much reaction from the international left, which is sympathetic toward terrorists. Then, when this "strategy of tension" succeeded and a military dictatorship took over with its cortege of arbitrary rulings, torture, imprisonment and executions, the Communists could assail Turkish fascism and mobilize against it a suddenly much more superciliously legalistic international left to exploit an already deplorable situation; the aim, of course, was to embroil the West in contradictions and safely discredit a country essential to Europe's defense.

Some democracies do manage to cleanse themselves of terrorism without distorting their natures. This happened in the early 1960s in Venezuela, which foiled a Castro-inspired insurrection; West Germany succeeded in eliminating its Red Army Fraction. But these are exceptions. For it is the supreme injustice of terrorism that the political regimes it can most easily attack are those in which it is superfluous: the democracies. Terrorism is unnecessary there because it is the democracies that provide procedures for nonviolent opposition. But terrorism is easy there because the democracies are also the sole regimes that cannot, without destroying themselves, tolerate close police control and all the other repressive shortcuts that, unfortunately, are the most efficient ways to stamp out subversion. A democracy cannot employ one citizen out of five in the police, cannot close its borders, restrict travel inside the country, deport part of a city's population if necessary, keep an eye on every hotel, every building, every apartment on every floor, spend hours scrupulously searching travelers' cars and luggage— *all* travelers'. If the democracies could borrow these totalitarian tricks, they would soon enough liquidate terrorism at home and intercept aid coming to it from abroad. Nor can they consider the kind of state counterterrorism used in Argentina against the *guerrilleros* and their supposed accomplices, many of whom were innocent.

Closed to democracy, too, are the techniques of terrorism by divine right that have prevailed in Iran since 1979; according to Amnesty International, 4,568 persons were executed there up to August 31, 1982. It is a bitter irony for the French to hear the presumptive Government of Iran accuse them of complicity in alleged anti-Khomeini terrorism when it was France that sheltered

Khomeini's terrorism in 1978. Iran uses state terrorism by taking diplomats hostage, by shooting, torturing, and stoning its citizens, but it accuses the United States and Britain of violating human rights when Iranian demonstrators are arrested for identity checks in those countries—and then released.

Democracy, then, is poorly armed to defend itself against terrorism whether it originates at home or abroad. The Italian Government cannot fight on an equal footing against killers masquerading as political militants who not only use all the guaranties the Italian judicial system offers the accused, but threaten to murder judges who dare to sentence them and journalists who take the liberty of criticizing them. Nor are these empty threats, as we know. Luckily, the terrorists have failed to kill Italian democracy. Some other countries, however, have less successfully preserved their democratic ethic. Totalitarianism takes the shape of terrorism to drive the democracies toward fascism and from there to communism. Its aim: that democracy perish where it now exists and die aborning where it has not yet been reached.

I cannot help thinking again of Demosthenes's warnings to the Athenians against Philip of Macedon. "For he knows very well that even if he became master of all the rest, nothing would be solidly in his grasp as long as you are a democracy . . . First of all, then, hold him to be an enemy of our Constitution, the irreconcilable adversary of democracy; for if this conviction is not seated deep in your souls, you will not give events all the attention they demand."[8]

Terrorism in the democracies is due to the ideological madness of minorities too unrepresentative of the people to acquire political weight by existing legal means. Their crimes are crimes against humanity, just as those of the Khmer Rouge and the Nazis were, and should be treated accordingly. Democracy must consider itself at war with terrorism, exactly as it was against naziism. If it does not, then, under external assault by totalitarian Soviet imperialism and from within by the convulsive degeneracy of terrorism, the life of our small democratic *presqu'île* will be very short indeed.

8. *Oration on the State of the Chersonesus*, pars. 41 and 43.

PART FOUR

THE MENTALITY OF
DEMOCRATIC DEFEAT

18

THE FAULT LINES

THERE'S NO WINNER without a loser. And when the loser cannot blame his defeat on the inferiority of his equipment, then he has to have lost either because he used what he had badly or because of some peculiar crack in his self-confidence.

Could communism's expansionist strategy have succeeded so well unless the West was predisposed to succumb to it? For years, the overall balance of power was in the West's favor; in many respects it still is. Isn't it reasonable, then, to suspect that behind the flexibility that too often takes the form of a low bow to the East lies not so much a lack of power as a lack of foresight and a tendency to back off as the enemy advances? The way in which a civilization faces difficulty is at least half determined by its mental and moral state and only half by its objective situation. The indolence that makes the democracies so easy to fool is at least partly the product of an intellectual failure in evaluating facts, gauging threats, choosing responses, and understanding the enemy's methods; we even lack intuitive perception of what the adversary is really like. Another source of weakness: the slackness of the democratic mind's resistance to totalitarian intimidation, which easily convinces it that it has lost its right to exist.

Perhaps it's exaggerated to suggest that our democracies are foreordained suckers. What I do know is that this is how our adversaries have long seen us. I won't go back over Hitler's estimate of us except to note how contemptuously and dangerously perspicacious it was. We can refer to a much earlier appraisal, just a sample from an extensive catalogue, made by Lenin in 1921. "As a result of my observation during my emigration, I must say that the so-called cultivated elements in Western Europe and America are incapable of understanding the present state of things and the balance of forces today; these elements should be thought of as deaf and dumb and treated accordingly . . .

"On the basis of these observations and in the light of the permanent struggle for world revolution, we must resort to special maneuvers that can accelerate our victory over the capitalist countries:

"a) to *appease the deaf-mutes*, we must proclaim the (fictitious) separation of our government and its institutions from the Party and the Politburo and especially from the Comintern, stating that these organisms are independent political entities that are tolerated on the territory of the Soviet Socialist Republic. *The deaf-mutes will believe this;*

"b) call for immediate restoration of diplomatic relations with the capitalist countries on the basis of total nonintervention in their internal affairs. Again, the deaf-mutes will believe us. They will even be highly pleased and will open wide their doors, through which the Comintern's emissaries and our agents will rapidly infiltrate these countries disguised as diplomats and cultural and trade representatives."[1]

Given Soviet imperialism's success since 1921, neither Stalin nor Khruschev nor Brezhnev nor Andropov nor Konstantin Chernenko has felt the need, understandably, to make the slightest change in Lenin's diagnosis, much less alter the methods it generated. Why tinker with a technique that works? Especially when you are striving to expand a society that *doesn't* work. For this is the paradox of totalitarianism's triumphs: it's the worst system that has demoralized the best so far devised.

This is not as mysterious as it seems. Totalitarian power's sole aim is its own survival, meaning that of its Nomenklatura, and the aggrandizement of its empire. A democratic leader is forever being

1. This passage was first published in 1961 by Yuri Annenkov in *Novy Zbournal.* See B. Lazitch and M. Drachkovitch, *Lenin and the Comintern* vol. I, (Stanford, Calif: Hoover Institution Press, 1972), pp. 549–50.

called on to prove to his fellow citizens—or at least persuade them
to think—that he is procuring tangible advantages for them, something new and better every day. The democracies' long-term common interests are often effaced by inevitable short-term rivalries.
Because their system slants inward, the democracies minimize danger from outside for fear of having to turn away from their domestic preoccupations of prosperity, unity, sociability, knowledge, culture. Sensing that the totalitarian threat cannot be dispelled by
compromise, at least by the kind of compromise standard in classic
diplomacy, democrats prefer to deny the danger exists. They are
even enraged by those who dare to see and name it. Rightly valu-
ing peace above all possessions, they persuade themselves that all
they need do to defend it is to renounce its defense, for this is the
only factor they control in the situation, the only merchandise they
can offer in quantity for negotiation. It is easier to win concessions
from yourself than from an adversary.

Western diplomats seem to have forgotten long ago that the object of negotiation is to wring concessions from their opponents. In
Geneva on March 16, 1933, six weeks before Hitler came to power,
British Prime Minister Ramsay MacDonald proposed sharp cuts in
French and British armaments. A widely respected left-wing journalist, Albert Bayet, an antifascist intellectual, prolific author, and
brilliant teacher, wrote at the time that "Mr. MacDonald's central
idea seems to be that we must at all costs prevent the rearmament
of the Reich and that, to do this, the nations not disarmed by the
Versailles Treaty must agree to substantial reductions."

A few days later, after Hitler obtained plenary powers from the
Reichstag and revealed the Nazi program to the world, Bayet,
while condemning the barbaric oppression foreseeable in Germany, nevertheless declared, "On the other hand, the Chancellor's
foreign-policy statements are so conscientiously moderate that it
would be unfair not to emphasize this."

Even before Hitler got his emergency powers, Bayet had sought
to persuade hotheads against making matters worse. "If Hitlerism
wins a majority of the Prussian Diet, it seems our nationalists are
going to unleash a sudden campaign of panic throughout the coun-

try, and they expect wonders of this campaign." Luckily, he went on, the French "will soon understand that the clearer the Hitler threat becomes, the more important it will be to have cool-headed, calm, thoughtful men in France, in the government, who are determined to preserve peace . . . So even if Hitler wins his two hundred thirty seats by force, the people of France will see in this profoundly regrettable event only one more reason to vote for men of peace."[2]

Idealists whose judgment was too much a prisoner of their intellectual systems to remain lucid were not the only ones who insisted on thinking that Hitler nursed a secret desire for peace even though all his overt actions denied it. At the time, the mania also infected the political realists. In a report on December 29, 1932, André François-Poncet, France's ambassador to Berlin, declared that "the disintegration of the Hitler movement is proceeding at a rapid pace" (Hitler would come to power on January 30, 1933, with 44 percent of the popular vote); three years later he detected with pleasure "how much the Führer has evolved since the period in which he wrote *Mein Kampf,*" adding, in a dispatch dated December 21, 1936, that this was an "inevitable evolution toward moderation." Convinced of the keenness of the insights he gained in his "frequent meetings with Hitler" (Ah, the childish myth of personal contacts!), His Excellency gave his government the benefit of his reliable predictions: "The occupation of the Rhineland will probably not take place in the coming weeks," he telegraphed at the end of February 1936. Hitler marched into the Rhineland on March 7, 1936. With time, this mortifying error was forgotten; in a dispatch to the Quai d'Orsay on February 18, 1937, we find our diplomat deliciously bathed in an "impression of détente" (what? already?). What better than a nice bit of détente to set the stage for the Wehrmacht's invasion and annexation of Austria in March 1938?[3]

2. The vote in the Prussian Diet preceded that in the Reichstag. These quotes from Bayet were taken from Bertrand de Jouvenel's book *Un voyageur dans le siècle* (Paris: Laffont, 1979).
3. These extracts from diplomatic dispatches were taken from Jean-Baptiste Duroselle's *La Décadence, 1932–39*, Paris, 1979.

François-Poncet's successor in Berlin, Robert Coulondre, invented a booby trap that was to go on exploding endlessly in East-West relations after World War II: the now standard distinction between "hawks" and "doves" in the Kremlin, with the concomitant need to support the doves. Merciful as well as discerning, Coulondre sympathized with the spiritual anguish he saw in the Führer, whom he had found "extremely indecisive" at their last meeting, he informed Paris, for the poor man was torn between the "hard-liners" (Goebbels, Himmler, Hess) and the "moderates" (Göring, Funk, Lanners). The latter, the French diplomat said, leaned toward "the Reich's return to the international circle." It is to be noted that the placidity attributed to some of the Nazi leaders would have come easily enough to them considering all they had won from the democracies in the Munich agreements signed three months earlier. Coulondre's dispatch was dated December 1, 1938. Hitler occupied Czechoslovakia in March 1939. World War II began on September 3 of that year.

It may seem too casually cruel to lampoon intelligent, patriotic men whose only fault was a shortage of the ideas they needed to understand what was, to them at least, a new political phenomenon: totalitarianism. Precisely because they were intelligent, we see their errors not so much as personal lapses, but as reflections of a fundamental lack of an interpretative framework. More serious is the fact that after the war we still lacked this framework for understanding Communist totalitarianism, despite the price paid by the West for the blindness of those "pioneers of détente" who considered Munich a response to Nazi totalitarianism.

Misunderstanding of communism stamped all postwar Western statesmen. They could not grasp its particularity, the laws by which it functions. They persisted in explaining it by its leaders' psychology. Or they likened it to the forms of political power with which they were familiar: czarism, the French Revolution, "socialism minus freedom." Some simply thought of it as a preliminary to freedom. "Roosevelt never understood communism," Averell Harriman said. "He viewed it as a sort of extension of the New Deal."[4] Perhaps the veteran diplomat should have noticed this when he was in a position to do something about it.

As regards Roosevelt, we review with amazement his derision of Stalin at the Teheran conference in 1943, where he even went in for elaborate jokes that rubbed Winston Churchill's prejudices the wrong way. After three days of talks during which Stalin remained icy, the President recounted that, at last, "Stalin smiled." A great victory for the West! It became total when "Stalin broke out into a deep, heavy guffaw, and for the first time in three days I saw light. I kept it up until Stalin was laughing with me, and it was then that I called him Uncle Joe."[5] Democracy was saved.

Even among democratic statesmen who think and feel alike, good personal relations can exert only a marginal influence on conflicts of interest. They are so artificial as to become sinister when the parties' mentalities and cultures are light-years apart. Stalin must have thought that a mug who reckoned he'd scored a political point by making him laugh was not worth arguing with.

Five years later, we see Harry Truman following in his predecessor's footsteps. In 1948, talking about the Potsdam conference, he told a reporter that he knew Stalin well and that "I like old Joe"; the dictator, he maintained, was a decent sort who could not do as he wished because he was the Politburo's prisoner.[6] Here we are, back to the hawks and the doves, a notion the Soviets would always know how to play on to extort one-way concessions.

This phantasmagoria stems from the Western habit of projecting the rules and realities of democracy on to contemporary totalitarian systems. It is like a historical anachronism in which we endow ancient civilizations with our own ways of acting and thinking. The idea that conflicts in the Politburo are of the same nature as the quarrels in a majority party or within a government in the democracies is always paired with a mirage of a Soviet "moderate"

4. Harriman made the statement in a television interview in January 1982 commemorating the one hundredth anniversary of Franklin D. Roosevelt's birth. He had been American ambassador to Moscow.
5. Paul F. Boller, Jr., *Presidential Anecdotes* (Oxford University Press, 1981).
6. New York *Herald Tribune*, 13 June 1948.

who must be backed by the West in his stern and perilous fight for détente because he is trying to liberalize his own society. In other words, he is the fabulous messiah who is going to "democratize" communism. In his 1943 book of memoirs, *On Mission to Moscow*, Ambassador Joseph E. Davies waxed tender over Stalin's apostolic boldness; Stalin, he said, was running enormous risks to his own power position and his leadership of the party in trying to liberalize the Soviet constitution. Democratic leaders and diplomats were to remain obsessed by this search for a conciliatory "partner" who deserved our support, both to save him from the intractable rivals hampering him and to win from him a pro-Western agreement.

The Communists quickly spotted this blind spot in us and learned how to exploit it. Several times in his memoirs, Kissinger describes how the unctuous Anatoly F. Dobrynin, Moscow's ambassador to Washington, begged him for a concession that would save a beleaguered Brezhnev from the animosity of the Supreme Soviet. To please the Americans, Dobrynin would sometimes report, Brezhnev had to act without the knowledge of certain men in the Politburo. Would the United States let him sink? If we did not have the hearts of hyenas, didn't we owe him that little favor that would allow him to face his colleagues again without blushing too deeply? Was there no future for détente?

These ponderous confidence tricks found takers, not the least of whom was Kissinger himself. Twenty years earlier, Charles Bohlen, considered one of America's shrewdest observers of the Soviet Union, glimpsed in Georgy Malenkov, who succeeded Stalin in 1953, a partner "better disposed toward the West than the other Soviet leaders."[7] You have to be on the lookout for every sign betraying a dove, including, for example, the fact noted by Bohlen that Malenkov did not drink—not, the diplomat added with scrupulous caution, at receptions, anyway. And if it had turned out that Malenkov was a secret tippler, would that have been a signal to the West to alter its strategy? Michel Heller, who cites these statements, remarks that "Western diplomats and politicians think

7. Charles E. Bohlen, *Witness to History*, New York: Norton, 1973.

they can influence the U.S.S.R.'s policy through Soviet leaders who are well-disposed toward the West."[8]

Not only is this fiction of close personal relations incapable of changing the internal logic of a system as implacably determinist as communism, but it can turn against its naive Western inventers and be used to manipulate them. Stalin persuaded Davies that his manifestly liberal tendencies were meeting hostility in the Politburo. To consolidate his shaky position, he asked Davies to intervene with Roosevelt to wangle two extra seats for him in the UN, for the Ukraine and Byelorussia. He got his two seats. Stalin had outdone himself; he even told the American diplomat that without this small consolation he would not dare show his face again to the "voters" in the Ukraine and Byelorussia!

Behind these tragicomic stories, and they make up a pitifully long anthology, lies a whole interpretative system, the result of a convergence in our minds of Soviet disinformation and our own inveterate and, to date, uncorrected misconceptions.

These turn on three main themes, not counting variants. The first is that foreign-policy "liberals," "reformists" and "moderates" in the Communist countries are in constant danger of losing their footing and that the West must prop them up by allowing them to win victories at our expense. The second is that our economic contributions will reinforce these Communist "liberals" or, if you prefer, will prevent the "hard-liners" from attempting desperate ventures that endanger the peace. And the third is that, since we know Moscow wants peace, it is always the West that must prove its good faith by making appropriate sacrifices.

In the days that followed Brezhnev's death in November 1982, the multitude of British and American Sovietologists and political figures interviewed from morning to night by the media urged that we "seize the opportunity" to give the Soviet Union proof of our goodwill. Most of them specifically recommended two measures: that the Americans immediately lift their embargo on technological transfers to the U.S.S.R., even those with possible military applications (this was done at once), and that we postpone for one

8. "La désinformation . . ."

year the deployment of the Euromissiles that were to comprise Western Europe's counterweight to the intermediate-range SS-20s Russia had already positioned on its Western frontiers.

Just what was this "opportunity" to be seized? The death of one leader and his replacement by another do not necessarily mean the country's policy will change. Only the new man's actions can show if he has taken a different tack. In the seven years preceding Brezhnev's death, it was Soviet foreign policy that was aggressive, not the West's. So it was up to Moscow to take the first step, not the West. There was no sign in Andropov's past of liberalism or pacifism. Then why offer him unilateral concessions before he had given the slightest indication of his goodwill or uttered a single word that sounded conciliatory?[9]

Why? Because, deep down, whatever they may say and write to the contrary, Westerners accept the Soviet Union's idea of them; they very nearly agree that they are at fault for the collapse of détente. We see ourselves through Moscow's eyes, we accept the myth of the Communists' desire for peace and acknowledge that it is we who are guilty of aggressivity endangering the world's stability. It is, consequently, our duty to take the initiative, even to disarm ourselves unilaterally to tranquilize what is really an involuntary Soviet impulse toward conquest. At best, we place East and West on the same plane. At worst, we believe that expansionism and the threat of war would vanish from the earth if the West spontaneously despoiled itself of its means of defense and refrained from contesting anything the Communists do. Sometimes we democrats—some of us, at least those who follow this line of reasoning to its extreme—think we are our own, and only, worst enemy.

When we read what some of the experts, especially in West Germany, say about strategic and nuclear problems, we get the impression that in their minds the Soviet military threat is a hypothetical X, a sort of unknowable, Kantian "thing in itself"; they seem to believe that its existence, or at least its metaphysical possibility, must be granted to the fearful to keep their delirium in check until

9. For further discussion of Western behavior during periods of Communist succession, see Chapter 23.

their ghosts can be gently exorcised. Gradually, these "experts" guide their readers toward a terrain where the Soviet threat dissolves; in its place, the public is treated to an undecipherable analysis of Allied misunderstandings. When you have eliminated the ultimate purpose of security, discussions on how to achieve it become ridiculous and the friction the question generates appears childish. In *Foreign Affairs* (Winter 1981/82), Christoph Bertram, director of the London International Institute for Strategic Studies, discoursed on the disarray among European NATO members before and after they decided to allow the stationing of new missiles on their soil. Not for one moment did they remember the virulent campaign of intimidation waged by the Soviets to block this modernization of NATO forces; the campaign, helped along, as usual, by accomplices in the West, had been going on for months and had included threatening letters of unprecedented bluntness from Moscow to each of the governments concerned. Yet without this light on the facts, all we can see are pitiful gesticulations and incomprehensible inconsistencies, mostly, of course, bearing on American clumsiness in dealing with Europe.[10]

Much the same situation prevails in regard to transfers of militarily useful technology to the Soviet Union; for that matter, just giving its industry a boost indirectly frees funds for increasing Soviet military strength. It is one thing for European and American firms to oppose restrictions on *open* transfers of technology. But it is strange to see them resisting attempts to balk *hidden* transfers effected through industrial espionage and technological pillage. In November 1982, a report (one of the many) by a United States Senate subcommittee revealed how damaging these have been to the West and, most significant, how much Soviet weaponry has profited from it, especially in the areas of electronics and lasers. This allows the Soviet Union, trailing the Americans, Europeans, and Japanese in technology, to bridge much of the gap with a minimum of risk, investment and research by using the world's oldest method: theft.

Information about this type of warfare (there is no other word

10. C. Bertram, "Implications of Theater Nuclear Weapons in Europe."

for it) is not confined to reports to legislatures; the most respected and widely read newspapers and magazines on both sides of the Atlantic have reported fully and accurately on the problem. So the danger—no, the defeat—has been solidly documented and attested. But when the United States Government timidly asked American universities early in 1982 to curtail visits by Soviet "scientific missions" to their research laboratories or at least to prevent KGB "scientists," "students" and "engineers" from circulating unsupervised through their buildings, the American scientific community indignantly refused. The same reception was given a request that, in certain cases, scientists defer publication of discoveries with possible military applications. It did the government no good to point out that the country was hemorrhaging technology, that almost all Soviet military development in recent years has been based on American research. To the scientists, it is the protective measures against pillage that violate "the spirit of détente," not the thefts themselves.

Why has détente failed? Because to Westerners it meant the Soviets had suspended their aggressiveness, while to the Soviets it meant that the West had suspended all reaction to that aggressiveness. But how could we Westerners have been so willfully blind to Soviet expansionism? Because all our notions about Soviet communism rest on the same supposition: that everything will straighten itself out. We think Russian communism is running into internal and external obstacles that will force moderation on it. What we must do, so goes the thinking, is to help this process along by making all necessary *preliminary* concessions to soften Soviet aggressiveness.

This notion forms the core of most theories about Soviet communism. It sterilizes them against political action, even when some of their components are correct. Here is a very incomplete catalogue of these soothing theories:

1. The Russians "respect the status quo." Therefore, we should understand that when they invade Hungary or Czechoslovakia they are operating within their zone. This is a false theory, one we should not, in any case, expect the Soviets to adhere to out of a

sense of honor. Since 1975, the Russians have thrust out of their "zone" into Africa, Southeast Asia, the Arabian Peninsula, Afghanistan.

2. Economic failure in the Soviet Union has obliged Moscow to abandon any overly ambitious foreign policy in favor of raising its people's standard of living. By helping to usher it into the consumer age, the West would foster a softer Soviet policy. It is not much use insisting on the fact that it was with our economic aid that Soviet imperialism reached global dimensions.

3. Communism's moral and ideological bankruptcy will finally sour people on it. In 1970, Nixon's national security adviser, Zbigniew Brzezinski, signed an article in *The New Leader* entitled "Communism Is Dead." He was forgetting that loss of moral prestige does not prevent the Communists from fooling people or extending their power.

4. The growth of national communism will limit the Soviet's worldwide influence. Titoism will become the rule. In 1975, after the fall of Saigon, the New York *Times* predicted that the Vietnamese Communists would soon be anti-Soviet.

5. The two systems will converge. In both societies, the same economic realities will place the same levers of command in the hands of the same race of technocrats and managers. This will generate a process of unification of the two systems. Supporters of this theory forget the absolute priority given to politics and ideology in the Soviet Union.

6. East-West trade will civilize communism. This is the principle that inspired the first massive transfusion of Western aid to the Soviet Union after 1922. After several years of Western liberality, what really happened was the forced collectivization of the land, extermination of the peasants, famine, purges and the Great Terror of the 1930s.

7. The conflict between China and the Soviet Union will replace that between the democracies and Soviet totalitarianism. Experience has shown, however, that the two conflicts are compatible and that the two totalitarian regimes can reduce tension between them.

8. Eurocommunism marks the end of the World Communist Church and constitutes a challenge to the U.S.S.R. No comment.

9. Soviet Moslems represent an explosive force within the Communist system. Moscow will have to compromise with the Islamic countries in the Near East so as not to touch off that explosion. This overlooks a better way to tranquilize these Islamic neighbors: invade them.

10. Its very expansionism is opening the Soviet Union to danger. The Russians are bogged down in Africa. Afghanistan has been no joyride for them. They have had their failures too: Egypt, Somalia. In fact, the Russians left Somalia voluntarily in favor of a more powerful client, Ethiopia. And Egypt had never been a Communist state. Becoming a satellite is very different from merely having Soviet advisers. Egypt showed its Soviet advisers the door when they failed to secure a victory for it in its war against Israel. True, imperialism secretes its own problems. Murderers often have serious difficulties. This never revives their victims.

11. The Russians invaded Afghanistan "out of weakness." This is the comic version of the preceding theory. Pity the poor Russians! The Afghans must dance for joy when they think of the moral anguish that triggered the Soviet offensive.

12. If we remain firm, we will "revive the cold war." As though this were up to us. The only choice we have is whether to let it widen. When the Communists invaded South Korea, the UN not only condemned the aggressors but sent troops to fight them. In 1956, for the invasion of Hungary the UN condemned the aggressor—and set up a committee of inquiry. Czechoslovakia, in 1968, didn't even rate a committee. And the Russians were admitted to the Olympic Games in Mexico. In the light of events between 1975 and 1985, what has its growing servility brought the West?

None of these twelve illusions is totally unfounded. Each rests on a partially accurate perception of the facts. It is our *exploitation* of the facts that is deficient. Soviet weaknesses do indeed exist, and so do Soviet failures, mistakes and rashness. But, I repeat, while the U.S.S.R. exploits weakness of the democracies, Western leaders avoid exploiting Communist failures. Worse still, they consider it their duty to help Moscow surmount these failures. The Soviets have never agreed to conduct both their foreign policy and ours, to defend their own interests and ours. It is not surprising, then, that a concept of détente that relied on such Soviet devotion went bankrupt. Even this may be doing it too much honor: to say a concept went bankrupt implies that it had a chance to succeed.

Two characteristics unite the body of prejudices and behavior patterns I have described: they have a long history, and they are common to both the right and the left. Just after World War I, and thus long before we made our analytical errors during and after the Second World War, Fridtjof Nansen, a Norwegian who knew Soviet Russia well and who was even named an honorary member of the Moscow Soviet for his immense services to the starving Russian people, concluded that Lenin would restore a free market and return to capitalistic trading practices. He let himself be deceived by the appearances of the NEP (New Economic Policy), which, to a Lenin with his back to the wall, was designed to extort capital and technical assistance from the West. The British Prime Minister then, David Lloyd George, made the same mistake: on February 10, 1922, he prophesied that the West could save Russia through trade because, he believed, trade has a moderating influence. He was convinced trade would end the "ferocity, rapine, and brutality" of bolshevism more surely than any other method.

Did the Stalinist hell of the thirties temper these opinions? Not in the least. In 1945, Sir Bernard Pares, the most eminent of the day's Sovietologists, serenely decreed that since 1921 Russia had been governed by Communists who no longer practiced communism.[11] We must not forget that this sort of nonsense nourished the thinking of statesmen since it emanated from experts who frequently acted as their advisers. All aside from Western Communists and agents of influence operating in full knowledge of what they were doing, other Western leaders, conservative and Christian-Democrat, centrists and socialists, Republicans and Democrats in the United States, have all more or less followed the same long-term, overall foreign policy toward communism. Or, perhaps

11. Sir Bernard Pares, *Russia and the Peace* (London, 1945).

it is the policies that lead the politicians. Occasionally, a leader will swim against the tide: a Reagan or a Thatcher among the conservatives, a Mitterrand or a Craxi among the socialists. What is remarkable is that their statements pass for "tough." Yet all they are usually doing is demanding the minimum a political leader must insist on or quit the game. For example, the speech about Euromissiles that Mitterrand made before the Bundestag on January 20, 1983, during an official visit to West Germany, was rightly considered firm and courageous; in fact, it was chiefly an exhortation to others, since none of the Euromissiles were to be stationed in France. And what was it the French President said? Simply that Western Europe should not reject its new armaments program before negotiations with the Russians produced a corresponding reduction in the Soviet arsenal. In other words, Mitterrand advised the West not to throw away all its bargaining counters before discussions even began. Of what was he reminding us but the rudiments of diplomacy?

That we had so forgotten these simple, commonsensical rudiments that we viewed Mitterrand's speech as an exceptionally vigorous policy statement underlines how timid our standards have become. When what should be our normal resolve echoes like an isolated exploit, it can only mean that we have become so accustomed to surrender that it is now the norm.

19

WHERE COWARDICE BEGAN: THE BERLIN WALL

To JUSTIFY the refinements of inertia that Western diplomacy devised after the invasion of Afghanistan and the return to totalitarian normalcy in Poland, our governments have been prodigal with ingenious excuses. Their lengthening catalogue includes an imaginary agreement at Yalta to share influence over the world and oaths of faith in the eternal fruitfulness of détente—not to mention the more realistic, if less glorious, admission of our military inferiority, recently affirmed and accepted with Christian humility. "The world now, at this century's end, is no longer that of American hegemony, nor that of two power blocs"—so the choir sings between each verse of the psalm in the *Prayers for Deliverance from Enemies.* "Remove from us, O Lord, the chalice of the blocs, turn away the dagger of the cold war and sprinkle us with the dew of North-South relations, or East-South or East-North or East-East or West-West, no matter which, but deliver us from East-West relations." For could we not find peace simply by erasing them from our minds?

The West's baffled impotence in the face of insolent Soviet aggressiveness is frequently blamed on new factors that allegedly have altered the state of the world since around 1970 and which we would be mad not to reckon with.

That there have been changes is undeniable. Weren't they inevitable? A more interesting question is whether they have been profitable or harmful to us. Many Western leaders and former leaders protest loudly that their policy was judicious and that they could not reasonably follow any other in attempting to reinforce the democracies' security. At the same time, with curious logic they point to the results of that policy to warn us that the counteroffensives and reprisals that were once available to us are no longer within our reach.

Our diplomats were supposed to make the democracies less and less vulnerable in an increasingly safe and stable world. Then how the devil could they have weakened us so? Does prudence henceforth dictate that we heed their advice and bow ever lower before the constantly rising tide of Communist violence? This is strange fruit to harvest from such long-cultivated diplomatic wisdom, so self-satisfied, so disdainful of political adventurism and the "cold war." If this is how things stand, then détente was, at the very least, a miscalculation. Yet I would almost be reassured to think our present weakness is simply a result of faulty reckoning. It would be no more, in that case, than the failure of a treatment based on a mistaken diagnosis that can be rationally reviewed and, unless it is already too late, corrected if necessary.

There is certainly nothing absurd or dishonorable in hoping that a process of reciprocal concessions and heightened cooperation might persuade the Soviet Union to moderate its policy and, for a while, respect the existing balance of power. But here is where the enigma begins: despite ready proof that the democracies' calculations have rebounded against them and that the conquest-bent Soviets have deceived them only so they could gain ground faster, the West still chooses to shut its eyes to its losses from a deal that has been so manifestly ruinous to them. This deliberate blindness, especially on the part of West Germany, has lasted well beyond the moment when it became clear that Western concessions were stiffening, not softening, Soviet policy. We may very well wonder, then, if détente really was a failure or if we were in fact seeking just that state of impotence into which it plunged us. Didn't we secretly hope to be forever spared the painful choice between resignation and firmness simply by stripping ourselves of the means to be firm? Was it the West's furtive wish to amputate its own decision-making faculty so as to avoid having to make any more decisions? And to excise its power of resistance in order not to feel humiliated by quitting when it could still resist? Perhaps this hard-won weakness has its compensation in the bitter but liberating quietude of irresponsibility.

If such notions were even remotely plausible, we would have to talk not of the failure of détente for the West but of its success as an honorable subterfuge for achieving weakness. An outlandish supposition, this, risky, futile, abhorrent—yet it sometimes haunts a mind buffeted by so many surrenders for which there seems no rational explanation.

The truth is that there was a time when the democracies could have stood firm at no risk to themselves, but they did not want to try. The intellectual roots of this litany of cowardice are sunk deep in the past.

If we could cite only one incident among the many available, the year 1961 is worth a connoisseur's attention, so touching was the West's zeal then to crawl to new heights of discomfiture in the sensational episode of the Berlin wall. This was a very mild Soviet display of force, since the glaring absence of Allied resistance made the use of force by the Communists superfluous. We'd be tempted to use the word "swindle" if it were not so inappropriate to a victim who voluntarily despoils himself of his wealth, leaving the crook nothing more to do than to modestly gather it up. It was a perfect occasion for black comedy, but it turned into farce instead; so eager was the West to open itself to ridicule that, bitterly noted Willy Brandt, then the mayor of West Berlin and future West German Chancellor, "the whole East, from Pankow to Vladivostok, burst out laughing."

Construction of the Berlin wall was a first version for chamber orchestra of the future symphony of détente, the glory of the succeeding decade. In the archeology of submission, it is comparable to those small Romanesque churches whose floor plans served as models for the great cathedrals that replaced them but which often reserve richer satisfactions for lovers of architecture. The summer of 1961 gives us a concise preview of that conjugation of factors which, for twenty years and more, would mold both the West's chronically anemic diplomacy and an increasingly bold Soviet policy.

The first characteristic of the 1961 crisis was destined for a brilliant future: it originated in a failure of communism and ended by weakening the democracies. The Communists built the wall to prevent East Germans from emigrating to the West via Berlin, the only point of free access between the two Europes. If so many East Germans were leaving, it was because of the dismal showing of the socialist economic system, already demonstrated by the 1953 workers' riots in East Berlin and more recently deepened by massive land collectivization. History shows that collectivization of land has always and everywhere been one of the primary tools of totalitarian subjugation—and one that ineluctably impoverishes farmers. So, from 1960 on, hundreds of thousands of people fled to the West, almost all of them through Berlin. Those who came were not just executives, workers, and technicians but also farmers from the rich soil of Mecklenburg who had no appetite for a new kind of servitude to replace what they had known under Hitler. Between January and June 1961, the exodus increased to a rate of nearly fifty thousand a month, then, in July and August, to fifty thousand a week. Particularly humiliating for the Communists was the fact that nearly half the emigrants were under twenty-five. The young were fleeing socialism, just as it had been the young who died in the front line of the proletarian rebellion against socialism in Budapest in 1956. In 1961, Communist East Germany was losing face along with the best part of its work force. The experience demonstrated, or, rather, confirmed, with terrible clarity that when the people in a socialist society have a choice, it's socialism they reject.

But, by a switch in roles that is still highly intriguing even if it has become familiar to us through repetition since World War II, it was not the Communists who had to support the consequences of their failure, but the West. As a rule, Westerners not only do not know about the weaknesses and internal difficulties of the Communist dictatorships and do not wish to exploit them, but they emerge diminished from most of the crises that should cost the Soviet Union dear. So the Soviet sphere of influence was enlarged and reinforced by the events of 1961, while the West's was shrunken and weakened. The sole difference between this misadventure and that of détente is that in 1961 the West merely went along with the Communist power play, but at least it did not add insult to injury by supplying economic and technological assistance as well.

A second characteristic of the Berlin wall episode, as during the invasion of Afghanistan eighteen years later, was the inaccuracy, indeed, the lack of Western leaders' forecasts and analyses. They were unable to interpret clear signals, to perceive obvious preparations. The hemorrhage that was emptying East Germany of its life's blood had become intolerably heavy for the Pankow regime and for Moscow. If the West's leaders had done their job, they would have considered every possible Communist move and every possible Western countermove. Early in August, for example, Brandt asserted that the Russians would never sacrifice the Berlin "contact point" between the two Germanies. And why not? Was it doing his job for Brandt to rule out this possibility in advance? Hans Kroll, the West German ambassador to Moscow, who was recalled to Bonn for consultation by Chancellor Konrad Adenauer, guaranteed the Soviets' "desire for peace." French Foreign Minister Maurice Couve de Murville, with his unique mixture of pretentious solemnity and political myopia, had long assured his ambassador in Bonn, François Seydoux, that the Berlin crisis was "slow-burning" and that "nothing was going to happen."

Similarly, in December 1979, while Soviet divisions were massing on the Afghan frontier, after the exasperated men in the Kremlin had been openly and vainly trying for a year and a half to anchor a satellite regime in Kabul, most Western heads of state and of government pooh-poohed the possibility of an invasion. When it did happen, they were greatly astonished and said so ingenuously, except for those who, like Valéry Giscard d'Estaing, were rendered speechless with surprise for weeks afterward.

Their surprise—the third Western characteristic—was equally total on August 13, 1961, when the Communists built the notorious wall in a single night. Not a single high-level Western diplomat in Germany was instructed to or thought it necessary to postpone his vacation. Western heads of state, prime ministers and foreign ministers, meanwhile, were relaxing in sylvan and marine retreats, demonstrating to posterity their love of nature, if not their political perspicacity. Adenauer was secluded on the shore of Lake Como. De Gaulle was meditating at his home in Colombey-les-Deux-Eglises, convinced the crisis was too trivial to warrant his return to Paris. British Prime Minister Harold Macmillan was believed to be grouse-shooting in Scotland—or was that his Foreign Secretary, Lord Home? French Prime Minister Michel Debré was honoring France's woods and ponds with his presence, like Couve de Murville, like the Quai d'Orsay's Political Affairs Officer, Eric de Carbonnel. Brandt was aboard a train heading toward the Mediterranean when he was hauled off at a middle-of-the-night stop and flown, frantic, back to his Berlin office.

I remember very well that August 13, 1961, was a Sunday, part of a long Assumption Day weekend. Twenty-five years earlier, Hitler had formulated a law that still held true: if you want to present the democracies with a fait accompli, do it over a weekend. But what justification can there be for the fact that there was no alarm system in place, no procedure for swift communication and emergency consultation? In diplomacy, improvidence is the child of incompetence. In private industry—on a newspaper, say—such negligence would be called a professional boner. But in public service, professional flubs are called prudence, circumspection, composure, the art of reducing tension. American Secretary of State Dean Rusk disappeared and only reappeared to watch a baseball game. President Kennedy was aboard his yacht off Hyannis Port; it was not until nearly noon, hours after the event, that a minor White House staffer got a radio message through suggesting that he come back to earth at once. Reading the dispatches ashore, Kennedy noticed that there was no question of the Communists blocking communications between West Berlin and the rest of West Germany. Reassured, he decided that the incident was not worth cutting short his stay at Hyannis Port. As far as he was concerned, he declared some days later, the crisis was over.[1]

And this is a fourth trait. We would detect it again in 1981, when

1. I have relied heavily here on the excellent book by Curtis Cate, *The Ides of August* (New York: McEvans, 1978), which describes these events almost minute by minute.

martial law was declared in Poland. In 1961, the Allies had been waiting a long time for a new increase in tension in Berlin, but they expected it to take the same form as the 1948 Berlin blockade. When the Soviets failed to act according to expectations, the West assumed that nothing had happened. In the more recent Polish events, the West had been waiting since the summer of 1980 for the only counterattack they could imagine against the Solidarity trade union in Poland: an invasion by Soviet tanks like the invasions of Prague in 1968 and of Budapest in 1956. But the Soviets had sought, and found, something new. In 1961, too, they had invented a new way to staunch the exodus of East Germans to West Germany, not by isolating all of Berlin from the West, a repetition of the 1948 blockade that the Allies would not have tolerated, but by cutting the city in two, which caught the West napping. In both cases, Berlin in 1961 and Warsaw in 1981, some Western governments were so willing to be tricked that they pretended they were not dealing with Soviet maneuvers, that only the Germans and the Poles, respectively, were to blame.

We could extend this catalogue of fundamental traits of Western behavior. It leads us to suspect a sort of preestablished harmony, of providential complementarity between Soviet aggressiveness and the Western will to capitulate. Even in 1961, the advisers who most importuned and irritated Western heads of government were the ones who advised firmness. Rusk devised a way of pleasing Kennedy by finding a line of reasoning that was to become so classic that it would be badly overworked later on: that resistance to an assailant is dangerous because he may become violent. In other words, opposing an aggressor may make him aggressive!

This was the rule on which all Western diplomacy was to be based. It goes without saying that once a Soviet power play has succeeded and Western resignation is well established, the democracies put out communiqués loudly and categorically condemning Communist aggression. The ritual was duly observed in 1961. They even mumbled some vague threats of trade embargoes, mere impotent yelping; the same warm breaths would again caress Soviet ears after the occupation of Afghanistan and after the military crackdown in Poland.

A few days after the Berlin wall went up, General de Gaulle, back in Paris at last, drew from the events the lesson he thought most judicious, namely that we had to negotiate as soon as possible with the Russians in order to "reduce tensions." As though it was the West that had created the tensions! He had just invented the principle of détente: as soon as the adversary violently takes something from you, try immediately to find the concessions you can make to convince him that you were not at all hurt by the damage he has inflicted on you and that you harbor no grudges. When De Gaulle made an official visit to West Germany in September 1962, he ostentatiously avoided West Berlin. For God's sake, don't irritate them!

Even during the summer of the wall, the world theater of festivities, propaganda and symbols remained open, to the Communists' great joy. In July 1961, with the fever rising daily in Berlin, the British Government saw no reason to postpone a tour of Britain by Soviet cosmonaut Yury Gagarin, who was hailed as a hero, lunched with the Queen and was acclaimed by schoolchildren. The courtesy heralded similar Western gestures in 1980, notably by the French, who insisted on participating in the Moscow Olympics after the invasion of Afghanistan. We Western democrats are crackerjack at protecting not only the interests but the pride of totalitarian rulers. Indeed, the Kremlin counts on our passivity; in 1961, several of its diplomats, including its ambassador in Washington, brazenly informed American newsmen of the lack of Allied reaction to the wall.[2]

It can be correctly pointed out that in 1962 the Soviets bet wrong on Western apathy when they stationed offensive missiles in Cuba. Washington's reaction was clear and vigorous, the Soviets retreated, dismantling their missiles and shipping them home. But why pin a heroic label on an elementary act of American self-

2. Articles on July 16, 1961, by Warren Rogers in the New York *Herald Tribune* and James Reston in the New York *Times* were based on interviews with the Soviet envoy.

defense? Must we see superhuman merit in a President who objected to installation of a nuclear arsenal ninety miles off the coast of the United States, or shouldn't we really conclude that a President who consented to the Soviet move would have been a bumbler or a traitor? For the Western spirit of resignation can also be measured by the ease with which we see our rare gestures of legitimate self-defense as epochal.

As for the observation, often repeated since then, that General de Gaulle, despite his customary anti-Americanism, took America's side and assured Kennedy of France's support in the Cuban missile affair, it too shows the modesty of Western standards in defining loyalty to an alliance. Since, until the rules are changed, an alliance consists in taking the ally's part rather than siding with the enemy attacking him, why was it so admirable that De Gaulle refrained from applauding Moscow's gambit? The least he could do was to lend his support, which was purely verbal anyway, to America's defensive posture. What is surprising is that we boast of it. True, had the Cuban missile crisis happened fifteen or twenty years later, it's to be feared that instead of siding with the United States the Europeans would have urged it to give in to the Soviets so as not to "compromise détente." But some heights of self-sacrifice in the face of aggression are not to be reached at the first try. It takes training.

On the other hand, it is arguable that the missile crisis, which brought the world, say the experts, to the brink of nuclear war, might not have happened at all if the Allies, led by the United States, had not surrendered in East Berlin the year before and so convinced the Soviet Union that they no longer even had the energy to claim their rights or manifest their instinct of self-preservation.

For the worst of it, in the tragedy of the wall, is that we could not use any of the specious reasons we usually drag up to excuse our nonchalance toward acts of Communist imperialism. Under the terms of the quadripartite agreement governing Berlin, all four occupying powers were responsible for the *entire* city; the Soviet occupation zone no more belonged to the Russians than the French zone did to France or the American zone to the United States. East Berlin was never included in the Soviet "sphere" by any Yalta agreement, not even a fictitious one. The demarcation line between East and West Berlin was not a frontier between two states. Forcibly isolating one sector of the city, therefore, was a treaty violation by one of the occupants. Which meant that an Allied military reaction would have raised none of the problems that stopped us from intervening in Hungary five years earlier and which would also apply to other aggressions committed elsewhere later. Moreover, we now know that if the West had sent a dozen tanks to disperse the East German soldiers building the "wall of shame" (under a rain of insults from their fellow Germans), who were not even armed, these masons in uniform would have scattered. They had been ordered to do so by their Soviet masters had such an eventuality arisen.

This needless capitulation by the West also shows the inanity of trying to distinguish between the "cold war" and "détente." The notion of a "cold war," appeals against the danger of "reviving the cold war," were weapons brandished after the Afghanistan invasion by those determined to prolong Soviet-style détente. How could the democracies be less active and more submissive, more passively conciliatory, than they were in Berlin in 1961, when, according to the theoreticians in international relations, the cold war was at its peak?

For the occasion, Kennedy even invented what would become the prime stratagem for dressing up our retreats in the era of détente: verbal resistance after the situation had become irreversible, condemnation as "unacceptable" of what we had already rushed to accept. In June 1963, standing before the wall, he uttered his famous *"Ich bin ein Berliner."* It is edifying that, after our deliberate capitulation, the detail that history chose to remember was the American President's pompous proclamation that "I am a Berliner"—one who had allowed the Communists to amputate part of Berlin to satisfy their imperial needs. It had a fine sound, this hollow phrase, worthy of the events that produced it and a fitting postscript to the sad farce of the Berlin wall.

In war, Sallust said, it is intelligence that counts most.[3] In the 1961 confrontation and most of the others before and since, the Soviets have simply shown more intelligence than the West. Working to a blueprint they were often to use later on, they took the initiative, jostled the democracies in the correct expectation that they would be paralyzed by the divisions in their own ranks; Moscow read things correctly, moved fast, and won without a fight. What better proof of higher intelligence is there, and what greater delight, than to win a battle you never even had to wage? It's no wonder the totalitarians showed their jubilation so immodestly when it was all over; we can understand the indecency with which, in 1971, the German and Russian Communists publicly celebrated the tenth anniversary of the building of the wall, that triumph of socialism. They had cause for celebration. For they had defied what was then an unfavorable military balance and ostentatiously trampled formal treaties underfoot with impunity; what's more, they had the satisfaction of seeing the democracies conclude that nothing was deeper than the Soviet desire for peace and nothing more urgent than to embark on a process of détente that was in all particulars advantageous to communism. Didn't this give them the right to feel superior to the adversaries they had tricked and to savor that superiority? This is why I do not put much stock in the "inferiority feelings" attributed to the Soviets by zealots of détente at any price, who are forever anxious to "reassure" Moscow with proofs of their goodwill. On the contrary, I think that over the years the Soviet Union has developed an enormous feeling of superiority over the West that has grown with every new confirmation of how easy it is for it to fool us.

After years of nourishing the illusion that they were waging a so-called cold war against the Soviets while maintaining a concessionary policy that, well before the 1970s, already prefigured détente, the democracies finally fell victims to a complementary illusion: that they actually *were* in a period of détente. They did not realize that this was really the Soviets' cold war against them.

3. *"Compertum est in bello pluramum ingenium posse"* (*The Cataline Conspiracy* 2).

20

THE PHONY "COLD WAR"

DURING THE "détente" era, which took its name officially with Brandt's *Ostpolitik* on the eve of the 1970s but of which De Gaulle was unquestionably the precursor in the middle 1960s, a favorite refrain of politicians, analysts, and journalists concerned the danger of "reviving the cold war." Manifesting the slightest alarm over creeping Soviet expansionism in Africa and Asia or over the Communists' patent violations of their treaties or voicing suspicion about the sponsorship of terrorist destabilization efforts was to descend to the ranks of "cold-war fanatics" whose obsolete prejudices had not yet melted under the warm sun of détente.

The mystery about this distinction between cold war and détente stems from the fact that, like so many inherited ideas in history, it substitutes words for a real situation with which they have little connection. Constant repetition of these words creates a state of public opinion that is generally impervious to reminders of the facts. From the Soviet point of view, there has been neither détente nor cold war. Moscow's policy during both periods was one of consolidation of its gains and of diplomatic and military expansion. It used the same method, counting almost always on Western passivity, in making its power plays; it brought the same art to dividing the democracies and, while destabilizing them from within, extorting territorial, military and economic concessions in exchange for promises of "peace" it never kept.

That this system earned the Soviets their greatest gains during the so-called détente period seems indisputable. But they viewed the period more as a development of the preceding one rather than a reversal of it. And when I say that to see this we must adopt the Soviets' viewpoint, I do not mean that we should believe what they say in international conferences, as Western diplomats usually do, but that we should observe what they do, analyze the victories and reversals that fall to them, and compare this list with the West's successes and failures.

Although it seems superfluous, we ought nevertheless to start by remembering—since the most elementary facts are almost always overlooked in this bizarre situation—that if there has been a cold war, it was initiated by the Soviets. We must really make the effort to recall or to ascertain that in 1947, after considerably expanding the Sovietization of Eastern and Central Europe and ringing down the Iron Curtain between the (henceforth) "two" Europes, Stalin ordered Western Communist parties, especially the Italian and French parties, which had abandoned their participation in coalition governments, to embark on a policy of destructive, even insurrectional, opposition. He founded the Comintern in September 1947 and inaugurated a foreign policy of conquest and belligerency. In the three years that followed, he engineered the Soviets' Berlin blockade and the invasion of South Korea by Communist North Korea.

The West went on the defensive against both these thrusts, and it was these straightforwardly defensive actions that, in a preposterous spirit of self-mortification, we then began to label as "cold-war behavior." America's airlift between West Germany and Berlin broke the blockade, but there were no reprisals to make the Soviets pay for their treaty violation. Having failed to annex Berlin to East Germany by force, Moscow simply reverted to its previous position. This is usually what happens in East-West relations: when the Soviet Union wins, it enlarges its sphere of influence; when it loses, it returns to the position it occupied before launching its attack. But it almost never retreats. To be sure, there have been a few exceptions to that rule—Stalin's loss of Iran in 1946, for example. But, in general, the U.S.S.R. is never punished for having attacked and lost. This principle alone explains why it cannot help but advance, which is what it has been doing since 1945.

The same pattern applied to the Korean War: the Communists invaded, provoked armed conflict, ravaged a country, caused the deaths of thousands of people, failed to achieve their ends, and withdrew to their previous bases without losing an inch of their terrain. American doctrine at the time was summed up in the notion of *containment* and not in the very descriptively named idea of *rollback* that was to sound so exaggeratedly bellicose to partisans of détente twenty years later. Theoretically, as far as the Kremlin is concerned, cold war is synonymous with containment, whereas détente translates into Western appeasement, relaxation of tensions, in short, nonresistance by the democracies. In practice, the Soviet Union has always arranged either to conserve its gains or to advance, but it can never be forced to retreat.

From the start, then, the confrontation between the Soviet Union and the West resembled a football game in which one of the two teams, the West, disqualified itself from going beyond the fifty-yard line. The best the West can do in such a contest is to tie, which, for the Soviets, is the worst possible score. Their only choice is between deadlock and victory, the West's between deadlock and defeat. Even then, the rule really applies only to the "cold war"; in the period of détente, some Westerners would see détente as too favorable to the West and seeking a tie score as provocation by the democracies.

The Vietnamese War was no exception to the rule. All the United States was trying to do there was to prevent the North Vietnamese Communists from taking over South Vietnam in violation of the 1954 Geneva agreement guaranteeing each country's independence. As always, the war began with a Communist attack; South Vietnam had not the slightest intention of invading the north, nor the Americans of helping it do so. The political topography and legal framework in Vietnam were exactly like those of the two Koreas in 1950, and the warmonger was on the same side. America's perseverance in trying to defend the status quo in Indochina, its obstinacy in struggling to achieve a tie score that finally eluded it, were enough to pin an ineradicable imperialist label on it in the world's eyes. By this standard, then, imperialism consists of opposing attempts by enemy armies, if they are Communist armies, from subjugating peoples who want no part of communism, as the South Koreans and South Vietnamese demonstrated when their countries were invaded from the north. There was a time when you were an imperialist if you invaded an alien territory and imposed on independent peoples an authority they rejected. Today you are an imperialist if you oppose such aggression, if you are a democracy and the invader is Communist.

At no time during the cold war, as we know, did the democracies try to exploit the internal illnesses of the Soviet system, certainly not the uprisings of the subjugated people in East Berlin in 1953 and Budapest in 1956. In what way were Eisenhower's administration (including Secretary of State John Foster Dulles, who was called "the traveling salesman of anticommunism") or the strongly anti-Communist governments of the French Fourth Republic or the Conservative governments of Churchill and Anthony Eden in Britain more intransigent than the zealots of détente in the 1970s? I see only one difference between them: the former refrained from making capital of the totalitarian empire's internal problems; the moderns have gone so far as to help the empire's masters surmount those problems by overwhelming them with money, food and understanding.[1]

Yet from the beginning of the cold war the West got into the habit of calling its deadlocks and even its defeats victories. Let's return to the Berlin wall briefly. This was a test of strength that the West lost. Instead of reacting, the democracies used all their talent in finding reasons to avoid reaction. The Soviets achieved their objectives with no effort, no concessions; they had no sanctions to support. Despite this inglorious surrender, the democracies all but congratulated themselves on how well the incident turned out: the Red Army didn't occupy all of Berlin, did it? It did not cut the city off from the rest of West Germany. This kind of rarified reasoning could transform the Franco-Prussian War into a

---

1. Dulles's favorite doctrine was that of "calculated risk," which prompted the comment from then French Foreign Minister Georges Bidault that "he calculates enormously and never takes a risk."

French victory, for while Germany did annex the French provinces of Alsace and Lorraine in 1871, it didn't absorb Champagne,
did it? The 1971 edition of the New York Times Encyclopedic
Almanac noted in its biography of President Kennedy that after
the Berlin wall went up he "called up army reserves and dis-
patched military units to the border *until the tense situation ceased*"
(my italics). Border? What border? If what was meant was the one
between the two Germanies, the move was the wrong response to
the Communist thrust. Allied capitulation doubtless eased the tension, but the situation remained unchanged and the Soviets scored
a definitive gain. This is how a defeat is recorded for posterity in a
big-circulation reference work: in the colors of victory. The *Times*
formula was picked up word for word in the 1973 Official Associated Press Almanac.

At that we are probably lucky when the victories of Soviet imperialism are not considered signs of Soviet weakness by the very
persons at whose expense they were won. One such remark was
the last straw in that summer of the wall. "At a meeting," Curtis
Cate reported, "several experts from the State Department's legal
section began propounding the thesis that the desperate measures
now being taken by the Ulbricht regime could not be considered
really offensive or dangerous enough to warrant a sharp American
reaction. They were only laying claim to what was already theirs,
and in doing so, they were revealing how vulnerable and unpopular this regime really was. The seal-off action along the sector
boundaries could only be regarded as 'a major setback and defeat
for communism.' "[2] This was the first of a series of analyses com-
posing the vast anthology of Western diplomatic stupidity. Two
different aspects of the situation are being confused here. Being
forced to build a wall to keep its inhabitants from escaping, as the
East German Communist regime had to do, is an incontestable
sign of a society's weakness. But to build that wall and get away
with it, despite treaty commitments and against the will of the
entire Western camp, was by no means a sign of weakness, but a
sign of strength.

2. Cate, *The Ides of August*, p. 336.

Since, in such circumstances, the West never likes to admit to itself that it has suffered a setback, it never asks the two questions that should be asked after a failure: who is responsible, and what lessons can be learned from the reversal?

No Western head of state or cabinet officer has ever resigned because his policy toward Moscow failed, as Prime Minister Eden did after the Suez fiasco in 1956 and British Foreign Secretary Lord Carrington did in 1982 for failing to foresee Argentina's invasion of the Falkland Islands. Whole series of setbacks, more serious than these trifles because they endangered the very survival of democratic civilization, have never been punished, never even recognized for the defeats they were, since they occurred within the framework of East-West relations. One leading figure was even elected to the world's most influential job after proving his lack of understanding of Communist strategy. For it was Dwight D. Eisenhower, in his role as Supreme Allied Commander in Europe, who made it possible for the Soviet Union to take over Central Europe in 1944–45. Not only was he not blamed for this blunder, but he was later given *two* terms in the White House.

How can the West extract precise and useful information from events if it refuses to see them as Soviet successes? It is taught lessons but never learns them. So the Soviets count increasingly on Western passivity. In every one of their repressive or expansionist operations, in Hungary, Czechoslovakia, Afghanistan, Poland, they present both the East and the West with a fait accompli. In this periodically replayed drama, the peoples of the East are the resistants and the victims, those of the West are the weakest link, passive and vaguely grumbling witnesses, de facto accomplices. The Kremlin knows that the only obstacle to its repressiveness is the courage of the people it martyrs, never of those in the West. Note that the Soviets do not try to tell the democracies that "the Afghan or Hungarian or Czech or Polish people are with us, so don't count on using them against us." They do just the opposite. They tell their subject peoples, the East Germans in 1953 and 1961, the Czechs in 1968, the Poles in 1982, "The West has deserted you and will always desert you. You resist in vain. The wisest thing you can do is to resign yourselves to the power of the apparatchiks we've chosen, accept your fate, and try to make the best of a bad situation." How can they disregard such good advice, so manifestly based on experience?

Two years after the Soviet Army entered Afghanistan, while systematic extermination of the country's mountain people was moving into high gear, the West had already shelved any possibility of aid to Afghan freedom fighters and of economic reprisals against the U.S.S.R. Three months after martial law was declared in Poland, the principal topic of debate among Western governments was the extent and promptness of the concessions to be made on the question of intermediate-range missiles so as to appease the Soviet Union. In the West, even purely verbal reprisals are seen within a matter of weeks as being in bad taste, as being shocking. Questioned by a reporter on the possibility of economic sanctions in reprisal for the martial-law decree, a startled former French President Giscard d'Estaing protested, "Let's not talk about sanctions. Let's talk about *measures.*"[3] Measures! How you do go on! Gracious! That will terrify the KGB, all right! Every time they grab a new advantage, martyr another people, the Soviets know they can count first on the inaction of the "great powers" in the West and then on their silence. For all the West can do is repeat the lament from Pierre Corneille's *Rodogune:*

> Over the grim blackness of so sad a scene,
> We must draw the curtain or wipe the slate clean.

Aside from a few comic-opera gestures, such as the dispatch of American Marines to Lebanon in 1953 and the Bay of Pigs fiasco against Cuba in 1961, Western "imperialism" during the cold war was purely defensive—and even the Lebanese and Cuban operations fall into this general category. It always came in response to a

---

3. *Paris-Match*, February 1982. Commenting on a strongly anti-Soviet statement by President Mitterrand, Giscard's former Prime Minister Raymond Barre told members of Parliament from the ex-President's French Democratic Union Party in September 1981 that "Mitterrand is compromising the traditional friendship between France and the U.S.S.R." This was a sequel to the Gaullist mirage that will be discussed in the next chapter.

Soviet offensive. These expeditions, like the destabilization of the anti-Western regime of Mohammed Mossadegh in Iran and the pro-Communist government of Jacobo Arbenz in Guatemala, were enough to brand the United States forever with the seal of ignominy. I do not propose to contest the justice of this disgrace; I will simply confine myself to the observation that the Soviet Union and Cuba and China successfully undertake and have always undertaken similar operations almost every day. And *their* operations are always carried out on their own initiative, as offensive, not defensive, actions. Yet the condemnation they draw down on themselves by world opinion is never so vituperative or long-lasting. When communism goes on the attack, it is said to be defending itself; when democracy defends itself, it is charged with aggression. This principle is common to both "détente" and the "cold war." And it is accepted, even in the West, by large segments of public opinion, the media and of political parties and their leaders.

A typical example is the popular interpretation of the Cuban missile crisis. Note that the state of alert that historians present as an American victory and a humiliation for the Soviet Union was a strictly defensive move by the United States. The real—and offensive—initiative of stationing nuclear missiles in Cuba came from the Kremlin. In what did the alleged Soviet "defeat" consist? In a reversal of its decision to install the missiles; in other words, as usual, *the U.S.S.R. went back to where it began, with no losses.* How did the United States win this "victory"? By *promising not to interfere with the Castro regime* and by *removing American missiles from Turkey.* In this transaction, then, it was the "winner" who paid a price and the "loser" who received a double bonus: the sanctuarization of Cuba and a weakening of NATO. The Soviet Union is a past master in the art of being paid *not* to do something that, of course, it will do later on.[4]

Twenty years later, in 1982, we find President Reagan offering economic aid to Nicaragua, a new Soviet satellite, if it will stop

4. In discussing this Cuban episode, we can only list the concessions *we know* Kennedy made. There may have been others. If not, how explain the fact that the American authorities, so prone to leak state secrets, have kept the Kennedy-Khrushchev correspondence under wraps since 1962?

inciting and arming guerrilla forces in El Salvador. Here the
White House was making the same mistake it made with Cuba in
1962: giving, or offering, a concrete, positive, material advantage in
exchange for hypothetical cessation of a negative activity; a tangible present asset is sacrificed for a promise not to make trouble in
the future; something measurable and manifest is traded for the
promise of something unmeasurable and unverifiable.

This negotiating principle is part of a wider technique: *prior
concession*. It consists of ceding in advance, even before negotiations
begin, what should be the subject of the negotiations and which
the West should propose at the end of the talks, not at the start, and
then only in exchange for a carefully weighed and at least equivalent counterconcession. The West has formed the habit of sacrificing its best assets too often on the altar of détente in the hope that
this will make its goodwill and openness of mind shine forth. It is
done in the naive hope that the Soviets, touched by such magnanimous conduct, will eagerly seek ways to repay the gesture and
fulfill the West's desires.

The Soviets, made greedy by inurement to such windfalls, find it
natural to propose negotiations on the prior condition that the
West renounce all its bargaining points in advance. This is what
Moscow proposed on the issue of intermediate-range missiles in
Europe. And the Soviets explode in fury when our governments,
with unaccustomed insubordination, hint that they might like to
go back to the grubbily capitalistic rules of diplomacy, of genuine
give-and-take—by suggesting, for example, that the Soviet Union
ought to dismantle its missiles before we agree not to deploy ours.
The normal procedure in Moscow's view, and, incidentally, in that
of many Western spokesmen, would be for us to agree immediately
not to set up our missiles in Western Europe *in order* to earn the
privilege of *talking* to the Soviets about opening negotiations at
which we would appear with empty hands.

Indeed, the Soviets would be making a serious mistake not to
maintain their usual intransigence and insist on prior Western
guarantees; to their delight, this remains the most popular and
warmly recommended procedure in the West itself. In the spring

of 1982, for example, four eminent American statesmen—
McGeorge Bundy, former national security adviser to Kennedy
and Lyndon B. Johnson; ex-Defense Minister Robert McNamara;
veteran diplomat George Kennan; and former SALT negotiator
Gerard Smith—jointly bylined an article in the magazine *Foreign
Affairs* urging Reagan to renounce America's right to a nuclear first
strike in case of a Soviet attack on Western Europe. Such a move,
well publicized in advance, would be the divine surprise of which
the Soviet Union has fondly dreamed for over thirty years. The
article provided the encouragement needed by European pacifist
groups, the partisans of unilateral Western disarmament. And,
please note, it did so just as the turbulent congress of Helmut
Schmidt's Social Democratic Party, the weakest link in the chain
of democratic resistance to totalitarian advancement, was getting
under way in West Germany, the citadel of defeatism.

We could list hundreds of such examples. In the West, what has
been labeled, with martial hyperbole, as the "cold war" was in
practice conducted along astoundingly moderate lines. Later on,
the architects of détente had only to soften them further without
having to make substantive changes. This tameness agreeably surprised Moscow. The Cuban crisis was the last in a series of incidents stretching over a decade, from 1953 to 1962. During this
period, the West—mainly, of course, the United States—had all the
means it needed to wage a political offensive, which does not mean
a policy of military aggression but a diplomatic drive to reinforce
the positions and guarantees of the prevailing balance of power.
Naturally the Soviets, who know how this game is played, expected precisely that of us in defense of our own interests. Our
incompetence amazed them.

Moscow never understood why the West failed to profit from
Soviet inferiority during those years, from Soviet vulnerability,
from the first popular uprisings in East Germany, in Poland even
then, especially in Hungary, by peoples that were beginning to
understand what a nightmare of poverty and slavery their strange
"liberators" had brought them. The West did not simply fail to
pressure the U.S.S.R. into relinquishing the territories it had ille-

gally grabbed and restoring the national independence of countries
it had colonized or in which it had set up client governments that
it could maintain only by military brutality and police terror; the
United States and its European allies failed even to profit from the
favorable opportunities that arose to negotiate settlements of the
prickliest and most dangerous postwar problems, especially that of
a divided Germany, so pregnant with peril, a carrier of incurable
weakness for the future of democratic Europe.

In August 1961, when the Allies passively let the Communists
build the Berlin wall, the American ambassador in Bonn was the
same man who, as ambassador in Vienna, had negotiated the Austrian peace treaty concluded with the Soviets in May 1955. On his
arrival in Bonn in 1959, the envoy, Walter Dowling, met a Soviet
diplomat named Timoshenko, who had also been stationed in Vienna when the peace treaty was initialed. Timoshenko said:

" 'Do you remember in Vienna when we used to say: "Yes, we
are going to get a state treaty?" '

" 'Yes indeed,' Dowling had answered, 'but now let's see if we
can do the same thing here.'

"At that, the Soviet diplomat had shaken his head sadly. 'No, I
am afraid that's impossible. You missed your chance in 1952.' "[5]

It was not only in 1952 that the West let a chance go by to
negotiate a German reunification treaty, which would have eliminated one of the most glaring weaknesses in the democratic camp
and one of Moscow's most effective means of blackmail. Truman
fumbled a first opportunity during the 1948 Berlin blockade when
he refused to send an armored train from West Germany to Berlin
to see if the Soviets would dare to attack it. Whether they did or
not, they were beaten and the United States could have capitalized
on their blunder to demand clarification of the German situation.
Instead, the American airlift eluded the blockade, in a sense, without really breaking it. Washington was unable to follow up its prestige victory with a diplomatic victory. When the blockade was
lifted in 1949, the Allies, as usual, returned to their old stances, as
shaky militarily as they were confused juridically. Under the ele-

5. *The Ides of August*, p. 368.

mentary rules of diplomacy, the Allies should have demanded that, in reparation for the Soviet treaty violation, Moscow negotiate an immediate German peace treaty. Their failure to do so is proof of their diplomatic incompetence. That the Allies failed to press the advantage granted them by the Soviet setback during that brief period when the United States had a monopoly on the atomic bomb, which gave it an absolute superiority unprecedented in history, has no rational explanation, however blind we may think Western leaders were at the time—an estimate we need not be tender about. There certainly would have been nothing immoral about using our atomic monopoly to force Stalin to agree to a German peace treaty, since we would have been using our military superiority not to make war but to eliminate a cause of future war or, at least, of permanent friction and of fundamental Western weakness.

When East German workers rose up against communism in 1953, the Allies should have been able to convince Moscow to abandon the unpopular Ulbricht regime and settle the German problem. This is what the Soviets expected. The question came up before the Politburo in the Kremlin, and so hopeless did it seem to Stalin's successors that they could hang on in East Germany that Beria himself urged that they seek an arrangement favorable to the West. But we find nothing in White House archives to indicate that any parallel attention was paid to the question of how to exploit the Allied advantage in order to win a German treaty. Moscow was ready to make concessions to Washington, but Washington never noticed this and never dreamed of demanding them. Yet at this point, the State Department was in the hands of superhawk Dulles, the gallant knight of the "cold war."

After Stalin died, the new Soviet Government saw two satellite countries as being vulnerable: Albania and the (East) German Democratic Republic (GDR), neither of which was linked by a "friendship" treaty to the Soviet Union. The lack of a GDR connection, especially, showed that Stalin and his heirs expected a Western initiative on the German treaty question. For Moscow had lost no time in signing "friendship" treaties with all the other East-bloc countries: Czechoslovakia, Yugoslavia, Poland, Romania, Hungary and Bulgaria. In 1947, Stalin had not yet even brought the East German Communist Party into the Cominform, so certain was he that the West would not allow the incorporation of East Germany into the Soviet sphere. Clearly, he had decided in advance that he would have to make a concession on Germany. He still did not know that there were no real negotiators left in the West, only "experts."

This self-generated Western paralysis was rooted in a key misunderstanding during World War II that led the democracies to a mistaken diagnosis of the cause, nature, and real objectives of the Soviet Union's entry into the war. In the immediate postwar period, this numbed the Western Allies' powers of political observation and plunged them into one of those stupors in which indolence joins with credulity to block comprehension and even perception.

It is impossible to forget or to omit mention of the fact that the U.S.S.R. rallied to the Allied side in June 1941 very much in spite of itself. The Soviet war plan was to hold to its 1939 alliance with the Nazis. Its objective was to gather up as much as possible of the spoils of Germany's war. Hitler upset this magnanimous calculation by unilaterally breaking his pact with Stalin and invading Russia in 1941. He caught the Soviets by surprise; the lack of preparation of its government and army cost millions of Russian lives. Communist propaganda has exploited their sacrifice since then, but there would have been many fewer victims had the men in the Kremlin been competent rulers.

So, involuntarily forced to fight the same enemy as the democracies, with the aid of American food and military equipment without which, of course, it would never have been able to resist the Wehrmacht, the Soviet leadership never did side wholeheartedly with the democracies or share their political objectives in the war. Far from seeking, as they did, to eliminate totalitarianism from the world, the U.S.S.R. did its best to extend the system. Although the inconstancy of the ally it would have preferred, Adolf Hitler, forced it reluctantly into the democratic camp as a belligerent, the

Soviet Union's political aims remained intact: to swallow up as much foreign territory as possible and impose its own totalitarian system on it. This shows us both the naiveté of pro-German collaborators in the Nazi-occupied countries who thought they were helping to fight bolshevism and that of the Western wartime leaders who thought the Soviet Union was going democratic simply because it was—unwillingly—fighting on their side. Pathetically ingenuous predictions of Stalin's imminent conversion to a vaguely Swiss-style political morality were frequent in American and British newspapers during and just after the war, as they were on the lips of Western statesmen.

It is obvious why the defenders of Western interests, armed with so brilliant a hypothesis, marched "backward into the future," as Paul Valéry put it.

After the Nazi collapse, the total dissymmetry emerged between the Soviet and democratic war aims. The democracies wanted to liberate the occupied countries, restore their national independence, and help them adopt democratic systems of government. This was achieved in Western Europe and Japan. All the Soviet Union wanted to do in the countries from which it had routed German forces was to take Hitler's place, annex them in turn, and impose its own system. For disguised annexation is the only honest description possible of the regimes forced on the so-called popular democracies.

This was when the false parallelism of Soviet and American "zones of influence" took hold on the ground and in people's minds, predestining the West to defeat in the cold war and the détente that followed it. Real parallelism would have meant that the United States, having liberated them, had annexed France, Italy, Holland, Belgium, Denmark, and West Germany and installed its own proconsuls there, governing through local lackeys, as the Soviet Union is still doing in Eastern and Central Europe, including East Germany.

The Americans, of course, evacuated their troops from everywhere in Europe except defeated Germany soon after hostilities ended. It was because of the Red Army's threat to Western European independence that the Atlantic Alliance was concluded, *at the Europeans' request,* in 1949. Western Allied troops were quickly demobilized after the war, their numbers shrinking from five million to under nine hundred thousand. The Red Army, four million strong, was kept on a war footing. From 1946 to the coup d'état in Prague in the spring of 1948, the Soviet Union extended its military dominion over nearly one hundred million people, from East Germany and Poland in the north to Albania and Bulgaria in the south. The North Atlantic Treaty was a reply to this threat. But there is and always has been a vast difference between the Eastern countries' strict subordination to Moscow and the freedom of judgment and maneuver the NATO countries enjoy vis-à-vis Washington. By the time the treaty was signed, however, public attitudes and postures in the democracies had crystallized into acceptance of the implicit principle of inequality of rights and of legitimacy between the Soviet Union and the West. Two symptoms of the gravity of Western democracy's resignation, of its zeal to share the views and the ambitions of those seeking to destroy it, became clear then. They are still visible today.

The first is our tendency to recognize Soviet conquests as legitimate even though they rest on pure force and violate international law, beginning with the UN Charter. It is disinterested recognition, with no cynicism behind it, no Western demands or Soviet promises of reciprocity—no promise adhered to, at any rate. This bizarre democratic self-mutilation climaxed in the 1975 Helsinki accords.

Thirty years earlier, on April 17, 1945, the French daily newspaper *Le Monde,* created only months earlier but already functioning as France's self-appointed conscience, ran an editorial justifying in advance the future incorporation of Central Europe into the totalitarian fortress. "The clock of history has struck the Slavic hour," it intoned. ". . . Only those who, consciously or not, are playing Germany's game will deplore this or be alarmed by it . . . It was great Russia that saved the Slavs from servitude or destruction, and it is normal that they now show their gratitude toward it by grouping under its aegis."

What flowers do we gather from this passage? An extravagant resurrection of the Pan-Slavism used as a cover for Communist totalitarianism. A sudden canonization of the Slavic community, into which, if I understand the piece rightly, the Hungarians, Romanians and Prussians were enrolled willy-nilly, in defiance of all known anthropological evidence. A sly accusation against anyone daring to contest this new Pan-Slavism that they were "playing Germany's game"—only three weeks after the German debacle. (A few months later, the charge would be "playing the Americans' game.") And, finally, a foolish assertion that out of "gratitude" to Moscow the peoples soon to be crushed under the Stalinist juggernaut were voluntarily gathering under their future hangmen's "aegis." An early demonstration of Westerners' deeply anchored tendency to toe the Soviet line.

The second symptom appeared when the Atlantic Alliance was formed. Asked by a defenseless Western Europe to fill the military gap from which it faced an alarmingly well-prepared East, the United States Government was reluctant to go along with the idea at first and made up its mind to sign the treaty only after overcoming strong domestic resistance. Yet it was not long before the Americans were being seen as aggressors, by some as an occupying power, as witness the hostile demonstrations that greeted General Matthew B. Ridgeway on his arrival in Paris as commander in chief of NATO forces.

So, early on was erected the mental framework of the cold war and détente. Defense became aggression; Europe's American ally, which became an ally in freely consented negotiations, became an "occupying power."[6] On the other hand, the countries being crushed by Stalinism were "grouping in gratitude under its aegis"; the liberal democracies, because they were led by the United States, were "rightist" reactionaries; the Soviet Union and its subject nations represented the "left" and progressivism. The peace lovers were those whose power rested wholly on the army, the

---

6. In 1961, writer Simone de Beauvoir, the companion of Jean-Paul Sartre, saw two American soldiers in a restaurant in Chinon. As soon as she recovered from this frightful shock, she told novelist Albert Camus, "I thought I was back under the [Nazi] Occupation" (*La Force des choses*).

police, the concentration camps and who were forever attempting new power plays like the ones in Berlin and Korea. It was the Americans who harbored the "criminal intention of triggering a third world war." At best, the United States might be given the benefit of the doubt and placed on the same plane as the Soviets by the champions of neutralism.

The actors are onstage, the parts have been distributed, the performance can begin. What is most mysterious about this play—in which the hero, the moral and material winner in each act until the final curtain can only be communism—is that it was written by the West, by the democracies. It was they who developed the plot and determined the action.

21

ON THE INVENTOR
OF DÉTENTE

GENERAL DE GAULLE was tormented by what has been described as a "Perrichon complex," named for the hero of a play who comes to hate the man who pulled him back from the edge of a cliff; the mere sight of his savior reminds him that he owes his life to someone else's intervention and not to his own courage alone.

Consumed with animosity toward those he called the "Anglo-Saxons," De Gaulle persistently displayed his resentment of the British, who had sheltered him during his exile after France collapsed in 1940, and especially of the Americans, without whose help the Allies would have lost World War II to Hitler. I would be straying from my subject here if I traced this bizarre rancor back to its sources; it was partly justified by the general's very real disagreements with the British over his uncertain status and by Franklin Roosevelt's undeniable psychological mistakes regarding him. Still, since a statesman is not supposed to behave like an offended prima donna eager to revenge her outraged pride, but like a leader responsible for the destinies of millions of people, the reasons, good or bad, for his rancor leave me cold. Not so its consequences. If these turned out to be harmful, then the man failed in his mission by giving his personal animosities precedence over the duties of his office. In a democracy, a statesman has no right to be touchy except in the name of the country he governs and the basic interests of his constituents.

De Gaulle's attitude toward the British and the Americans regarding NATO rested on a sound principle: each member of an alliance must claim a sovereign state's independence of decision while participating fully in group decisions; this claim must be pressed especially against the most powerful country in the alliance, which inevitably tends to make its own decisions in the group's name.

But De Gaulle went on to conclusions and conduct that contravened the very notion of an alliance. For one thing, his assertion of an "independent" foreign policy that was really anti-American and that paid less and less attention to the fact that France was, after all, a member of the Atlantic Alliance was based on sophistry. Any nation, any individual signing a contract automatically alienates some independence. A party to a contract maintains full freedom of action *before* signature, while discussing its clauses and calculating its benefits and obligations. Once he has signed, while he does not sacrifice all his independence or sovereignty since without them there would be no contract, he does lose absolute freedom of decision. For example, a musician who signs an exclusive contract with a record company may not go off and record for someone else. What is unreasonable is to claim the right, on the grounds of "independence," to belong to an alliance while behaving as if you did not, the right not to respect a contract you have signed.

In practice, this alteration of the notion of independence led De Gaulle, especially beginning in 1962, into a very odd foreign policy that consisted mainly of fighting his own allies instead of combating the common exterior danger the alliance was formed to guard against. Using the alliance's adversary to thwart the influence of France's allies, especially the most powerful of them, became the guideline for French diplomacy.

To justify his determination to dismantle the democratic camp from within, De Gaulle devised—no, he revived—the old neutralist theory of an exact equivalence between the two power blocs. "We are happy to have you to help us resist pressure from the United States," he told a delighted Khrushchev, although he did, it's true, add, "just as we are very glad to have the United States to help us resist pressure from the Soviet Union."[1] Clearly, for the

1. Cited by André Fontaine in *Un seul lit pour deux rêves, histoire de la "détente"* (Paris: Fayard, 1981).

French chief of state the two forms of pressure were compensatory; there was no fundamental difference between democracy and totalitarianism. De Gaulle forgot, or repudiated, the alliance's deep meaning and its goal: to safeguard a civilization based on freedom. For the Atlantic Alliance is a treaty among nations that do not wish to end up like Bulgaria and Poland.

The Gaullist myth of perfect equilibrium between, say, Canada and Hungary, each of them as members of their respective blocs, won a following. It also revealed the degeneration of French political thought over the course of the twentieth century: it is hard to imagine anyone in 1937–38 seeing genius in a French leader who told Hitler that "we are happy to have you to help us resist pressure from the British." And people would have feared for the mental health of any French head of government then who formulated a "multidirectional" defense policy operating in a spirit of perfect impartiality between France's British ally and its potential enemy, Nazi Germany. Yet this was the strategic doctrine adopted by Gaullist France in the 1960s.

Hatred of the United States, then, became stronger than fear of control by the Soviet Union. "As seen from Paris, the major danger came from the West" and "De Gaulle unleashed an anti-American offensive at every level," wrote André Fontaine—a serious accusation and a striking one from an author who admired the general and who, as a journalist, was more than a little reserved toward "Atlantism."[2] All the testimony echoes this Gaullist peevishness, which had no place in sober political analysis. In an interview with the French monthly magazine *Franc-Tireur* in March 1982, former Algerian President Ahmed Ben Bella spoke of the De Gaulle he knew then. "He was obsessed by the Americans and, in this sense, we were objectively allies. I can even tell you that at one point De Gaulle proposed to me a conference in Paris with Fidel Castro." The frenetic excessiveness of the general's anti-American diatribes went far beyond the aim of restoring a healthy power balance within the alliance; it in fact weakened that alliance. "American hegemony is *smothering* Europe," the French President

2. Ibid., p. 77.

told Willy Brandt, "blocking an *understanding with the East*, and is troublesome in *every* way."[3]

Armed with this diagnosis, General de Gaulle also reached extraordinary heights of virtuosity in wielding diplomatic weapons I have already recommended to anyone with suicidal tendencies: prior concessions, provisional gifts, preliminary renunciation of bargaining points, prophylactic capitulation. He was to make this technique a fad among Western negotiators. For example, in anticipation of an official visit to the Soviet Union De Gaulle, who had already decided to take France out of NATO's military command, publicly announced the good news *before* leaving for Moscow. This considerate gesture, he supposed, would improve the Soviets' mood and prove our goodwill, and this would certainly stimulate their generosity and impel them to repay us. A correct estimate, except, of course, for that last bit about generosity and repayment. You had to be totally ignorant of communism (and it is true that De Gaulle took more pleasure in the Victor-Lucien Tapié's useless and old-fashioned book *Richelieu* than in Boris Souvarine's current and indispensable *Stalin)* to imagine for one moment that it was good tactics with the Soviet leadership to dispose of your bargaining counters before sitting down to negotiate. It's not even a good idea when dealing with civilized people, but it is positively farcical when you are wrestling the alligators in the Politburo.

Nevertheless, delighted with his inspiration and feeling himself in a decidedly generous streak, De Gaulle, the first of the chatty traveling presidents, pranced off to the Soviet Union to praise a "Russia prosperous, powerful, and *filled with peaceful ardor*" (my italics); only the second qualification, unfortunately, escapes the category of mere pompous stupidity. That category should, however, include the masterful words De Gaulle sent floating into the wind of history as the banners of his future policy toward the East. "Détente, entente, and cooperation" and, especially, his famous "Europe from the Atlantic to the Urals." Both these slogans were irresponsible—sterile voids that no political substance would ever

3. Willy Brandt, *From the Cold War to Détente*, published in France by Gallimard in 1978. The italics are mine.

fill, futile illusions since dispelled by history. Yet posterity considers their author, even more than his contemporaries did, as a model of perspicacity in foreign policy. For time often builds reputations on bases as fragile as that of any faddish celebrity. De Gaulle's visits to the Communist countries in the naive belief that he could establish real and different relations with them are now seen to have been equally vain, and for the same reasons: his ignorance of the satellites' real position, the mirage of parallelism between the countries of East and West, his refusal to recognize that the governments with which he thought he was dealing were not, like his, independent and that they were no more masters of their decisions than they were representative of the peoples by whom they arranged for him to be acclaimed.

The Soviet tanks rolling into Czechoslovakia in August 1968 failed to open De Gaulle's eyes to the nature of communism and the Soviet system. He attributed that "accident en route" to the "policy of blocs" and the damage done by the "Yalta agreements," thus again displaying his ignorance of just what those agreements were, since the Czech question was not touched on at Yalta. His dream of a Europe in harmony "from the Atlantic to the Urals" seemed no more unlikely to him after the Red Army occupied Prague than it had before. "Let us guard against excessive language," the general said at a French cabinet meeting on August 24, 1968. "Sooner or later, Russia will return [to its old ways] . . . We must build Europe. We can construct something with the Six [of the original Common Market], even build a political organization. We cannot build Europe without Warsaw, without Budapest, and without Moscow."[4]

All the future illusions and surrenders in détente are contained in that statement: De Gaulle's acceptance of Moscow's fait accompli, his unwillingness to consider sanctions to punish a crime against freedom, his de facto alliance with Soviet imperialism, which he forgave all sins. Add to this his lack of understanding of Communist reality, in short, his incompetence and his blind trust in the Soviet Government's desire and ability to become part of a

4. Reported by Jean-Raymond Tournous, *Le Feu et la cendre* (Paris: Plon, 1979).

harmonious and homogeneous Europe—which, be it noted, General de Gaulle thought Britain had no right to join!

While doing his best to torpedo the Atlantic Alliance, De Gaulle worked to prevent the unification of Europe's defenses. In 1954, under the French Fourth Republic, his party, the French People's Rally (RPF) joined the Communists to prevent French ratification of the European Defense Community. This was a success for Soviet diplomacy and Moscow's secret services. Ten years later, De Gaulle's Government similarly annihilated a plan for a European Multilateral Force. Clearly, the principal beneficiary of a French foreign policy designed to weaken the United States and balk a concerted defensive effort in Western Europe could only have been the Soviet Union. So it was, and so it continued to be for a long time. De Gaulle's rejection of "bloc politics" systematically worked out in favor of Soviet interests. In 1980, Giscard d'Estaing did not consider the Soviet Union guilty of the vice of playing "bloc politics" when it invaded Afghanistan, but the United States was when it called for sanctions against Moscow. France, he felt, should therefore dissociate itself from America on the issue.

De Gaulle had made "Atlantism" and anti-Sovietism infamous. Down deep in his heart, who did he think would profit from his handiwork?

22

YALTA: THE MYTH OF WHERE IT ALL BEGAN

It is an occupational habit for actors on the political stage to distort the truth, for reasons and in ways that vary with the nature of the power they hold. Autocrats, in direct control of all means of communication and expression, disguise the present and rewrite the past. Democrats, whose influence depends, happily, on their persuasiveness, expend so much energy trying to show their undertakings in the best possible light that they eventually lose the habit of thinking about the issues' substance. Their skill in presenting their case almost entirely replaces their interest in the facts. So that in free societies the past is sometimes misrepresented, not, as in slave societies, by crude state censorship and lies, but suavely, through legitimate persuasion and the free propagation of an adulterated or entirely bogus version of an event. With repetition, this version joins the body of accepted ideas, those the masses believe; it acquires the status of truth, so firmly that hardly anyone thinks of checking the original facts for confirmation.

The widespread image of a "dividing up of the world" at Yalta in early February 1945 is one of the purest examples of this sort of retrospective hallucination. It would not, of course, have been so generally accepted if it had not answered a need by the people of Europe that the top decision-making politicians both detected and stimulated. Remember the fable of the "stab in the back" that was used to convince German war veterans after 1918 that the armistice was a betrayal for which there was no military justification. This later enabled Hitler's propaganda machine to prepare German opinion for another war to efface the stigma of the Versailles Treaty.

Such fictions are like the stories children make up when they invent imaginary ancestors—the "neurotics' family fable," Freud called it. Since 1945, Yalta has been the "fable of the origins" of European diplomacy, a myth whose disconcerting survival prompts us to try to analyze its psychic and political function.[1]

When we examine the minting of the Yalta myth in the standard —and generally accepted—political propaganda between 1960 and 1980, the years of Gaullist influence on Western diplomacy and the decade of détente, we find certain basic postulates.

At Yalta, as we have seen, the world is supposed to have been "divided up" between the two superpowers (the collective memory, anticipating a still distant future, had already erased, or at least blurred, Britain as a major power, which was a historical mistake). Europe was then allegedly divided into spheres of influence corresponding to what are now Eastern and Western Europe, separated by an iron curtain across which the cold war would be fought. If all this seems a little compressed, it is because the sin of historical anachronism mixes the period under study with events that occurred later in other places. European egocentrism, we might note in passing, ignored arrangements for Asia, which occupied a prominent place in the Yalta discussions and which, incidentally, were disastrous for the democracies.

The supposed Soviet-American carving up of Europe gives rise to a third postulate: consolidation of the superpowers' worldwide spheres of influence into two rival blocs. This provided a convenient theme for European diplomacy: rejection of a "two-bloc policy." Rejection could take the extreme form of Gaullist "independence," which also meant being as anti-American as possible. Or it could tread more softly, adopt fewer postures, be less explosive and more ambiguous. This was both riskier and potentially more prof-

1. In her book *Roman des origines et origines du roman* (Paris: Grasset, 1972), Marthe Robert pointed out that Freud, before his 1909 paper on family fables, had first used the expression *Entfremdungsroman*, or "romance by which one distances oneself from reality" or becomes a stranger to it, the word suggesting a "psychotic denial of reality."

itable, as West Germany's "opening to the East" proved to be. But the central idea in either form was to "escape the blocs," even if that sometimes came down to mere whimsicality. True, European governments usually hasten to specify, when pressed to follow their reasoning to its conclusion, that they are primarily loyal to the Atlantic community. Yet after Afghanistan was invaded, for example, both France and West Germany proclaimed their disdain of a two-bloc policy.

What else could this mean in practice but that these countries saw no difference between the occupation of an independent country by a foreign army, in this case the Red Army, and Washington's appeal to its allies to join in inflicting economic sanctions on the invader? Europe's particular vocation, we were told, was expressed in its rejection of both types of behavior as being equally injurious to détente. How profitable this equation is to the Soviet Union is obvious: Europe's policy prevented the use of sanctions, but it certainly had no influence on the war in Afghanistan. Similarly, Europe's refusal to reply to martial law in Poland by cutting off technological aid to the Soviet Union must be seen as a not very convincing attempt to "maintain an even balance" between the "two blocs." It is hard to spot what the cause of freedom gained in this business and what the totalitarian cause lost.

We cannot help supposing, then, that the false symmetry of "two blocs" anchored in the Yalta myth allows the Europeans to bow to Soviet power while thinking of and presenting their passiveness as a choice, an active policy. One frequent function of the myth is common to both Western Europe and the United States: the idea that because the Yalta conferees "granted" Central and Eastern Europe to the U.S.S.R., we should not stick our noses into what happens there. To this we immediately add, with superb disregard of the need for consistency, that because Afghanistan was not touched on at Yalta, we ought not to butt in there, either.

A second use of the Yalta myth is peculiar to Western Europe. It is the aforementioned balanced rejection of both blocs, which is like money in the bank for Moscow, since claiming to reject both blocs gives the Europeans power only to weaken their own, the one they belong to.

Just how useful the Yalta myth is was shown again in the hardening of repression in Poland. In his New Year's greetings to the French on December 31, 1981, President Mitterrand declared it is "dangerous that the two powers I am talking about [the Soviet Union and the United States] can coexist on the basis of a division of Europe as it existed nearly forty years ago . . . Anything that gets us out from under Yalta will be good . . . The Polish tragedy is a consequence of that contradiction." Four days later, in an interview with the New York *Times*, West German Chancellor Schmidt urged the West to shut its eyes to the Polish problem because, he said, the West had decided at Yalta to divide Europe, for all practical purposes, into spheres of influence. Since then, he went on, the West has agreed that "the countries beyond the Elbe are not under the West's rule." Against the troublemakers who insisted on supporting the Solidarity movement, Schmidt brandished the ultimate riposte: he branded them as warmongers. Forgetting Yalta, he concluded with splendid simplicity, "would mean war."

No less! The admonition was clear enough: if you protest against what is happening in Warsaw, you will blow up the world. Let's not even think of sanctions because then, good heavens, who knows what we might blow up. Maybe the whole solar system! This is what is called "maintaining a balance between the two blocs."

These European leaders could not have found a better way to expose the myth's deepest roots, to show that to them Yalta is not a fact but a state of mind that enables them to escape their responsibilities in any situation that makes a diplomatic or economic confrontation with the Soviet Union inevitable. How, in good faith, could these eminent statesmen have shown such ignorance of the real contents of the Yalta agreements, an ignorance that fifteen minutes' reading would have dispelled? Indeed, several European journalists and historians undertook to inform them of the truth through the press in 1981–82. Refutations of the Yalta myth regarding Poland erupted with an energy and precision that were sure signs that what had amounted to censorship, conscious or not, had suddenly been lifted. The enormity of blaming Yalta for the Sovietization of Poland exceeded the limits of tolerability and plausibility, even in amnesiac societies.

We will understand better what an enormity this was if we add to the list of the myth's functions that of a "memory screen" to hide a more recent, more exemplary and better documented capitulation: the surrender at Helsinki. It was there in 1975, and not at Yalta in 1945, that the West formally recognized the legitimacy of the Soviet Union's postwar annexations and colonizations. The world was really divided up in Helsinki, not in Yalta. But Yalta provides a better alibi for Western leaders' inaction. Invoking Helsinki might oblige them to demand that, in return for our rejection of sanctions, the Soviets keep the promises they made at this very recent conference. Doing that would have brought us back to firm diplomatic ground where nothing is ceded except in exchange for something else. Obviously, it is less tiring to attack the Americans when the Soviets step out of line.

Not only was nothing whatsoever "divided up" at Yalta, but, for the Soviet Union, the conference represented a bonanza of unilateral Western concessions. The common ancestor of all the conferences studding the succeeding forty years, it prefigured them all by developing fully perfected prototypes of their most calamitous traits. It displayed the West's inability to understand communism and thus to negotiate with the Communists. It especially showed our incapacity to prevent the Soviets from illegally grabbing territory or from subjugating countries by forcing vassal regimes on them. Yalta, with its sister conferences at Teheran and Potsdam, simply delivered Eastern and Central Europe over to Stalin without sharing in anything. Similarly, in Asia the Allies allowed Stalin to appropriate Manchuria and annex the Kuriles and the southern part of Sakhalin Island in exchange for a last-minute Soviet declaration of war against Japan that, in 1945, brought no gains to a United States that was already sure of victory in the Pacific. Note that the Americans, who for four years bore the full weight of the war against Japan, took nothing for themselves after the war, while the Soviets, who were merely sham, last-minute belligerents in the Pacific, gobbled up vast stretches of territory. The states of mind that led the West to these paradoxical diplomatic disasters in both Europe and Asia merit as much attention as the results themselves. For it was this mentality, more than any real balance of power, that explains the movement of history in the second half of the twentieth century.

As noted earlier, Roosevelt relied on his charm to democratize Stalin. He thought it his duty to shower the Soviet leader with proofs of his goodwill without demanding anything in return. In so doing, he laid down the principle that would long govern diplomatic relations between East and West: that the West must at all times demonstrate its good faith by granting uncompensated concessions. The proof of American good faith, wrote Roosevelt's Secretary of State Cordell Hull in his memoirs, did not reside in Washington's recognition of expanded frontiers, but in its determination to . . . etc. It was not Stalin, the former ally of the Nazis who was betrayed by Hitler, who was expected to demonstrate his good faith, but the Americans. To an Admiral Leahy alarmed by American benevolence toward Russia, Roosevelt wrote that while he was not disputing his ally's arguments, because they were fair, nor the Briton's reasoning, he had a feeling that Stalin was not the man he was thought to be. Truman, said Roosevelt, had the same feeling, that all Stalin wanted was his country's security. Hence the President's notion that if he gave Stalin everything he could give without asking anything in return, "noblesse oblige," the Soviet dictator would not think of annexing anything but would work with Roosevelt toward a democratic and peaceful world.

This would remain the West's diplomatic philosophy, implicit or avowed, for the next forty years in its relations with communism of whatever variety. And why not? Hadn't Joseph E. Davies, who as American ambassador to Moscow from November 1936 to the spring of 1938 was present during Stalin's purges and show trials and mass executions, said in *Mission to Moscow* that all the facts supported his personal opinion that the Soviet Government's word of honor was as good as the Bible? Roosevelt's trust in Stalin's democratic instincts prompted him to beg that famous philanthropist to attend the Yalta conference because, he cabled the Caucasian despot on July 27, 1944, "such a meeting would help me domestically." In that year, Roosevelt summed up the new philosophy in the assertion that "the Soviet Union needs peace" and was prepared to pay for that peace with "democratic cooperation with the West." The idea took hold in the American press and among the new generation of State Department bureaucrats; it would resurface intact, despite the years of the so-called cold war, during the period of détente.

This basic postulate came wrapped in the wildest conjectures on the inevitable transformation of communism into a free market economy, the imminent conversion of Stalin to political pluralism, and the possibility, in face-to-face meetings, of convincing him to accept the Christian way and democratic principles. As gratuitous as it is indestructible, this postulate, assuming Moscow's desire for peace, explains why Stalin triumphed so easily at Yalta and in Teheran. It also explains the scatterbrained attitude of Westerners as they marched ahead openly and unsuspecting and their optimistic vision of Soviet intentions, which was the source of their errors and weaknesses—their mistaken understanding of each side's assets in negotiation, gross overestimation of Stalin's strength, heedlessness in insisting on Soviet guarantees for the future, one-way concessions not conditional on Soviet respect for promises or treaty commitments, even their deadly, almost incredible carelessness in revealing their plans or, to be exact, their lack of planning. At Yalta, for example, Roosevelt was even forthcoming enough to tell Stalin he did not think American troops could remain in Europe for more than two years after Germany's surrender. Besides, he said, he did not believe in maintaining strong American forces in Europe. He couldn't have been more obliging. By informing Stalin in advance that American troops would be withdrawn and when, Roosevelt was behaving like a home owner who put up posters to tell local burglars when he planned to take his vacation and leave his apartment unguarded.

Armed with this assurance, Stalin could calmly lay his postwar plans. First he demanded that the Allies grant him full control over the areas Germany had promised him in the 1939 Hitler-Stalin pact, the only real agreement to divide up territory signed in the twentieth century. He was instantly granted the Baltic states and chunks of Finland and Romania—in other words, everything Hitler had awarded him in 1939. But Poland, the subject of Western leaders' 1981 invocation of the Yalta agreements, was not delivered over to Stalin in any of the accords reached in February 1945. He took it by trickery and force. The worrisome historical truth is that Western negotiators let themselves be fooled by Stalin because they believed his promise to respect the Polish people's right to self-determination by organizing free elections there. After ceding the eastern third of Poland to the Soviet Union, another of Hitler's promises, the West, either through unspeakable cowardice or gigantic error, recognized the legitimacy of the provisional government of the soon-to-be-"liberated" Poland "pending elections." This was the Lublin regime, made in the Soviet Union and headed by Stalin's Polish counterpart, Boleslaw Bierut, who was to plunge the Poles into totalitarian darkness until the 1956 Polish workers' uprising. The London-based Polish government in exile, the only one the Poles saw as representing their resistance to Germany and their legitimate future leadership, was disavowed. The few minor figures who were tempted home from Britain to take part in a government of "national union" with the Communists had little time to savor the joys of their new partnership; soon disenchanted, they fled just in time to save their skins.

The Communist machinery for appropriating monopoly power was already operating at full blast by then. When Harry Truman complained angrily to Molotov at Potsdam in 1945 that the free elections promised in Poland had yet to take place, the Soviet Foreign Minister declared himself insulted; no one, he protested, had ever "spoken to him that way" before. But then, he did have a balm to soothe his wounded sensibilities: the Soviet Union already owned Poland. By then the die was cast; it was too late to save the country.

A painful epilogue, this, when we remember that Poland had been the first nation to try to resist Nazi invasion, one week after Stalin signed his treaty with Hitler; that Polish flyers had played a key role in the Battle of Britain; that on the day the Yalta conference opened, one hundred and fifty thousand Polish soldiers were still fighting the Wehrmacht on the Italian front. What augured still worse for what was left of free Europe was that Poland's reduction to slavery came not through any cynical betrayal by the Western Allies but because of their ignorance of communism. Believing that Stalin would agree to free elections was nothing but sheer incompetence.

Allied docility and credulity has often been blamed on their fear in 1943–44 that Stalin might sign a separate peace with Hitler. That they did fear such a turnaround is true enough, but it is only one more manifestation of the same old Western credulity. Again, it could only have arisen from faulty analysis of the facts. Having been double-crossed once by Hitler, and depending entirely on the war equipment the Americans delivered free under their lend-lease program, Stalin knew that he did not dare face his brother dictator unarmed again. Yet as early as the Teheran conference in 1943, with the Wehrmacht still holding vast stretches of Soviet territory and well before Yalta, the West had already granted him everything he asked.

For it was not the Allies who had appealed for Stalin's help. He had called on theirs. Without lend-lease, he was lost. True, Hitler's attack on the Soviet Union was a break for us. But we should have insisted on specific commitments from Moscow in return for our aid. Stalin would have been annihilated without Allied assistance; that was the time for us to drive a hard bargain with him. But our lack of familiarity with the Communist machine is now glaringly obvious.

To negotiate means to trade. This is what the Allies did not understand and what the West has yet to relearn. In return for their lend-lease supplies, the democracies failed to demand Soviet good-conduct guarantees after the war. Yet the sole cause of Moscow's switch to the Allied camp was Germany's offensive against the Soviet Union; it was Hitler who broke their pact, not Stalin. This fact alone should have inspired a minimum of distrust and caution in Western negotiators.

The obligation was especially pressing because Hitler and Stalin had been conniving long before their surprise treaty in 1939. William C. Bullitt, the American ambassador in Moscow and a personal friend of Roosevelt, later declared that no government in the world was as well-informed about the exact progress of the relations between Hitler and Stalin as the American Government was. Without spending a penny on a spy or informer, he went on, United States diplomatic representatives were able to tell Roosevelt in the fall of 1934 that the Soviet dictator wanted an arrangement with the Nazi dictator and that Hitler could get a treaty from Stalin on request.

We should be less surprised than we are at Bullitt's report that the secret negotiations between Stalin and Hitler in the summer of 1939 were carefully reported, day by day and step by step, to Roosevelt. The British and French governments were informed by Washington that Stalin was using his negotiation of a pact *against* Hitler as a screen behind which he could prepare his pact *with* Hitler undisturbed. Despite the warning, neither of those governments could bring itself to believe such duplicity, and they were as surprised as they could be when the Soviet Union and Germany signed their nonaggression treaty on August 23, 1939.[2]

No one can deny Stalin's right to reach an understanding with Hitler. I will limit myself to suggesting that the West at Yalta

2. William C. Bullitt, "How We Won the War and Lost the Peace," in *Life* magazine, 27 September 1948. Several of the statements by American political figures used in this chapter were taken from the article.

   That this carefully matured alliance also fed on the similarities between the Communist and Nazi systems is suggested in an odd story reported by Bertrand de Jouvenal in his book *Voyageur dans le siècle:* "Another memory retained from Moscow is so strange that it disturbs me to tell it. It was a simple enough incident: I was walking down the stairs at the big hotel we'd been assigned to. A young man I passed on a landing stopped and greeted me. He was one of the young Nazis I had met in Berlin in January 1934. I asked him what he was doing there and he told me he had come to study the Soviet [concentration] camps."

should not have forgotten that it was not the Kremlin that had ended that understanding and that the Soviet Union had been pushed into the war against its will. Stalin's record was such that a few precautions against similar exploits in the future would not have been insulting. We did not take them.

In an article in the Belgian newspaper *Le Flambeau* in September 1955, career diplomat Anatole Muhlstein, commenting on Yalta in bitterly incisive terms, cast a harsh light on postwar East-West relations. "To discern in 1945 the potential of communism on the march would have required the practiced eye of a real diplomat. Unfortunately, the Allied democracies had soldiers, economists, scientists, orators, but they no longer had diplomats. In the final analysis, this diplomatic decadence is the profound cause of all Europe's troubles."

The Western Allies' war aim was to restore independence to the countries liberated from naziism and institute democracy even in the Axis nations, Italy, Japan, Germany itself. Moscow's war aim was to subjugate the countries it liberated and absorb them into its orbit by disguised annexation. In his book *Conversations with Stalin*, Yugoslav dissident Milovan Djilas says that while he was visiting Moscow in April 1945 Stalin told him how he thought of "liberation." "This war is not like those of the past; whoever occupies a territory imposes his own social system on it. Everyone imposes his system as far as his army can advance. That is how it has to be." Yet the West was so unaware of the danger that in 1945 Truman ordered Eisenhower to halt the Allies' advance on Berlin to give the Soviets the satisfaction of capturing the German capital. We know now how costly that elegant gesture was and still is to European security. Stalin's plans, once the Soviet presence was consolidated in Central Europe and East Germany, naturally overshadowed Western Europe after the departure—so obligingly announced in advance—of American troops from the war zone.

This is why it is almost comical, grimly comical, to hear talk now, forty years later, of "double hegemony" and a "Russo-American condominium" or, better yet, to be told that it was at Yalta that the United States arranged its "domination" of Europe. Even cruder was De Gaulle's diplomatic misconception in enlisting Russian support to combat "the consequences of Yalta" when the Russians were Yalta's only real beneficiaries. It is a supreme irony that France was the country most fiercely assailed by Stalin and Molotov at Yalta. "The truth is," they asserted (France was not present), "that France has contributed very little to this war and that it opened its doors to the enemy." Yet De Gaulle, after a trip to Moscow in December 1944 to meet Stalin, believed he had won the Soviet dictator's support. Blind innocence! At Yalta it was the "Anglo-Saxons" so berated by De Gaulle who fought for hours against "France's friend, Stalin"[3] in defense of French interests, holding out until France was awarded an occupation zone in Germany and a seat on the armistice control commission, a concession the Soviet leader refused as long as he could.

After 1947 and, especially, following the Communist coup d'état in Prague, when the Western Europeans realized that the Red Army was on their doorstep and that they were utterly defenseless, they turned to a reluctant United States to ask its protection. Negotiations began then and ended on April 4, 1949, with the signing of the North Atlantic Treaty. But Europe's historical memory has retouched this picture as it has travestied Yalta. It has repressed the fact that the Europeans were the petitioners who had to force America's hand, not vice versa. The Europeans needed over eighteen months of laborious, persevering negotiation to wring a military guarantee from the United States. How quickly the notion of a "dividing up" of Europe collapses under pressure from the readily available facts!

To reply to the shady imposters whose mission it is to "get us out from under Yalta"—which, to them, is a code expression for siding with the Soviet Union against the United States—I will refer once more to Jean Laloy, who was present during De Gaulle's conversations with Stalin. "It is not Yalta we must get out from under," he wrote, "but the Yalta myth." Can we do this? And what good would it do us? Just as a dream can express a desire, a myth may be a mask for resignation. Lying to the point of claiming

3. De Gaulle signed a "friendship" treaty with the Soviet Union in Moscow.

that the Yalta agreements were to blame for the communization of Poland is an oblique way of capitulating in advance to Soviet domination of Europe. Once the decision has been made to surrender without a struggle, isn't it honorable to seem merely to be abiding by a treaty? Capitulating because we respect a contract is more honorable than surrendering to a violation of that contract. And if there is no contract, we invent one.

23

MIRACLE IN MOSCOW:
THE COMEDY OF SUCCESSION

IN THE SPRING of 1982, after a group discussion on pacifist movements in Europe, I lunched in Paris with a few friends, among them the exiled Soviet writer Vladimir Bukovsky. Speaking of Brezhnev's impending death, he launched into a monologue parodying what he was sure would be the West's reaction to the expected choice of Andropov as the Soviet leader's successor. "Andropov the liberal . . . Think of it! He speaks English, he likes jazz. He has a Hungarian tailor. He listens to the BBC . . . He is *very* Westernized. Don't discourage him. Show him he has our good wishes, anticipate his goodwill, support him against the hawks in the Kremlin. The success of the Andropov *opening* will depend on the West." Bukovsky predicted Western thinking in the near future more accurately than a good many professional pundits.

In fact, he was simply putting his finger on a recurrent phenomenon. Most Western reactions to events in the Soviet Union *are* recurrent phenomena anyway, persistent stereotypes that seem to indicate that we have learned nothing from history to help us revise them. Transfers of power in the Kremlin invariably produce the same Western clichés. They excite irrational, emotional reactions that, by their nature, contradict each other, drifting in a fog of ambiguity. In retrospect, the departed leader suddenly becomes "a man of peace, stability, caution." We fear the advent of "adventurists, hard-liners, hawks" in the Kremlin. The successor is immediately draped in a "liberal's" spotless chasuble: he is going to "start from scratch" and democratize the Soviet Union while easing relations with the West.

In 1924, Westerners deplored the death of Lenin, who they thought was on the point of scuttling communism because, with an economic knife at his throat, he had authorized the NEP in 1921. At the same time, they welcomed Stalin to power because, as a partisan of "socialism in a single country," he was a moderate, to be preferred to Trotsky, the preacher of permanent revolution. In 1953, the West deplored the uncertainty left by the death of Stalin, whose domestic policy may have been a shade brutal but who was "prudent" and "nationalistic" in foreign policy and who had managed "to maintain peace." It took a lot of faith in human goodness to pin a "man of peace" sticker on a leader who, in ten years and a few months, had signed a pact with Hitler, perpetrated the Katyn massarce in Poland, annexed the Baltic states and nearly half of Poland, attacked Finland and, after the war, grabbed Central Europe, attempted a power squeeze in Berlin and ordered the invasion of South Korea.

Western gratitude for such amiability did not prevent us from hoping for even more of Stalin's successor. In 1954, Isaac Deutscher, then (wrongly) considered the best of the Sovietologists and Stalinologists, prophesied that "if the Communist bloc must follow a policy of voluntary restraint and peaceful coexistence with capitalism, its leaders may judge it useful to prevent any further extension of communism that might affect the status quo."[1]

In the United States, the State Department's top experts on the Soviet Union, George Kennan and Charles E. Bohlen, shared Deutscher's opinion, gratuitously attributing friendly feelings to Georgy M. Malenkov, who briefly replaced Stalin. When he was eliminated by Khrushchev, the new man was smoothly cast in turn in the role of the messiah awaited by the West. For the West did not understand that the Khrushchev "thaw," his report to the twentieth Soviet Party Congress and, in 1962, his authorization to *Novy Mir* to publish *One Day in the Life of Ivan Denisovich* were not really steps toward democratization but political operations directed against old Stalinists. Khrushchev was consolidating his power by instituting a new rule: that members of the Nomenklatura, even

---

1. Isaac Deutscher, *La Russie après Staline* (Paris: Seuil, 1954).

those thrown out of office, needed no longer fear deportation or liquidation. But in foreign policy his moderation was displayed, among other sensational feats and notwithstanding his speeches about the "coexistence of systems," in the bloody suppression of the 1956 Hungarian revolt, construction of the Berlin wall in 1961 and the attempt to station nuclear missiles in Cuba in 1962.

Then Khrushchev fell and, after a brief spate of fulsome flattery, the West suddenly awakened to his "adventurism" and the danger of his shifting moods, his impulsiveness, which it contrasted with Brezhnev's imperturbable, methodical, balanced personality. Eighteen years of power finally shattered this safe and harmonious vision. But the tributes to Brezhnev as a "man of peace" after his insolent violation of the Helsinki accords, the increase in Soviet armaments, the conquest of Yemen and part of Africa and the invasion of Afghanistan were not as lavish as those Stalin received. Was the public blasé? Luckily, the politicians made up for this lack of enthusiasm by redoubling their applause and, more important, by hastening to express their anticipatory confidence in Andropov's peaceful and liberal tendencies; in this they were followed, supported and sometimes preceded by the pushy cohort of Sovietological soothsayers. Almost all of them strained their imaginations to find the concessions the rest of us Westerners could immediately grant to prove our goodwill toward the new Soviet leadership.

A strange intellectual process. For if Andropov really was a liberal, it was up to him to prove it, one would think, and not up to us. Especially since his record was not such as to prejudice us in his favor. For that, we needed more information about this former boss of the KGB, the man who fiercely choked off Soviet dissidents merely because they were urging respect of the Helsinki accords, the man who standardized the use of psychiatric hospitals for political purposes, who almost succeeded in having Pope John Paul II assassinated, made disinformation the rule, intensified guerrilla action and terrorism throughout the world and found a way for KGB agents on the ground to suffocate the Polish workers' movement without recourse to Soviet tanks. A liberal who has managed to hide the fact for sixty-eight years deserves encouragement, of course, but he could have begun with a slightly more concrete public demonstration of his miraculous conversion to tolerance. When Andropov was made head of the KGB in 1967 there were only three "special" psychiatric hospitals in the Soviet Union; when he left it in 1982, there were over thirty. Could he, perhaps, have shut down all but the original three? That would have been a good start. How did the France-U.S.S.R. Association feel about this? And the Kalevi Sorsa group? Olof Palme? Willy Brandt and the Socialist International?*

In foreign policy, Andropov was at pains to warn us in a speech on November 22, 1982, that we were not to expect any prior concessions from him. And he added, "Let no one expect unilateral disarmament on our part. We are not naive." An elegant way of insinuating where the innocents really are and of conceding Western supremacy in the lovable art of taking the first step. The short-term aims of Soviet policy after Brezhnev's death were unchanged from what they had been before: maneuvering for the indefinite postponement of Euromissile deployment in Western Europe, exploiting the Socialists' political victory in Madrid to promote Spain's withdrawal from NATO. Under the immutable rules of Soviet diplomacy, these concessions must be extorted in advance from the West in exchange for promises of restraint that Moscow will then have no reason to keep, since it will have obtained everything it sought.

The democracies' mistake when power is shifted in the Kremlin is not, of course, to seek to profit from it to improve the world situation, but *not doing so*. We democrats reason as though a change in Communist leadership were in itself a positive event, like a favorable astrological conjunction from which we must hasten to benefit. The Soviets, we figure, did all that could reasonably have been expected of them by burying Brezhnev and replacing him with someone else, in this case Andropov. With this gigantic effort completed, we feel, they have a right to expect that we will match

---

* Aside from what seems mere dutiful echoing of the Brezhnev-Andropov line, Chernenko has so far said too little to analyze. Even the West has trouble seeing itself in so cloudy a mirror.—TRANS.

it with an effort of our own. If this silly reasoning is taken literally and pushed to its extreme, we would have to put one of our leaders under the ground to demonstrate our desire for peace. Since all the Soviets have to do to prove theirs is to die!

In celebration of Andropov's elevation, a number of "authoritative sources," as we call the professional patsies, rushed to counsel at least a one-year delay in Euromissile deployment by NATO and were outraged that Reagan pressed for development of the MX missile in the United States.[2] What this amounts to saying is that the West should have suspended all its defense programs merely because Brezhnev died and was succeeded by another man. Did we hope Brezhnev was immortal or that, if he had to die, he would never be replaced and the Soviet Union would remain without a government? If the succession of one leader to another is in itself so prodigious a sign of goodwill, then the democracies, which change their leadership far more often than the totalitarian countries, ought to insist on lavish gifts from Moscow after every election, every time a majority changes, each time a President or Prime Minister gives way to another.

We see how confusedly the West projects its own image on totalitarianism, to its own detriment. Brezhnev's death was a biological, not a political fact; his replacement was not in itself a gesture for or against détente but an institutional necessity. It seems to me, therefore, that it was the West's duty to wait for the new leader's first actions, his first proposals, and to weigh them cautiously. He had no business hoping for congratulatory gifts on his accession to power. If the inevitable succession consequent on a leader's death implies political change, it is for the successor to demonstrate this, not for us. Our normal duty in such cases is to wait, at most to signal that we will respond to any favorable initiative with open minds and a willingness to negotiate.

2. On May 16, 1984, Congress approved by a very narrow margin funds for fifteen MX missiles instead of the forty requested by the administration. Moreover, those funds would only become available in April 1984 *if* by then the Soviets had not resumed the Geneva talks. This meant a Soviet advantage of one year over the United States for the modernization of nuclear forces. By merely resuming the talks in April 1984 without any intention of reaching an agreement or making concessions, the Soviets would be in a position to forever freeze the MX program.

This reversal of roles is, once again, explainable by the West's inability to understand the Communist system. The system is based on continuity, not rupture. Even such partial breaks as Khrushchev's revisionism and Deng Xiaoping's pragmatism are reversions to normality, to a true continuity that had been pathologically interrupted. Stalinist terror could not pursue its massacre within the Nomenklatura indefinitely without finally destroying the whole power system; the Maoist delirium of the Cultural Revolution that plunged China into chaos and economic ruin would, had it continued, have swiftly wrecked Chinese communism. But the so-called liberalization by Khrushchev and Deng soon reached their limits; it was pressed just far enough to *save* the Communist system, never far enough to begin *transforming* it, much less abandoning it. The continuity of what must continue always triumphs.

What is it that must continue? What changes and what does not in Kremlin successions? What must continue, what must not change, are the system's two pillars: its ideology and structure. What does change? Men. Sooner or later, the men in power must be replaced. Unfortunately, the West looks exclusively to the men; the decisive importance of personality in a democratic politician's career leads us into the error of carrying the standard over to totalitarian systems, where men reach the top not through the impact of their personalities on the public but via the machine, that is, via the state's structure and ideology. Seeing personality as all-important, Westerners bet on a new Communist leader even before they know who he is, underestimating the continuity of structure. So many pages were written to affirm that communism would change from top to bottom with Stalin's death in Russia, with Mao's in China, blithely sweeping aside all previous analyses of communism as obsolete. These peremptory pages quickly faded into oblivion. Yet with each new Kremlin power shift there are always new "experts" ready to rewrite them. Because such shifts are infrequent in Communist states, the West always forgets the preceding ones. The apotheosis of Andropov confirmed this rule. Wrongly interpreting the nature of change in Communist systems, the democracies limit their initiatives when change does occur to proposals for concessions. They are convinced that this is what they absolutely must do, when in fact they should seize periods of transition as opportunities to demand concessions from the Communists or at least to coldly analyze existing power relationships in a search for what the change can bring them, not what it can bring the Soviet Union. Let the Soviets make their own foreign policy, something they do extremely well. Let's not try to make it for them. We have enough of a job making our own. This, at any rate, is what every Western leader should say when power is transferred in the Kremlin.

But they say just the opposite. During his visit to India at the end of November 1982, Mitterrand declared that Afghanistan is a "poison in the Soviet body" and suggested that the West, along with such neighboring countries as India and Pakistan, could help the Soviet Union purge itself of the poison with a "political solution." This probably meant whittling down the Soviet occupation force while maintaining a vassal government in Kabul. Well, in the months following Brezhnev's death, no sign of goodwill, none of the expected signals throbbed from Moscow concerning Afghanistan, nothing even resembling Brezhnev's clownish announcement in the spring of 1980 that he would withdraw a few divisions from the theater of operations—pure propaganda, but it had briefly fooled Giscard d'Estaing at a meeting in Venice of Atlantic Alliance countries. The truth is that the "signals" of a conciliatory opening which the West, it seems, would be criminal not to grab on the wing have seldom been less visible on the international horizon than they were during the weeks when Brezhnev's successors were settling into power. This added an extra touch of comedy to the insistence with which Western commentators struggled to decipher the signals they thought they saw. In Brezhnev's last speech he had threatened merciless reprisals if the United States and its allies pursued the "arms race." Translation: if they persisted in trying to set up American cruise and Pershing II missiles in Western Europe to counterbalance the Soviet SS-20s. Andropov's first speech contained the same warning, delivered in the same tone. His logic matched his predecessor's: European defense is aggression in Soviet eyes, and any Western attempt to restore a balance of armaments is a threat to the Kremlin. On November 30, 1982, his warning was reinforced by a furious dispatch from the Novosti agency threatening Western Europe with an "immediate riposte" that would inevitably lead to a nuclear "world" war should the West fire one of the new missiles, "even accidentally." The dispatch was timed for the eve of a NATO ministerial meeting at which deployment schedules were to be set. Novosti's warning was double-edged, since there is no reason why a missile can't be "accidentally" fired from the East as well as the West, but the bull thundered forth from Moscow was aimed at frightening the ill-informed and providing an argument to pacifists and champions of unilateral disarmament, notably the Roman Catholic bishops in Italy and the United States.

This outrageously crude fear campaign, however, had little effect. Nor, incidentally, did it say much for the "finesse" so liberally attributed to Andropov by Western analysts. In any case, there was nothing to indicate that the new Soviet leader's aims were any different from his predecessor's except the desperate longing of some Westerners to find a favorable signal. During a visit to Bonn in January 1983 by Soviet Foreign Minister Andrey A. Gromyko— one more example of impudent Soviet pressure during an election campaign in a democratic country—the Foreign Minister's remarks were no more than the eternal mixture of threats, blackmail, intimidation and offers of (Western) concessions.

Profiting from power transfers in the Kremlin should mean anything but what we make of them. It should mean using possible instability in the Soviet leadership in defense of our interests. It is true that any incoming Communist leader faces internal difficulties that may force him to appear more conciliatory abroad. But he will not be conciliatory if he can help it. And he can avoid it if the West simply waits for him to volunteer concessions. What we should do is to play the cards we hold when Moscow's hand is weak, not call off the game until its hand is strengthened.

During the months, even the three or four years, following Stalin's death, when no preparation had been made, as it was in

Brezhnev's case, for a successor, the West utterly failed to exploit the confusion in the Kremlin. Between 1953 and 1956, the situation was ideal for the West to act; it did not act.

In June 1953, the people of East Germany rose against the occupying power, but the West failed to seize the opportunity to insist on peace-treaty negotiations that would have ended the dangerous division of Germany, still one of the Soviet Union's principal means of blackmailing the United States and Europe. At the time, no Western government had yet officially recognized the East German Communist government.

In the summer and fall of 1956, the Polish people rose; we let the Soviets arrange matters their way, by bouncing Bierut and replacing him with Wladyslaw Gomulka. Instead of acting like indifferent spectators, the West could have dusted off the promises made at Yalta—the real ones—committing Stalin to organize free elections in Poland. The balance of power, then highly favorable to the United States, would have made such a demand eminently realistic and, we must insist, in no way "imperialistic"; it would in fact have been the moral thing to do, in support of a people's right of self-determination and in the interests of that peace that the Polish tragedy in the heart of Europe has continually threatened in the twenty-five years since then.

Shortly after the Polish October came a new explosion, the even more widespread and more violent uprising of the Hungarian people, directly challenging the Soviet presence there and communism itself, without prompting from the West. With Moscow's agent, the Stalinist Erno Gero, swept out of power, the most popular man in the country, the only one available in that time of disintegrating power structure, was old Communist Imre Nagy, a former Premier who had been ousted a year earlier. The only program he could come up with was a sort of neutralization of Hungary on the Austrian model approved the year before, which would have taken the country out of the Soviet bloc. A mere flip of the finger by the West could have been decisive then. Caught off balance, with their guard down, the Soviets were being condemned throughout the world, and they were at a strategic disadvantage. Had the West overcome its irresolution and formulated its demands, it would not even have had to use its military power.

Why, after all, was Khrushchev so frightened? Why did he feel a need to cover himself with Mao Tse-tung's "authorization," and why did he consult secretly with Tito? Why did he hesitate so long before moving, sending in his tanks only when he was sure the West would merely boo the play without interrupting the performance?

With the situation so fluid, the West also failed to try to bring Albania back into the Western camp, even though, as I have already noted, Stalin was so uncertain of hanging on to the country that he never concluded with it one of those "friendship treaties" that, in his eyes, sealed a sister nation's irreversible enslavement. It was a noteworthy exception—that no one in the West noticed.

In their first communiqué, on March 6, 1953, Stalin's successors declared their support for a policy that could guarantee "the prevention of any kind of disorder and panic." Why those two words? A month and a half earlier, the Eisenhower-Dulles team had come to office in Washington brandishing the rollback policy they had proclaimed during the election campaign. Stalin's heirs did not know much about the "imperialists" facing them then, and they had forgotten Lenin's observations on the "deaf-mutes" in the West. Except for Molotov, they had had almost no personal contact with Western political figures. But they did know how fragile the situation was within the Soviet system, including its satellites. They readily perceived how disadvantaged they were by the conjunction of three factors:

1. the overall balance of power favored the West;
2. the new team in the White House was calling for a rollback of communism;
3. Stalin's death had created a situation of weakness in the Communist sphere, both at the party summit (as witness the trial and execution of First Deputy Premier Lavrenty P. Beria) and among the subject peoples (the East German uprising in June 1953).

It was both normal and reasonable, therefore, for Stalin's successors, as alert leaders, to anticipate a more aggressive Western policy. Nothing of the sort happened. The West did not budge. What conclusions can we expect the Soviet leaders to have reached at the end of this period, so dangerous for them, when the West could have forced the reunification of Germany and the signing of a fair peace treaty without shedding a drop of blood?

It may be pointed out that Stalin's heirs put other concessions into the scale during this period: the armistice in Korea on July 27, 1953; Moscow's reconciliation with Tito's Yugoslavia; the 1954 Geneva conference that ended France's war in Indochina; the Austrian peace treaty in 1955. Looked at more closely, however, these Soviet concessions show a disturbing and familiar texture; under a microscope they take on an odd look of Western, not Soviet concessions.

The Korean armistice implied no concession by the Soviets; the situation simply reverted to what it had been before the Communist invasion. As a Japanese colony until 1945, Korea was supposed to regain its independence after Japan's defeat. An agreement at Yalta provided for a transition period to allow the victorious armies, American in the South, Russian in the North (although the Soviets never really fought on that front) to liquidate the vestiges of colonialism and guide the country toward independence. As they did in East Germany, the Soviets remained in North Korea instead of pulling out their troops when the transition period ended, setting up a vassal regime there in line with their principle that all the countries they "liberated" after World War II were in fact conquests that became their permanent possessions.

With North Korea safely under lock and key, Stalin was ready for his second play: sending the Korean Communist Army against South Korea. After coming within an ace of conquering the South, the attack stalled before the unexpectedly determined resistance of the United Nations defensive force. Stalin's successors preferred to end the adventure and return to the previous demarcation line. So their attack, and its failure, in Korea cost them no territory at all. The armistice confirmed the existence of a Communist Korean state born of a violation of an international convention and incubated under the forcible occupation by a foreign power.

The United States, which had supplied the bulk of the UN "police" force, had paid with thirty thousand dead and one hundred and fifteen thousand wounded for the privilege of going back to its starting point, with a threat of another invasion from the north [that still hangs over the south today,] thirty years later.

Nor was the Kremlin's "goodwill gesture" in the decolonization of French Indochina any more advantageous to the democracies. They had not meant for the vital process of decolonization to turn to international communism's profit: they were concerned first of all for the welfare of the Vietnamese people, who now are among the unhappiest in the world under the tyranny of their country's Nomenklatura. Contrary to the legend, the Geneva conference does not deserve to be seen as a Western diplomatic achievement.

Khrushchev's memoirs, which appeared in 1971, revealed, first, that the Vietnamese military situation had been worse than the French thought and that the Chinese were not in a position to help the rebels. Second, he disclosed that France's Geneva negotiators began by giving away too much. "At the first session of the conference," Khrushchev wrote, "the French head of state, [Pierre] Mendès France, proposed to restrict the northern reach of the French forces to the seventeenth parallel. I'll confess that when we were informed of this news from Geneva, we gasped with surprise and pleasure. We hadn't expected anything like this. The seventeenth parallel was the absolute maximum we would have claimed ourselves. We instructed our representatives in Geneva to demand that the demarcation line be moved farther south, to the fifteenth parallel, but this was only for the sake of appearing to drive a hard bargain. After haggling for a short time, we accepted Mendès France's offer, and the treaty was signed. We had succeeded in consolidating the conquests of the Vietnamese Communists."[3] History has yet to invalidate this song of victory. International communism will surely take over all of Indochina. In 1954, France was undeniably at a moral, political, and military dead end. That the agreement it reached, in good faith, with Stalin's successors represented a real concession on their part and reflected a Soviet desire for a stable peace can no longer be argued without the spiritual help of belief in the occult.

It is also to be noted that the Soviet Union was not reconciled with Yugoslavia until it chose to be and that, when the time did come, the Kremlin managed to repair the damage done by Stalin's excesses without having to pay too high a price. Yugoslavia did maintain its special status in the Communist world, for this had become almost irreversible, but it could not really force the U.S.S.R. to atone for its conduct during the years of estrangement.

3. *Khrushchev Remembers*, London: Andre Deutsch, 1971.

Tito stopped behaving like an enemy of the Soviet Union the minute Khrushchev and Bulganin stretched out their hands to him—and no bills were clapped into those hands. Similarly, the Austrian peace treaty, the most positive accomplishment during that period, did not result from any Western diplomatic triumph, but from a Soviet policy reversal; at no time did the Kremlin lose control over the proceedings.

What this brief summary of the post-Stalin period points up is that the West was unable to summon the strength to impose conditions on the Soviets or to negotiate except on terms laid down by Moscow. It limited itself to reacting with febrile eagerness to all the Soviet Union's signals. And the Kremlin's new masters, while ridding themselves of the most visible of Stalin's excesses (for example, they buried the insane "doctors' plot"), altered neither the direction and tactics of Soviet foreign policy nor the principle of Central European subjugation nor Moscow's long-term ambitions in Western Europe.

Indeed, it was to weaken Western Europe that Stalin's successors, carrying on his peace movement, won a first-class trophy in 1954: the dismantling of the European Defense Community, which collapsed when France refused to join it. On August 30, 1954, Communists and Gaullists in the French National Assembly combined to vote against ratification of the treaty calling for a European Army. Not only were the Gaullists hostile in principle to any supranational organization, but they had been subjected for a full year to a classic, insistent Communist campaign of penetration, intoxication and propaganda.

Moscow's pounding against the EDC in 1954 was a dress rehearsal for the 1982–83 Soviet assaults against reinforcement of NATO's military potential and for a weapons freeze, a propaganda theme floated by the Soviets with the understandable aim of preserving their military advantage. The nuclear-freeze slogan, detached from its Soviet origins, which were soon forgotten, seduced people of good faith. What nobler crusade is there than opposing atomic war? In nine American states where nuclear-freeze resolutions were hooked on to the 1982 midterm elections, eight voted in favor, with only Arizona rejecting the idea. On the following day, *L'Humanité,* the French Communist organ, described the eight states' votes "against war"—meaning *for* unilateral weakening of the West—as the most important result of the election.

Brezhnev's successors did not drop or even change the Kremlin's aims of expansion and domination any more than Stalin's had. True, every new team in the Kremlin prunes dead tactical branches obscuring the Soviet Union's good name, but this is entirely cosmetic; nothing basic is ever sacrificed. The release of a few political prisoners in Poland, suspension of martial law there after repression had done its work, did not change the fact that the Roman Catholic Church had given in to the Communist Party and that the Solidarity movement had been castrated.

The "overtures" the West should have made to the Soviet Union to mark Andropov's accession to power, to "help him out of a tight spot" and "put détente back on the track," were ready to hand, for the most part. Brezhnev's successor had only to seize on them to reopen the East-West "dialogue," and the opportunity is again open now to Chernenko. For example, in July 1981, Secretary of State Alexander Haig and Britain's Foreign Secretary Lord Carrington, who spoke for the European Economic Community, proposed the neutralization of Afghanistan and Cambodia and replacement of all foreign troops there by a UN peacekeeping force in anticipation of free elections and nonaligned status for both countries. The Soviet Union instantly and without discussion rejected the proposal as "unrealistic." To Moscow, "realism" would have meant our negotiating with Babrak Karmal, the KGB agent the Kremlin had placed at the head of the Afghan Communist government; this would automatically have brought the regime international recognition. Simply calling for negotiations would have left us with nothing to negotiate.

With the grim humor of which, unwittingly, he is such a master, Gromyko has declared that talks about Afghanistan cannot begin until "foreign intervention" ceases there; naturally, the Soviet Union does not count as an intervening power despite the roughly ninety thousand men it maintains there, a figure that is sure to increase. Fine. But if Soviet intransigence in 1981 was due to Brezhnev's influence and if Andropov was just waiting for the old man to die before showing his flexibility, what prevented him in November 1982 from reopening conversations about the Haig-Carrington proposal? And what prevents Chernenko from doing so now? It might be answered that the Communists cannot agree to free elections anywhere. True enough. But in that case, it's the system that blocks solutions to problems, not the men it throws up. Nor is progress being stalled by a lack of Western proposals. For what can the West suggest—eternal Soviet occupation of Afghanistan? This, of course, would be one "overture" of which Moscow would approve highly. But is this even necessary? Don't the Soviets know that we have already in effect accepted the fait accompli in Afghanistan? The only grain of sand in the Soviet machine for conquest is the resistance being put up by the Afghan mountaineers. We in the West have no part in this. We are giving the freedom fighters very little help. True, we have not been asked to make the supreme concession and take the Soviets' place as the Afghans' butchers. Perhaps, though, to prove our interest in reviving détente and winning Moscow's confidence, we could put together an "independent" study group to examine that possibility. It could be made up of, say, Messrs. Willy Brandt, Olof Palme, Kalevi Sorsa, Edgar Faure, Tony Benn, and Ted Kennedy.

In the absence of any such grandiloquent gesture, nothing seemed to activate Andropov's better nature. Instead, on December 5, 1982, Afghan officials—in other words, the Soviets—announced that ten "terrorists" had been shot. There was nothing new in the execution of Afghan resistance fighters; the novelty came in the official announcement of executions carried out in all due form, a clear message to the West that fell lamentably short of the eagerly awaited signals of moderation.

Andropov did indeed show his love of détente, Communist style, by demanding that the West disarm and, particularly, by protesting against the stationing of MX missiles in Wyoming. The protest awoke many echoes in Western Europe and the United States. In November 1982, Moscow charged that the MX project violated the SALT agreement. Which one? SALT I, long obsolete, did not apply here and, anyway, it has so often been violated by the Soviet Union that its effectiveness is merely a distant memory. SALT II was being debated in the Senate when the Red Army invaded Afghanistan and wrecked its chances of ratification. Then what right have the Russians to invoke a nonexistent treaty? Even in this case, however, couldn't the Kremlin backtrack and welcome the Western initiative? If it simply pulled its troops out of Afghanistan, the Senate would resume its consideration of SALT II, which now, of course, needs revision. Clearly, there is no lack of conciliatory gestures from the West; the trouble lies in Moscow's refusal to concede anything at all in exchange for what it is offered.

Western belief in a miraculous softening of Soviet intentions whenever power is transferred in the Kremlin is another of the many traps we set for ourselves, with the aid of Communist disinformation, naturally. The extent and ingenuity of this disinformation was again disclosed by a minor incident that happened soon after Andropov, the new Muscovite Saint Francis, ascended to Stalin's throne. A Canadian college professor, Hugh Hambleton, appeared in a London court late in November 1982 to answer charges of spying for the Soviet Union, to which he transmitted secret documents while working for NATO. A humdrum event, routine, almost reassuringly banal. What was instructive was Hambleton's account during his trial of a personal meeting in Moscow a few years earlier with his boss Andropov, then heading the KGB. The eminent, jazz-loving, English-speaking Chekist suggested that his intellectual spook drop the estimable but subordinate trade of spying and go into politics, with the aid, needless to say, of a brotherly subsidy from good old Yury; he was to try to win a seat in Parliament from which he could influence Canadian politicians and public opinion in favor of the Soviet Union. There was no question of his running as a Communist candidate—a rare breed in Canada; Moscow needed a "peace-loving liberal" as an agent of influence. Since it is doubtful that Andropov and his acolytes tailored this scheme uniquely for the obscure Hambleton, I leave it to the reader to speculate on how many independent voices are raised in the world's parliaments when the Kremlin needs their help to pursue its uninterrupted ascension toward peace. It especially needs them to nudge the West into making concessions when the Soviet leadership changes, those magical interludes when our own leaders, like the three kings of old, bow deferentially before the new wunderkind's cradle.

I must repeat, I am not suggesting that the West has nothing to gain from the fluid situation surrounding any change of political personnel in Moscow or Peking or anywhere else, though the chances for profit are slighter in the East bloc than elsewhere. Nor am I suggesting that the way for us to do this is to bombard the Soviets with ultimatums. I am simply saying that the best way for us to exploit such situations certainly is not to behave solicitously in the hope of meriting Soviet benevolence, nor is it to stand pious watch for "signals" from Moscow that, for the most part, exist only in our imaginations. Again, I feel that this ingenuousness that substitutes wishes for analysis, this saintly diplomacy in which sacrifice replaces negotiation, are rooted in our ignorance of how Communist apparatusses and societies function.

Early in October 1982, it was announced that Averell Harriman was making an initial grant of one million dollars to Columbia University to stimulate study of the Soviet Union. A number of experts agreed that Sovietology had reached "its lowest level since World War II."[4] Whereas the Ford Foundation once spent forty million dollars a year supporting Slavic and Soviet studies, it paid out only two million in 1982 because of a lack of candidates in the field.[5]

From 1950 to 1969, when Communist power was confined to Eastern Europe and the Far East, two major Western democracies, the United States and Britain, were rich in formal institutes for the study of communism in the Soviet Union and elsewhere. I hasten to add that, to its honor, France has never sponsored any such bodies, which makes it, thank heaven, the only country where no decline in this line of activity has been noted. Since that period,

4. *International Herald Tribune,* 8 October 1982.
5. Ibid., 24 September 1982.

cruising along the peaceful stream of détente, communism has spread to every continent, but methodical study of communism has dwindled steadily in the United States and Britain; a host of British publications specializing in the study of communism, most of them supported by the Foreign Office, has disappeared. In consequence, democratic statesmen in the late twentieth century are even more ignorant of the subject than the postwar generation.

It is no secret, for example, that the Soviet invasion of Afghanistan on December 26, 1979, surprised key Western leaders. President Carter admitted it did more at a stroke to change his mind about the aims of Soviet policy than everything else that had happened since he took office. Chancellor Schmidt scurried to make a last-second change in his New Year's message, in which he had planned to assure the world of Moscow's peaceful intentions; one shudders to think how embarrassed the clear-sighted Chancellor would have been had the invasion been delayed until January 2. In Paris, President Giscard d'Estaing even projected his own surprise on the Soviets themselves, describing their action as improvised and hasty. Yet Lenin's heirs are not in the habit of improvising, as the history of the past sixty years has shown. But Western statesmen do not study history; they wait until they are elected to begin their on-the-job reading.

These statesmen belie Heraclitus's observation that "one never bathes twice in the same river." In the river of forgetfulness of the West's perception of communism, intermittently fed by the sterile influxes of Kremlin power shifts, they have bathed again and again, have bathed daily, and always at the same spot.

24

THE DOUBLE STANDARD

FROM THE DAY President Truman declared that "it must be the policy of the United States to support free people who are resisting attempted subjugation by armed minorities or by outside pressure,"[1] the democracies were locked of their own free will into an almost insurmountable bind. For they laid down the condition that to have the right to resist absorption into the Communist empire a country must be irreproachably democratic. In so doing, the West condemned itself to failure or opprobrium. It became the prisoner of an insoluble, self-imposed dilemma: either it allowed most of the planet to sink under Communist domination or, too often, it would be called on to protect countries that did not have democratic governments.

The trap was a boon to Communist propaganda, which on this point was widely supported by the liberal left in the democracies. And honesty does command that any democrat with consistent ideas deplore the hypocrisy of defending human rights and individual freedom while supporting authoritarian governments. The best of these may be no more than relics or revivals of archaic power structures; the worst are violent, police-run fascist regimes or pseudodemocracies where elections are held only spasmodically. Rarely, if ever, are they genuinely faithful to the ideal of the rule of law on which the West claims to base the legitimacy of its diplomacy and its defense.

From the outset, then, the game was unfair, since it is unthink-

1. Cited by Norman Podhoretz in *The Present Danger* (New York: Simon and Schuster, 1980).

able to insist that Communist empires respect democratic rules or limit their alliances to countries that do respect them. No one would dream of denying the Soviet Union's right to include the bloody dictatorship of Ethiopian Lieutenant Colonel Mengistu Haile Mariam among its satellites simply because he has refused to reform or because he did not come to office in an election of Swiss-quality probity and has not made democratic freedoms the rule in his country.

We all know the refrain: "Domestic affairs . . . No interference . . . The less developed countries have a right to put off elections as long as they institute progressive reforms . . . It's normal for them to turn toward the Soviet Union and away from the former colonial powers . . . Parliamentary democracy is a luxury the poor cannot afford, certainly not as a priority," and so on. It would be absurd and presumptuous to ask the Soviet Union to give up its strategic bastion in North Korea unless that protégé goes democratic. Yet the democracies are constantly vilified in Communist and "progressive" propaganda as well as by prominent liberals at home because they cooperate economically and militarily with, say, the very undemocratic government in South Korea.

To a totalitarian regime, strategic necessity is justification enough for Soviet presence in another country or alliance with or aid to that country. Anyone calling for further excuses is requested, even in the West itself, to mind his own business. A democracy, on the other hand, is not granted the right to defend the vital barricades of its own security unless the democratic imperative is obeyed. If it is not, the West's duty, if we understand correctly, is to cede the territory in question to the Communists, who are unhampered by this democratic obligation.

Similarly, defending the independence of South Vietnam in the 1960s and 1970s was tinged with infamy because the South Vietnamese regime was hardly of exemplary purity. But the Hanoi regime had no need to furnish guarantees of its democracy to win the right to defend itself or to attack its neighbors. Progressive and even centrist opinion throughout the world granted it "popular" legitimacy on trust which its history after 1975 did not support but which its totalitarian and aggressive behavior never seemed to diminish. And since 1981 we have been assured by the Socialist International and the media in Europe, Latin America and the United States that the West cannot be true to its principles unless it lets El Salvador go totalitarian—unless, of course, it could guarantee simon-pure political, economic, and social democracy there. The general feeling is that only hidebound reactionaries could question the legitimacy of Nicaragua's pretotalitarian, pro-Soviet regime or withhold economic or military aid from it in the name of human rights, political pluralism and democracy.

Better still: the Soviet Union is allowed to ally itself with traditional-style fascist regimes that dispense with even a facade of progressivism if Moscow's worldwide strategic interests require it. And it can do so without bringing down on itself the vehement criticism that world opinion levels at any democratic nation attempting the same expedient. The Soviet Union and Cuba, for example, loudly took Argentina's side against Britain in the 1982 Falkland Islands War simply because it was obviously in the Kremlin's interest to oppose the Western democracies; suddenly, no one in the Communist world minded the evil international reputation of the "odious and bloody fascist dictatorship" in Buenos Aires. It is true that the Soviet leaders must have laughed up their sleeves over the free world's indignation at the Argentine junta's crimes, which were extremely amateurish by comparison with those of any Communist dictatorship. After all, didn't the Buenos Aires fascists ship wheat to the socialists in Moscow in 1980 when the United States tried timidly to punish the Soviet invasion of Afghanistan by embargoing grain sales to the East?

The Soviet Union, then, is licensed by most people to safeguard its economic interests and capitalize on its strategic advantages by realistic links with any government notorious for its disregard of human rights. But we hear only clamor and vituperation when a Western country is cornered into collaboration—by its nature sinful—with South Africa or the Shah's Iran or Turkey.

I am all in favor of world opinion judging the democratic countries' compromises more sternly than it does the socialist countries'. I merely note that this double standard gives the Soviet empire an automatic advantage over the West: it not only can defend itself and expand without having to bother about the rules governing the democratic powers' foreign policy, but its satellites and clients are also exempted. This is really a two-pronged advantage: although it need not respect human rights at home, the Soviet empire is free to condemn violations, real or fictitious, anywhere else, to exploit them and set its agents to exploiting them. It can even provoke violations, using terrorism to elicit repression in the Western countries or those associated with them.

The Soviet Union, then, enjoys the privilege of being entitled not only to defend its empire, but to enlarge it without being judged on the basis of its subject states' standards of living, social justice, political freedoms or respect for human rights. When subjugated peoples rise against communism, the West usually refrains from helping them, thus recognizing the legitimacy of Communist domination in all circumstances. The Communists, on the other hand, recognize the legitimacy of no government outside their empire, least of all in the democratic countries.

Conversely, the democracies suffer the theoretical handicap in their struggle with the Soviet Union of being responsible on all the abovementioned grounds not only for their own behavior but for their allies' as well. For example, when military governments took over in Greece in 1967 and Turkey ten years later, the question immediately arose in the democracies of whether these countries, which had broken faith with democracy, deserved to remain within the Western defense system. But when Poland, which was already totalitarian, declared a state of martial law to allow its Army to shore up the shaky Communist Party dictatorship, Westerners immediately argued that no real liberalization is possible in a country like Poland because *it is a vital strategic zone for the Soviet Union.* Yet Turkey is just as essential to the West as Poland is to the Soviets. Driving it out of NATO, or even suspending weapons shipments to the Turkish Army (which was done because of the Greco-Turkish conflict over Cyprus in 1974) means opening a fatal breach in the Atlantic Alliance's southern flank. No one would suggest with a straight face that the Soviet Union enjoin Poland to restore democracy there or be booted out of the Warsaw Pact. Yet this is precisely what many eminent Western political, labor and journalistic figures have recommended to NATO to purge Turkey of its antidemocratic humors. Here again, the imbalance between the democracies' obligations and those of the totalitarian countries leaves little doubt as to which side has been whipped in advance.

Detractors of the United States and the "free world"—the expression is usually employed as a term of derision, as though there were not really a free world and a slave world—have always rightly maintained that we cannot fight in democracy's name by consorting with nondemocratic countries. The answer to this, in the first place, is that since World War II the West has not fought or, at any rate, has not taken the offensive. It has defended itself and, on the whole, has retreated. The handful of democracies that make up the "free world" have merely tried to survive in the competition with communism. Are they sure they have the right? We are free to doubt that they are; as I just noted in passing, it is instructive that the West formed the habit early on of placing quotation marks around the phrase "free world" but not around the phrase *popular democracy*.

Second, it would obviously be ideal if the democracies could survive without having to defend any but other democracies. In most cases, however, this moral ideal runs up against local traditions of government or de facto situations the West cannot easily alter. If it tries to do so, it is at once accused of neocolonialism. President Carter's human-rights policy, under which he suspended American aid to the dictatorships in Argentina, Chile, and Bolivia, produced no political improvement in those countries, but the Soviet Union leaped into the breach to increase trade with them. In Iran, Carter hastened the fall of what was certainly a detestably tyrannical regime—that was succeeded by a much worse one.

It takes a profound ignorance of history to blame American imperialism alone for the long Latin American tradition of coups d'état, military dictatorships, civil wars, corruption, revolution, bloody terror, and repression; this goes back to the very founding of independent states there nearly two centuries ago. It is striking that one-man, one-party rule has triumphed almost everywhere on the African continent, in North Africa and Black Africa, in the former French colonies as in the former Belgian and British colonies, in "progressive" and "moderate" regimes alike. Even such leaders as President-for-Life Kenneth Kaunda in Zambia and Zimbabwe's Prime Minister Robert Mugabe, after opting when their countries received their independence for multiparty systems, soon changed their minds without arousing indignation in Europe; their reason: one-party systems are more in tune with the African character. Some of the most barbarous examples of internal genocide, like the slaughter in Burundi, had nothing at all to do with Western "imperialism"; neither have some of Africa's most monstrous tyrants, such as Uganda's Idi Amin. And for the people of Uganda, the country's "liberation" by troops from "progressive" Tanzania inaugurated an era of suffering and martyrdom every bit as abominable as the one that preceded it.

It must be admitted, nevertheless, that the political longevity of another bloodthirsty lunatic, the Central African Republic's Jean-Bedel Bokassa, was partly France's fault. France did not produce him, but it helped keep him in power until he went too far and was run out of the country by his own people. The United States was guilty of the same moral fault in supporting Nicaraguan dictator Anastasio Somoza Debayle, who ruled too long by terror supported from abroad.

In any case, the free world's moral turpitude and political inconsistency are recognized, proclaimed and condemned whenever it collaborates with largely or wholly undemocratic governments that violate human rights, whether it merely accepts them passively or assists them actively. To escape this contradiction and avoid condemnation before the tribunal of free-world opinion, the West must therefore deny itself the support, in its struggle against Soviet expansionism, of any country that is undemocratic and disrespectful of human rights. This principle means the democracies' right to defend themselves must be subordinated to the conversion of the whole world to democracy. Clearly, it can only lead to the disappearance of what subsists of democracy in today's world.

I am not quarreling with the principle's validity. I cannot repeat often enough that my aim in this book is not to decide who is "right" and who is "wrong," but to lay bare a mechanism. I submit that the mechanism of international relations and world opinion is so rigged that in almost every situation it imposes an almost insurmountable initial handicap on the West. When the Soviet Union appropriated South Yemen as a base for destabilization of the Persian Gulf countries and a training school for international terrorists, no one insisted that it begin by making the Yemenis paragons of democratic virtue. This would be a forbidding task anyway, even for the most pious missionaries of Scandinavian socialism at the top of its form.

In short, without always going so far as to approve we nevertheless consider it natural for the Soviet Union to defend its interests, increase its power, install its henchmen in Yemen or elsewhere through a craftily spaced series of coups d'état and purges. No one asks these imperialists to make the people they capture happy; no one thinks the Communists can be scolded into retreating. Nor does anyone in the democratic camp recognize his own right—not openly, at least—to fight Soviet imperialism with its own weapons. Instead, the free world again risks being accused of impure complicity with a reactionary "feudal" regime when it defends Saudi Arabia, say, against the undermining and subversion that the Soviet Union and its agents, including the Libyans, have been carrying on there for years. The moral is that the Soviet Union must be allowed to take over the Arabian Peninsula unless all the countries on it mold themselves to Western democratic ideals, an eventuality I would wish for but scarcely expect, at least in the immediate future, which is all that counts.

Also at stake in the immediate or very near future is the fate of southern Africa, especially that of the Republic of South Africa, which has earned the rightful hostility of all defenders of human rights for its official policy of racial segregation. That it should be excluded from all international sports events is not surprising—

until we remember that the Soviet Union, the People's Republic of China, North Korea and Romania, which have as many or more human-rights blots on their records, do take part in these events.

A professional tour of South Africa by a British cricket team in March 1982 aroused more criticism in Britain than the news, which broke at the same time, of Russia's use of chemical weapons in Laos and Afghanistan or the stiffening of totalitarian rule in Poland. The team went to the land of apartheid against the express wishes of the British Government; Britain's Labor opposition even accused the Tory Government in the House of Commons of unpardonable weakness in failing to jail the cricketers. Their illicit trip, it was feared, might bring reprisals in the form of refusals by Pakistani and Indian cricket teams to play in Britain. Yet no one has threatened to boycott any of the countries that sent athletes to the Moscow Olympics in 1980.

This is another example of the double standard. But athletics is just a side issue here. What really matters is whether the West should, as the most enlightened and respectable voices of Western public opinion recommend, refuse any political and strategic cooperation with South Africa until apartheid has been eliminated. Considering that, at best, it would take a long time to end racial segregation in South Africa, that the Soviet Union is already strongly entrenched in the region, and that the slow process of reform might be radically accelerated by an uprising of South Africa's blacks, the West might gain little from abandoning South Africa and would certainly be seriously weakened. For, as we know, the sea route around the Cape of Good Hope is the main channel for our supplies of oil from the Persian Gulf. Moreover, South Africa's soil holds most of the world's deposits of rare minerals outside the Soviet Union, supplying most of the metals needed by the industrialized countries.

In other words, if South Africa were to come under Soviet influence, Moscow would control not only its own vast mineral resources but also those of South Africa and Namibia, where the pro-Communist SWAPO (South-West African People's Organization) is likely to take power. In short, it would have a stranglehold on most and, in some cases, all of the minerals vital to our industries. It could block oil shipments to us—if it hadn't already shut them off at the source along the Persian Gulf. That kind of economic power would make the Soviet Union master of the West without recourse to war, nuclear or conventional, in Europe.

The Soviet Union's great strength lies in its freedom to invade areas where history has left the decaying remnants of archaic regimes that are important to the West's security or are sources of vital materials. Never mind that these regimes are replaced, as they always are, by bloodier, more repressive Communist police states and that the change leaves the area's poor more starved than they were before. The U.S.S.R. still comes out ahead. For local and world opinion perceive the *relative* advantages of the old regime and the horrors of Communist putrefaction only after the new regime is in power and irreversible.

When the West tries to protect archaic regimes or those of "modernistic authoritarians" like the Shah of Iran from disintegration or attempts to restrain their abuses, it cannot help seeming to defend the right against the left, the past against the future, the billionaires against the poverty-stricken masses. The fact that when the Communist left overturns the right it brings with it rampant famine, the camps and the boat people, that it is the left of Cambodian genocide and Khomeini's firing squads, never works as a *preventive.* If the West tries to pressure an archaic regime into becoming more liberal, either it is accused of "interference" by outraged nationalists or its well-meaning proselytizing shoves the country into unforeseeable chaos, as exemplified by the Islamic revolution in Iran. And while the ayatollahs' bloody terror may now be partly anti-Communist, for essentially religious reasons, the Kremlin knows very well that in the long run, when the brink of the pit of anarchy is reached, Iran may topple into the Soviet camp, but it is unlikely ever again to tip back over into the free world.

The Soviet Union's advantage over the free world is that neither world opinion nor, of course, its own muzzled public expects it to preach to its allies before associating with them or to hold on to its satellites by any way but sheer force; it is not even required to provide enough food for the peoples it absorbs into its imperial system.

But "international opinion"—the phrase describes part of the free countries' public opinion plus Soviet propaganda—will not accept violation of the rules of democracy by the West's friends. Even when such countries as Taiwan, South Korea, Malaysia and Singapore develop thriving economies that most other nations in the Third World envy and that would bring cries of admiration from the Western left if they blossomed under Soviet banners, they are not appreciated. For they have curtailed their citizens' freedom. The socialist regimes, of course, have obliterated freedom without even achieving comparable prosperity.

The hostility toward the United States inspired in men of goodwill by the horrors of the Vietnamese War is understandable. Yet we now see that the regime that won the war, with help from the Russians, the Chinese and world opinion, was the worst possible for the Vietnamese, for their neighbors, for the independence of Vietnam and the countries around it, for human rights and an adequate standard of living, and for peace in the area. Had the United States won, South Vietnam would doubtless have been subjected to the "imposed democracy" experienced in Japan after World War II—and which has not done too badly by the Japanese. But the Russians would probably have maintained terrorism there and a prosperous South Vietnam would be disturbed by demonstrations against "imperialist domination" and for "the liberation of Vietnam." The demonstrations would spread to the rest of the world, especially to the United States.

International communism uses peoples' aspirations to well-being, freedom, dignity and independence to eliminate the democracies. It is not afterward compelled to satisfy these aspirations; it merely safeguards its own political and strategic interests. The free world, on the other hand, seems not to have the right to consider *its* own political and strategic interests unless it has first fulfilled all the other conditions—has instituted social justice, political democracy and economic prosperity. It is very practiced at this and tries to meet the terms whenever it can.

When the democracies do take on a reactionary regime as an ally, it is not at all because they prefer such governments or even because they need it to realize their primary objective. This contradiction is a source of perpetual trouble; it makes the democracies vulnerable to hostile propaganda and is often a prelude to the worst kind of political upheavals. Whenever possible, the West much prefers that the countries on which its security depends be democratic. Unfortunately, this is not always possible.

The United States knows, for example, that NATO would be stronger if Turkey were governed by a stable democracy instead of bouncing back and forth between anarchy and military dictatorship. But the anarchy created by the failure of democracy in Turkey left the country with two alternatives: radicalization that would have opened it to a Communist putsch or rule by the Army. The West was incapable of restoring democracy to Turkey, at least for the near future. Does this mean we should have broken with the military government, ejected Turkey from NATO? This is precisely what the Soviet Union would have wished, what it has sponsored ten years of terrorism there trying to achieve.

Such dilemmas never confront the Soviet Union. Because it is a totalitarian power, the world thinks it natural that it set up and maintain devoted totalitarian regimes in its image in the countries with which it is "allied." These are vassal regimes, forced to mimic the Soviet state, but any attempt to challenge their legitimacy is greeted with strong objections in the West and icy disdain by Moscow. Only on the West does the contradictory duty devolve of leaving every ally free to choose its own political system while trying to persuade it to conform to democratic ideals. By the same reasoning, each country allied or associated with the West must be free to leave the alliance at any time—a liberty that no one in the East or the West would dream of claiming for a Soviet satellite.

This inequality of duties that so favors the Communists over the free world prevents no one from turning around and equating the two sides when argument requires it. The technique for doing this seems fair but is in fact discriminatory: it simply lumps them together in iniquity.

The free world has incomparably less power over its affiliates than the Communists have over theirs, but it has far greater responsibilities toward them. The United States is held directly responsible for the poverty of every Latin American peasant, whereas no direct responsibility is ascribed to the Soviet Union for the poverty in Vietnam. The liberal left, backed up by many "conservatives," long believed that there was only one kind of imperialism: American imperialism. When it finally had to resign itself to recognizing the existence of Soviet imperialism, it immediately developed a purification ritual: calling a plague on both their houses. This is only one verse in the long chapter of false parallels. Doubtless there is such a thing as Soviet imperialism, there are Soviet violations of human rights, Soviet economic setbacks. But for every case of Soviet aggression, each violation, any setback, the left hastens to seek a way of pinning exactly equal guilt on the West: the Soviet Union and communism are dangerous, of course, but no more so than the United States and free enterprise; communism is criminal, but no more so than the free world; they cannot rescue humanity from want, but neither can we.

Almost throughout the twentieth century, the politically cross-eyed left in the democracies has unsheathed its fury only against the crimes of the capitalist world. Around 1970, the amnesia that periodically rejected unsavory disclosures about the Communist world began to show cracks. Telltale scars remained after each new cleansing absolution. Soon the mass of facts grew too dense to deny out of hand. This is when the lumping-together hoax was devised.

It consists of admitting the existence of Communist crimes and failures provided these can instantly be matched by equivalents in the capitalist world. Binary obsession, apocalyptic symmetry, mania for linkage, fussy egalitarianism—all working to see to it that both pans of the scale hold exactly balanced doses of horror. They are zealously checked and, when necessary, readjusted with a sly flick of the finger to maintain their absolute equilibrium. Communism is now absolved not because it never sins but because the democracies sin as grievously.

In this new dialectical game, everyone is free, without necessarily being dishonest, to retail the misdeeds and failings of totalitarian communism, but on condition that we hasten to present their capitalist twins. Any derogation from the rule is immediately vilified as "selective indignation" and earns the cheat the severe censure of impartial players. A serene mind is obliged, as soon as it observes a flaw or social sore behind the iron, bamboo, sable, sugarcane or coconut-palm curtains, to scramble to find the thug charged with seeing to it that a matching canker is pinpointed on this side of the silver curtain, in the capitalist sphere.

The lumping-together technique is really just the modern way to routinize communism and grant it a plenary indulgence. When everyone is equally guilty, no one is, with the possible exception of capitalism, which does not, after all, have the same excuses to plead as a rival that will not share its concern for building a more just society.

For example, a doctrinally pure French socialist, Louis Mermaz, President of the National Assembly since 1981, replied to a reporter's question about the gulags, "I am as horrified as you are by the gulags, which are a perversion of communism. But I ask that you also condemn that monstrosity of the capitalist system: hunger throughout the world that kills fifty million people each year, thirty million of them children."[2] The retort, remarkable for its speed, is less so for its objectivity. For the parallel is only apparent: the gulags are a "perversion" of communism, but famine, according to the Socialist leader, is a product of the basic nature of capitalism. And while the magic of parallelism makes the Communist sin almost venial, that of capitalism remains mortal. Indeed, absolution is usually a one-way grant—to forgive the horrors of communism. It seems unlikely that, if questioned on famine in the world, Mermaz would have replied with a diatribe against the gulags; he would have protested violently against the shocking malnutrition of some of our fellow humans, and he would have been right. That the gulags exist does not make Third World poverty

2. The statement was made during radio station Europe 1's "Press Club" program on July 5, 1981.

any less morally intolerable. But by what sorcery is the reverse true?

Besides, the magician was using phony statistics. As demographers know, some fifty million people die in the world every year. They can't all die of starvation, and three fifths of them can't be children. The fight against infant mortality in the poor countries has reduced its incidence, which is why their populations are increasing. Nutritionists estimate the number of deaths annually due to malnutrition at 10 percent of the total, *and this includes the Communist countries*, which slightly weakens the indictment of capitalism. Starvation deaths in the Communist world may be better hidden, but the victims are just as dead as any others. Mao's successors have confirmed what demographers had already determined from their study of Chinese population patterns: that some sixty million Chinese died of starvation in 1960–70.

A final objection to the Mermaz comparison: the gulags came into being by *deliberate* political decisions of Communist governments, whereas the direct connection between capitalism and famine is far more conjectural. I know it is a Third World rallying cry, but it has never been scientifically tested, although it has been subjected to rigged tests whose inconsistency has been pointed out by Paul Samuelson, the Nobel prize-winning economist, and he is not a conservative.[3]

Historically, capitalism has in fact rid Europe of the periodic famines that plagued it until the middle of the eighteenth century, as they now do in the less developed countries. It has even begun to relieve starvation in some of the poorer countries, India and Brazil, for example, which now export foodstuffs. Much, enormously much remains to be done everywhere before all mankind can enjoy the high nutritional standard that not even the capitalist West reached until the nineteenth century. But this problem has nothing whatever to do with the question at issue: the deliberate creation by an organized political regime of a repressive concentration-camp system that doubles as a system of government.

Whatever conclusions we may come to on these matters, the

3. See "The Unequal Exchange," in *Commentary*, spring 1982.

truth is that the lumping-together process is designed to make evil relative—which, in the last analysis, means to excuse it. The procedure also implies tailor-made interpretations of available data, and this must lead to error and prevarication: you cannot artificially equate events and faults that are rarely comparable without jerryrigging the facts.

When a political-science professor entitles his article on El Salvador "A Western Cambodia?"[4] not even the question mark saves it from being a soothing balm to many of his readers. The genocide by the Khmer Rouge Communists in Cambodia daubed socialism with a stain that no socialist laundering, however "perverted," can wash away. By suggesting, even tentatively, that the West is saddling itself with a Cambodia in Latin America, the article restores the balance. Communism is not the only guilty party. Everybody back to square one. The weakness in this Solomonic impartiality lies in the author's almost total ignorance of the situation in El Salvador or his refusal to learn about it. It is not discounting the deaths there to point out that, fortunately, there have been far fewer of them than in Cambodia. Moreover, seldom have two historical situations been more different than the genocide in Cambodia and the civil war in El Salvador.

In Cambodia, a fourth to a third of the population was methodically exterminated by a handful of ideologists who aimed to purify their society by restricting it to people who knew nothing about capitalism, money, consumption or culture. We sometimes forget to cite one of the most effective of the many ways mankind has found to commit suicide: utopia. This has no part in the Salvadoran civil war, which, if we can speak this way of human suffering, had far more "classic" causes. Again, no one is trying here to minimize or excuse or accuse, only to understand. But this is precisely what we are prevented from doing by obsessive attempts to use El Salvador as a rag to wipe away the stain of Cambodia. And that of Afghanistan, another case with which the Central American problem cannot be compared. The stubborn pursuit of equivalences has led some excellent politicians to willfully neglect

4. By Maurice Duverger in *Le Monde*, 15 January 1981.

available information about El Salvador. Hence their disappointment at the fact that elections there have been held as regularly as possible, under close international observation; their chagrin has been deepened by the results of these elections, for which the voters have turned out in force to show unequivocally that the rebels have only minority support in the tiny country. This is mortifying. No one likes to see his theories upset by the facts; the tendency is to avoid this by deforming those facts still more. Example: the Socialist International, meeting in Bonn, rejected the election held in El Salvador on March 28, 1982, as "manipulated." Whatever else might be said about that election, it is for once impossible to allege it was faked. If it had been, the incumbent government would not have been defeated.[5]

The brokers of repression have also circulated the slogan "Turkey and Poland: the same fight." There is no need to be indulgent toward the Turkish regime since the military takeover there on September 12, 1980; no one should shut his eyes to the trials of Turkish labor leaders, and we would do better to exaggerate the rumors about torture and summary executions there than to ignore them. But we nullify in advance whatever positive influence we might have over the Turkish leaders when we start by failing to understand that no two cases could be more dissimilar than those of Poland and Turkey in 1981–83.

Since 1956, the Polish people have tried periodically, and vainly, to throw off a totalitarian regime imposed on them from outside by a foreign power after Poland's forcible absorption into the Soviet empire. They have never been given a chance to vote in free and honest elections, terms that cannot apply to the dreary sham balloting customary in Communist countries. Since 1961, Turkey had functioned within democratic institutions administered by political parties that took turns governing the country. Unfortunately, it had also been infested since 1975 with political terrorism—I will leave it up to the malicious-minded to guess who instigated it—that between 1975 and 1980 was responsible for one thousand deaths a year. Lacking leaders who could guarantee their security by lawful

5. See Chapter 17.

means, the Turkish people resigned themselves, without enthusiasm, certainly, but with absolutely no hostility, to rule by soldiers who, as a French newspaper commented, "enforce order without using terror."[6] Even if we are entitled to be severe toward these military governors, we must admit that it was the Turks who put their own house in order.

Asserting that Turkey depends as closely on the United States as Poland does on the Soviet Union is another example of that false symmetry that can be defined as an asylum for ignorance. Testimony to this is the quarrel that erupted between Washington and Ankara over the 1974 Greco-Turkish war and led Turkey to close some of the American bases on its territory. In Poland, even at the peak of its official "renewal," not a single voice, neither in the Church nor in *Solidarność* nor anywhere else was heard demanding that a single Red Army soldier leave the country.

Infinitely preferable to this spurious equivalence is the frank bias of Greek Socialist Prime Minister Andreas Papandreou. After rightly inviting the world's scorn for Colonel George Papadopoulos and the military junta that asphyxiated democracy in Greece between 1967 and 1974, the Prime Minister refused at the beginning of 1982 to endorse a European communiqué denouncing martial law in Poland. In other words, Papandreou approves of Papadopoulos when his name is Jaruzelski. This political gymnast has stuck to the old horizontal bar; he is going to have to learn about the discreet charm of parallel bars.

The device of lumping East and West together is based on a respectable concern to which we should all subscribe: to denounce injustice wherever it may be found, without, for partisan reasons, shielding those responsible. But in practice this has become a sort of witch's trick for blaming others to acquit the side we prefer. Moreover, trying too hard to deal aces to their friends gets people into the habit of inventing artificial equivalences. The more astute we become in dreaming up these correlations between really unre-

6. *Le Monde*, 29 December 1981. The Turkish referendum in the fall of 1982 confirmed its judgment.

lated ills, the less capable we are of understanding those ills, much less curing them.

Equitable in appearance, parallelism—the lumping-together technique—really favors Soviet propaganda and power. It presents as pure routine the conquests that substantially and tangibly increase the Communist empire's power by discounting them against a collection of "balancing" but, in fact, disparate free-world actions that either are not conquests at all or do not begin to match the Communist conquests. Here again, we are dealing with a shrewdly assembled system whose postulates, although recognized as equivalent by both parties, lead ineluctably to a long-term loss for one of them. This is what happens when the future loser agrees to a double standard under the rigged rules of political bookkeeping.

Since 1973, Chile's General Augusto Pinochet has been one of international communism's most effective servants, just as the Spanish generals would have been had their attempt at a coup d'état in Madrid succeeded in February 1981. And if the Spanish Army had tried again and won just after the declaration of martial law in Poland (on December 13 of that year), the Kremlin would have been overwhelmingly grateful. We can be sure it would have exploited this providential boon with consummate virtuosity.

Pinochet, at any rate, is still on the job and ready for action. There he is, on call twenty-four hours a day, seven days a week to soothe troubled socialist souls. For the cry of "Pinochet! Pinochet!" can exorcise any devil, all the Cambodian and Afghan and Ethiopian and Czech and Tibetan devils. Since the Greek colonels left us, he is almost alone in manning the front-line psychotherapy service that ministers to the left's sense of guilt.

Just how important the post is can be measured by the strength of the resistance that, since the fall of Salvador Allende, has made it difficult to know exactly what happened to push Chile under a military dictatorship. Or rather, that has rendered the knowledge useless by making it a disgrace even to consider the true facts. For the facts themselves are well known, they've been published, they are available to anyone who really wants to learn about them.[7] My

7. See the second part of Kissinger's memoirs, *Years of Upheaval*.

purpose here is not to rehash them or to try to change the minds of those whose moral stability rests on mistaken beliefs. I certainly have no intention of whitewashing Pinochet, any more than I would seek to "justify" an explosion that destroys an apartment building because the tenants forgot to turn off the gas.

It is because Pinochet fills a double function that opposition to examining the case of Chile is so passionately fierce: he masks the mainly intrinsic reasons for the economic and political failure of a socialist experiment, and he lends credence to the myth that the United States put him in power in Chile in the same way the Soviet Union put, say, János Kádár in power in Hungary in 1956. Utopia cannot be saved or the legend of equivalence between Eastern and Western imperialism be maintained except by a lying reconstruction of the past, an art at which, as George Orwell noted long ago, the Marxist-Leninists excel because their power is fed by it. International communism benefits from this reconstitution because most people in the democracies and the "nonaligned" nations sincerely believe the United States alone was responsible for the military coup d'état against Socialist President Salvador Allende in September 1973; especially important is the fact that *non*-Communist opinion believes it (for the real Communists, the professionals, know perfectly well what really happened). They further believe that the United States single-handedly supports and maintains Pinochet in power, blocking any chance for a return to democracy in Chile just as, again, the Soviets are propping up Jaruzelski in Poland and Karmal in Afghanistan. As usual, the West loses by the comparison, but in Chile it was in a no-win situation anyway.

When the military coup got under way, Allende, who was already guilty of a number of illegalities and who was opposed by the majority of Chileans, could only hang on to power by suspending the Chilean constitution and modeling his regime on Castro's—something he had long since been heading toward. Had he succeeded, Chile would have entered the Soviet orbit while the West looked on impotently as its sphere of influence shrank. When he lost, the West was blamed for his fall. And because the Army won the final shoot-out when it took Allende's Castroists by surprise, the West lost on different grounds: it was charged with having assassinated a democracy and its President, which discredits its alleged fight against totalitarianism.[8]

As a rule, then, if the Soviets succeed in taking over a country, they score a net gain; if they destabilize it but fail to control it and cannot install a client dictator there, the story is that they were defeated by a "rightist plot" and the democracies are seen as reactionaries. Why is the West so viewed? Because of a widespread sophism that identifies the forces holding communism in check in any country as invariably being creatures of the West, particularly of the United States. Either the democracies lose the battle on the ground or they lose on the propaganda front, which includes their own public opinion; this inevitably weakens them and paves the totalitarians' way to future victories.

A dictatorship like Pinochet's is infinitely more useful to the Soviet Union than a bland, Western-style democracy. It is the most valuable of allies because the Communists' bête noire, their worst enemy, is a capitalistic, welfare democracy that works reasonably well. A rightist dictatorship is a redoubtable weapon for the Soviets to wield in subverting the democracies everywhere in the world: if they succeed in their subversion, they rack up another satellite; if they fail, they have at least created the conditions for a rightist dictatorship that, for years afterward, their propagandists can throw in the West's face. What makes this weapon so effective is that these dictatorships *really are* evil; the Soviet Union has only to insist that they exist by the will and design of the free world.[9]

8. A referendum, for which machinery existed in the constitution, could have settled the conflict between the majority of the population and the "illegalists" who favored outright radicalization of the regime and who pushed Allende toward Castroism. All through 1972 and most of 1973 the President refused to call a referendum because he knew he would lose it. When he finally made up his mind to it, on September 10, 1973, it was too late. The coup d'état took place September 11.

9. During the summer of 1983 Augusto Pinochet's autocratic power began to be seriously shaken by political opponents and street demonstrations. In spite of a callous and bloody repression Pinochet was unable to completely curb the wave of protest and the move of the country toward change. The process of return to democracy had begun in Chile. These events show once more the difference between the "classical" dictatorships of the military-fascist type and the true totalitarian

It is obvious, then, why the Soviets become so furious when a Western political leader unmasks their game, as happens from time to time, by stating publicly what his peers secretly think. Mario Soares was treated to a display of this Communist anger. During the winter of 1981–82, the head of the Portuguese Socialist Party, who is now the country's Prime Minister, commented frankly on the Basque terrorism plaguing Spain by declaring publicly that "it is the Soviet Union's intention to destroy democracy in the Iberian Peninsula." As Prime Minister in 1975, Soares had had to cope with Soviet attempts to confiscate the young Portuguese democracy and convert it into a Stalinist military dictatorship. He knew terrorism in the Spanish Basque provinces had long since ceased to be a wholly indigenous movement and now depends not on the backing of the Basque people but on logistical support from the East.

Soviet officials are so used to being treated circumspectly by Western politicians that the Prime Minister's remark shocked them profoundly. The Soviet ambassador in Lisbon, wild with rage, so far forgot himself that in an *official* communiqué he described Soares as insane and suggested he would benefit from confinement in a rest home. It was an ill-chosen insult for the envoy of a state known for its political use of mental hospitals; it shows how sensitive the Soviets are and how easily they are shaken when someone puts a finger on the East's particular contribution to détente: the organization and use of international terrorism to Moscow's profit.

Italian President Alessandro Pertini and French Interior Minister Gaston Defferre were similarly insulted by *Pravda* for having replied to terrorist killings in their countries by giving the public a peek at secret documents normally available only to members of the government. But Portugal was the only one of the three countries that demanded, and received, an apology, even though, by that time, Soares had left the government.

When the Soviet Union faces a messy situation within its em-

---

systems. The former must, sooner or later, accept a process of liberalization or be overthrown from within. The latter is devoid of any capability of self-transformation to a democratic regime and is much better equipped to resist and suppress any kind of internal opposition.

pire, it can distract attention from it by ordering its mercenaries to stir up terrorist or guerrilla activity in the West. The repression this elicits can range, depending on the country, from perfectly legal responses through varying degrees of brutality to the most abject savagery. "Lumping-together" specialists in the West can then protest that the capitalist world is essentially and sometimes functionally "as totalitarian" as the Communist world. We cannot even imagine arming potential Lithuanian or Tatar guerrillas who would then enjoy the sympathetic understanding of Soviet newspapers and television.

This is why the lumping-together method, while seemingly objective, is actually a clever way to legitimize Soviet imperialism and totalitarianism. The evils of the free world certainly do not proceed from a guiding principle and a central command system, as the misdeeds committed in the Communist world do at the explicit orders of its masters and their agents. Free-world structure is far too loose to allow for such tight centralization. On the one hand we have actions caused by the decisions of a centralized totalitarian authority; on the other are those resulting from a multitude of causes in a polycentric civilization where political authority is often powerless to influence events. Any scale that purports to give both types of phenomena identical weight is necessarily prejudicial against the West.

These, however, are factors I would as soon avoid here. Although I have come to believe that a capitalist society does far less harm than totalitarian systems do, I want to assume for purposes of demonstration that they are equally guilty. My aim is not to prove that either of the two worlds is better than the other but to show how and why one of them is devouring the other—never mind now whether for better or worse. And I conclude that even the assumption of equal weight for the failures, errors and crimes committed in both worlds automatically grants an advantage to the totalitarian side.

The reason for this is that any denunciation of capitalist misdeeds stirs dissension, crises, dispute, sometimes rebellion and revolution in the democratic world. Such is not the case in the totalitarian camp. Even supposing all things equal—which they are not—the capitalist world comes under ceaseless attack from within and without. The Communist world is seriously challenged only from outside, and then how flabbily! Because of the effectiveness of its totalitarian instruments of defense, communism far more easily suppresses domestic challenges, usually has little difficulty in parrying those from abroad, and, most important, never has to deal with both at once, which is its key formula for undermining the West. Thus, for its smallest weakness, for any flaw of which the totalitarians are equally guilty, democracy pays twice the basic price that Communist dictatorships pay. To lump them together, then, is to send the democracies to their grave.

25

THE TWO KINDS OF MEMORY

HENRI BERGSON distinguished between two types of memory, habit-memory and recall-memory. In the former, the past is preserved but blended into the present so that we can use it automatically in daily life. The latter preserves the past as such, the past delimited in time, the memory of a unique and original experience that happened at a specific moment of our lives, with its emotional tone, happy or painful. Habit-memory enables us to circulate unerringly in a familiar city while thinking of something else. Recall-memory brings back our beginnings in that city, when it was new to us and we were getting to know it. I think this psychological distinction can be applied to politics: in the democratic countries' historical consciousness, communism's past is part of habit-memory, capitalism's of recall-memory.

As things are now, it seems that only the West's failures, crimes, and weaknesses deserve to be recorded by history. Even the West accepts that rule. The ordeal of capitalism's Great Depression of the 1930s still haunts historians, journalists, politicians, and Western schoolbooks like an indelible stain on the capitalistic system despite the prodigies the system later accomplished in surmounting the added disaster of World War II to bring about a society of abundance. But the deaths of tens of millions of people as a result of a direct, deliberate policy of Communist leaders in the Soviet Union during the forced collectivization of the Soviet economy in those very years, from 1929 to 1934, have only a vaporous reality in the West's historical memory, as objects of scholarly curiosity.

Reality to us is what Soviet leaders are preparing to do *now* and, especially, in the future to stimulate the country's agriculture. By "now" we can mean 1945 or 1953 or 1964 or 1982 or any other date when the Western press revives the classic vaudeville show entitled *A Great Reformer Prepares to Spur Soviet Agricultural Productivity*. The production has also been dubbed into Chinese, Cuban, Vietnamese, Tanzanian, Algerian, Romanian, etc. The show's plot revolves around the very much overworked idea of Hungary's "new economic mechanism," which is nothing but a camouflaged and clumsy approximation of capitalism. We will *never* learn that socialism does not begin to work until it is jettisoned.

Thus communism's past loses its reality, melting into the eternal present of a reform the bureaucracy claims it is always about to unveil. Communism's past is always a *stage* en route to a future that, when it comes, is invariably as dismal as the past, but which is in turn promoted to the rank of a *stage*, etc.

Capitalist slumps, however, do not rank as "stages" even when they are followed by brilliant recoveries. Nor are the economic breakthroughs of capitalist countries in the Third World—Taiwan, South Korea, Singapore, even Indonesia—given any standing in the West's memory. All we remember is these countries' authoritarian politics. But the authoritarianism, to use a mild term, of the Algerian political system, for example, is not remembered, any more than the penury that Algerian socialism has inevitably caused, as state socialism always does. When Algerian citizens are permitted to leave their country, which is rare, they stock up on staples bought from their "reactionary" neighbors, Tunisia and, especially, Morocco, where a still traditional farming system still floods world markets with produce. These are countries of poverty but not penury, for only a socialist bureaucracy can arrange for permanent shortages in fertile countries.

The distinction between the two types of memory is useful not only in conditioning the West to accept fundamentally inequitable differences in the two worlds' attitudes toward living standards, political systems and human rights. It also serves to blur socialism's misdeeds while keeping those of capitalism fresh in people's minds. The Vietnamese War is still an open wound, the guilt it produced still vivid in America's consciousness and in the free world's image of the United States. But habit-memory effaced the bloodbath in Ethiopia and the Cambodians' martyrdom almost as soon as they happened. How many Westerners have even an inkling of the number of Cambodian refugees who were parked just inside the Thai border at the end of 1982?

The Soviet suppression of the 1956 Hungarian uprising, a rebellion the West did *not* provoke, was quickly legitimized by the world's indifference, as Albert Camus angrily lamented in 1958,[1] then legitimized formally in 1975 by the Helsinki agreement. But the CIA's destabilization in 1954 of the Arbenz government in Guatemala, which was definitely linked to the Soviet Union, will live on for posterity as a crime of American imperialism.

General Jacobo Arbenz Guzmán, who was elected President of Guatemala in 1951 and overthrown in 1954 at the instigation of the United Fruit Company, is one of the heroic martyrs in the progressives' calendar of saints. As recently as 1982, a historical pamphlet appeared on the subject in the United States. It was coauthored by Stephen Schlesinger, the son of Kennedy adviser Arthur Schlesinger, and Stephen Kinzer, and it carries a preface by former New York *Times* correspondent Harrison Salisbury. Its title, *Bitter Fruit*, refers to United Fruit, which once dominated Guatemala economically and politically and which, as I said, prompted the coup d'état against Arbenz. The line the piece takes is pure Marxism: private capital summoning its lackey, the pseudodemocratic and imperialist state, to its rescue. There is some truth in it. The relations between the United States and Guatemala were semicolonial. But it ignores what was probably the decisive element: the international aspect of the coup d'état's cause, its imbrication into East-West relations.

1. In his preface to *L'Affaire Nagy* (Paris: Plon, 1958), Camus wrote, "In October 1956 the world rose up in indignation. Now the world is sated . . . In October '56, the UN lost its temper . . . Now the Kádár government's representative sits [in the General Assembly] in New York, where he regularly defends peoples oppressed by the West." It must be conceded that the decay of Western energy described by Camus has repeatedly and identically recurred in connection with other issues. His protest can be reused indefinitely simply by changing the names of the places and people involved.

It was Rómulo Betancourt, the former President of Venezuela and the father of democracy in his country, who made me most sharply aware of that aspect. That was in Caracas in 1978, during a conference in which the senior Schlesinger, John Kenneth Galbraith, and the present Spanish Socialist Prime Minister, Felipe González, also took part. Betancourt, who, as head of the Democratic Action Party (a member of the Socialist International) had prepared the way for nationalization of Venezuela's oil industry and had resisted terrorist subversion, was obliged that day to reply to an American writer, Richard Goodwin. Attacking America's good faith in Latin America, Goodwin had cited as examples the deplorable fates of Arbenz in Guatemala and of the Dominican Republic's Juan Bosch in 1963. Betancourt spoke from first-hand knowledge because during the period of Arbenz's ouster he was a political exile living mainly in Central America.

"Richard Goodwin got the impression from my remarks this morning," he said, "that in connection with the overthrow of certain democratic governments, I attributed the blame exclusively to errors committed by the heads of these governments, who were brought to power by popular suffrage, and that I neglected to give sufficient importance to [other] external and internal forces, especially the external forces, particularly the multitentacular CIA and the embassies of the United States in Latin America.

"There is no doubt that the very mysterious and shadowy CIA has contributed to the overthrow of a number of governments in Latin America, including governments elected through popular suffrage, and that its operations were sometimes carried out directly by the United States embassies. This was established and illustrated in the detailed report to the Senate by the Church Committee in the United States. But what emerges as most dangerous for the stability of democratic governments in Latin America is that every time a government is overthrown, we can say the CIA overthrew it, the State Department overthrew it. Carlos Rangel wrote a book[2] with which I basically agree and which aroused broad international debate, since it was not only a bestseller in

2. *Del buen salvaje al buen revolucionario*, Caracas, 1976.

Spanish, but was also translated into English and French. He warns us against the convenient tendency of Latin American governments, when they are overthrown because they were incompetent, because they were corrupt, because they did not show a sense of responsibility toward the obligation the electorate placed in their hands, to explain these difficulties and falls as being due uniquely to external maneuvers.

"Goodwin cited to us the case of General Arbenz, who was overthrown in 1954 by an insurrectional movement wholly fabricated by the CIA. But General Arbenz, who had been placed in power by a popular vote, surrounded himself with a communist staff as soon as he took over the government.[3] Guatemala became a rallying point for communists of various origins, European and Asian as well as Latin American. Arbenz bought arms from Czechoslovakia. When Stalin died, he asked the Guatemalan Parliament to stand in silence for two minutes to show its grief.[4] When Lombardo Toledano, the Mexican communist labor leader, went to Guatemala, General Arbenz, surrounded by his *entire* cabinet, went in person to the airport to greet him. Yet all this was combined with extraordinary corruption on the part of the team in power. These defenders of the proletariat were unbridled in enriching themselves while in office. I have precise information on all that and when we Venezuelan socialists learned of the situation in Guatemala, we sent an emissary to President José Figueres of Costa Rica with a letter explaining what was happening. Arbenz was overthrown and Arbenz left for the Eastern countries. Then he went to Cuba. I do not wish to be cruel, because he is dead, but I must be frank: since he was not a very useful imbecile, the communists dropped him and [he] disappeared.

3. In the interests of clarity, note that the popular vote could in no way have authorized domination of the Guatemalan Government by a more than negligible Communist Party of which the vast majority of voters knew nothing. In addressing a Latin American audience, Betancourt saw no need to specify that Arbenz had been elected on a social-democratic, reformist, and nationalistic platform.

4. To put the Guatemalan Parliament's gesture in perspective, we ought to note something Betancourt seems not to have known: that the entire French National Assembly, except for one Socialist Deputy, stood to hear a memorial eulogy for Stalin.

"In the case of Juan Bosch, to which Goodwin also referred, there is usually some confusion. President Bosch was really overthrown by a military movement that he saw coming and did nothing to oppose. Throughout his term in office, he did not once call a meeting of his government. One fine day he suddenly decided to dissolve his own party, the party that had brought him to power, the Dominican Revolutionary Party. He distanced himself widely and aggressively from his democratic companions, took it on himself to tighten relations with Fidel Castro's Cuba, and was overthrown by the military. It was really not until a year later that the United States intervened, when the Caamano movement arose, which does not alter the fact that the United States's intervention in the Dominican Republic was one of the gravest and most reprehensible mistakes that government ever made. But there would have been no occasion for making that mistake if Juan Bosch had not begun by totally denaturing the mandate entrusted to him by the Dominican people."[5]

I protested too much in the previous chapter against the "lumping-together" process, or what can be called "mutual absolution for heinous crimes," to insinuate now that Afghanistan or Hungary could "balance" an injustice perpetrated by a non-Communist power. I want to bring out a different point here. It is that the West really accepts the idea that the Soviet Union "could not" give in over Poland or Czechoslovakia or Hungary, that it "could not" let those countries slip out of the Warsaw Pact, that its "lines of defense" and its "vital strategic interests" were at stake in these upheavals, and that, as Chancellor Schmidt declared in 1981, challenging its right to intervene in those countries meant "revising Yalta" and thus "endangering the peace."

The democracies therefore agreed to recognize communism's right to political realism, to maintain the primacy of reasons of state, especially in its so-called sphere of influence, which is really an occupation zone. But the United States is denied these natural rights in protecting its vital interests in Central America, among

5. I have reconstituted Betancourt's statement from notes I took during the session and from another transcript shown me by his widow.

its nearest neighbors. It is expected to consent unreacting to open Communist subversion in the Caribbean, to Arbenz's obvious manipulation by Moscow. Yet the Soviet Union defends its presence in Afghanistan with the argument that "it cannot tolerate a hostile regime in a country with which it has a common border." This is a principle the West and the UN accepted when "signals" were transmitted concerning a "political solution" in Afghanistan at the end of 1982. For "political solution" read "an arrangement recognizing the Soviet Union's 'special position' in the country and enabling it to maintain its political domination there without having to fight for it." The democracies are the first to admit that Communist might makes right.

Fuzzy perception, murky recollection, anger that dies aborning or evaporates within a matter of days—these are the mechanics of our awareness of totalitarian activity. No one better understands our forgetfulness than the Communist leaders; we may not know them very well, but they know us. They coined the monstrous euphemism of "normalization" to describe redoubled totalitarian ferocity toward peoples who dare rebel, even fleetingly, against their masters. The term is equally precise in describing Western public opinion and leadership. We too are normalized as our indignation deflates, and it is notably short-winded. We soon find that the abnormal is normal. It's not our patience that is limited, it's our impatience. It runs out in a few months. The Soviet Government and Western Communist Party bosses know from experience that after a year of martial law in Poland nothing of our indignation remained afloat but the memory of half a dozen demonstrations, a few million *Solidarność* buttons and a wound in the West's side from the most bitter economic conflict between Europe and the United States that has occurred in a very long time.

So the phrase "lumping together" is not altogether adequate. Or, if you prefer, reciprocal absolution really works, feloniously, in one direction only, almost always in favor of totalitarianism and its allies. Some people say that "as long as we have Pinochet, Marcos, South Africa and the Argentine *desaparecidos* we will not have a moral right to pillory the suffocation of Poland." Nobody ever says "as long as they have Poland and Afghanistan, we do not have a moral right to denounce apartheid and Pinochet." The most ecumenical among us talk about "the same fight," but this is wrong: it is not the same fight, and there is no real equivalence between reaction to Communist dictatorships and reaction to other dictatorships.

The last time Franco had a Basque resistance fighter[6] executed was in 1975, and the protest demonstration in Paris was so large and so angry that the neighborhood in which the Spanish embassy stood was devastated for half a mile around. Who ever heard of a demonstration, even a silent, nonviolent one, against the murder of some three thousand Ethiopians summarily executed by Lieutenant Colonel Mengistu in Addis Ababa alone? No one, and we know why. And we remain discreet despite, or because of, the presence in Ethiopia of a massive contingent of Soviet "advisers," whose prominence in the revolutionary purges there we would be unfair to deny. Until his last moment in power, another African dictator was surrounded by Soviet advisers: Francisco Macías Nguema, who could not have immolated up to a third of his fellow countrymen in tiny Equatorial Guinea without the consent or at least the silent complicity of his Russian friends. Yet when Macias in turn perished by the sword, his Soviet entourage scuttled back to Moscow, *zitti zitti, piano piano,* without anyone, as far as I know, having criticized the Soviet Union for failing to curb its protégé's little excesses.

On the other hand, a butcher on a less industrial scale, the Central African Republic's Bokassa, had his "capitalist" allegiance to thank for making headlines the world over as a murderer and alleged cannibal of schoolchildren. He put his allies in so awkward a position that his French protectors themselves had to unseat him. During the Korean War, an unfounded charge that the Americans were using bacteriological weapons, one of history's great examples of mass disinformation, launched a worldwide wave of protest

6. I am deliberately using the term "resistance fighter" here because the Spanish Government then was not democratic. With Spain now a democracy, the expression is inappropriate, unless we are talking about resistance to democracy.

that was not entirely calmed by subsequent refutation of the lie, as often happens in such cases.

In 1982, a number of eyewitnesses and several investigative committees, including one from the UN—and we can imagine how languid and cowardly its curiosity was—established beyond a reasonable doubt that the Soviets were using biochemical weapons (the mysterious yellow rain) in Afghanistan and had supplied them to Vietnam for its campaigns in Laos and Cambodia. Were consciences stirred or politicians aroused in the West and the Third World? The only campaign I can remember in this connection was not waged to force Moscow to halt this abominable practice— heaven forfend that trade be interrupted!—but against the New York *Times,* which scrupulously insisted that the accusation had not been conclusively proved, by *The Wall Street Journal,* which charged its rival with refusing to face the facts. It was the *Journal* that came off best in the row, and it had plenty of time to enjoy its victory, since the Soviets went right on dropping their yellow rain on Asia with stony indifference to the timid Western yawping they knew was, as usual, totally innocuous.

The radar screens of Western perception lost sight of the Vietnamese boat people only a year or so after their mass exodus began, allowing Castro's friend Gabriel García Márquez to castigate them as "currency smugglers" and "exporters of capital" and still receive a Nobel prize. The flight of hundreds of thousands of Cuban boat people showed that communism is decidedly the same at any latitude. Yet none of these lessons helped Western seers to view, say, the Sandinista revolution in Nicaragua in its true light.

When the Sandinistas took over the government, the few commentators who ventured to predict that they would run out every other political grouping and establish a one-party police state were accused in all good faith of being Somoza sympathizers. And when it became impossible to deny that Nicaragua was becoming a Castroist state, attention shifted to the issue of how non-Communist the rebels in El Salvador are. While they doubtless receive Cuban —thus Soviet—aid, it was affirmed, the revolution's basic causes were social injustice and poverty.

And so they were. But communism has never eliminated social injustice or poverty; it has always and everywhere accentuated scarcity and privilege. Descriptions of Nicaragua since 1982 attest that the process is holding to form there too, so much so that Nicaraguans are beginning to murmur that food shortages and corruption are "worse than under Somoza." It is all very classic, very wearying. The penury is acute in Poland and Romania too, but no one seriously advocates those countries' deserting the Communists for the capitalists or pleads that social injustice there would justify a guerrilla uprising backed by NATO. Yet the United States is expected to consent to the Sovietization of countries on its doorstep, even if this would not bring these neighbors either freedom or well-being but would eliminate what little they have and effectively block any chance for them to acquire more.

I by no means contend that all Good is on one side and all Evil on the other. I am simply describing the "two-memory" syndrome, the amnesia that afflicts Westerners who applaud the guerrillas in El Salvador while completely forgetting the lesson administered by those in Nicaragua. For example, most of the media assumed, before the March 1982 elections in El Salvador, that the guerrilla boycott of the vote would be massively supported. In other words, they overestimated the Farabundi Marti Front's popularity. As late as noon on election day, ABC television newscasters were incautiously predicting a low voter turnout when, in fact, word was beginning to filter in that the peasants were defying the guerrillas' call for a boycott despite the risk of rebel reprisals. In the end, the turnout was 80 percent (versus 50 percent in 1972) with only minor voting irregularities. Indeed, confidential surveys made beginning in December 1981 had indicated that between 70 and 85 percent of the population planned to vote. But American reporters simply refused to take the surveys seriously because they contradicted their convictions. Many commentators, observers and politicians have great difficulty in understanding such complex situations as those described above by Betancourt, in which it is true that social injustice has brought a country to crisis point, false that communism can remedy that injustice, but true again that it is skilled at exploiting such situations to achieve its political and strategic objectives.

When it comes to mass extermination, communism has to polevault to prodigious heights to reach the threshold of Western perception. And even that threshold merely represents an average. Papandreou's threshold of perception, or Palme's, for example, is higher than any Communist vaulter could ever reach. The Nicaraguan Sandinistas would have been wrong to forego their minigenocide, the slaughter of several thousand Meskito Indians, reportedly under conditions of savagery the West will be arguing about for a long time to come. When in doubt, hold your tongue.

The finest display of reluctant perception and swift forgetfulness, however, is still the West's awareness and dismissal of genocide in Cambodia.

Reading catalogues can be interesting. I am in a position to provide this pleasure for those of you who enjoy lists. For I went to the trouble of combing my files to record a long list of articles about the Cambodian Khmer Rouge that appeared in publications in the United States, Britain, and France in 1975–76. Here are the headlines, in chronological order:

1975

March 25–26	*Le Monde*	"Government Reshuffle May Signal Ouster of Marshal Lon Nol"
April 25	*Le Monde*	"Three-Day Celebration Organized for Khmer Rouge Victory"
April 28	*Le Point*	"A Village Under the Khmer Rouge"
May 5	*Newsweek*	"We Beat the Americans"
May 5	*Time*	"A Khmer Curtain Descends"
May 6	*International Herald Tribune*	"Ford Says Reds Slay Lon Nol Aides, Wives"

May 8	*Le Monde*	"Travel Log from Phnom Penh to the Thai Frontier"
May 9	*Le Monde*	"The Khmer Enigma" (editorial)
May 10	*Int. Her. Trib.*	"Phnom Penh: Victory of Peasants; Eyewitness Report"
May 10	*Le Monde*	"Who's Governing Cambodia?"
May 10	*Le Monde*	"Tens of Thousands of Refugees on the Roads"
May 11	*Sunday Times* (London)	"Diary of a Doomed City"
May 12	*Le Point*	"Phnom Penh: Two Million Deportees"
May 12	*Le Nouvel Observateur*	"The Fall of Phnom Penh"
May 12	*Int. Her. Trib.*	"The Last Days in Phnom Penh: Sorrow, Selfishness"
May 15	*Int. Her. Trib.*	"A Famous Victory (A Bleak View of Cambodia)"
May 19	*Newsweek*	"Cambodia's 'Purification'"
May 19	*Time*	"Long March from Phnom Penh"
May 26	*Nouv. Obs.*	"A Frenchman, Bernard Hazebrouk, with the Khmer Rouge"

May 26	*Le Figaro*	"Doum Uch's 25th Hour (The Story of a Man 'Liberated' by the Khmer Rouge)"
June 22	*Sunday Times*	"Cambodia Refugees Tell of Deaths and Famine"
July 18	*Le Monde*	"A Touchy Yen for Independence Guides Revolutionary Leaders"
July 20	*The Observer*	"Cambodia Opens a Swop-Shop"
July 27	*Sunday Times*	"What About the Executions? Only Traitors Have Been Killed"
August 18	*Le Monde*	"Cambodia, China and Indochina" (editorial)
August 18	*Newsweek*	" 'Organization' Men: a Report from Refugees"
August 23	*The Economist*	"News from No-Man's Land"
August 25	*Nouv. Obs.*	"The Return of Sihanouk"
Sept. 2	*Le Monde*	"Daily Life in the Country: Khmers May Not Own Money or Travel Between Provinces"
Sept. 8	*Newsweek*	Interview with Ieng Sary at nonaligned congress in Peru

Sept. 9	*Le Figaro*	"The Prince's Revenge (Sihanouk's Return to Phnom Penh)"
Sept. 10	*Le Monde*	"Sihanouk's Return to Phnom Penh"
Sept. 14	*Int. Her. Trib.*	"A Proposal to Overrun Cambodia"
Sept. 17	*Le Monde*	"Ieng Sary's Private Visit to Paris"
Oct. ?	*Le Point*	"Sihanouk: Chief of a State Without People"
Oct. 4	*Le Monde*	"Portrait of Prince Sihanouk During Press Conference"
Oct. 11	*Le Monde*	"Sihanouk: 'We Want to Be Neutral, Like Austria, Switzerland and Sweden'"
Oct. 12	*Sunday Times*	"My Visit to the Revolution" (by Prince Sihanouk)
Oct. 12	*Le Monde*	"Disappointed by the New Regime, Some Fifty Khmers in Peking Refuse to Return to Their Country"
Oct. 15	*Le Figaro*	"Cambodia: A People's Calvary"
Oct. 19	*Le Monde*	"Cambodia's New Leaders (Government Formed)"
Oct. 24–25	*La Croix*	"A Revolution Born in Terrible Pain" (series)

Nov. 3	*Le Point*	"Peking: Sihanouk in the Red Circle"
Nov. 8	*Le Monde*	"The Critical Difficulties in Supplying Food May be Remedied in 1976"

1976

Jan. ?	*France-Soir*	"Resistance Being Organized in the Tropical Forest" (series)
Jan. 18	*Sunday Times*	"A Peep into Cambodia Through the Eyes of Those Who Fled"
Feb. 11	*La Croix*	"The Productivist Revolution"
Feb. 17	*Le Monde*	"Cambodia Nine Months After" (series)
March 8	*Le Point*	"The Helots of the New Regime"
April 5	*Nouv. Obs.*	"A Door Ajar into Cambodia"
April 6	*Le Figaro*	"Sihanouk Leaves the Political Scene"
April 6	*Le Monde*	"Sihanouk 'Retires' "
April 11	*The Observer*	"Thousands Flee Land of Genuine Happiness"
April 16	*Le Monde*	"Cambodia and Its Revolution"
April 16	*Le Point*	"Sihanouk: 'It Was Untenable' "
April 17	*Le Figaro*	"The Smile of Angkor"
April 17–18	*Le Figaro*	"Cambodia Under the Khmer Rouge"

April 17–19	*Libération*	"The Secret Revolution" (series)
April 18	*Sunday Times*	"Cambodia Is Convulsed as Khmer Rouge Wipe Out a Civilization"
April 18–19	*Le Monde*	"Tiev Chin-leng Reports: 'A People Controls Its Destiny' "
April 18–19	*Le Monde*	"The Story of Yen Savannary" (A refugee under the Khmer regime for two hundred days)
April 23	*Times* (London)	"A Nation in Chains"
April 24	*Paris-Match*	"Terror in Cambodia"
April 26	*Time*	"Why Are the Khmer Killing the Khmer?"
April 29	*Le Monde*	"Selective Indignation"
May 17	*Newsweek*	"Two Views from Inside"
May 17	*Nouv. Obs.*	"Cambodia as Seen from Hanoi"
May 21	*Le Monde*	"Report from a Former Resident of Païlin"
May 26	*La Croix*	"Refugees Report on Life in Cambodia"
May 31	*Le Figaro*	"Cambodia: A Mad Experiment with a New Order"
June 7	*Le Point*	"They Returned from the 'Land of the Dead' "

Sept. 18	*Le Monde*	"In a Camp Near the Khmer-Thai Border, Refugees Tell of the Lack of Freedom and the Difficulties That Forced Them to Leave"
Sept. 28	*Le Monde*	"No Victories for the Anticommunist Resistance"
Oct. 29	*Far Eastern Economic Review*	"When the Killing Had to Stop"

You will notice, to start with, that a historian five hundred years from now who has nothing but this list of headlines from which to draw an idea of what happened in Kampuchea in this crucial period (and even this is a lot more than the documents we have concerning some periods of antiquity and of the Middle Ages) could in no way guess that methodical genocide had taken place there that exterminated between a fourth and a third of the population. Translated into statistics closer to home, this would represent twelve million to twenty million people in France, West Germany, Britain or Italy, sixty million to eighty million in the United States.

In only three or four of the seventy-four headlines do the words "death" or "executions" or "land of the dead" or "two million deportees" appear to guide us through that cemetery. Our historian would probably conclude that a new regime might have executed a few dozen people from the old order. How could he guess that millions of human beings in Cambodia in the late twentieth century had their brains beat out with clubs and picks like the baby seals in Greenland? I agree that many of the articles under those headlines supplied full details about this orgy of exploding skulls. It is nevertheless odd that so many headlines were so moderate as to provide only the merest glimpse of the nature and extent of what really happened.

Some of them were deliberately easy on the Khmer Rouge. At worst, they mention "critical difficulties in supplying food," but these, of course, are on their way to being "remedied," as they have been in all Communist countries since 1917.[7] Even the accusatory articles or those testifying to the horror in Cambodia were given fairly neutral headlines. When we read that Sihanouk wanted to turn his country into another Switzerland or Austria, we figure that, in that case, things can't be too bad there. The expression "disappointed by the new regime" might well be used by French voters disillusioned with Mitterrand's perfectly constitutional and democratic Socialist administration. And "it was untenable" could just as well describe one of Italy's revolving-door cabinet crises. Understatement is really the order of the day in references to refugees' complaints of "lack of freedom" and "difficulties." Do we say the Jews were "disappointed in naziism" or that they ran into "difficulties" in 1942 because of some undefinable impression of "lack of freedom"? In the headlines given, the words "killing," "killed," "slay" seldom appear, and even then "slay" refers only to ex-Premier Lon Nol's followers, which gives us no hint of mass slaughter.

Remember, too, that we are dealing here solely with reports received while the events were happening. Since then, the tides have swept the beaches of memory clean. Habit, indifference, and time have completed this task of purification.

In my list of sample headlines I did not include any from Communist publications because they obey other laws than those of perception and memory. They observe the laws of Soviet foreign policy. This is particularly true of the French Communists, and it is worth glancing rapidly at how the party newspaper *L'Humanité* covered the Cambodian genocide.

As long as the Cambodia liberated by the Khmer Rouge did not ally itself with China—for Moscow's peace overtures to Peking were still well in the future—the Cambodian revolution rated

7. "Within a maximum of ten years we should cover the distance separating us from the most advanced capitalist countries." Joseph Stalin, *Pravda*, 5 February 1931, and Nikita S. Khrushchev, *Pravda*, 1961.

L'Humanité's dithyrambs. On April 23, 1975, it headlined, "Phnom Penh: Peace and Prosperity Are Independent Cambodia's Top Priorities." A farsighted prophecy if ever there was one! The paper's staff was plainly devoting itself to defending newly Communist Cambodia against the "campaign of intoxication" being waged by the bourgeois Western press, which carried early stories of the horrible conditions under which Phnom Penh's population was being forced out of the capital. When President Ford called for UN intervention "to avoid a bloodbath in Phnom Penh," *L'Humanité*'s managing editor, René Andrieu, violently counterattacked on April 18, ridiculing these imperialist alarums as odious and hypocritical.

It is striking that three years later, on January 9, 1978, the same newspaper would lambaste the "frightful spectacle" in Cambodia, reporting a "gigantic attempt at authoritarian regimentation, massive deportation, families separated, summary executions, unfortunately probably wholesale." On January 29, 1979, *L'Humanité*'s correspondent with the invading Vietnamese troops found prisoners of the Khmer Rouge "with slashed throats, crushed skulls, arms severed, traces of shovel blows all over the bodies. Phnom Penh . . . A soulless city. A nightmare city. A city over which constantly floats the obsessive smell of death." In other words, the bloodbath predicted in 1975 by President Ford, whose foresight Andrieu was careful not to recognize.

As a matter of fact, the atrocities reported in the Communist newspaper in 1978–79 were not exactly new. The Communist press does not go in much for scoops. What is interesting here is why, in hurling its anathema at Cambodia, it overtook and passed the worst excesses of language the bourgeois press had been guilty of in its "campaign of intoxication." There are two main reasons for this: first, the Cambodians' chose China as their protector rather than accept Soviet satellite status; second, and more important, was the invasion and occupation of Cambodia beginning in October 1977 by the forces of unfailingly pro-Soviet Vietnam. From that moment on, the Communist press geared its propaganda machine to an all-out defense of the invasion and its benefits for the Cambodian people. This meant coming down hard on earlier

Khmer Rouge atrocities so as to depict the Vietnamese troops as liberators.

Some spokesmen for the non-Communist left invested even more time and ill will than the Communists in refusing to recognize genocide in Cambodia. But they had very different reasons for finally resigning themselves to it. The Communists no longer believed in the Khmer Rouge revolution. They now believed only in conquest. The non-Communist left still believed in the revolution; at first it had seen the change in Cambodia as a pure "cultural" revolution, the sort of total change of society it had dreamed of so long. So for more than a year it had remained aloof from the indigestible reports coming out of regenerated Kampuchea. Then, when the effort to ignore them became superhuman, it adopted another attitude: preening itself for being the first to condemn the genocide before the court of world opinion when, in fact, it had been the last, even behind the Stalinists.

This sort of trumpery is a refined form of cliquishness: if the left itself damns monstrous leftist deviations, they remain the left's business, become mere mishaps in its historical advance, symbols of its capacity for self-criticism and self-purification. In that case, the overall socialist explanatory system is not ruined by genocide, by the Vietnamese reeducation camps, by the boat people, by Castro, by Nicaragua, or by the annihilation of *Solidarność*. Denunciation of these crimes and errors is merely the constantly repaired springboard to the left's eternal ascension, its growing lucidity. This is why it is so important to erase criticism and even news from "the right," to bury them in the rubble of forgetfulness, for they attack the system's roots, its fundamental cause, which, wherever it is planted, produces its inevitable and always identical fruit.

I am not questioning the unusual scale of the Cambodian massacre. But wasn't its prototype Stalin's mass extermination of the millions condemned as "kulaks" in the early thirties? Then why should the West have been "surprised" again by the "unexpected" and "unforeseeable" Cambodian bloodbath? For one reason only: the delicate care with which it had wiped its memory clean of the Stalinist precedent, refusing to analyze or explain it and so becoming incapable of foreseeing a repetition, much less forestalling one.

26

THE DEMOCRACIES VERSUS DEMOCRACY

In most cases, then, the democracies take the attitudes and decisions Communist leaders want them to take. This acquiescence is both ideological and functional. Broad sectors of public opinion and of the West's political and cultural elite see the democracies as more reactionary, more damaging to the Third World, more aggressive militarily, especially as regards nuclear warfare, than the Soviet Union and its satellites. Westerners who favor an effective nuclear deterrent and a verifiable balance of forces are still viewed as "conservatives," "right-wingers," "warmongers," or, at best, as "cold warriors." Those advocating unilateral disarmament or, at any rate, prior and increasingly juicier concessions to the Soviet Union without reciprocal guarantees are considered "leftists," generous souls who love peace.

In practice, what these "liberals" are really promoting is an imbalance that would enable the Soviet Union to force its economic and political will on a growing number of countries without going to war, thus enlarging an already spacious orbit. Yet history teaches us that never, anywhere, have concessions coaxed the Soviet Union into making concessions. From this unhappy truth, for which they are in no way responsible, the democracies do not conclude that they must change their diplomatic approach but that they must concede still more. Apparent Soviet concessions, Moscow's flashiest sucker bait, find plenty of takers in the West; the few Western political observers competent enough to see these maneuvers as no more than deceitful propaganda cannot swim against so many currents of opinion, which will not forgive them for neglecting any "windfall opportunity" magnanimously offered by the Kremlin.

Anyone with his ear to the political ground might think the only danger to the West is Western arms and Western diplomacy. For example, the New York *Times* of April 2, 1982, worried that "An Adverse Impact Among Allies Is Feared After Reagan Remark on Soviet Superiority." That is, the real danger to America's European allies is not seen as possible Soviet military superiority but in America's plans to counter it by reinforcing our defenses. Any President of the United States visiting Western Europe is treated to demonstrations so hostile that an unsuspecting spectator would think he were the worst enemy Europe ever had.

True, people often show better judgment than their elites and their activists. In 1982, a survey[1] showed that all the peoples of Western Europe except the Spanish thought the growth of the Soviet military potential was more important in explaining international tension than the growth of America's military potential. This had its clownish side, however: by a margin of 45 percent to 21 percent, the French people believe that American interest rates and the dollar's role in international finance are much more serious causes of tension than Russia's bulging arsenal. Let us note in passing that the people of every Western country made the mistake of blaming the arms race as a cause of tension when it is really a consequence of tension.

Despite an improved and, by 1981, clearer perception of Soviet power or perhaps because of the realism of that perception, most Europeans, and not just militant pacifists, say that if their countries were invaded, they would rather submit than resist. Asked in another poll, "If the Soviet Army entered French territory, do you think the President of France should immediately open peace talks with the Soviet Union?" 63 percent of the French answered yes, 7 percent favored the use of nuclear weapons, and 21 percent

1. Louis Harris poll conducted in September 1982 for the Atlantic Institute of International Relations and the *International Herald Tribune*.

thought France should fight, but without using its nuclear missiles.[2]

Now, one may very well prefer servitude to death. But we can also avoid putting ourselves in a situation in which this grim choice is all that is open to us. Yet the will to avoid such a situation is precisely what we seem to lack. The relentless Soviet "peace offensive," therefore, has every chance of succeeding, that is, of persuading the West and the rest of the world to accept permanent military inferiority by portraying this as an absolute guarantee against war.

Any normal person naturally hates the idea of war, and, of course, this antagonism interferes with proper public information about strategy, as though the information itself were dangerous. But let's face the fact that the Soviet "peace" we are accepting is synonymous with subjugation, for which we are already being psychologically conditioned, and that its continued pursuit will lead us by imperceptible stages to a state of undeclared but total satellization. Even economic weapons, not to mention military deterrence, have been forbidden to us, or rather we've forbidden ourselves to use them. Our refusal to apply stern economic sanctions against the Soviet Union must have vastly reassured the men in the Kremlin. And if the West can no longer resort to a credible strategic deterrent or to economic weapons, what is there to prevent the Soviet Union from continuing to trample the sovereignty of other countries, other continents, of the whole world?

What practical conclusion must we expect Communist leaders to draw from our military and economic passiveness? That they can go right on doing what they have been doing. In their place, isn't that what we would think? Former Giscard d'Estaing cabinet minister Jean-François Deniau quotes a high Soviet official as having told him, "We took Angola and you did not protest. We even saw that you could have beaten us in Angola—the government was on our side, but it was within an ace of giving up—and that you did nothing to win, on the contrary. And when, to save ourselves, we

2. Survey by the French Research Corp. published in the magazine *Actuel* in January 1981.

sent in thirty thousand Cuban soldiers, Ambassador Young, a member of the American cabinet,* said it was a positive step and an element of stability. All right, we noted the fact and included it in our analyses. Then we took Mozambique. Forget it, you don't even know where it is. Then we took Ethiopia, a key move. There again we noted that you could have replied via Somalia or Eritrea or both. No reply. We noted that and put it into our analyses. Then we took Aden and set up a powerful Soviet base there. Aden! On the Arabian Peninsula! In the heart of your supply center! No response. So we noted: we can take Aden."[3]

Still more favorable to Communist imperialism than our diplomatic inertia is a powerful ally of that very inertia: the West's assent to the Communists' condemnation of our civilization. Not even they believe what they say about us; they know full well what sort of human values they have cultivated in their civilization, but they go on condemning us because, after all, we love to be insulted. While claiming to have learned the truth once and for all about Stalinism, about totalitarian communism, many people in the democracies still cling to the old standards of classification, even in their jargon, as though they had never learned the truth at all, which casts doubt on how much they really have learned. Anticommunism is still thought of as reactionary. What a mockery is this so-called awakening to the vices of Stalinism when the "right wing" still rejects anti-Stalinists, even accusing them of behaving . . . like Stalinists. Capitalism and free enterprise are flayed with one voice from the academic chair and from the pulpit; cult and culture unite to preach the wildest whims as axioms that discredit the industrialized democracies, blaming them for the Third World's poverty. On what bases, with what motivation, can freedom be defended when so many opinion molders, educators, thinkers have always, openly or secretly, maintained that our civilization is "fundamentally bad"?

Maybe they're right, but where the devil will children who are taught that their society incarnates evil find the determination to

---

* Andrew Young was then American ambassador to the UN.—TRANS.
3. Jean-François Deniau, "La détente froide," L'Express, 3 September 1982.

defend it later on? Many schoolbooks throughout the West are indictments of capitalism, as violently caricatural as they are contemptible scientifically. But defenseless schoolchildren lack the information they would need to read these books critically.

The Lutheran Church in West Germany is fat with tax money if poor in churchgoers. To recruit an audience, it espouses pacifism, just as the Roman Catholic clergy in Latin America offers revolution to the masses it cannot hold with theology alone. The archbishop of Paris, Cardinal Lustiger, has written, "A rich nation that loses its soul is a nation of the dead. A sumptuous culture that loses its soul is a culture of the dead. And a nation whose soul is dead, a culture that has lost its reasons for living, economic and social systems that, in practice, contradict the goals they profess, can only give birth to nothingness and destruction."[4]

We can say in all modesty that it's us he was writing about, and no one could be rash enough to doubt for a moment that the society that is giving "birth to nothingness and destruction" is the capitalist society. Without going so far as to suggest that the Communist society is giving birth to a surfeit of Being and Creation, the archbishop is nevertheless helping to drive home the notion that democratic capitalism unquestionably, necessarily, is reactionary, selfish, destructive. Which implies with compelling logic that its opposite is leftist, altruistic, progressive.

I am not going here into why industrial capitalism, the first and only system of production that has wrested people from penury and that could perform the same service for those still experiencing penury, is the most decried. Nor will I waste time arguing at length that since the eighteenth century the nations where industrial capitalism has developed also happen to be those where modern democracy took root. This does not mean that these countries have kept consistent faith with democracy or that democracy is found wherever capitalism goes. But it does mean that two centuries of history are witness to a general concomitance between capitalism and democracy. I will only note that this monumental file of evidence has been filched and that the democracies themselves have

4. *Le Monde*, 12 February 1982.

adopted the Communists' image of the world and their perspective on history.

The falsest and most pernicious characteristic of this image and this perspective lies probably in the antithesis between socialism and capitalism, between totalitarianism and democracy. This functions in most minds as an interpretative grid, even for those opposed to socialism. Its imposition is not the least of disinformation's victories, for this disinformation no longer bears on events, but on ideas; it is philosophical disinformation, a sort of ideological mole that has burrowed into the understanding most of us have of these forces.

Adopting this grid means accepting the principle that any regime that is less than perfectly democratic may be likened to totalitarianism and so loses its right to defend itself against communism. Since the world is full of governments that are neither totalitarian nor democratic, their futures are sealed. For one thing, because no democracy, even those recognized as such, is perfect, and since there are oppressive features to any society, which regime can claim a genuine right to defend itself against communism? None. And, following the same line of reasoning, if all that need be done to legitimize communism is to show that capitalism has its faults, its vices and crises, then let's turn world power over to the Communists at once on the principle that the best way to correct a limp is to cut off both legs.

The real antithesis is not that of totalitarianism to democracy or communism to capitalism, but of totalitarian communism to all the rest. Communism is a necrosis of economics, totalitarianism a necrosis of politics, of the body civic and of culture. As a dead society, totalitarianism can be contrasted with countless social forms now and in the past that cannot be called democratic as the term is understood in a few societies today but which were not and are not dead, either. Medieval Europe, Ming China, African, Polynesian and American societies before their contact with Europeans, the France of Louis XV and Napoleon III, Elizabethan England, the Spain of Philip IV, India under the Gupta dynasty, and the Germany of Kant's day were neither democratic nor totalitarian, but they were all living societies that, each in its own way, created valuable civilizations.

The existence of injustice, persecution, oppression in a group is one thing; for a group to be a negation of human nature in *every* aspect of its structure and ideology is something else again. This is the group to which totalitarianism belongs. True, today we believe that to fulfill themselves all societies should aspire to democracy, progress toward it and finally achieve it. I certainly do. Nevertheless, thousands of social organizations down through history, while not comparable to modern democracies, were not negations of humanity or freedom and did contribute elements of civilization to our present patchwork culture.

I am not talking about the political scientists' classic distinction between authoritarian and totalitarian regimes. Unlike the latter, authoritarian regimes are, so to speak, biodegradable; from time to time we see Latin American-type dictatorships grow more moderate, cross back over the frontier toward an approximation of democracy, take on a pluralist structure, and open out. But communism, like a ship, cannot open without sinking.

These are rudimentary notions. I have in mind a very different, more profound, more radical distinction. It separates a body of political systems advancing in stages from autocracy to democracy, deserving of severe criticism but compatible with more or less normal civic life, with a *custom* from the totalitarian system whose mission is to destroy all social, cultural and individual autonomy.

The contrast between capitalism and socialism is more apparent than real. To begin with, capitalism was never conceived as a unified ideological system to be clamped violently and arbitrarily over societies that did not want it. It is a fusion or juxtaposition of a myriad individual behavioral fragments that have come down to us from the dawn of time, that are unified only in our minds, and that we have finally assembled into a general, erratic and imperfect concept. Capitalism is a bundle of modes of economic behavior. Communism, however, is not an economic system, it is a political system that must necessarily asphyxiate an economy. We should therefore refuse to lump communism in with other authoritarian systems or them with it. Totalitarianism endangers not democracy alone, but life itself. Communism is not simply one despotic political system among many or one inefficient and unjust economic system among others. In normal life, despotism and inefficiency are among the rare qualities that can be corrected, as is shown by all of history—except the history of communism. To survive, communism seeks to destroy not just existing democracy but every possibility of democracy.

Any society of any type in the world today can accede to democracy, with a single exception: communist society, which cannot go democratic without destroying itself. Understandably, then, totalitarian strategists try to reverse or block this tendency in the still malleable world around them. What is less easy to understand is that they can recruit some of their most assiduous disciples from among democracy's guides and thinkers.

CONCLUSION

NEITHER WAR
NOR SLAVERY

As YOU NOW SEE, the aim of this book has not been to compare the merits of capitalism and communism, of democracy and totalitarianism, but uniquely to explore the question of which of the two systems is forcing the other to retreat. Nor, I must insist, has my objective been to examine possible internal "sicknesses" of democratic societies and their institutions. An already fat collection of works, both classic and recent, deals with democracy's "crises," its "plunge toward suicide," its "twilight," in which democracy is seen as a condition of a free society, a method of delegating power, a system for the control and exercise of power. Most of these works deal with democracy in itself, as an isolated phenomenon, and could have been written even if no mortal danger had arisen outside the geographical perimeter in which the democratic societies are located.

This is also true of all the literature devoted to "the crisis of capitalism." True, the constraints in democracy, which are bonded to its advantages, largely explain its vulnerability to its external enemy. But this can be incorporated into our reckoning of the balance of forces without our having to decide if it is a symptom of "decadence," whether the term is used seriously, as Spengler did in *The Decline of the West*, or ironically. The issues to which I have confined myself revolve around a central theme: must the democracies consent to war to escape slavery, or accept slavery to escape war? Or, worst of all, must they fight a war that will end in their enslavement? What I hope is that they still have the time and the capacity to spare themselves both war and slavery.

Throughout the course of relations between the Communist and democratic worlds, the question of "which will destroy the other" has always been obscured on the democratic side by adventitious side issues. Communism's leaders have never concealed their belief that this is the only question that counts and that they are determined to answer it with a total Communist victory. No temporary compromise, they feel, can alter the final judgment of history. If people in the West find it hard to bear this vision of merciless struggle between the two forms of society, if they sometimes drive it out of their minds, it is partly because the socialist cause was forged within the democracies themselves in the nineteenth century, was one of their offspring that became an independent component of political life. We have trouble understanding that this offspring's heir presumptive, twentieth-century communism, has assumed the historical mission of destroying the democracy from which it issued. We persist in viewing it as just another political persuasion that may have degenerated but which can mend its ways, calm down, participate someday in a global concert. To think otherwise, we feel, sins against tolerance. Unfortunately, the democracies are not making the rules in this game. The Communists in no way share their concern for tolerance and the coexistence of systems.

Communism considers itself permanently at war with the rest of the world, even if it must occasionally agree to an armistice. This is nothing to be indignant about. We must simply recognize it; unless we do, we obviously cannot begin taking suitable political countermeasures. The Communists' war is fought in many ways. If necessary, this includes military action, but to communism's leaders all forms of action are part of this war, beginning with negotiation, at least their very particular notion of negotiation.

In their minds, the aim of negotiation has never been to reach a lasting agreement but to weaken their adversary and prepare it to make further concessions while fostering his illusion that the new concessions will be the last, the ones that will bring him stability, security, tranquility. The Soviets' "peace" propaganda, which to them means convincing others not to defend themselves, always overlies a threat of war, of implicit intimidation that exploits our very justifiable fear of an atomic cataclysm. This belligerent demand for peace merely summons the democracies to buy their security with slavery; it is an elaborate way to say "surrender or be wiped out." It has been called "attack through pacifism."

One of the most active and fecund techniques of this novel form of pacifism is incessant bombardment of Western leaders with proposals for disarmament and nonaggression treaties. Andropov maintained this offensive and even intensified his fire. We will note that Moscow's arms-reduction proposals always provide for a margin in the Soviet Union's favor. It is also noteworthy that the men in the Kremlin are seldom wrong when they bet that Western leaders will have to take them seriously sooner or later. Public opinion, the media, the political parties and the legislatures in their countries will force them to do so on the very civilized theory that you cannot ignore an offer indefinitely. Fear that the offer may be booby-trapped seldom prevails against pressure from advisers urging that the proposal be taken up in good faith. "Negotiate, negotiate!" millions of voices clamor, "you always gain a little," as though negotiation were an end in itself and not just a means to an end, effective or not as the results in each particular case attest. And the results in most cases are that democratic leaders feel they must agree to reductions in both conventional and nuclear arms, then to cuts in their military budgets and, finally, to the supreme diplomatic pantomime, a summit meeting with the masters of the Soviet Union.

Some historian should draw up the long list of calamities that have been pumped up by these summit conferences and dumped on the democracies since World War II. Given the meager benefits these encounters produce, you would think the West had learned to be wary of them, but, no, it persists in wasting its energy at them. Worse yet: most candidates hoping to become head of state or of government in the big democracies now feel they must make the pilgrimage to Moscow before launching their election campaigns. And the Kremlin's patrons make a point of returning the courtesy, indicating by heavy-handed signs which party or candidate they favor. Sometimes they even dispatch Gromyko or Zagladin or some variant thereof to the scene to add a personal touch to the campaign, instruct the natives in how to separate the grain from the chaff, and deliver a deserved rebuke to the "enemies of peace, of rapprochement among peoples and of disarmament." Western TV networks devote plenty of airtime to these Soviet emissaries, without a hope of reciprocity, needless to say. Once the campaign has taken off in this direction, Western pacifists, opposition parties and Moscow's front organizations jump noisily on the bandwagon; anyone trying to breast the tide risks being isolated, unpopular, mired in sarcasm and opprobrium. Who would have predicted only twenty years ago that candidates for the democracies' highest offices would so have needed Moscow's prior endorsement?

In its fight against the democracies, communism has so far won much more than it has lost. It is a Western weakness to take comfort from those losses when what is crucial in learning from experience is whether they outnumber the gains. In this contest, figures talk. I won't linger over this except to note that communism has indeed suffered reverses, faced fearsome difficulties, and lives with weaknesses that are chronic and, as time has shown, incurable because they are inherent in the socialist system. Net losses are rare, however, and Westerners are too quick to see unsuccessful attempts at expansion as definitive setbacks when they are not really losses at all, merely delays in making gains. Example: the Indonesian Communist Party's unsuccessful attempt at a coup d'état in 1965; the fiasco led to a frightful massacre of Communists throughout the country, not by the government or the Army, but by the Indonesian people, with each town and village seeing to its own "purification" and the "liquidation" of its Communists. Another example is Moscow's failure in 1982 to maintain and harden its grip on Lebanon through the occupation of the country by its Palestinian and Syrian clients, its inability to push back the Israeli Army's drive and to keep political control there. In a delayed spasm, it did engineer the assassination of Bashir Gemayel only days after his election as Lebanon's President.

But none of this represents a loss unless we assume that Indonesia and Lebanon belong by rights in the Soviet orbit. Note too that these incidents grew out of accidental and untypical local situations, not from the West's foreign policy as it is conceived by the governments that make it.

Among Moscow's reverses can also be listed its increasing difficulty in keeping the Communist International firmly in line. Communist parties like France's that bark obediently whenever the Kremlin whistles are becoming fewer and more isolated. Their declining strength at the polls is one of the interesting developments of the 1975–85 decade. Brezhnev's warning to a Western Communist leader who objected to the use of Soviet tanks in Prague in 1968 that "we can whittle you to a splinter group" is being made good in a number of countries, but not for the reasons Brezhnev had in mind.

Even though external Communist parties no longer obey like players in a symphony orchestra, as they did in the great days of the Comintern, some of them are still entrusted with specific and important tasks. We have only to observe how artfully the French Communist Party has profited from its presence in the government since 1981 to seize the levers of command in the bureaucracy, in industry and over channels of information. What's more, it has patiently edged France into economic isolationism that, while dealing a blow to the Common Market, has also fulfilled a long-standing Kremlin objective. As has been stressed in this book, Moscow has modernized its techniques for influencing public opinion and governments in the big industrial countries and in the Third World. It is working less and less through the too-visible Communist parties and increasingly through subtler, less suspect, often invisible channels.

The collapse of communism's political and human prestige as a social model unquestionably represents the loss for the Soviet Union and the other socialist countries of a capital asset that was invaluable in opening the way to Communist and pro-Communist ideologies between the wars and up to around 1970. I am not referring here to communism's atrocities; throughout this period they only moderately hampered the spread of socialism. I mean mainly socialism's economic failures, the debacle of the hopes it had raised, of the happiness, justice and equality it had promised. Since 1970, the Soviet Union has even managed to be the only industrialized country where infant mortality has risen steadily.

Public opinion today is reasonably well-informed about life under communism. Fewer textbooks in France and Italy are presenting the censured, falsified, embellished picture of Soviet and Chinese history with which their authors cynically deceived generations of youngsters. The saga of the Vietnamese and Cuban boat people has tarnished the legends gilding socialism in the Third World. In France, for example, respect for the Soviet Union is at its lowest point since the end of World War II, as witness the results of a survey carried out there in December 1982. Asked if "the results of the socialist system as it functions in the U.S.S.R. and the popular democracies seem to you to be rather positive or rather negative," 69 percent replied "rather negative" and 11 percent "rather positive." Ten years previously, 43 percent had said "negative" to the same question and 28 percent "positive." To another question, "In looking back over recent years, would you say the Soviet Union was sincerely seeking peace?" 50 percent replied "no" and 29 percent "yes," which shows that the mass of the population is more clear-sighted than many of its leaders. The comparison, not with 1972 but with June 1980, six months after the invasion of Afghanistan, gave 46 percent "no" and 24 percent "yes." Nine percent of the "undecideds" had made up their minds in the interval.

In its social system as in its foreign policy, then, communism is meeting increasing reproval. This is probably why Communist leaders do not rely much any more on honey to catch their future victims (except, perhaps, in some badly informed Third World countries). Having given up trying to seduce the unwary by pretending to represent leftist ideals, they are stripping off their mask and using pure force. Unlike the Western leadership, which is tormented by remorse and a sense of guilt, Soviet leaders' consciences are perfectly clear, which allows them to use brute force with utter serenity both to preserve their power at home and to extend it abroad. In *La Nomenklatura*, Michael Voslensky brought out this external aspect, the danger the Nomenklatura represents for world peace, its vaingloriousness, aggressiveness, xenophobia, its global ambitions. The Soviet *machine for conquest* must be awesomely efficient if it can go on working despite communism's inefficiency in everything else.

For I agree that we should make a point of communism's failures. Their list is so impressive that it frightens me; a system that has grown so strong despite so many failings, that increasingly dominates the world even when no one wants anything to do with it, at least not the majority of the people in the countries it seeks to penetrate, and that, where it is in power, everyone except the Nomenklatura longs to be rid of—this system must nevertheless embody a principle of action and monopolization of power more effective than any mankind has ever known before. Communism and the Soviet empire are unprecedented in history. None of the classic concepts that make the past intelligible explains Communist imperialism. It does not follow the bell-shaped expansionist curve of previous empires. Yet the democracies persist in believing it will decline of itself and inevitably grow more moderate.

The longer Soviet communism lasts, the more expansionist it becomes and the more difficult it is to control. Other Communist states, notably Cuba, Vietnam and North Korea, have shown similar propensities for conquest. It does not follow that because communism is showing signs of rot and suffers reverses that it will turn into the path of peace. Except when they were disintegrating, few other empires had to deal with as many national and popular rebellions as the Soviet empire has since 1953. But *it* has withstood and quelled them without going to pieces. And these difficulties have in no way slowed its expansionist thrust.

Frequently, part or all of a Soviet ruler's reign is scarred by serious setbacks. This happened under Stalin in 1925–35. It happened during the reign of Khrushchev, who for a while seemed to be digging the empire's grave, and in the years immediately following his fall: the break with China, the loss of Albania, North Korean and Vietnamese neutrality in the Moscow-Peking quarrel, insurrections in Poland, Hungary and Czechoslovakia, Romania's new standoffishness, cracks in the monolithic Communist International. Yet never had the empire expanded so much or so boosted its military power as it did in the years following this critical period. The closer we get to the end of the century, the more Communist imperialism becomes the chief problem of our time. Indeed, no other threat to world freedom has endured as long in the twentieth century, and it is still unabated. Other totalitarian systems were defeated or simply crumbled with age. In many other unhappy countries that have been or still are ruled by dictators, democracy and dictatorship—or, at least, adulterated forms of dictatorship (and democracy)—have swept in and out like tides. Only Communist totalitarianism is both durable and immutable.

To the question of what should the non-Communist countries do, I am tempted to answer by turning back to Demosthenes. "Some people," he said, "think they can stump the man who mounts the tribune by asking him what's to be done. To those I will give what I believe is the fairest and truest answer: don't do what you are doing now."[1]

This is not as summary an answer as it seems, even to today's problems. What, indeed, *can* we do? To go on as we have been would guarantee the continued advance of totalitarianism, for, as experience has shown, it will not be stopped by the system's weaknesses and internal failures.

A second option is based on the hope that communism will change its ways voluntarily if we acknowledge its place in the sun and show clearly through concessions that we have no intention of attacking it. Anchored to peaceful coexistence and détente, this option has too adequately proved its harmfulness to warrant further discussion. But since we have yet to scrap it, I can only warn people not to count on it to save us. It will keep us out of war by ushering us into subordination or slavery.

A third choice proposed, reviving—horrors!—the "cold war," which we are so repeatedly admonished not to do, really does not exist, since there has never been a cold war. It has simply been a

1. *Oration on the State of the Chersonesus*, par. 38.

toned-down version of détente that has certainly not attained its theoretical goal of "containment." The democracies selfishly thought to use détente to guarantee their security by signing treaties finally and officially confirming the subjugation of the peoples already under Communist dictatorship. In this they have failed. All we have succeeded in doing is to abandon these enslaved peoples to their masters. In *To Build a Castle*, Bukovsky found a cruel symbol of this complicity: "The chekist, who took off my handcuffs, remarked for my edification, 'These handcuffs, incidentally —they're American.' And he showed me the stamp. As though I had waited this long to learn that since the Soviets took power, or just about, the West has been supplying us with handcuffs, literally and figuratively."

Yet this complicity has not brought us the security we expected from it. Never were the democracies more vulnerable, more baffled, more exposed to the blows of Communist imperialism than they were when the so-called détente period ended. The years 1981–83 have been especially tragic, with confusion sown in the democratic camp by the Polish and Afghan affairs, by the democracies' gradual but irresistible acceptance of Soviet superiority despite the more and more threatening, impudently biting and brutal way the Kremlin talks to them.

War, then? Some responsible thinkers are pessimistic enough to believe that the West has become so docile that it can no longer call a halt without risking war. I have reached the opposite conclusion. I am convinced that the Soviets are not sincere in their attempt to blackmail us with the threat of nuclear apocalypse and that they have only intensified it from year to year because of the enormous profits it has and still does bring them. But the regime is in no condition to resist a war.

While I think it is an illusion to count on the totalitarian system disintegrating in peacetime by its own dynamic, it seems to me equally probable—and must seem even more so to Communist leaders—that the peoples it has enslaved will refuse to sacrifice themselves to the Nomenklatura's lunatic ambitions. It is not for nothing that Soviet soldiers wounded in Afghanistan were treated in East German hospitals and not in the Soviet Union. When the Nazis invaded Russia in 1941, large segments of the population saw the war as an opportunity to turn against the Communist regime for reasons that had nothing to do with any alleged sympathy for fascism, as Solzhenitsyn has explained and shown with utterly convincing examples. Under normal circumstances, the Communist system is virtually impossible to dismantle from within by internal dissidence or even by massive popular uprisings, as the history of the popular democracies so sadly proves. But the system would be immensely fragile in war precisely because of the weaknesses we wrongly count on to work miracles in peacetime but whose explosive potential would wreak havoc in the prodigious disorder a world war would inflict on an already inefficient and disorderly society.

The Soviets are intent on maintaining their nuclear superiority over Western Europe as a way to increase their pressure on us *without* being dragged into a general war while gradually disengaging the United States from the continent of Europe. This is why they were so furious when Helmut Kohl's Christian-Democrats won the West German elections in March 1983, thus annihilating Communist hopes of neutralizing the Federal Republic in the near future.

Being certain they would not risk a Western nuclear response would not, however, prevent the Soviets from resorting to classic military operations in the more or less distant future. I would even say that such a certainty would encourage them to wage conventional warfare. Localized Communist military operations have always succeeded because they are based on the theory that the West, though unable to oppose them with conventional power, would nevertheless rule out a nuclear riposte. Thus the Western nuclear deterrent remains the principal guarantor of peace it has proved to be for the past thirty-five years. The Nomenklatura doesn't want to die either.

Once this is well understood, the second article of a worthy foreign policy would be to reply to any Soviet encroachment with immediate reprisals, mainly economic, and to make no further concessions without manifest, equivalent and palpable counterconcessions. I think I have supplied enough examples in these pages of cases in which we have done exactly the opposite so that I needn't repeat myself here.

Put it another way: our policy should be to practice and insist on *genuine* détente, one that works both ways, not for the Soviet Union's benefit alone. We have a plethora of trade and propaganda weapons and means of action against the Soviet secret services and their agents of influence and especially against Communist expansionism in the Third World. We must systematically reject all Communist demands, even those for (phony) disarmament talks, as long as the Soviet Union maintains its expansionist policy. Why didn't we demand the total and immediate evacuation of Soviet troops from Afghanistan as a precondition to talks on reducing the number of intermediate-range missiles in Europe? This would have been standard, classic diplomacy. Then why did no Western statesman dare to propose it in 1982–83? It is the Soviets who have been eager since 1980 to talk about the Euromissiles, they who have been pressing for negotiations, not us. Given this position of strength, what did we do with it? The answer is simple: nothing. How have we used it? Same answer: we haven't. The non-Communist countries' revised foreign policy must and can have a precise objective: to make the Soviets understand once and for all that the irrevocable prior condition for resumption of negotiations and the granting of concessions of any kind is a definitive halt to Communist imperialism everywhere in the world.

Activating this new policy, which really would be no more than a return to normal diplomacy, presupposes an almost total Western intellectual reconversion, sound understanding—at last—of what communism is and how it works, and a hitherto unprecedented harmonization and coordination of policy among all the democracies. This amounts to saying that while this new diplomatic departure appears objectively possible, it seems to me highly unlikely because of the intellectual frivolity, indecisiveness and discord of the men called on to apply it.

My function here is not to be optimistic or pessimistic. I am stating a case. It's the case that is pessimistic, not the person stating it. Democracy's fate will be fixed in the closing years of this century. I mean our fate, for history may be reckoned in millenia, but life is short. In the words of Achim d'Arnim, "the history of the world begins anew with every man, and ends with him."

INDEX

Aden, 341

Adenauer, Konrad, 234, 235

Adler, Fritz, 154, 155

Afghanistan, 15, 23, 25, 34, 36, 37, 38, 40, 49, 51, 54, 55, 61, 63, 65, 71, 75, 83, 93, 104, 105, 112, 113, 114, 118, 121, 128, 135, 142, 143, 146, 153, 159, 183, 184, 193, 209, 227, 230, 234, 237, 239, 246, 247, 263, 266, 279, 283, 290–94, 297, 302, 309, 313, 323, 326, 357–58, 359; Soviet censorship and, 171–72

Africa, 23, 24, 37, 58, 94, 96, 99, 106, 115, 116–17, 169, 195, 200, 226, 227, 241, 279, 300, 301–3. *See also* specific countries

Agence France-Presse, 198, 200

Albania, 252, 255, 286, 355

Algeria, 58, 106, 112, 319

Allende, Salvador, 115, 312–14

Amalrik, Andrei, 131

Amin, Idi, 300

Amsterdam-Pleyel Movement, 151, 152, 154, 155, 157

Andrieu, René, 336

Andropov, Yuri, 74, 111–12, 135, 153, 158, 194, 216, 223; described, and Soviet succession, 277, 279–84, 290–93

Angola, 26, 58, 59, 70, 71, 114, 115, 116, 125, 209, 340–41

Anti-Americanism, 165, 183, 192, 193, 198, 275, 304, 339; De Gaulle and, 258–63, 265, 275

Anti-War Congress, 154

Arabian Peninsula, 105, 226, 301, 341. *See also* Arab nations; Middle East; Persian Gulf

Arab nations, 105, 206; oil crisis and, 99, 104–6. *See also* Arabian Peninsula; Middle East; Persian Gulf

Arbatov, Georghi, 192, 193

Arbenz Guzmán, Jacobo, 248, 320, 321, 322

Argentina, 80–81, 115, 132, 208, 211, 246, 297, 299

Arms race, 26, 66–74, 75–85, 92–98, 99–108, 109–22, 123, 133–35, 145–59, 179, 189, 191, 192–93, 289–90; controls and disarmament (*see* Disarmament; specific aspects); conventional weapons, 68–74; nuclear weapons (*see* Nuclear weapons); "struggle for peace" and, 145–59 (*see also* Peace movement)

Asia, 23, 94, 167, 226, 241, 268–69, 326. *See also* specific countries

Assad, Hafez, 172

Atlantic Alliance, 45–46, 66, 71, 73, 122, 142, 193, 255, 256, 266, 283, 298; De Gaulle and, 258–63. *See also* North Atlantic Treaty Organization

Atomic weapons. *See* Nuclear
  weapons
Aubuisson, Roberto, 195
Austria, 93, 107, 146, 251, 285, 287,
  289

Balance of forces (balance of
  power), 25, 66–74, 216–29, 231–
  40, 285–86, 338, 349. *See also*
  specific countries
Baltic states, 56, 97, 109–10, 156,
  271, 278
Barbusse, Henri, 154, 155, 157
Barre, Syad, 117
Batista, Fulgencio, 128
Bayet, Albert, 217–18
Beirut, Boleslaw, 271, 285
Belaúnde Terry, Fernando, 116
Belgium, 56, 166, 191, 193, 254
Belgrade conference (1978), 37, 131
Ben Barka, Mehdi, 186
Ben Bella, Ahmed, 260
Benin, 58
Benoist, Alain de, 28, 29
Bergson, Henri, on memory, 318
Beria, Lavrenty P., 252, 286
Berlin: blockade and airlift, 152,
  242, 251–52, 257; Soviet capture
  of (W.W. II), 274; wall, 128, 232–
  40, 244–46, 251, 279. *See also* East
  Berlin; West Berlin
Berlinguer, Enrico, 45, 115
Bertram, Christoph, 224
Besançon, Alain, 94
Betancourt, Rómulo, 321–23, 327
Big Con, The (Maurer), 167
Biological (biochemical) warfare,
  23, 171, 183, 302, 326
Blum, Léon, 190
Boat people, 23, 91, 303, 326, 337,
  354
Bohlen, Charles E., 221–22, 278
Bokassa, Jean-Bedel, 300, 325
Bolivia, 115, 299
Boris II, King (Bulgaria), 208
Bosch, Juan, 321, 323
Brandt, Willy, 118, 192, 193, 205,

232, 234, 235, 261, 280, 291; and
  Ostpolitik, 241
Brezhnev, Leonid, 20, 36, 65, 73,
  74, 75, 76, 77, 103, 111, 127, 138,
  191, 192, 216, 221, 280 n., 353;
  death of, 222, 223, 290; and
  "peace struggle," 148–49, 158;
  and Soviet succession, 279, 280–
  81, 283, 284, 291
Bukovsky, Vladimir, 277; *To Build
  a Castle*, 141–42, 357
Bulganin, Nikolay A., 110, 289
Bulgaria, 107, 119, 204, 208, 253,
  255, 260
Bullitt, William C., 273
Bundy, McGeorge, 250

Cambodia, 23, 59, 183, 290, 303,
  321; Khmer Rouge terrorism
  and, 212, 328–37
Camus, Albert, 320
Canada, 100, 292
Capitalism, 28, 44, 126–27, 148,
  216–29, 230–40, 341–45, 349–60;
  Communist propaganda and,
  175–87; double standard in
  judging, 308–17, 318–37;
  economic weapons of, 84–85 (*see
  also* Economy; specific aspects).
  See also Democracy; specific
  countries
Caribbean area, 23, 93, 115, 121.
  See also specific countries
Carlos (terrorist), 209
Carrington, Lord, 246, 290–91
Carter, Jimmy, 37, 73, 132, 134,
  178, 294, 299
Casanova, Laurent, 62–63
Castro, Fidel, 42, 128–29, 133, 148,
  169, 194, 197, 217, 260, 323, 326.
  See also Cuba
Cate, Curtis, 245
Censorship, 25, 115, 167, 168, 171–
  72; Communist control of the
  media and, 198–203; self-,
  democracy and, 25
Central America, 83, 94, 99, 115,

116, 309, 321–24, 326–27. *See also* specific countries

Central Europe, 8, 24, 36–54, 57–65, 93, 137, 153, 242, 246–57, 278; Yalta agreements and, 266–76. *See also* specific countries

Chaliand, Gerard, 112 n., 113

Chandra, Romech, 154–55

Chernenko, Konstantin, 158, 216, 280 n., 290–91

Chevrillon, Olivier, 204

Cheysson, Claude, 39, 51, 52

Chicherin, Georghi V., 150

Chile, 37, 115, 132, 299, 312–15

China, Communist, 5, 19, 25–26, 45, 55, 59, 62, 112, 167, 168–69, 189, 197, 200, 248, 280, 282, 286, 288, 302, 308, 354; Soviet Union and, 89–90, 226–27, 335, 336, 355; and Tibet, 59, 173–75

Church, the (religion), 163, 189; KGB and, 177, 179; and peace movement, 284, 342; Roman Catholics, 284, 290, 342. *See also* specific individuals

Churchill, Winston, 220, 244

CIA, 40, 182, 183, 186, 320, 321

Cold War, 152, 192, 215–29, 230–40, 356–57; détente and, 239–40, 241–57 (*see also* Détente); phony, 241–57. *See also* specific aspects, countries

Collectivization of land, 233, 318

Colonialism, 55–65, 114; decolonization and, 56, 57; neocolonialism, Soviet Union and, 55–65, 96–98, 209, 250–51, 254, 268. *See also* Expansionism; specific aspects, countries

COMECON (Council for Mutual Economic Assistance), 48–49

Committee for European Disarmament (CED), 146

Common Market. *See* European Economic Community

Communism, 3–6, 7–11; democracies and, 3–6, 7–11 (*see also* Democracy; specific aspects); détente and, 123–35 (*see also* Détente); dividing of the West and, 136–43; double standard in judging, 295–317, 318–37; economic aspects (*see* Economy); and expansionism (*see* Expansionism); future of and response of democracies to, 338–45, 349–60; global strategy (world conquest aim) of, 21–29, 66–74, 75–85, 89–98, 99–108, 109–22, 123–35, 136–43, 144–59, 160–87, 188–212 (*see also* specific aspects); ideological warfare and disinformation and, 160–87 (*see also* Propaganda); patience of the system, 112; and "peace struggle," 144–59 (*see also* Peace movement); and political piracy and perversion, 188–212 (*see also* specific aspects); succession (leadership changes) and, 277–94; weaknesses and failures of, 3, 19, 20, 90–91, 112, 113, 125–26, 352–60 (*see also* specific aspects, developments); weaknesses of democracy versus (*see under* Democracy). *See also* Socialism; Soviet Union; Totalitarianism; specific developments, events, individuals, organizations

Communist International (Cominform, Comintern), 107–8, 120, 127 n., 150, 190, 208, 216, 253, 353, 356; founding of, 153, 242

Containment doctrine, 243

Convergence theory, 226

Costa Rica, 116

Coulondre, Robert, 219

Couve de Murville, Maurice, 53 n., 234, 235

Craxi, Bettino, 79, 229

Cruise missiles, 73, 283

Cuba, 26, 45, 55, 58, 59, 60–61, 64, 70, 71, 89, 97, 114, 116, 117, 128–

29, 142, 167, 195, 197, 206, 209,
211, 247, 248, 297, 323, 341, 355;
boat people (exodus), 23, 169,
326, 354; missile crisis, 110, 128,
237–38, 248–49, 250, 279
Czechoslovakia, 43, 44, 52, 57, 62,
64, 102, 113, 159, 197, 219, 225,
246, 253, 262, 323, 356; Prague,
23, 35, 62, 113, 236, 255, 275

Debray, Régis, 42
Debré, Michel, 235
Decline of the West (Spengler), 349
Defense (military) budgets, 19, 47,
68, 82, 124, 281, 283–84, 351
Defferre, Gaston, 205, 315
Democracy (democracies), 3–6, 7–
11, 12–15, 16–20, 21–29; and
arms race and military strategy,
66–74, 75–85, 89–98, 99–108 (*see
also* Arms race; specific aspects);
and balance of forces, 25 (*see also*
Balance of forces); communism
as enemy of, 3–6, 7–11 (*see also*
Communism; specific aspects);
Communist global strategy and
(*see under* Communism);
democracy against itself, 125–26,
338–45 (*see also* specific aspects);
and détente, 123–35 (*see also*
Détente); divided, Communists
and, 136–43; double standard in
judging, 295–317, 318–37;
economy and (*see* Economy);
future of, response to
Communist threat by, 338–45,
349–60; as a historical accident,
sense and duration of, 3; and
ideological warfare and
disinformation, 160–87 (*see also*
Propaganda); inadequacies, real
and imagined, 8–11; internal and
external enemies, 3–6, 15 (*see also*
specific aspects, groups); public
opinion in, 12–14 (*see also* Public
opinion); self-blame and
criticism in, 5, 7–8, 9–10, 18;

Soviet expansionism and (*see*
Expansionism); Soviet
leadership succession and, 277–
94; Soviet piracy and perversion
and, 188–212; Soviet terrorism
and, 203–12 (*see also* Terrorism);
Tocqueville on, 12–15, 18;
weaknesses versus communism,
3–11, 215–29, 230–40, 241–57,
258–63, 264–76, 295–317, 318–37,
338–45, 349–60 (*see also* specific
aspects); worldwide attack on,
10–11, 15 (*see also* specific
aspects, countries). *See also* West,
the; specific countries, events,
individuals
Democracy In America (Tocqueville),
15
Deng Xiaoping, 282
Deniau, Jean-François, 340–41
Denmark, 156, 158, 191, 193, 254
Despotism (dictatorships), 5, 13,
94, 196, 344, 345. *See also*
Fascism; Totalitarianism;
specific countries, individuals
Destabilization, 188–212, 215–29,
241, 248, 314, 320. *See also*
specific aspects
Détente, 33–34, 38, 46–47, 52, 67–
68, 69, 72, 82, 94, 97, 100, 103,
112, 121, 123–35, 177, 191, 192,
219–29, 232–40, 258–63, 266, 270,
291–94, 356–60; Cold War and,
239–40, 241–57, 356–57; De
Gaulle and, 258–63; failure of,
153, 155, 169, 223–29, 232–40,
258–63; "linkage" and, 130, 133,
135; "peace struggle" and, 148–
49 (*see also* Peace movement);
Soviet "targets of," 129–35, 137,
138, 139, 148–49
Deterrence strategy, 69–74, 78,
111, 338. *See also* Arms race;
Nuclear weapons
Deutscher, Isaac, 278
Disarmament, 26, 68, 72–74, 76,
110–12, 121, 123–24, 165, 166,

191, 192–93, 195, 351; SALT talks and, 124–25, 129, 133–34, 137, 292; "struggle for peace" and, 145–59, 166 (see also Peace movement); unilateral, 76, 165, 179, 189, 193, 223, 250, 280, 284, 290–94, 338, 359. See also Arms race; Missiles, nuclear; Nuclear weapons; specific aspects
Disinformation, 48, 161, 166, 176–87, 279, 292
Djilas, Milovan, 20, 274
Dobrynin, Anatoly F., 221
Dominican Republic, 321, 323
Dowling, Walter, 251
Duarte, Napoleon, 195
Dulles, John F., 244, 252, 286

East Berlin, 44, 113, 233–40, 244–46. See also Berlin; East Germany
Eastern Europe, 35–54, 56–65, 81, 82–83, 93–98, 137–43, 206, 242, 252–57; Yalta and, 265–76. See also Yalta agreements; specific countries
East Germany, 58, 64, 70, 102, 136–37, 158, 185–86, 242, 246, 250–51, 252–53, 254–55, 274, 285; Berlin wall and, 128, 233–40, 244–46, 251, 257, 279; uprising, 252, 285, 286, 287
Ecevit, Bulent, 210
Ecologists, 166, 179, 188
Economy (economic aid, aspects, problems): 16–20, 26, 33–34, 36–37, 38, 40, 45–54, 55, 60–61, 68, 79–85, 90, 99–106, 135, 140–43, 188, 196–97, 222–23, 226, 268, 340; loans, interest rates and, 33–34, 36, 47–53, 83, 100, 103; sanctions, 26, 40, 45–54, 80–83, 247, 266, 272, 340, 358–59; Siberian gas pipeline and (see Siberian gas pipeline). See also Trade; specific aspects, countries
Eden, Anthony, 244, 246

Egypt, 60, 71, 104, 105, 227
Einstein, Albert, 155
Eisenhower, Dwight D., 244, 246, 274, 286
El Salvador, 115, 194, 195, 249, 297, 309–10, 326, 327
Equatorial Guinea, 58
Estonia, 57, 151
Ethiopia, 26, 58, 93, 97, 115, 117, 197, 209, 227, 296, 320, 325
Eurocommunism, 227. See also specific countries
European Defense Committee (EDC), 146
European Defense Community (EDC), 152, 263, 289–90. See also North Atlantic Treaty Organization
European Economic Community (Common Market), 80, 102, 120, 122, 290, 353
Expansionism (annexations, territorial imperialism), Soviet, 15, 16–20, 22–29, 33–54, 55–65, 75–85; democratic weaknesses and (see under Democracy; specific countries); détente and Cold War and, 241–57 (see also Cold War; Détente); economic weapons and resistance to, 55, 60–61, 79–85 (see also Economy); future of, response of democracies to, 338–45, 349–60; and "peace struggle," 144–59 (see also Peace movement); phony Cold War and, 241–57; propaganda and, 160–87 (see also Propaganda); tools of, 89–98, 99–108, 109–22, 123–35, 136–43, 144–59, 160–87, 188–212; Yalta and, 264–76. See also Colonialism; Imperialism; Totalitarianism; specific aspects, countries

Falklands Islands War, 80–81, 246, 297
Fascism (fascist regimes), 8–9, 152,

167, 168, 174, 175, 194, 208–12, 295–317 *passim*, 318–37 *passim*, 344. *See also* Despotism; Totalitarianism; specific aspects, countries
Faure, Edgar, 291
Fauvet, Jacques, 41
"Fechteler Report," 181
Figueres, José, 322
Finland, 57, 97, 107, 110, 117–21, 146, 151, 192, 271, 278; Finlandization and, 117–21
Fishing agreements, 93
Fontaine, André, 259 n., 260
Food shortages (famine), 17, 19–20, 196, 304, 307–9
Ford, Gerald, 114, 131, 328, 336
Forgeries, 176–77, 181–82
For Lasting Peace, For Popular Democracy, 153–54
France, 8, 9, 19, 28, 34, 39, 56, 69, 71, 77, 80, 102, 105, 112, 116, 152, 163, 181, 184, 186, 211–12, 217–19, 237, 244, 254, 255, 263, 287–88, 289, 293, 300, 335, 339–40, 343, 354; CGT, 41, 43, 190; Christian-Marxists, 28–29, 44–45; Communist Party, 41–45, 62–63, 95, 109, 120, 138, 140, 146, 157, 189–90, 203, 208, 242, 335, 353; De Gaulle and détente and, 258–63; Gaullists, 28, 42–43, 53, 79, 113, 138, 152, 181 (*see also* Gaulle, Charles de); and NATO, 59, 77, 78–79, 258–63; and "New Right," 9, 28; and "peace struggle," 144–45, 146, 152, 157; and Siberian gas pipeline, 139–42; Socialist Party, 41, 42–45, 95, 109, 189–90, 191–92, 205; and Soviet expansionism, 25–26, 28–29, 39, 41–45, 50–54 (*see also* specific countries); and terrorism (Paris), 204–5, 208–9; and Yalta, 264–67, 275
François-Poncet, André, 218–19
Freedom (liberty), 13, 15, 94–98;

conditional, 94; as an inherent weakness in democracies, 13, 15; movements, 94–98 (*see also* specific countries, movements). *See also* Gulags; Human rights and freedoms; Labor, forced; Slavery, war or
Freud, Sigmund, 265
Fried, Eugen, 208
"Friendship treaties," 93, 119, 252–53, 275 n., 286. *See also* Nonaggression pacts
Gagarin, Yury, 237
Gandhi, Indira, 199
García Márquez, Gabriel, 42, 326
Gaulle, Charles de, 28, 53 n., 59, 235, 237, 238, 258–63, 265, 275; and détente and NATO, 258–63; and Yalta, 265, 275
Gemayel, Bashir, 183–84, 352
Geneva conferences: arms talks, 166, 217, 281 n.; on Indochina, 243, 287
Genocide. *See* Mass extermination
Georgia (Georgian Republic), 100, 118; Soviet annexation of, 61–62
Germany, 8, 27, 100, 103–4, 107, 119, 170, 174–75; Nazi era (W.W. II) (*See* Nazis; World War II); pre-W.W. I, 245, 343; splitting of, 136–37, 251–56, 264–76 *passim*, 285, 286; Yalta and, 264–76. *See also* Berlin; East Germany; West Germany
Gero, Erno, 285
Gherasimov, Alexander, 132
Giberti, Louis, 154
Gide, André, 155
Giscard d'Estaing, Valéry, 19, 25–26, 46, 77, 130–31, 173, 184, 234, 247, 263, 283, 294
Gomulka, Wladyslaw, 138, 285
González, Felipe, 71, 182, 193
Goodwin, Richard, 321–23
Gourmont, Rémy de, 76
Grain (wheat) sales, 49, 83, 103, 297

Grenada, 93, 115, 194
Great Britain, 8, 56, 60, 80–81, 91, 102, 103, 105, 165, 166, 199, 217, 235, 237, 244, 246, 258, 260, 293–94, 302, 343; and Argentina and Falklands war, 80–81, 246, 297; BBC World Service 201; Labour Party, 145, 165, 191; and Siberian gas pipeline, 80–81, 139–40; and Yalta, 265, 269, 272
Greece, 8, 92, 298, 311; CP, 185
Gromyko, Andrey A., 284, 290–91, 352
Guatemala, 64, 115, 248, 320–22
Guerrillas (guerrilla movements), 115, 121, 195, 279, 316, 327; and terrorism, 206, 208, 209–10
Guinea, 58
Gulag Archipelago, The (Solzhenitsyn), 132 n., 133, 140, 165
Gulags, 133, 140–42, 165, 173, 307–8
Guyana, 115

Haig, Alexander, 36, 290–91
Hambleton, Hugh, 292
Harriman, W. Averell, 219–20, 293
Heller, Michel, 46, 177, 221–22
Helsinki conference (1975), 36–37, 38, 50, 51, 52, 53, 58, 65, 84, 94, 99, 103, 107, 109, 130–32, 136, 146, 201, 255, 268, 272, 279, 320
Hitler, Adolf, 52, 54, 57, 97, 119, 123, 126, 161, 170, 191, 215, 217–21, 233, 235, 253–54, 258, 260, 265; and Stalin pact, 56–57, 97, 103–4, 119, 136, 151, 208, 253–54, 269, 271, 272–74, 278. *See also* Nazis
Holland, 15, 56, 72, 158, 166, 191, 193, 254
Honduras, 84
Hull, Cordell, 269
Humanité, L', 140–41, 203, 290, 335–36
Human rights and freedoms, 37,

130–32, 135, 140–42, 204–12, 295, 298, 299, 306–8, 319–37 *passim;* Helsinki agreements and *(see* Helsinki conference). *See also* Freedom; Gulags; Labor forced; Slavery, war or
Hungary, 43, 44, 48, 62, 64, 87 n., 102, 107, 119, 165, 180, 225, 227, 239, 246, 250, 253, 256, 279, 285–86, 313, 319, 320, 323, 356; Budapest, 23, 35, 113, 128, 233, 236, 244

Ideology (ideological warfare), 160–87, 338; disinformation and, 161, 166, 176–87; terrorism and, 212. *See also* Propaganda; specific aspects, countries
Imperialism, 15, 16–20, 22–29, 55–65, 128; economic, 55, 60–61, 79–85 *(see also* Economy); propaganda and, 163–87; Soviet piracy and perversion and, 188–212; terrorism, 203–12 *(see also* Terrorism); "two imperialisms," 55. *See also* Colonialism; Expansionism; Totalitarianism
India, 173, 174, 183, 197, 198, 199, 284, 308, 343
Indochina, 107, 287–88. *See also* specific places
Indonesia, 304, 352–53
Intellectuals, "peace struggle" and, 155–56
Internal History of the Communist Party (Robrieux), 127–28
Interparliamentary Union, 189
Iran, 63, 96, 99, 114, 132, 211–12, 242, 248, 297, 303; Communist Tudeh Party, 63, 96; Shah, 297, 299, 303; and terrorism, 63, 96
Ireland, 206
Iron Curtain, 242, 265
Israel, 71, 227; and Lebanon, 112–13, 172, 183–84, 352
Italy, 8, 9, 54, 72, 77–78, 79, 80, 100, 119, 182, 200, 254, 274, 284,

315, 335; Christian Democrats, 207, 209; Communist Party, 45, 206–8, 242; fascist, 8, 9, 54; Red Brigades and terrorism, 182, 186, 204, 206–8, 209, 212; SID, 186; Socialist Party, 79; Social Movement, 9 n., 79

Japan, 22, 60, 200, 224, 254, 269, 274, 287, 304
Jaruzelski, Wojciech, 43, 51, 313
John Paul II, Pope, 204, 279
Joliot-Curie, Frédéric, 155
Jospin, Lionel, 192
Jouvenal, Bertrand de, 273 n.
Juan Carlos, King (Spain), 176

Karelian Isthmus, 119
Karmal, Babrak, 290, 313
Kaunda, Kenneth, 300
Kekkonen, Urho, 110, 121
Kennan, George, 25, 250, 278
Kennedy, Edward (Ted), 291
Kennedy, John F.: and Berlin wall, 235, 238, 239–40, 245; and Cuban missile crisis, 237–38, 248n.
KGB, 25, 37, 128, 155–56, 158, 189, 204, 225, 247; Andropov and, 279–80; and "disinformation," 166, 176–77, 184–85, 186; and technology thefts, 225
Khomeini, Ayatollah, 211–12, 303
Khrushchev, Nikita S., 20, 127, 128–29, 132, 133, 134, 165, 168, 216, 248, 259, 286, 288, 333n, 355; succession as Soviet leader, 278–79, 282, 286, 289
Kissinger, Henry, 26, 66, 69–70, 92, 106, 111, 221; and détente, 69–70, 123–25, 126, 129–30, 131, 133–34, 135, 137, 221
Kohl, Helmut, 358
Korea, 107, 114–15; Korean War, 151, 152, 243–44, 257, 287. See also North Korea; South Korea
Kosik, Karel, 26

Kroll, Hans, 234
Kurile Islands, 57, 268
Kuwait, 184

Labor, forced, 140–42, 160, 174. See also Gulags; Slavery, war or
Laloy, Jean, 275
Lang, Jack, 28
Langevin, Paul, 155
Laos, 59, 183, 302
Lasers, 224
Latin America, 23, 64, 114–15, 121, 169, 194–95, 199, 200, 297, 299–300, 306, 321–24, 326–27, 342; terrorism in, 204, 206, 208–10, 321–24. See also specific countries
Latvia (Letts), 57, 151
League of Nations, 107
Leahy, Admiral, 269
Lebanon, 112, 172, 183–84, 247, 352–53
Lend-lease program, 272–73
Lenin, Nikolai (Vladimir Ilyich Ulyanov), 22, 75, 100–1, 190, 228, 278; on "deaf-mutes" in the West, 215–16, 286; and "peace struggle," 148, 149–51
Less developed countries (LDCs), 196–212; Soviet piracy and perversion and, 196–212. See also Third World; specific countries
Libya, 58, 106, 133, 301
Lithuania, 57, 151
Lloyd George, David, 228
Lon Nol, 328, 335
Luanda Government, 116
Lustiger, Cardinal, 342
Luxembourg, 193
Lysenko, T. D., 20, 132

MacDonald, Ramsay, 217
Macías Nguema, Francisco, 58
Macmillan, Harold, 235
McNamara, Robert, 250
Madagascar, 58, 71, 84
Madrid Conference on European

Security and Cooperation (1980), 37, 50, 51–52, 131, 146, 176
Malenkov, G. M., 221–22, 278
Malia, Martin, 84–85
Manchuria, 268
Mannerheim, Carl Gustaf, 118, 119
Mao Tse-tung, 5, 148, 167, 168–69, 170, 280, 286
Marchais, Georges, 41
Marcuse, Herbert, 162
Marenches, Alexandre de, 25
Marshall, George C., 101–2
Marshall Plan, 101–3, 120
Marxism-Leninism, 136–43, 206, 207–8, 313. *See also* Communism
Mass extermination (genocide), 167, 168, 170, 172–75, 211–12, 303, 328–37
Maurer, David W., 167
Mauroy, Pierre, 41–42, 47, 50, 52, 80
Maurras, Charles, 28
Media, the (newspapers, radio, TV), 42, 45, 67, 71, 112, 115, 124, 125, 222–23; Communist propaganda and, 167, 170–75, 179–85; control and censorship of, 198–203; and détente, 124, 125, 131; and double standard in judging the democracies and the Soviet Union, 297, 319–23, 327, 328–37; and peace movement, 124, 125, 131, 351
Meinhof, Ulrike, 209
Mengistu Haile Mariam, 296, 325
Merkulov, Vladimir, 156
Mermaz, Louis, 307–8
Meskito Indians, 328
Middle East, 94, 104–6, 206. *See also* specific countries
MIRV tests, 133–34, 137
Missiles, nuclear, 68–70, 72, 73, 74, 76, 77, 78–79, 110, 133–34, 166, 283–84, 340, 359; Cuban crisis, 110, 128, 237–38, 248–49, 250, 279; Euromissiles, 78–79, 111–12,

152, 166, 179, 193, 223, 224, 229, 280, 281, 284, 359; intermediate-range, 247, 249, 359 *(see also* specific kinds); MIRVs, 133–34, 137; MX program, 281, 291–92. *See also* Arms race; Disarmament; Nuclear weapons
Mission to Moscow (Davies), 221, 222, 269–70
Mitterand, François, 39, 41–42, 45, 50, 51, 79, 191–92, 205, 229, 247, 267, 283–84, 335
Molotov, V. M., 100, 102, 271–72, 275, 286
Monde, Le, 41, 43, 53 n, 73, 181, 182, 204, 255
Mongolian People's Republic, 62, 118
Moro, Aldo, 182, 208
Morocco, 64, 186
Moscow Radio, 179–80
Moslems, Soviet, 227
Mossadegh, Mohammed, 248
Mourousi, Yves, 184
Mozambique, 58, 70, 341
Mugabe, Robert, 300
Muhlstein, Anatole, 274
Munich agreements (W.W. II), 219
Münzenberg, Willy, 154
Mussolini, Benito, 8
My Country and the World (Sakharov), 104, 105–6

Nagy, Imre, 285
Namibia, 116–17, 209
Nansen, Fridtjof, 228
Nasser, Gamal Abdel, 60, 105
National-front governments, 62
Nationalism (national liberation movements), 96, 189, 194, 198–212. *See also* Revolutions; specific countries
Nazis (Nazi Germany), 4, 9, 44, 56–57, 66, 136, 170, 174–75, 191, 212, 215–21, 251–56, 269, 272–74, 285, 386, 358. *See also* Hitler, Adolf; specific aspects

Nehru, Jawaharlal, 197
Nepal, 173, 174
Neutron bomb, 72, 73, 78, 178–79, 193
New York *Times*, 245, 267, 326, 339
Nicaragua, 26, 59, 62, 94, 115, 167, 194, 209, 248–49, 297, 300; Sandinistas, 59, 326–28, 337
Nin, Andrés, 208
1984 (Orwell), 13
Nixon, Richard M., 26, 93, 123, 124, 135; and détente, 123–24, 125, 129–30, 131, 135
Nomenklatura, 4, 48, 90, 91, 106, 202, 216–17, 278–79, 282, 288, 355, 357, 358
Nomenklatura, La (Voslensky), 4 n.
Nonaggression pacts, 109–10, 112, 118–19, 351. See also "Friendship treaties"; specific pacts
Nonaligned Countries Movement, 58, 188, 197–203; Algiers conference (1973), 197; Colombo conference (1976), 198–99; Lusaka conference (1970), 197
North Africa, 106. See also specific countries
North Atlantic Treaty Organization (NATO), 27, 40–41, 59, 95, 110–11, 121, 152, 156; De Gaulle and, 258–63; and Euromissiles, 69–70, 72–73, 76–77, 78–79, 111–12, 152, 166, 179, 193, 223, 224, 229, 280, 281, 284, 359; and neutron bomb, 178–79. See also Atlantic Alliance; specific countries
North Korea, 242, 243–44, 287, 296, 302, 355
North Vietnam, 107, 112, 243–44, 288
North Yemen, 58
Norway, 110, 191, 193
Novosti agency, 193, 284
Nuclear weapons (nuclear war), 23, 66–74, 75–85 *passim*, 110–12, 123–25, 133–35, 178–79, 193, 252, 338, 349–60; control of and disarmament *(see* Disarmament); peace movement and *(see* Peace movement); resolutions to freeze, 289–90. See also Arms race; Missiles, nuclear

Oil supply, 184, 303; crisis, 99, 104–6
Olympics: Mexico City (1968), 227; Moscow (1980), 23, 36
One Day in the Life of Ivan Denisovich (Solzhenitsyn), 132, 278
Orwell, George, 13
Outer Mongolia, 62

Pacem in Terris conference, 126
Pakistan, 65, 114, 171, 182–83, 284
Palestinians, 114, 352–53
Palme, Olof, 118, 193, 280, 291, 328
Papadopoulos, George, 311
Papandreou, Andreas, 311, 328
Pares, Sir Bernard, 228
Passivity (resignation), 24, 27–29, 34, 51, 237–40, 241–57, 340–41; Berlin wall episode and, 237–40
Peace movement (pacifism), 22, 67–68, 73–74, 78, 106–7, 166, 173, 177, 179, 186, 188, 191, 192–93, 217–18, 222–23, 234, 241, 251–57, 270, 285, 289–94, 340, 350–52, 354–55, 356; Soviet funding of, 156–59; "struggle for," 144–59, 166, 350–52
Pershing II missiles, 69, 73, 78 n., 283
Persian Gulf area, 63, 104, 184, 301, 302–3. See also Arabian Peninsula; specific countries
Personal-contacts myth, East-West relationships and, 218, 220, 221–22, 269
Pertini, Alessandro, 204, 315
Peru, 115, 116, 209–10
Petersen, Arne Herlov, 156
Philip of Macedon, 67–68, 159, 212

Phnom Penh. *See* Cambodia
Picasso, Pablo, 155
Pinochet, Augusto, 312–14
Pipes, Richard, 25, 26, 85
Plato, 12, 14–15
Poland, 3, 10–11, 15, 23, 34–53, 55, 57, 63–64, 76, 79, 82, 83, 85, 97, 99, 102, 107, 114, 131, 135, 138, 142, 143, 149, 151, 153, 230, 236, 237, 246–47, 250, 253, 255, 260, 266, 267, 268, 271–72, 276, 278, 279, 285, 290, 298–99, 302, 310–11, 312, 323, 356; KOR, 183; Lublin regime, 271; Solidarity, 36, 165, 236, 267, 290, 311, 337; Yalta and, 266–68, 271, 276
Ponomarev, Boris, 192
"Popular democracies," 95–96, 196
Popular Fronts, 152, 190–91
Portugal, 56, 94–96, 204, 209, 315; CP, 94–96, 189, 209; fascist, 8, 54; "Revolution of the Carnations," 116, 189
Potala monastery (Lhasa, Tibet), as sole surviving monastery of the Chinese invasion, 175
Potsdam conference (1945), 50, 107, 268, 271, 272
Poverty (the poor), 5, 16–20, 46, 47, 196–97, 306, 307–8, 327, 341–42. *See also* specific aspects, countries, groups
Pravda, 34, 40 n., 132, 157–58, 315
Press, the. *See* Media, the; specific periodicals
Prior-concession principle, 249; De Gaulle and, 261
Propaganda, Soviet expansionism and, 21–29, 40, 60, 115, 118, 126, 161–87, 289–90, 295, 312, 359; ideological warfare and disinformation and, 160–87; media control and censorship and, 198–202; "peace struggle" and, 144–59, 350–52
Proust, Marcel, 12
Psychological warfare, 161–87. *See*
also Ideology; Propaganda; specific aspects
Public opinion (world opinion), 12–14, 95, 100, 104, 109, 112–15, 124–25, 147, 170–87, 204, 338, 351, 354; double standard and, 303–17; ideological warfare and disinformation and, 160–87; and "peace struggle" and, 147–59, 351, 354; Tocqueville on dictatorship of, 12–14

Qadaffi, Muammar, 133
Quillot, Roger, 80

Raab, Karl, 185–86
Radio Free Europe, 180
Radio Liberty, 180
Radio stations and broadcasts, 179–80, 184; control and censorship of, 198–202. *See also* Media, the
Rangel, Carlos, 194–95, 321–22
Rapacki, Adam, 111
Reagan, Ronald, 27, 33–34, 36, 76, 176, 229, 250, 339; and MX missile program, 281; and Poland, 36, 40; and Siberian gas pipeline, 49, 76, 81–82
Reale, Eugenio, 153–54 n.
Red Army, 25, 35, 61, 62, 84, 94, 103, 145–46, 193, 244, 247, 254–55, 262, 266, 292
Refugees (escapees), 23, 158–59, 169, 232–40. *See also* Boat people; specific countries
Religion. *See* Church, the
Repression, 17, 20, 33–54, 90–98, 131, 196, 298, 310–17. *See also* Terrorism; specific countries
Réunion, 146
Reuter's, 198
Revolutions (coups d'état), 94–98, 99, 103, 115–16, 118, 127–28, 149, 163, 173, 301, 313, 320, 326; Soviet piracy and perversion of, 188–89, 194. *See also* Nationalism;

specific aspects, countries, groups, individuals
Rhineland, German occupation of, (W.W. II), 218
Ridgeway, Matthew B., 256
Riesman, David, 13
Robrieux, Philippe, 62–63, 127–28
Roehl, Klaus, 209
Rolland, Romain, 155
Roman Catholic Church, 284, 290, 342
Romania, 57, 82, 102, 107, 119, 253, 256, 271, 302, 327
Ronchey, Alberto, 207
Roosevelt, Franklin D., 219–20, 222, 258; and Stalin and Yalta agreements, 269–71, 273
Rose, François de, 78
Rossanda, Rossana, 207
Rusk, Dean, 235, 236
Russell, Bertrand, 155
Russia. See Soviet Union
Ruthenia, 57

Sakhalin Island, 57, 268
Sakharov, Andrei, 104, 105–6, 130
Sakharov Committee, 140
Salazar, António de Oliveira, 54
Salisbury, Harrison, 320
Samuelson, Paul, 308
Satellites, Soviet, 20, 24–25, 26, 57–65, 68, 103, 105, 113–14, 197–212, 226, 252, 262, 305, 309, 340. See also specific countries, groups
Saudi Arabia, 37, 104, 301
Scandilux, 193
Scandinavia, 73, 110, 156, 301
Schlesinger, Arthur, 320, 321
Schlesinger, Stephen, 320
Schmidt, Helmut, 40, 46, 51, 205, 267, 294, 323
Schroeder, Patricia, 26
Seydoux, François, 234
Shepilov, D. T., 104
Shifrin, Avraham, 141
Shliapnikov, Aleksandr, 149
Siberian gas pipeline, 49, 50, 75–

83, 138–42; slave labor and, 140–42
Sihanouk, Prince, 331, 332, 335
Sinclair, Upton, 155
Singapore, 304, 319
Slavery, war or, 349–60. See also Gulags; Labor, forced
Slavs (Pan-Slavism), 255–56
Slovaks, 57
Smith, Gerard, 250
Soares, Mario, 204, 315
Socialism, 10, 28, 43–45, 53, 196–97; future of, response of democracies to, 343–45, 349–60; "with a human face," 62–63; and "peace struggle," 145–59; "in a single state," 278; and territorial expansion, 62–63 (see also Expansionism). See also Communism; specific aspects, countries, organizations
Socialist International, 54, 95, 118, 145, 150, 154, 155, 188, 190–97, 198, 280, 297, 310; Palme Committee, 193; Sorsa Group, 192, 280, 291
Solzhenitsyn, Aleksandr, 132, 133, 141, 358
Somalia, 117, 227, 341
Somoza Debayle, Anastasio, 300, 327
Sophist, The (Plato), 12
Sorsa, Kalevi, 192, 280, 291
South Africa, 297, 301–3
South Korea, 60, 114–15, 152, 227, 242, 243–44, 278, 287, 296, 304
South Vietnam, 171, 243–44, 296–97, 304. See also Vietnam
South West Africa People's Organization (SWAPO), 117, 209, 302
South Yemen, 58, 104, 105, 301
Souvarine, Boris, 97, 261
Sovietology, 293–94
Soviet Peace Fund, 158
Soviet Union (Russia, U.S.S.R.), 5, 10, 16–20; appeasement of, 16–

20, 21–29, 33–54, 79–85, 215–29, 230–40, 241–57 (see also Passivity; specific aspects); and arms race and military strength and strategy, 66–74, 75–85, 92–98 (see also Arms race; Nuclear weapons; specific aspects); and China (see under China); Communist Party, 191, 192, 216; and détente (see Détente); and dividing-the-West strategy, 136–43; double standard in judging democracies and, 295–317, 318–37; and economic aspects (see Economy); and "fear of encirclement," 26, 65, 89–98; future of, response of democracies to, 338–45, 349–60; and global strategy (world revolution and domination aim), 21–29, 66–74, 75–85, 89–98, 99–108, 109–22, 123–35, 166, 206 (see also specific aspects, events); "hawks and doves" in, 219, 220, 222–23, 277; and ideological warfare and disinformation, 160–87; and leadership succession and changes, 277–94; and "peace struggle," 144–59 (see also Peace movement); and personal-contacts myth, 218, 220, 221–22, 269; and persuasion by force, 75–85, 89–98, 99–108 (see also specific aspects, kinds, places); Politburo, 216, 220, 221, 222, 252; and political piracy and perversion, 188–212; and propaganda, 21–29 (see also Propaganda); Red Army (see Red Army); stinginess in aid to LDCs, 196; and territorial expansionism, 15, 16–20, 22–29 (see also Expansionism); and terrorism, 188, 203–12 (see also Terrorism); and treaties and agreements, 84, 93, 106–8, 109–12, 118–19, 124–25, 130, 133–35,

136, 251–56, 264–76 (see also specific countries, kinds, treaties); twelve myths concerning, 225–29; weaknesses and failures of, 3, 19, 20, 90–91, 112, 113, 125–26, 352–60 (see also specific aspects, kinds) See also Communism; Socialism; specific aspects, individuals.
Spadolini, Giovanni, 71
Spain, 8, 54, 73, 91, 92, 176, 182, 200, 208, 339, 343; Basque ETA terrorism and, 204, 205, 206, 210, 315; and NATO, 73, 77, 280; Socialists, 190, 191, 193, 210, 280
Spheres (zones) of influence, 254; Yalta agreements and, 267
SS-11 missiles, 134
SS-17 missiles, 134
SS-18 missiles, 134
SS-20 missiles, 69, 73, 78, 137, 223, 283
Stalin, Joseph (Stalinism), 50–51, 97, 103, 107, 119, 132–33, 148, 165, 191, 194, 220, 221, 242, 252–53, 256, 335 n., 337, 341; death and successors of, 278, 282, 284–90 passim, 292, 322; FDR and, 269–71, 273; and Hitler pact (see under Hitler, Adolf); and "peace struggle," 148, 151, 153–54; and terrorism, 165, 168, 170, 228, 282, 337; at Yalta, 268, 269–75, 285
Stockholm Appeal, 151–52, 155
Strategic Arms Limitation Treaty talks (SALT), 124–25, 129, 133–34, 137; SALT I and II, 133–34, 292
Submarines, nuclear, 69, 77–78
Subversion, 4, 143, 167, 181–82. See also specific aspects, kinds, organizations
Suez Canal, 105
Suriname, 84, 115
Suslov, Mikhail, 149, 192
Sweden, 77, 146, 193

Swiss radio, 180
Syria, 184, 352; and Hama bloodbath, 172

Taiwan, 304, 319
Tanzania, 300
Tass (news agency), 200
Technology, 266; embargo on transfers of, 222, 224; Soviet thefts and, 224–25
Teheran conference (1943), 107, 220, 268, 270, 272
Television (TV). See Media, the
Terrorism, 9, 93, 115, 166, 171, 181, 188, 203–12, 241, 298, 300, 315–16; leftist ("red"), 9; rightist ("black"), 9; Soviet support of, 188, 203–12, 279 (see also Gulags; Labor, forced; Mass extermination; Repression)
Thatcher, Margaret, 80, 156, 229
Third World, 5, 18, 47–48, 160, 189–212 passim, 307–17, 318–37, 338, 349, 354, 359; disinformation and, 177–87; propaganda and, 160–87; Soviet expansionism and, 56–65 passim; terrorism and, 290–12. See also specific countries
Tibet, 59, 173–75
Tito, Marshal, 197, 286, 287, 289
Tocqueville, Alexis de, 12–15, 18
Toledano, Lombardo, 322
Totalitarianism (authoritarianism), 3–6, 8–11, 15, 17, 18–20, 22–29, 33–54, 55–65; democracies' weaknesses and, 215–29, 230–40 (see also under Democracy); and dividing the West, 136–43; double standard in judging, 295–317, 318–37; economic resistance to, 84–85, 340 (see also Economy); future of, response of democracies to, 338–45, 349–60; ideological warfare and disinformation and, 160–87 (see also Propaganda); and "peace struggle," 144–59, 166 (see also Peace movement); and terrorism, 203–12 (see also Terrorism). See also Expansionism; Imperialism; specific aspects
Trade, 81–83, 138–40, 163, 226, 228. See also Economy; specific aspects, e.g., Siberian gas pipeline
"Transferable ruble," 48–49
Treaties (agreements, pacts), 84, 93, 106–8, 109–12, 123, 124, 130, 133–35, 136, 230, 251–56, 264–76. See also specific countries, kinds, treaties
Trotsky, Leon, 118, 208, 278
Truman, Harry S., 220, 251, 269, 271–72, 274, 295
Turkey, 27, 73, 248, 297, 298–99, 305, 310–11; Ottoman Empire, 91; and terrorism, 210–11

Uganda, 300
Ukraine, 222
Ulbricht, Walter, 245, 252
United Fruit Company, 320
United Nations, 107, 111, 183, 188, 221, 227, 287; charter, 199, 201, 255; Declaration of Human Rights, 201; UNESCO, 198, 199–203
United Press (UP), 198, 200
United States, 26, 50–51, 111–12, 124, 138–41, 192, 197, 202, 212, 248–49, 258–63, 281–94 passim; and anti-Americanism (see Anti-Americanism; specific aspects); and Bay of Pigs, 247; and Berlin blockade and airlift, 242, 251–52; and Berlin wall episode, 235–40, 244–46, 251; and Cold War and détente (see Cold War; Détente); and communism, future of and response by democracies to, 338–45, 349–60 (see also Communism; specific aspects);

Congress, 114–15, 124, 281 n.;
and containment doctrine, 243;
and Cuba, 110, 128–29, 237–38,
248–49, 250 *(see also* Cuba;
specific developments); and De
Gaulle, 258–63; double standard
in judging, 295–317, 318–37; and
economic aid and problems, 16–
20, 33–34, 45–54 *passim (see also*
Economy); and Grenada, 93,
115, 194; and Latin America
(Caribbean, Central America),
93, 115, 194, 320–24, 326–27 *(see
also* specific countries); and
Lebanon marines, 247; and
Marshall Plan, 101–3; and
NATO *(see* North Atlantic
Treaty Organization); and
nuclear arms race and Soviet
strategy, 66–74, 75–85 *passim,* 111
(see also Arms race; Nuclear
weapons; specific aspects); and
Poland, 34–54 *passim;* and
Siberian gas pipeline, 75–83;
Soviet global strategy and, 66–
74, 75–85, 89–98, 99–108, 109–22,
123–35, 136–43, 144–59, 160–87,
188–212 *passim (see also under*
Soviet Union; specific aspects;
and Soviet ideological warfare
and disinformation, 160–87 *(see
also* Propaganda); and Soviet
leadership succession, 281, 283,
284–94; and Soviet territorial
expansionism *(see*
Expansionism); State
Department, 25, 26, 28, 47–48,
125, 245, 252, 270, 278, 321; and
Vietnam, 93, 112, 113, 114, 170–
71, 173, 193, 243–44, 304, 319–20;
and weaknesses of democracy
versus communism *(see under*
Democracy); and Yalta
agreements, 50–51, 264–76 *(see
also* Yalta agreements). *See also*
Democracy; specific

administrations, individuals,
organizations
Uruguay, 115, 208

Venezuela, 115, 194, 209, 211, 321,
322
Versailles summit meeting (1982),
33–34
Versailles Treaty (W.W. I), 265
Vienna disarmament talks, 26
Vietnam, 55, 58, 89, 90, 93, 107,
112, 113, 114, 142, 197, 208, 304;
boat people, 23, 326, 337, 354;
and Cambodia, 59, 336–37;
North, 107, 112, 243–44, 288;
South, 107, 171, 183, 243–44,
296–97, 304; Vietnam War, 93,
112, 113, 114, 170–71, 173, 193,
243–44, 304, 319–20
Voice of America, 180

Wagner, Ingmar, 158
Wall Street Journal, 326
Warsaw Pact nations, 69, 75, 110,
111. *See also* specific countries
Washington Monthly, The, 25
Watergate, 124
West, the: and appeasement of
communism *(see under* Soviet
Union); and arms race and
military strategy *(see* Arms race;
Nuclear weapons; specific
aspects); dividing by
Communists of, 136–43; double
standard in judging, 295–317,
318–37; future of, response to
the Communist threat by, 338–
45, 349–60; and ideological
warfare and disinformation,
160–87 *(see also* Propaganda); and
"peace struggle," 144–59, 166 *(see
also* Peace movement); and
phony Cold War, 241–57; and
Soviet expansionism, 55–65 *(see
also* Expansionism); and Soviet
leadership changes, 277–94; and
Soviet repression in Poland, 35–

54 (see also Poland); and "two imperialisms," 55; weakness versus communism of (see under Democracy). See also Western Europe; specific countries, events, individuals, organizations

West Berlin, 232–40. See also Berlin; West Germany

Western Europe, 16–20, 339; and appeasement of communism, (see under Soviet Union); balance of power and threat to, 23–29; Communist propaganda and 21–29, 160–87 (see also Ideology); military expenditures by, 82 n.; and "peace struggle," 144–59, 166 (see also Peace movement); and phony Cold War, 241–57; Soviet economic exploitation of, 79–85, 102; and Soviet expansionism (see Expansionism); and Soviet leadership succession, 279–94; and Yalta, 265–76. See also Democracy; West, the; specific countries, organizations

West Germany, 8, 9, 67, 72, 75–77, 80, 136–37, 223–24, 229, 254, 266, 267, 342, 358; Baader-Meinhof group, 204, 206, 209; and Berlin blockade and wall, 128, 232–40, 242, 244–46, 251–52, 279; CP, 209, 251; ecologists (Greens), 166; elections (1983), 358; and French summit conference (1982), 34; neutralism and defeatism in, 59–60, 75–77, 223–

24, 229, 231, 250; and "peace struggle," 145, 158, 166; Red Army Fraction, 205, 211; and Siberian gas pipeline, 75–77, 80, 139; Socialists, 191, 193, 205; and Soviet repression in Poland, 39–40, 46–47, 50, 51–52; terrorism in, 204, 205, 206, 209, 211

Westmoreland, William, 181

World Council of Churches, 189

World Peace Council, 154–55

World War I, 8, 27–28, 106–7, 123, 153, 228

World War II, 8, 9, 19–20, 21, 28, 36, 53, 56–57, 66, 102, 103–4, 106–7, 118–19, 123, 136, 151, 181, 217–21, 228, 233, 251–55, 258, 262, 287, 299, 318; Yalta agreements and, 264–76 (see also Yalta agreements). See also specific countries

Wriston, Walter, 48

Yalta agreements (1945), 50–51, 53, 107, 230, 239, 262, 264–76, 285, 287; and "two blocs," 265

Yellow rain, 23, 326

Yemen. See North Yemen; South Yemen

Young, Andrew, 341

Yugoslavia, 253, 287, 288–89; Tito, 197, 286, 287, 289

Zagladin, Vadim, 73–74, 192, 352

Zaire, 71

Zhdanov, Andrei A., 120, 132–33, 153–54 n.

Zhukov, Yuri, 158